Praise for *A Re...*

No sincere question about God is out of ... ...ost apologists offers insightful answers to challe... ...ow to help people get past their spiritual sticking points.

> —LEE STROBEL, **author of** *The Case for Christ* **and** *The Case for Faith*.

The premise of this very helpful volume is stated up front: "questions are our friends." I couldn't agree more, and that's why I love this new book. Dr. Craig's responses to questions he's been asked over the years will stretch you, but with Joe Gorra's assistance you'll gain the benefit of understanding new insights. You won't regret the journey.

> —JOHN STONESTREET, **author and speaker for Colson Center for Christian Worldview (BreakPoint.org) and Summit Ministries (Summit.org).**

What a book! Combining a top-notch reference work with solid, practical instruction, Bill Craig and Joe Gorra have created a unique and innovative title that will help all Christians grow and minister. Bill's sharp insights answer the biggest questions surrounding Christianity, while Joe's analysis and framework provides real-world wisdom that can be employed by the evangelist as well as the philosopher.

A Reasonable Response not only gives you the answers but shows the value of apologetics and helps the reader be a more effective communicator of the gospel message. This is a rich resource for the pastor and apologist, and an effective tool for personal growth.

> —LENNY ESPOSITO, **founder and president, Come Reason Ministries (ComeReason.org).**

As a pastor for more than 30 years, I know firsthand the importance of apologetics in the life of the church and the personal journey of believers. I've faced the questions of confused believers and disgruntled skeptics. *A Reasonable Response* has comprehensive content yet a user-friendly approach that leverages a Q&A format. Dr. Craig strikes an impressive balance between gifted philosopher and compassionate sage. Of special interest are the appendixes, which provide practical advice to pastors on recommendations for doing apologetics in the local church.

> —DR. BRENT STRAWSBURG, **Equipping & Outreach Consultant, Conservative Baptist Association of Southern California**

Dr. Craig's credentials are well known, so it will not surprise the reader that serious questions about God and the Christian life are answered with wisdom and respect. An added bonus to this work is how well the church and pastor are handled. I don't know of another book that answers the seeker, trains the Christian, and models the apologetic task in the context of the church as well as this one does.

—PHIL STEIGER, senior pastor, Living Hope Church (Colorado Springs)

Unlike similar books that repackage the same tired answers to perennial questions, *A Reasonable Response* offers thoughtful and philosophically astute, yet succinct, answers to some of the most challenging queries of both skeptics and believers. You'll gain valuable insight from reading Bill Craig's winsome, enlightening approach to apologetics.

—JOE CARTER, editor, The Gospel Coalition (TheGospelCoalition.org)

If learning is often by example, then *A Reasonable Response* can be a valuable source of encouragement to current and emerging leaders in apologetics. Read it for your own equipping. Read it to gain confidence in answering people's tough questions. Every Christian at every university should have a copy on their bookshelf!

—RICK SCHENKER, president, Ratio Christi: A Student Apologetics
Alliance (RatioChristi.org).

This is a Q&A book that goes well beyond mere questions and answers. It will linger with you, inviting you into the practice of thinking itself. If you study this book carefully, you will certainly gain a rich storehouse of Christian answers. But more importantly, it will equip you to think for yourself so that eventually you're able to arrive at answers on your own. And when you can do that, you will be well-positioned to help others discover satisfying answers to their deepest questions.

—BRETT KUNKLE, Student Impact Director at Stand to Reason (STR.org).

Dr. Craig not only tackles some of the toughest questions people are asking today, but we get an "insider's glimpse" as to how and why he answers them as he does. This book will be helpful to beginners and experts alike.

—SEAN MCDOWELL, educator, speaker, and general editor for *The Apologetics
Study Bible for Students*

When I am preparing for a debate or a presentation before an atheistic college audience, there is no one I rely on more for clear arguments than William Lane Craig. Now the most important of those arguments appear in this one volume! *A Reasonable Response* should convince anyone who is truly reasonable that Christianity is indeed true.

> —Dr. Frank Turek, president of CrossExamined.org and coauthor of *I Don't Have Enough Faith to Be an Atheist*

For many years, William Lane Craig has thoughtfully and graciously engaged in answering questions from people around the world. *A Reasonable Response* combines some of the most difficult questions Dr. Craig has received with the answers he has given into one incredibly valuable resource! Not only will the reader gain insight into Dr. Craig's arguments, but she will see an excellent model of how to be an ambassador for Christ. Here's a resource that not only attends to the life of the mind but also challenges Christians in the daily practice of Christianity. This is a timely work in the field of apologetics!

> —Mary Jo Sharp, assistant professor of Apologetics, Houston Baptist University, founder, Confident Christianity Apologetics Ministry

William Craig is one of the top Christian thinkers in the world today. *A Reasonable Response* is a classic collection of his responses to readers' questions. Readers will be delighted to see how Dr. Craig handles even the most difficult questions people ask today. Read this accessible book to sharpen your own skills in apologetics.

> —Dennis McCallum, author, *Discovering God: Exploring the Possibilities of Faith*, and a lead pastor at Xenos Christian Fellowship (Ohio).

For the Christian ambassador seeking to master his subject and become a tactful communicator, there is no better example than William Lane Craig. In *A Reasonable Response*, budding apologists will find not only a rich resource of scholarly content but wisdom and insight for engaging others with gentleness and respect.

> —Brian Auten, founder of Apologetics315.com and director of Reasonable Faith Belfast

A Reasonable Response is God's gift to Christendom. We not only benefit from Dr. Craig's cogent and insightful answers to tough perennial questions, but we get a glimpse into what really excites the heart of the author—one who is passionate and dedicated in reaching the genuine seeker through the defense of the truth claims of Christianity. His example is one to emulate. This is a must-read.

—HARRY EDWARDS, **founder and director, Apologetics.com**

Christians today have access to tremendous informational resources for defending the faith —but information by itself is not enough. *Apologetics is relational*; questions and objections come from real people, whether they are family, friends, coworkers, or even strangers on the Internet. *A Reasonable Response* provides a valuable resource for Christians who seek both to have good answers to questions, and to share those answers in a way that will be genuinely respectful and helpful. The question-and-answer format makes *A Reasonable Response* a handy reference guide while also modeling how to graciously answer questions. A further benefit of this book is the extensive introduction, conclusion, and appendixes that explore crucial ideas about apologetics dialogue as a ministry.

—DR. HOLLY ORDWAY, **chair of the department of apologetics, Houston Baptist University**

A REASONABLE RESPONSE

WILLIAM LANE CRAIG

Answers to Tough Questions on

GOD • CHRISTIANITY
AND THE BIBLE

AND JOSEPH E. GORRA

MOODY PUBLISHERS

CHICAGO

Scripture quotations marked NIV are taken from the *Holy Bible, New International Version®*, NIV®. Copyright © 1973, 1978, 1984 by Biblica, Inc.™ Used by permission of Zondervan. All rights reserved worldwide. www.zondervan.com.

Scripture quotations marked NKJV are taken from the *New King James Version*. Copyright © 1982 by Thomas Nelson, Inc. Used by permission. All rights reserved.

Scripture quotations marked ESV are taken from *The Holy Bible, English Standard Version*. Copyright © 2000, 2001 by Crossway Bibles, a division of Good News Publishers. Used by permission. All rights reserved.

Scripture quotations marked RSV are from the *Revised Standard Version of the Bible*, copyright 1952 [2nd edition, 1971] by the Division of Christian Education of the National Council of the Churches of Christ in the USA. Used by permission. All rights reserved.

Comment policy in Appendix 3 from jpmoreland.com appears with permission of J. P. Moreland, copyright 2012.

Edited by Paul Braoudakis and Mikel Del Rosario
Interior Design: Ragont Design
Cover Design: John Hamilton Design, LLC
Cover Photographer: Jan Craig
Photo Credits: Jan Craig.

Library of Congress Cataloging-in-Publication Data

Craig, William Lane.
    A reasonable response : answers to tough questions on God, Christianity, and the Bible / William Lane Craig, with Joseph E. Gorra.
      pages cm
    Includes bibliographical references and index.
    ISBN 978-0-8024-0599-9
    1. Apologetics—Miscellanea. I. Title.
BT1103.C745 2013
239—dc23

2013013929

To Peter and Heather May,

who help put the "Great" in Great Britain.

"This happy breed of men, this little world,

This precious stone set in the silver sea,

Which serves it in the office of a wall

Or as a moat defensive to a house,

Against the envy of less happier lands,—

This blessed plot, this earth, this realm, this England."

King Richard II. act ii. sc. 1.

CONTENTS

ACKNOWLEDGMENTS

We are most grateful for the engaging readers and inquirers of ReasonableFaith.org. Without your ongoing interest to discover answers to your questions, this book would not have been possible.

Special thanks to Moody Publishers, and specifically to editors Chris Reese and Paul Braoudakis, publicist Janis Backing, and audience development manager Parker Hathaway. We are encouraged by your enthusiasm for this project, your faithful editorial care, and your eagerness to connect readers with the benefits of this work.

We are also grateful for the diligent representation of our agent, Steve Laube. Thanks for your behind-the-scenes work, and for your persistence in advancing our conceptualization of this project's scope and benefits.

I (Joe) cannot overstate my gratitude and affection for my wife Fera, son Samuel Isaac, and daughter Ella Joy. Each of you gave me immeasurable patience and space during this project. My dear Fera, you are the inspiration of "Questions are our friends!" and Ella and Sam, you are astute students of your mother! I am also grateful to Bill Craig for his trust and entrustment to me of this project and for his patience with me along the way. Bill, with this book, I cannot think of a more fitting way to conclude ten years devoted to serving you with your research and publishing needs. Thank you, brother!

Introduction

A MEDITATION ON THE PRACTICE AND MINISTRY OF ANSWERING QUESTIONS
by Joseph E. Gorra

Questions are our friends!" That's what I have often commended to students and pastors over the years . . . and then one day my three-year-old, loquacious daughter got wind of this saying, and my wife and I have never been the same!

Seriously, though, I think questions can be our friends because if something can help us discover what is true about reality, it is a friend, not an enemy; a "companion along the way." Questions can help us get at things. Questions are means for excavating what is known and what can be known. They're a valuable tool, whether in the crucial work of introspection or in dialogue with a fellow explorer of what is real.

A Reasonable Response is a celebration and example of the practice and ministry of answering questions. These questions are the result of correspondence that Dr. William (Bill) Lane Craig has received personally. In fact, we've chosen to keep the questions in their original context. Consequently, you the reader can gain an appreciation for how and why a person may have inquired about issues that they care deeply about. This is important to recognize. For example, two people may ask about whether there are good arguments for God's existence. Even if posed as the same question, it does not follow that an identical answer should be given. For two people could ask the same question out of different needs and desires, background, degrees of care, assumptions, concerns, etc. So, we have tried to dignify the inquirers (who are real people on the other end) by keeping the context of their correspondence intact.

Why This Book?

When conceiving of this work, Bill and I felt there were various needs and opportunities for a book like this. Some of which, perhaps, have even attracted you:

First, we think that Christian and non-Christian readers want more than just "Bible answers" to ultimate questions. At the very least, interested readers want to understand what is a "Christian worldview" perspective of the biblical vision about the "big questions." There are other books that do Q&A by offering more or less a biblical theological answer to a question. To be sure, those books have their place and do fulfill a genuine need. But we wanted to offer more than just "what does the Bible say about this topic?" So, it will not be surprising to find that some of Bill's answers work at some cross-section of theology, metaphysics, and epistemology, for example.

Second, we find that readers crave clear, substantive, and succinct answers to challenging questions. Today there is an explosion of solid Christian thought resources from a variety of authors and organizations. We are grateful for this work. But what if a reader can be served with a substantive answer to a tough question without having to read a chapter, journal article, or even an entire book on the subject? For example, take the controversial issue of whether the God of the Old Testament committed "divine genocide" by having the Canaanites driven out of the land of Canaan. Now, this is a big question. Myriad books have been written on the topic. Entire conferences have been created to deal with this issue. But consider Bill's answer to this question. It is a few pages long. It is clear. It gives you much to chew on and will challenge you to work through your own beliefs on the matter. If you want to study further, I have recommended resources in the introductions to each part of this book where you can learn about further contributions from Bill and others.

Third, we think it is important to value the doing of apologetics instead of just talking about apologetics. Over the last twenty years alone, Bill and many of his colleagues and friends have written some influential books about apologetics. These often offer helpful and informative frameworks for thinking about the task of apologetics and dealing with quintessential apologetics questions. But it is also valuable (and, indeed, in some cases it may be more valuable) to promote actual examples of doing apologetics as a way of learning about apologetics. That reason alone compels us to offer this book for your encouragement.

Bottom line: we present this book to you not only because of the value of the content but also because of the value of the educational opportunity. Learn to be attentive to the way in which Bill answers these questions. Consider the experience of reading or perusing this book as its own school of thought.

ON THE INTENT AND SCOPE OF THIS BOOK

Producing *A Reasonable Response* involved making what I would describe as some "canonical judgments" for the sake of encouraging a type of experience with this material. Yes, there is intelligent design at work ... or at least, design! With all the hundreds of correspondences that Bill Craig receives, we had to choose what to feature or refrain from featuring in a book like this. We've tried to be choice in our choice, as I like to say. We don't claim this to be a comprehensive compilation.

But what decisively distinguishes this corpus of writing from what can be available online? Answer: the sort of reading experience that we seek to foster with this book. The conditions for that experience are shaped by everything from the fact that you don't have to be screen-dependent to enjoy this content, to how we have arranged this correspondence thematically and sequentially.

More substantially, this book contains what I would describe as "para-texts" along the way that act as a kind of strategic annotation to the main text, seeking to help the reader notice what's going on in an answer to a question or to emphasize how Bill might be modeling something teachable for us in the moment. I talk more about these **Insights** boxes below. Later in this introduction, I offer some specific recommendations for how to maximize the learning opportunity with this book. We also provide some brief contextual remarks at the beginning of each part, attempting to shape reader expectations and encourage study of recommended resources in a particular area. In addition, the Conclusion and the Appendixes are designed to add further perspective concerning how to enact in various environments the ministry of helping to answer people's questions. Again, this focus is motivated by the fact that Bill's practice of answering questions can help us to strengthen our own work in this area, and if I might say, even extend it further and farther than Bill has been able to do through ReasonableFaith.org (he is a powerful clearinghouse of content, and not just that ... but he is still only one man. To you the reader, I think carpe diem may be in order here!).

The correspondence in this book is arranged into six different parts.

> Part One: Questions on Knowing and Believing What Is Real
> Part Two: Questions about God
> Part Three: Questions about Origins and the Meaning of Life
> Part Four: Questions about the Afterlife and Evil
> Part Five: Questions about Jesus Christ and Being His Disciple
> Part Six: Questions about Issues of Christian Practice

In many ways, these parts represent broad themes in Bill's writing and speaking. Part of what I wanted to do in this book was not only to offer to you, the reader, more of what Bill is known for, but to also help you come to appreciate his work on other (perhaps lesser known) affiliated areas of thought (e.g., those in Part Six). Yet, we also think that these six themes represent some of the more popular and consequential areas of study when considering the plausibility of the Christian worldview. As mentioned above, at the beginning of each part, we provide some introductory remarks to prepare your expectations for what can be studied and learned. There are two recommended resource lists at the end of each introduction, which are designed to (1) encourage further study within the range of Bill's own work on a theme, and not just his books and articles, but his vast library of audio and video content (we provide helpful links to this content). But we also want to (2) encourage study in light of other people's worthwhile work. The opportunity to gain direction about how to study further a theme of your interest is one of the benefits of this book. Each of the recommended lists categorizes resources as either

- "Beginner" (introductory, requiring a high school level of comprehension)
- "Intermediate" (requires some knowledge from a specific discipline or field and more specifically focused)
- "Advanced" (graduate degree required, carefully honed, scholarly material recommended).

We aim to strengthen readers at a variety of levels and backgrounds and so want our recommendations to be user-friendly.

WHY THESE QUESTIONS?

We do not claim that these questions embody the most important questions ever to be asked, nor do we claim that these are the only questions that one should learn to answer. It was more art than science to make some "canonical judgments" about which questions to select from the hundreds that Bill receives. Yet, it was not a whimsical process. For example, most of these judgments centered around three questions.

Is it interesting?

Is it insightful?

Is it instructive?

Any of the questions vary in differing degrees related to the above factors. For example, some are more interesting than instructive, perhaps because of the way Bill answered a question or by virtue of the way a question was posed. So, we don't claim that all the questions rank at ultra-high levels in all of the three areas. We do think that what we offer is a meaningful sampling of interesting, insightful, and instructive answers to questions. Part of what makes these instructive is that they aren't revised from their original contexts; we didn't attempt to make the questions sound smarter or more stupid. We sought to keep these as natural and as authentic as possible for our publishing purposes, since human beings and not robots were involved in both asking and answering.

ON THE EXPERIENCE OF READING THESE "REASONABLE RESPONSES"

There are at least two main types of experiences when reading the main body of *A Reasonable Response*.

First, we experience the value of becoming acquainted with someone's background and biography. This happens at a variety of levels. Most questions posed by inquirers in this book are communicated in some sort of relevant context. Rarely do correspondents merely ask a question. Perhaps they go public with their reasoning on some issue, or explain how and why their spiritual journey is relevant to them asking a question. This is all valuable background for the context of their leading questions in the foreground. But we also discover interesting (and maybe even surprising) aspects about Bill. For example, you can come to realize (even humorously) as a result of this book that . . .

- Bill not only enjoys quoting Al-Ghazali but also Hugh of St. Victor.
- He's not some one-note wonder when it concerns knowing God. He recognizes the benefit that arguments for God's existence can offer a sincere inquirer; but he also recognizes that such arguments are not merely for the sake of leading someone to a "generic deity." Bill's evangelistic: he wants to help people encounter the living Christ!
- The research professor of philosophy who has two PhDs can also be pastoral and attentive to people's emotions and feelings as he helps them work through their questions.
- His life has been challenged by a debilitating neuromuscular disorder, known as CMT, which has also shaped his character by how he has chosen to address it with care and self-discipline.
- The scholar who has authored nearly one hundred peer-reviewed journal articles and has a wealth of knowledge on many things academic, is also thoughtful about how he thinks of marriage, productivity, and priorities (truth be told, it's probably because of his discipline in the latter that he can accomplish the former).

During the ten years working directly with Bill to support his research and publishing efforts, I have observed up close several of Bill's virtues, which often get played out in public contexts like this book. For example: his tenacity for truth and clarity, his childlike teachability and sheer joy to learn something new, and his enthusiasm to be "caught up" with God's kingdom causes in the world.

Second, reading the correspondence in this book is similar to reading other letters; we get to experience only part of an incomplete process of exchanging thoughts between people. The benefit of this experience is that it does make it conducive to learning on-the-go or learning along the way. You read for the nuggets. You read for the distilled knowledge, wisdom, or insight. Reading the correspondence is not like reading a lecture (even if it is instructive), nor is it like reading an exposition of ideas from an academic course (even if there is expositing and explaining involved).

A Reasonable Response can be read from start to finish; it's nearly like being a fly on a wall in a philosophy, theology, and apologetics course with Bill Craig. Or you could read this book in a more piecemeal fashion, whether dipping into a particular part over another or skipping from one question to another. I have found that it's even enjoyable to randomly pick a question and enter the conversation that way; it's like being justified to be a curious busybody of someone else's conversation! On the other hand, perhaps one could make it a practice to contemplate one of the Q&A's each day for the next couple of months.

To help you in noting concepts and strategies in Dr. Craig's response to each question, I have added **Insights** about the suppositions and approaches Bill employs. These **Insights** appear in many of the responses to help you understand both the claims and their appeal when addressing inquirers who want to understand issues of theology, philosophy, and apologetics. The purpose in responding, of course, is not to win arguments, but to remove barriers that keep the inquirer from seeking further, all the while responding in a gracious and patient manner.

AN EXERCISE IN USING THIS BOOK

I encourage you to consider what it might mean to read the correspondence in this book as an opportunity to exercise other-mindedness. This will be especially valuable if you are a pastor or if you seek to practice listening for the sake of caring for someone's soul.[1] As

---

1. This important issue is related to pastoral care and spiritual direction. For a helpful, substantive, and accessible treatment of spiritual direction, I recommend the Web series by Biola professor Ryan Bradley at jpmoreland. com (http://bit.ly/SDBradley).

such, I encourage you to read the correspondence as "case studies" (at the very least). You don't need to read the whole book in this way. But I do commend it as a valuable way of reading choice selections.

Consider the following steps:

Step 1: Read a question directed to Bill.

Step 2: After you read the correspondence and understand what is being asked, pause, don't rush to Bill's answer, but ponder the following two questions:[2]

What is this person revealing about the question(s) they ask? (e.g., assumptions of their mind, "reasons of their heart," role of their passions in the question-asking).

How would I directly respond to this person if I had an opportunity to enter into real, give-and-take communication?

Step 3: You may want to briefly document your thoughts to the two questions so that you can compare what you would say with what Bill says. In so doing, you can open up your thought process to be weighed by Bill's approach, and then also assess his approach in light of your own take on the matter.

The experience of this exercise can be enriching if for no other reason than that it can help you move from being a passive reader to an engaged participant in the process of thinking through the various questions surfaced in any of these correspondence. You could also supplement your reading of a discussion in this book with a meditation on a passage of Scripture that would be relevant to the topic before your mind.

The genre of letters/correspondence can be useful for fostering this kind of dialogue with a text. It's not impossible to have a similar experience when reading/listening to a

---

2. You might also want to experiment with a third reflection, which might be useful: Consider someone in your life or in the life of a close acquaintance or friend of yours. Do they have similar questions as those of the original inquirer? This will help you to put a "human face" on the inquiry. Imagine them in the place of the person corresponding with Bill. What would that be like? How would you respond if you were Bill?

lecture or reading a paper that exposits or analyzes. But I have found interviews/correspondence reading to be more engaging, and at times, even more rewarding.

The benefit of doing the above exercise with correspondence (or interviews) is that you become acquainted in a concrete way with the intended audience. Bill is not responding to the masses but to a particular inquirer. His answers are fitted for that person. We can learn something about his approach. This isn't rocket science, but it is worthwhile to recognize. The payoff is immense. For example, it's one thing to have a prepared, even generic case to respond to atheistic objections to theism. It's another matter, though, to skillfully and wisely contextualize what you might say in general so that it is fitting to the particular inquirer at hand.

While reading through Bill's answers, sometimes I had the experience of wondering, Why didn't he say, x, y, or z to that claim? or simply wondering, It's interesting to note what he could have said (given all that he knows about a topic) versus what he actually said. I had these questions not because I thought Bill's replies were incomplete. I had them mainly because those questions are helpful for conceiving of a range of possible answers in light of what was actually said.

A simple yet consequential communication lesson is appropriate here: *Know your audience and communicate in a way that they find compelling.* This is an important word of encouragement to any public communicators, and not the least of which includes all of us who are spokespersons for Jesus Christ and His mission in this world, whether we are pastors, college students, parents, business leaders, educators, politicians, or a whole diverse range of other colorful vocations that shine through the beautiful body of Christ.

Tough questions not only require tough-minded answers, but the skillfulness to know how to say what needs to be said in order to help others come to understand this for themselves. In that regard, we should seek to have patience, to stay with people in their question-asking and *communicate for the sake of educating* insofar as they *want to know* what it is that they *need to know*. Ultimately, the practice and ministry of answering questions, like most anything else that is meaningful in life, is for the "whosoever is willing."

On the Practice and Ministry of Answering Questions

In the second part of this introduction, I invite you to consider how the practice of answering questions is a ministry to others. In so doing, not only can we gain an appreciation for this very work in our own lives but also become better acquainted with Bill Craig's contribution in public. For in many ways, no matter what image you might have of Bill's role in public (e.g., being an internationally recognized debater), one thing is definitely true: the man knows how to thoroughly ask questions and thoroughly offer answers. Q&A is the lifeblood of his work, even if it is not always presented in that form.

ON A PROPER "HOME" FOR ASKING QUESTIONS

Bill not only knows his stuff, but he knows how to prepare; he values good questions and their integral role in acquiring understanding. He's really a disciplined, lifelong learner at heart. I'm convinced that's his "secret."[3] Having two PhDs didn't indicate for him that he had arrived at all that he needed to know, even for those chosen areas of formal study!

Learning and inquiring are staple foods for Bill's appetites, not merely because he is intellectually hungry, but because he learns and inquires as a *representative and spokesperson* of One greater than himself. We might say that he inquires *in order to be prepared to give an answer.* For him, curiosity alone is not the only reason to inquire. To inquire in order to be prepared to answer is not some mere "1 Peter 3:15 branding" over his style of ministry. No, this is deeply real for him; it cuts to the core of how he views his vocation. He does not want to be taken off guard. He wants to be on guard. This is what it means to be "prepared." For Bill Craig, to be prepared is not primarily motivated by a fear of embarrassment or wanting to be known as a know-it-all. That is not the sort of character that nurtures preparedness. For him, being prepared is a *settled confidence* distilled into the manner in which he conducts himself before others as a spokesperson for the claims and cause of Jesus Christ in our Father's world.

Bill literally believes that by virtue of the witness of his work he can bring the name of God either praise or blame by how he conducts himself. Now, that attitude is not surprising when measured by the ruler of Scripture's instruction concerning how we are to practice our lives before others. But it is nearly a radical posture, a countercultural orientation, when viewed from the standpoint of how the work of Christian scholarship is usually construed

---

3. In a correspondence in this book, I am reminded of one of Bill's insights: ". . . we need to realize the feebleness and finitude of our human knowledge. I can honestly testify that the more I learn, the more ignorant I feel. Further study only serves to open up to one's consciousness all the endless vistas of knowledge, even in one's own field, about which one knows absolutely nothing. I resonate with a statement Isaac Newton once made, reflecting back on his discoveries laid out in his great treatise on physics, the Principia Mathematica. He said that he felt 'like a boy playing on the sea-shore, and diverting myself now and then finding a smoother pebble or a prettier shell than ordinary, whilst the great ocean of truth lay all undiscovered before me. How feeble, uncertain, and unstable are our own intellectual attainments!'" ("On Protecting against Spiritual Failure," pages 324–28).

in the twenty-first century. It's not uncommon for Christian scholars to have a habit of living as if their scholarship (even integrated with other disciplines) is for the academy and seeks to be "Christian" yet often divorces itself from seeing such work as actually seeking to *represent* and *advocate* for Jesus' message and ministry in academe. But such a divorce, however unintentional, would be unconscionable for Bill.

In one sense, it's easy to see how that "divorce" would be foreign to Bill's work since he is known as an apologist; he's expected to defend Christian truth, right? True, but I think he is compelled to represent and advocate in the way that he does because he ultimately believes that is what is involved when being a disciple of Jesus through the vocation of a scholar.[4] Consequently, I think there is this rationale for these types of questions that often run through his mind as he is working: *Will I (whether by my debating, lecturing, publishing, etc.) bring not only honor to Christ but will I also help the people "back home" become more confident that the Christian tradition has a lot going for it?* Or, *Will I bring shame to the name of Christ and to the work of His church by doing what I do in public?* How Bill conducts his life and ministry is suggestive to me that he is circumspect about such types of questions. For him, it is a sober-minded recognition that his work is as a public witness, and that witness is in the form of representing and advocating for Jesus.

I have taken the time to mention all this about Bill because it is important to recognize that questions, especially if they are from our friends, need and deserve a nurturing "home" in order to be strengthening to one's life. That home is one's character and is demarcated by one's witness in the world. If one's character is full of cynicism or suspicion of others, that will shape the conditions, outlook, and outcomes of the questions that spring forth from that character. With Dallas Willard, "to witness means to help someone come to know what you know to be true."[5] If one views life as having no bearing on one's witness, but is instead isolated from affecting others, that will also shape how one raises questions (e.g., we will become inattentive to speaking to the questions of the "other"). For scholars and graduate students, there is great temptation to be so into our own questions for the good of our own projects (in an individualistic and isolationistic manner) that we think our inquiries will affect only us and not the ones we serve and represent. Questions can have a way of

---

4. For more on this, see William Lane Craig and Paul M. Gould, *Two Tasks of a Christian Scholar* (Wheaton, Ill.: Crossway Books, 2007).

5. See Dallas Willard's "Knowledge for Life: Learning to Trust and Grow in Spiritual Knowledge," Vineyard Anaheim Conference (April 17, 2010), http://bit.ly/WillardVA. The quote is from Vineyard Anaheim Conference notes.

opening us to or closing us off from a world depending on our character and how we view our lives as a witness before others.

Character involves virtue and overall moral/spiritual formation. According to J. P. Moreland, our mutual friend and colleague at Biola University, "A virtue is a skill, a habit, an ingrained disposition to act, think, or feel in certain ways." In general, virtues are what make a person advance in excellence at living well. In *Love Your God with All Your Mind*, J. P. goes on to survey "five groups of virtues that are especially important for cultivating a Christian mind."[6] In summary, here is what J. P. proposes:

Group #1	*Group #2*	*Group #3*
Truth seeking	Trust	Humility
Honesty	Hope	Open-Mindedness
Wisdom		Self-criticality (we might call this *circumspection*)
		Non-defensiveness

Group #4	*Group #5*
Ardor	Fidelity to God
Vigilance	Dedication to God's cause in the world as one's chief end
Fortitude	

These virtues of one's character, and the overall moral/spiritual formation entailed, can be as a "home," enabling a habitable environment for the nurturing of our asking and answering of questions. Our inquiring practices will be developed and formed in view of these virtues.

I suggest that if you take stock of the life and ministry of Bill Craig, you can notice how character and witness shape the practice of his question-asking and the ministry of answering people's questions. For example, for any of his public projects, whether providing arguments for the existence of God or defending the historicity of the bodily resurrection of Jesus, all these were "birthed" out of his own personal questions or the questions (often as skeptical objections) of others. That's what *compels* these projects. When he develops these projects, whether for scholarly, peer-reviewed contexts, or for non-academic readers, he's mindful of his witness, of the stakeholders of that witness.

6. J. P. Moreland, *Love Your God with All Your Mind: The Role of Reason in the Life of the Soul*, revised and updated (Colorado Springs, CO: NavPress, 2012), 121–27.

People have all sorts of different images of Bill and his highly visible work. For example, a dominant image for many is Bill as debater. Or, for others, Bill is known as lecturer and conference speaker. Or, Bill as published author. Still others see Bill as campus spokesperson for Christ. Regardless if you are talking about thousands in the audience for a major debate in the UK, or a group of students in a graduate philosophy of religion program at Talbot School of Theology in Southern California, Bill not only seeks to be himself, but he's open to the opportunity for questions to shape his projects. In that sense, openness to questions is responsiveness to others. His work is not merely about "propagation" and "perpetuation" of what's always been believed or thought. For he does believe that tradition can do real work for addressing the questions and problems of today, and, indeed, can foster new or recovered questions for us to consider. You can take any of his debates, books, or journal articles and peel them back and discover that there is a lead question that animates his work. Regardless of the size of his audience or the occasion, Bill is attuned to the question(s) at hand.

Conveying knowledge, wisdom, and insight in the form of questions and answers is as old as human knowledge. We are question-asking creatures. Coming to know an answer to a question, and observing how other people's questions are answered, is one of the most effective and time-tested ways to learn and grow.

The Good of Questions, Connecting Us with Reality

"Questions are the gateway to reality," says Benedictine sister Joan Chittister. For "to ask a question simply means that we want to know more about something we consider important," she says. On the other hand, "to fail to ask a question that ought to be asked means that we are ignoring human issues for which we should be holding ourselves responsible."[7] Do you see how questions can have a kind of hold on us? It is true that we are often gripped by the questions we ask, habitually.

Question-asking can serve several goods in a conversation with someone. Writer Matthew Lee Anderson observes that questions can

1. Focus the attention of discussion participants
2. Make the familiar unfamiliar, which can help us see it more clearly

7. Joan Chittister, *Seeing with Our Souls* (Oxford: Sheed and Ward, 2004), 77.

3. Expose our presumptions and thoughtlessness

4. Engender curiosity by pointing our attention to the unknown.[8]

To his list, I would also add that questions can help us to

5. Practice self-discipline with the range and intent of our claims by suspending our claims (even if only momentarily) for the sake of converting them into a hypothesis to be tested.

Questions can have a way of deflating an authoritarian dogmatism. Take the claim, *"God does not exist because there is evil in the world!"* Now, that's hard to dialogue with. But the claim could be practically converted into a hypothesis for open consideration. Notice the invitation involved in saying, "If evil exists in the world, does it follow that God does not exist?" Now, with a proposal like that, you can work on it. It offers opportunity for consideration. It is not, in principle, a "conversation stopper."

6. Foster "Come, let us reason" invitations so that mutuality in inquiring can be profitable. Answering questions can give birth to dialogue and then to community, the result of mutual work.

Related to my last point, Anderson discerns that

In a way, a question dignifies the world or the subject as that which is different than ourselves and as a thing that is worth knowing. It draws us out of our complacent relationship with the world and makes us attentive to its other-ness, its distinctness. The more we ask questions, the more we are able to love the object as we seek an understanding of it.[9]

If I acknowledge that I do not have all the answers to the questions at hand, I am more inclined to be open to dialogue, and to enter into a mutually beneficial learning experience

---

8. Matthew Lee Anderson, "Four Things Questions Can Do," MereOrthodoxy.com (March 15, 2011), http://bit.ly/AndersonQuestions. See also Anderson's *The End of Our Exploring: A Book About Questioning and the Confidence of Faith* (Chicago: Moody, 2013).

9. Ibid.

with someone who might know something more than me (that "other" may be in the form of a book, or a real, living and breathing conversation partner!).

7. Remind us of our creaturely dependence on God and others. But in Christ is the fullness of all knowledge and wisdom.

The practice of question-asking and, indeed, answering questions, is not merely a "Christian practice," but a *human* practice. That we want (or even have need) to ask questions is, to me, one of the beautiful facets of being made in the image of God; for we are designed to reason, as reality-discovering and reality-recognizing creatures. Of course, this does not mean that we know all things or even know them with certainty. Knowing an answer to our questions rarely (if ever) requires that scope or degree of knowing. Questions (unless they are a pure rhetorical device) seem to be reliable indicators of knowers who are coming-to-know something, even if only barely grasping what can be known. Thus, question-asking reminds us of our quest for understanding. And for this, we should be grateful. For in what meaningful sense would our question-asking exist if we were all just machines? That is also a question worth pondering.

8. Acknowledge that we do in fact live in a God-saturated world.

The epistemic and social stature of question-asking is valuable because this is God's world; for it is a revelatory world; a speak-and-respond kind of reality. Reality is meant to be discovered and not merely constructed. Reality is conducive to seeking and finding; of knowing and being known. God, who is ultimate reality, is discoverable. That's our world, and that's where the practice of question-asking lives and moves and has its place. That's how questions and answers are environed, even if it exists in different ecosystems.

It's not surprising that the Q&A-energized practice of *catechizing* would be regarded as a prominent historical means for educating entire Christian communities. For it is an illuminating example of the practice of question-asking *for the sake of formation*. It reminds us that questions are not just "about issues out there" but they reflect what we care about "inside here"; they can be informing as well as forming.[10]

---

10. One might also think about the long tradition of rabbi and apprentice relationships and practices. Or, the medieval *summa* and its longstanding learning attitude of "faith seeking understanding."

QUESTIONS AS INTEGRAL TO DISCIPLESHIP

One of the earliest recorded accounts that we have of the young Jesus is of Him being found by His parents in the temple. Do you remember that story? It is one of my favorites. In Luke 2:46, notice the posture of Jesus' life: *sitting among the teachers, listening to them and asking them questions.* The passage offers an impressionable image of the vocation of a student or a learner.

Asking and answering questions are integral to the life of a disciple of Jesus in at least two main ways: (1) they help us deal with doubt and (2) they can help energize the spiritual discipline of study.

Questions and Dealing with Doubt[11]

Raising doubts about what we believe or know is not itself problematic. In many ways, it's what we do with such doubts or what we permit these doubts to become that matters long term. You can begin to see the role that the virtue of self-discipline plays here. In one of the questions in this book, Bill is asked about doubts. Here's some of what he says:

> Remember: Doubt is not just a matter of academic debate or disinterested intellectual discussion; it involves a battle for your very soul, and if Satan can use doubt to immobilize you or destroy you, then he will.

> I firmly believe, and I think the Bizarro-testimonies of those who have lost their faith and apostatized bears out, that moral and spiritual lapses are the principal cause for failure to persevere rather than intellectual doubts. But intellectual doubts become a convenient and self-flattering excuse for spiritual failure because we thereby portray ourselves as such intelligent persons rather than as moral and spiritual failures. I think that the key to victorious Christian living is not to have all your questions answered—which is probably impossible in a finite lifetime—but to learn to live successfully with unanswered questions. The key is to prevent unanswered questions from becoming destructive doubts. I believe that can be done by keeping in mind the proper ground

---

11. Some of what follows in this section is adapted from my articles "How the Holy Spirit Is Restoring God-Confidence Among Youth," RedPointMag.com (5/13/2011), http://bit.ly/RedpointGodConfidence, and "Beyond an Evangelical 'Mere Spirituality'? Reflections on the Kingdom Life and Practical Theology," *Journal of Spiritual Formation and Soul Care* 4:2 (2011): 290–313.

of our knowledge of Christianity's truth and by cultivating the ministry of the Holy Spirit in our lives.[12]

In many ways, questions need to be environed by a settled peace in order to be fruitful. Bill counsels that "the really important thing is learning to live with unanswered questions without allowing them to become destructive doubts." Could it be that the virtue of contentment has more going for it with regard to seeking answers to questions than what might otherwise be expected?

I would contend that authentic discipleship to Jesus is a healthy way to surface and address doubts. Why? Because we can honestly and vulnerably share our doubts with others before God and learn to effectively deal with them with support and resources from the Christian tradition (yes, there is an important word to be said here about having churches that foster this kind of environment, which I'll address below). For Jesus affords us space to deal with our doubts. The story of "doubting Thomas" is evidence of His embrace, for example. Notice that Jesus didn't say to Thomas "deny your doubts" or "pretend that they aren't real." But He gave Thomas the occasion—direct acquaintance with the personified evidence of Himself, raised from the grave!—to reckon with and adjust his doubts.

For our purposes here, this is the important point to be made about doubts in the life of faith. We want to learn to deal with our doubts to the degree that we can, and we want to grow in our confidence in God. If we do not want to grow in our confidence, then we might as well settle for living some sort of bifurcated life between "following Jesus" and being "inattentive to addressing our doubts" and, like weeds, permitting them to become overgrown. This is the choice we have to face with others before God. But do we really want that? It ends up being a bifurcated kind of life because there is not a willingness on our part to recognize Jesus' lordship over all areas of life. Clay Jones, our mutual friend and colleague at Biola University, is fond of telling students that:

When Christians hear skeptical arguments that they can't answer, they tend to push their doubt deep down inside. The trouble is that as they hear more and more of those arguments it begins to build a wedge between them and real confidence in Jesus. Thus I find "apologetics" to be deeply spiritual because you can't love the Lord with all your mind and secretly suspect that Christianity can't answer the hard questions.

12. In this book, from the question "On the Hard Yet Rewarding Work of Dealing with Doubts," pages 311–19.

We should have an intentional purpose for why we are to deal with doubts. Is it to play with them, like someone being entertained in an old "curiosity shop"? Is it to just expose them or only bring them to our awareness? Is it to stew in them and merely settle for their meaningful cohabitation in our soul? The goal of dealing with doubts is to remove them insofar as they stand between a person's interactive relationship with God and His authority in their life.[13]

Why this goal? Because a doubt is a way of distrusting what is the case; it very often can distract and redirect the heart (sometimes through the mind or the desires of our heart) to question what is true and what is known to be true. In fact, doubts can often manifest in the form of questions-as-objections (of course, notice that not all questions or all questioning are examples of doubts). Doubts come in all sorts of shapes and sizes. Sometimes they are "intellectual doubts" and sometimes they are "emotional doubts" or even "spiritual doubts." Quite often a person's doubts about God and His trustworthiness are eclectic in nature; a combination of any or all of the above. Perhaps they are "existential doubts." A doubt often has a felt need associated with it (e.g., a feeling of wanting to be accepted). Thus, when someone raises questions-as-objections there is often a non-articulated felt need that accompanies it. We must learn to treat the need with the objection.[14] Regardless of the classification, doubts are real and they appear in both the heart and mind of non-Christians and self-identified Christians alike.

How can we lift a doubt? We can do so by offering counter-reasons and evidences to help defeat it so that it does not have the power to stand between us and the growth of our confidence in God. Through even questions of a circumspect type, we can learn to doubt our doubts. Again, this does *not* mean deny them, but to learn how to *deprive* them of their power. For example, perhaps people question whether God cares and sees them. Maybe He seems distant. If it is the case that such people are willing to open up themselves to

---

13. Here, I am drawing from some of philosopher Dallas Willard's treatment of doubts. For example, consider his "Knowledge for Life: Learning to Trust and Grow in Spiritual Knowledge," Vineyard Anaheim (April 17, 2010), http://bit.ly/WillardVA.

14. I am here reminded of philosopher and theologian James Beilby's attentive observation that "while intellectual causes of unbelief occur when there are unresolved intellectual objections to Christianity, affective causes of unbelief are the result of being wounded or having unresolved personal pain associated with Christian belief. ... Affective objections to Christian belief might occur even if a person has not personally experienced pain or abuse. It is often enough to look around and see others in pain or being abused. In fact, an affective objection to Christian belief might even occur in the absence of profound pain and suffering. Whenever there is a gap between expectations and reality, an affective objection is possible," in James K. Beilby, *Thinking about Christian Apologetics* (Downers Grove, Ill.: InterVarsity, 2011), 171.

have their doubts identified and examined, they might be able to discover reasons to doubt their doubts (e.g., evidence for how God has, in the past, made Himself known to such people; how feelings are not an adequate guide to lead our lives; how God cares for us and administers His grace through other people). But perhaps the same doubt is rooted deeply in a person's outlook. If that is the case, maybe the doubt is empowered by the appeal of a particular worldview (e.g., atheism). For example, instead of just dealing with the specific doubt per se, an endeavor should be made to offer reasons to doubt the very viability of the worldview assumptions that might contribute to the doubt.

So, in this context, questions are as much a tool for diagnosing and clarifying as they are a means to question the power of the doubt and to help the mind and heart to be open to counter-reasons and evidences. But we also want to learn to practice questioning for the sake of discovering answers to the very questions that inform, if not empower, our doubts. In that regard, questions can be useful for both "deconstructing" a doubt and "recovering" confidence that has been lost.

Questions and the Spiritual Discipline of Study

When one typically thinks about "study" these days, perhaps the dominant image that comes to mind is one related to school, books, and the drudgery of homework (aka "busy-work"). If so, that image can (re)shape how we conceive of the role of questions in the work of study. For example, we might be led to think that the place of questions in study is just to master prepared answers. Or, perhaps, as a result of this idea and image of study we construe questions as the things to be studied as an end in itself. Thus, always questioning, never answering, always seeking, never finding. But thanks be to God that the practice of study does not rest on a conceptualization that is the result of contemporary, academic experiences.

To grasp the significance of the role of questions in study as a spiritual discipline, we must first recognize the value of avoiding (like a plague!) a reductionist account of study. For example, *study is not identical* to reading books, attending a lecture, going to a conference, mastering a topic, doing assignments in a classroom, or performing "pure research" (whatever that is!), nor is it an activity reserved for thinkers, intellectuals, scholars, and formal students alone. Now, study may involve these matters, but it does not have to, and when it does, it is not just a reference to them alone. So, in some significant sense, I want to say that we need to ransom study from an "academic-ization" impulse; an over-reaching, over-bearing, over-defining of life, ideas, and practices in terms of academic values and functionalities.

Consequently, when you pull back all that layering, all the social constructs of what "study" has come to be primarily represented as (e.g., in the form of such ideas, dominant images, roles, and practices mentioned above), you can begin to discover how study is rather humane, dignifying, and integral to whole-life flourishing. You discover, for example, how study is *a way of training our whole sight (physical, moral, and spiritual) to notice and integrate what is noticed in all of life*. With J. P. Moreland, study should "be approached as a set of training activities, as spiritual and intellectual exercise. Study is a discipline that strengthens the mind and enriches the soul. . . . Seen as a discipline, study becomes a means of building my character, ingraining habits of thought and reflection, and reinforcing in my own soul the value of the life of the mind."[15] Isn't that interesting, inspiring, and inviting?

The relevant Christian formational literature is keen to represent study as a spiritual discipline of "engagement" versus one of "abstinence." The goal of the latter is to "abstain to some degree and for some time from the satisfaction of what we generally regard as normal and legitimate desires."[16] Why do we abstain? To torture, shame, and penalize ourselves into believing something? No! Among other reasons, we are learning to practice abstaining for the sake of strengthening our trust and confidence in God's provision even without our various attachments and their trappings. So, as a discipline of engagement, study "is the chief positive counterpart of solitude,"[17] since solitude "is choosing to be *alone* and to dwell on our experience of isolation from other human beings."[18]

According to Dallas Willard, a discipline for the spiritual life is "nothing but an activity undertaken to bring us into more effective cooperation with Christ and His kingdom."[19] So, how is study a spiritual discipline?

First, in study "we engage ourselves, above all, with the written and spoken Word of God."[20] It is to engage our whole life, and not merely our "religious" or "spiritual" life, with a holy attentiveness. In such study we work to understand our life in a circumspect manner under and in subject to the authority of God. Think of it this way: your life is like a school, where you are not the teacher but the student of your life. The Father through the Son and

15. Moreland, *Love Your God with All Your Mind*, 128.

16. Dallas Willard, *The Spirit of the Disciplines* (San Francisco: HarperSanFrancisco, 1991), 159.

17. Ibid., 176.

18. Ibid., 160.

19. Ibid., 156.

20. Ibid., 176.

by the Holy Spirit is your Teacher and Master. To be "enrolled" in this school means to learn to be addressed by and to respond to God Almighty about your life in Him. Perhaps you can begin to see the value of being addressed by God through Scripture, for example. For the goal in studying Scripture is not mere "mastery of the text," but ultimately being mastered by it, being formed by it; it is the practice of experiencing God speak to us as learners of His ways, students of our lives. I am here reminded of something that J. P. Moreland once told me (and I paraphrase) about when he was a student at Dallas Theological Seminary. The late Howard Hendricks used to tell his students that they should first and foremost learn to be "scholars of themselves" and then scholars of ideas. That's good. I think it helps to convey this notion of study and the work that is involved. Perhaps it is here that we can come to hear and receive advice from Hugh of St. Victor, who wrote in his *Didascalicon* (1125):

> Now the beginning of study is humility. Although the lessons of humility are many, the three which follow are of especial importance for the student: First, that he hold no knowledge and no writing in contempt; second, that he blush to learn from no man; and third, that when he has attained learning himself, he not look down upon everyone else.[21]

Second, in study we also work "to see the Word of God at work in the lives of others, in the church, in history, and in nature."[22] Notice the intentional recognition of integrating how God is at work in us and how God is at work in others. How do we do this? "We not only read and hear and inquire, but we *meditate* on what comes before us; that is, we withdraw into silence where we prayerfully and steadily focus upon it."[23] Notice the interrelationship between the study of the Word and works of God. This is by intelligent design. Why? Recall the goal of a spiritual discipline: it is to bring us into more effective cooperation with God and His kingdom. It is learning to be at work where God is at work in our work with others. But such work is not mere laboring or striving. It is a prayerful way of

21. Jerome Taylor, *The Didascalicon of Hugh of St. Victor: A Medieval Guide to the Arts* (New York: Columbia University Press, 1961, 1991), 94–95.

22. Willard, *The Spirit of the Disciplines*, 177.

23. Ibid.

being in the world. It "is simply talking to God about what we are doing together," says Willard.[24]

Finally, notice the role of meditation in the work of study. It animates study. "Study has been called a prayer to truth,"[25] says A. G. Sertillanges in his classic book, *The Intellectual Life: Its Spirit, Conditions, Methods.* How? Sertillanges says that "it seeks out and honors the traces of the Creator, or His images, according as it investigates nature or humanity; but it must make way at the right moment for direct intercourse with Him."[26] Given what study seeks, is it surprising that it would lend itself to the disciplines of worship and celebration of God?

So, how might questions operate in study as a spiritual discipline? Here are some brief, relevant observations about their theological character:

1. The ultimate goal of asking questions is not for idle chatter or for satisfying mere curiosities. Questions are a powerful tool for becoming acquainted with the reality of God's Word and work in His world. In that respect, perhaps one of the more consequential questions to ever ask is this: *How is God at work in my world? How can I learn to cooperate with His work?*

2. Christ-shaped questions are integral to study. We ought to value (a) asking questions that Jesus would be interested in asking[27] and (b) learning to ask and answer

---

24. *The Divine Conspiracy* (San Francisco: HarperSanFrancisco, 1998), 243. Willard goes on to say that "prayer is a matter of explicitly sharing with God my concerns about what he too is concerned about in my life. And of course he is concerned about my concerns, and in particular, that my concerns should coincide with his. This is our walk together. Out of it I pray."

25. A. G. Sertillanges, *The Intellectual Life*, Mary Ryan, trans. (Washington, D.C.: The Catholic University of America Press, 1987, 1998), 69.

26. Ibid., 29.

27. It is interesting to note that there have been some books in recent years that have tried to take seriously the role of questions in the life and ministry of Jesus. For example, some of the more interesting ones include Stan Guthrie's book *All that Jesus Asks: How His Questions Can Teach and Transform Us* (Grand Rapids: Baker, 2010); Winn Collier, *Holy Curiosity: Encountering Jesus' Provocative Questions* (Grand Rapids: Baker, 2008); John Dear, *The Questions of Jesus* (New York: Image Books, 2004); Conrad Gempf, *Jesus Asked* (Grand Rapids: Zondervan, 2003).

them in the *manner* in which He would do so.[28] For part of what it means to be His disciple is to adopt His "worldview." And, indeed, not just *adopt* but *conform* our view to His. He is our Good Teacher. We are His apprentices. Our life in the world is His schoolroom. The practice of study can help us habitually see and take stock of reality in the way of Jesus.[29]

3. The ministry of helping people seek answers to their questions is a service to others that God has also accomplished in human history through patriarchs, prophets, apostles, teachers, and most brilliantly, the ministry of Jesus. Consider how each is an example of God working through people's vocations to bring answers to questions that communities of people (especially the people of God) ask throughout "redemptive history."

4. The goal of asking questions as a Christian, at least in the context of study, should *not* involve us in endless discussions and disputes of ideas so that questions, even our precious questions and "projects," become an *obsession*. They are an obsession when they interfere with our ability to live well by loving God and loving our neighbor. Cultivating virtues of temperance and prudence are important both for the health of our question-asking and for their place in our life. Our goal should be to inquire in order to be able to more effectively love God and serve our neighbor. That should be our ultimate goal here. To borrow from philosopher Paul Moser, we should learn to inquire not merely in the "discussion mode" but in the "obedience mode."[30]

---

28. For more on this, see Paul K. Moser, ed., *Jesus and Philosophy* (New York: Cambridge University Press, 2009); Moser's "Jesus on Knowledge of God" (586–604) and Dallas Willard, "Jesus the Logician" (605–14), both from *Christian Scholar's Review* 28:4 (1999). Finally, see Willard's *Knowing Christ Today* (San Francisco: HarperSanFrancisco, 2009).

29. Moreover, it would not be far-fetched to read the epistles of the New Testament as examples of how to take on "the mind of Christ" and apply Jesus' worldview to a whole range of issues, questions, and concerns.

30. See Paul K. Moser, "Jesus and Philosophy: On the Questions We Ask," *Faith and Philosophy* 22:3 (July 2005): 261–83. Moser describes the modes of being human. "An obedience mode," he writes, "responds to an authority by submission of the will to the authority's commands. A discussion mode responds with talk about questions, options, claims and arguments" (273). His point is, *who has the authority to lead our life?* If Jesus has this authority because He is Lord then that should form our priorities, regarding both how we approach Him and how we live our life before others. It is not enough to merely "think Christianly" about all truth that can be sought even if "all truth is God's truth." For what matters is that a Christian mind and Christian thinking be obedient to Christ. What does that mean? It means we must do what He says. "In giving us love commands as supreme (love God, love neighbor), Jesus calls His followers into not just reflection but primarily a mission, the lived mission of witnessing to the good news of His Father's self-giving love (particularly in Jesus Himself)" (268). Will we "go for broke" with Jesus, as Moser would ask?

5. Study is integral to spiritual warfare. We are in a battle. The apostle Paul says that "the weapons of our warfare are not of the flesh, but divinely powerful for the destruction of fortresses. We are destroying speculations and every lofty thing raised up against the knowledge of God" (2 Cor. 10:3–5). J. P. Moreland has argued that these "fortresses" are "speculations, theories, patterns of ideas raised against *knowledge* of God."[31] If so, study plays an important part in the destruction of these fortresses. At one level, it is examining what is "raised up against the knowledge of God." But this is more than just a study of competing worldviews against Christian truth, although it may include that. It is seeing fit that all things, including those "fortresses" in my life and among my contexts of living, are altogether subjected under the authority of God and His revelation; specifically, that my *knowledge of God* (or at least what is depicted as that) is subjected to the *reality* of God. In short, through study (in the spiritual discipline sense), we can learn to deal with idolatry, which is, among other things, "knowledge raised up against God."[32]

I encourage pastors, parents, educators, and others who lead in the name of Christ for the sake of His church to pay attention to the above observations and seek to help others cultivate an awareness of them in light of the discipline of study.

HEALTHY FOR THE LOCAL CHURCH

If what I say is true and beneficial about the good of asking questions and the ministry of answering them in light of our discipleship to Jesus, how might we think of the work of the local church in light of these matters? I contend that the church as a culture and community is where the mutual work of answering questions can be effectually accomplished. How? Well, an answer to that is related to another question: "Who are the stakeholders of the ministry of helping to answer people's questions through the local church?" I try to suggest a perspective in Appendix 2. I'll only emphasize here that the ministry of answering

---

31. For example, see J. P. Moreland, *Kingdom Triangle: Recover the Christian Mind, Renovate the Soul, Restore the Spirit's Power* (Grand Rapids: Zondervan, 2007), 32–33.

32. Here I am reminded of how Paul Moser helps to serve the members of his own church through his creative and fruitful "Idolatry Project" (http://bit.ly/Idolanon). This project is specifically focused on surfacing idolatry-related questions in order to help people become aware of spiritual transformation in Christ. This is a formidable way to enact the ministry of answering people's questions through the local church.

people's questions is *not only* the job of self-identified pastors, teachers, and apologists. It is for everyone who self-identifies as Jesus' follower. We enact this ministry through our vocations. But for our purposes here, let me suggest why the church is valuable to this ministry and how this endeavor is edifying to the church.

First, if it is helpful to dealing with people's doubts and fostering study in the ways mentioned above, why wouldn't this be in a church's interest? Of all places, the local church should be an invitational, welcoming, and belonging place to discover answers to the big questions of life, belief, knowledge, and practice. If not the church, then the *university* as a source of moral and spiritual knowledge about reality? Good luck!

Second, the church is at least a representation of Christianity as a knowledge, wisdom, and affective tradition. I have a confession to make. I am sometimes envious of Christian Science Reading Rooms. They open their literature and guides to the public. Why? Because they at least seem to recognize a range of resources available at their disposal to address the wandering inquirer. What if a local church had that reputation in her community? What if she were known as a culture and community intent on offering content to be discussed and debated with all people? I am not saying that the local church should become a library, but it should be known for having a reputation as a place and a people where understanding about life can be discovered and experienced.

Third, by fostering contexts in our gathering (whether weekly or monthly) to regularly ask questions, we will enable our teaching and preaching to become even more open to being responsive to the questions that our members and "onlookers" are asking in our midst. What could be more negatively consequential for people's formation, and our preaching and teaching than to be *unresponsive* to people's deepest questions?[33]

---

33. Please see the appendixes for more specific suggestions about fostering contexts for Q&A in the local church. I would like to also add here that if pastors and teachers in the local church are only at the church's location all week long, and not present in their respective communities interacting with others beyond their own staff and members, this will affect the pastor's and teacher's ability to "double listen," as the famed and late John Stott would say. For preaching and teaching to be relevant to how we live today, which it surely must aim to be, it must be conversant with the questions that people are asking, generally and locally speaking. It must be responsive to listening both to the "Word" and the "world" (see John Stott, *The Contemporary Christian* (Downers Grove, Ill.: InterVarsity, 1992). "Our calling is to be faithful and relevant, not merely trendy," says Stott (27). "'Double listening'... is the faculty of listening to two voices at the same time, the voice of God through Scripture and the voices of men and women around us. These voices will often contradict one another, but our purpose in listening to them both is to discover how they relate to each other. Double listening is indispensable to Christian discipleship and Christian mission" (29).

On How We View the Ministry
of Answering People's Questions

Much has been said in this introduction about the merit of asking and answering questions. To help summarize and apply, I want to now offer some thoughts on what it might mean to view this ministry as a way of being led by God to serve others. In what manner do we serve others with helping them come to know answers to their deepest questions? I want to underscore five main features:

1. ANSWERING QUESTIONS AS *GOD'S AMBASSADORS*

We must be mindful of the fact that we do not "speak on our own accord" or "on our own behalf" alone. We are "sent ones"; commissioned to bear witness. And we are sent not because of our mere ability to answer or due to the prowess of our intellectual skill or accomplishment. These are tools, and not conditions for service. We are called and commissioned to be prepared "to give an answer" because we are meant to produce good works as God's workmanship. Serving people with answers to their questions is one among many ways to work. We work as His ambassadors wherever we are in public. There is not "the public square." There is only where my life and your life are lived before others, and that is the public with which we are to take our place and represent Him who is the Fount of all knowledge, wisdom, and understanding.

2. ANSWERING QUESTIONS AS *REPRESENTATIVES OF CHRISTIAN TRADITIONS* OF UNDERSTANDING AND PRACTICE

While God is the ultimate one we represent, as His ambassadors we also stand within various Christian traditions. We do not represent members that are part of our own contemporary communities alone; we have heritage, even inheritance, to steward an ancient faith for the benefit of others. This is significant for several reasons: *First*, it means that we do not need to make up our answers or reinvent the wheel. To be sure there is some creative improvisation and renewed discernment involved in *appropriating* Christian thought and practices for learners, yearners, and inquirers of all sorts. But we need not offer (or act as if we need to) answers *creatio ex nihilo*. We must study and understand our traditions in order to discern how they might help to do work for us today. *Second*, just as our question-asking is bounded by our character and Christ's shaping of our questions, so too, we ought to earnestly seek answers to our and other people's questions from within the vast and diverse resources of our various Christian traditions. Scripture, as our ultimate and indispensable source of knowledge and wisdom, is not the only source, but should enable us to discern how the Spirit is at work extra-biblically. *Third*, we must be mindful of how we represent Christ and Christian traditions to others so as not to cause shame or ill repute to the church. A practical implication of this concerns how we even talk about other Christians and their "tribe." I may be fully convinced of the merit and good of Lutheranism, but it does not follow that by seeking to represent "Christian tradition" to others, I must do so by merely cheerleading for my own tribe.

3. ANSWERING QUESTIONS AS *DIAGNOSTIC, SOUL CARE WORK*

When being confronted by someone's questions, first we should listen well, and it may be the case that our initial answer is in the form of a further question. One of the most dignifying acts that we can offer a conversation partner along the way is to help them gain clarity and understanding of the very question they are trying to answer, including how that question is situated within one's soul.[34] How does it bear on other matters? What might the Spirit of God, who is the Spirit of wisdom and understanding, desire to communicate through, or in spite of, this question and its longing? Sometimes the value of interviewing an inquirer can be the best first step when helping such a person come upon answers to questions. The goal here is not to analyze and critique questions per se, but to help inquirers come to gain an understanding of the context of the question from within their own life in light of the Spirit's work. There are at least four main "factors" from which to listen here, as we seek to help people answer their questions:

> ➤ Factor 1: We listen to the actual questions as they are embedded as part of someone's story, season, or stage of life, and as they relate to one's vocation and overall biography, including the longings of their heart.
> ➤ Factor 2: We listen for the identity-forming factors related to a question and how the need for an answer to be sought shapes the very "hearing" of an answer.
> ➤ Factor 3: We listen to what the Spirit of God might be saying and doing as we listen to people's questions, including how they process a question and answer.

---

34. I am here reminded of "rabbinic evangelism" as articulated by Randy Newman, *Questioning Evangelism* (Grand Rapids: Kregel Publications, 2004), 31–38.

➤ Factor 4: We listen and pay attention to how the culture-shaping, reality-defining, and image-producing institutions and spheres of society (e.g., media, government, business, education, technology, family) "color" the questions, loves, beliefs, ideas, images, longings, and desires of those inquiring.[35]

Sometimes listening with all these factors in mind is essential in a conversation. Rarely is only one at work. Listening with all four factors might become complicated real fast if the overall conversation is not focused and intentional or if what you want to accomplish with the conversation is front-loaded with unrealistic expectations. To listen with these four is not so much about simultaneous multitasking, as much as helpful means for surfacing relevant considerations about how to intentionally listen and serve people with answers to their questions.

4. ANSWERING QUESTIONS AS *EDUCATING FOR GROWTH*

Answering questions is a process in a journey of understanding. If our aim is to "get people out of our hair," we will be less likely to walk with the inquirer and more likely to miss out on the fruit to be grown by steadfast patient endurance with inquirers and their questions. Hurriedness and busyness kills nurturing. To be sure, not all inquirers that come our way will merit attention for the long term. Listening to Wisdom's voice is essential. But to those who want to open themselves up to being led, and who act on what is discovered, we should endeavor to stay with them for as long as they are willing to journey. To answer questions as a way of educating for growth is to take the "long view" on such an endeavor; it can't be merely "taught" in a class. It is often better "caught" in the process of journeying with people and their questions. For we are to help people move toward response and obedience to God's revelation in Jesus Christ. It is to consider these types of questions with sincere inquirers:

---

35. Part of what might powerfully shape people's assumptions, and even stand as blind spots in their thinking, is how they perceive Christians. These perceptions, especially if they are at the level of frustrations and disappointments with Christians and the institutional church, should be handled with care and discernment. Perhaps part of what needs to be accomplished in this area is helping people have their social perceptions confronted by reality, whether bona fide cases of Christians who defy their perceptions or openness to how the socialization of their perceptions might be more informed by image-shaping institutions (see Bradley R. E. Wright, *Christians Are Hate-Filled Hypocrites . . . and Other Lies You've Been Told* (Minneapolis: Bethany, 2010).

> Where are they now in light of where they are going in their growth?
> How might God be at work in the process of their inquiring and discovery?
> What are the blind spots or roadblocks to their growth?
> What shapes their assumptions?
> How do they think of themselves and why?
> What do they deeply hold to make up the good life? What do they consider worth pursuing?
> What do I envision, hope, and yearn for as a preferable future for this person and their journey?
> How can I strengthen them and offer my service for the journey?
> How might there be further means and opportunities for their growth?

At the very least, these questions make clear that the ministry of answering questions is not for mere casual bantering back and forth with each other's thoughts and ideas about some topic. Apologetics is not a sport; a kind of intellectual Ping-Pong. *It is intentional answering for the sake of growth.*[36]

5. ANSWERING QUESTIONS AS *HERALDERS*

When answering people's questions, not only must we "go beyond" what is in the fore-ground and help people discover a background, but we must also help direct people's attention to how God is at work in their lives and in the lives around them. We announce how the kingdom of God is near to them. We invite them to acknowledge this, not because we are trying to "close a deal" between them and God (for He's really good at completing good work that He's started), but because we owe it to our fellow human beings to let them in on the "divine conspiracy." This is not a call to be loud and noisy with our answers, or to be "triumphalist" in our answers, but to find meaningful ways to declare, herald—yes, verily,

---

36. Some of these questions have been adapted from Gregory E. Ganssle, "Making the Gospel Connection: An Essay Concerning Applied Apologetics," in *Come Let Us Reason: New Essays in Christian Apologetics* (Nashville: B&H Academic, 2012), 3–16.

and truly, *preach*—in order to bring attention to what is in their midst![37] After all, doctors, meteorologists, and pundits of society and the "good life" do this all the time; they bring knowledge (hopefully!) to bear on our life.

If we are sincerely interested in offering answers, we must not shrink from the opportunity of helping others notice how the gospel of the kingdom of God, indeed, Jesus Christ Himself, is near to us by the ministry and presence of the Spirit, and can be found whenever He is sincerely sought. To draw attention to Jesus' authority, presence, ministry, words, deeds, knowledge, wisdom, mission, and even His very questions and answers is to herald Him. How sad it would be if we answered people's questions but did not seek to help them pay attention to the living and risen Christ who is here, and not far off. How incomplete it would be to grant them wisdom to their questions but not invite them to be encountered by the Fount of all wisdom and understanding. In short, we might understand heralding as calling people to be confronted by the significance of the moral and spiritual authority of God for their life.

On How to Benefit by Reading This Book

If there is one benefit that I hope you experience as a result of reading even only selections of this book it would be this: that you, as a follower of Jesus, would be encouraged and strengthened with faithful confidence that people like Bill Craig are publicly offering answers to tough questions but that you too, with love and self-discipline, can also be sent out through your vocations into this world to serve people by answering their questions.

37. It seems to me that part of the challenge that is at play here is threefold: (1) Preaching has suffered at the hands of major reductionists, where preaching has come to mean (as a potent image and idea) "being preachy" or "being a babbler." (2) Due to the (over-)specializations, and to some extent "professionalization," of apologetics and evangelism work, there is in the mind of some a false dichotomy between the task of apologetics and evangelism. To be sure, some of their features are distinguishable but to foster a gulf between them, such that "apologists" are not to be concerned with "evangelism" (or vice versa), is regrettable, if not a distraction to our witness in the world. (3) We need a renewal of thinking and practicing regarding what it means to herald, and that not only entrusted by the vocation of the pastor but enacted by all Christians through their vocations in the world. For example, what does heralding look like for the professional (regardless of his or her industry)? What does it look like for the civic leader? How about for works in the diverse service industry? How might an enriched notion of heralding strengthen the witness of parents in their vocation? A pressing need exists for a theology of preaching that is rooted in a theology of vocational stewardship and work, of the mission of God in the kingdom of God by the Spirit of God. For more on this, see my article with Clay Jones, "The Folly of Answering Distracting Atheistic Arguments," *Christian Research Journal* (July/August 2013).

In light of what I offer above as an exercise in using this book, I think there are at least three main benefits to reading this book that will help realize *the good of question-asking and the ministry of answering people's questions*. But first, recognize what is the genre of this book. Again, this book is mostly a compilation of questions and answers. The experience is similar to reading a letter. That is, as "secondary" and not "primary" readers we enter this discussion midstream, as it were. You've probably had this experience when you read the New Testament letters or a collection of letters from a famous author. As such, we are reminded of this hermeneutical concern: Even if our questions might be identical to those being asked in this book, nonetheless, these questions are someone else's questions, excerpted from someone's season of life, out of someone's need or interest. So, in one sense, I want to counsel that we readers approach these questions with that sort of mindfulness. As a routine exercise, we may even wish to consider how a particular question in this book reflects, and is even situated, in our own soul. How does it resonate—and not just *why* does it resonate?

Here are three ways to benefit by reading this book.

First, *read it for your own interest, insight, and instruction*. In short, see this book as a gateway to discovering answers to your own questions, whether in whole or in part.

With the introductions at the beginning of each part, not only can you gain a feeling for some of the benefits in studying Bill's answers, but there are lists of resources that can be used toward developing your own "curriculum" for self-study. To self-study with these resources, I recommend the following general approach:

> ➢ Decide on a selection of choice questions that would be most relevant to your own life and its service to others (perhaps this might be a whole part in this book).
> ➢ Study the correspondence on its own merit in light of the above-mentioned exercise.
> ➢ Choose two or three recommended resources from the lists provided in the introduction to each part. Pick items that are both closest to your level of understanding and slightly advanced in order to give you a little challenge.
> ➢ Develop a realistic schedule to learn from your chosen resources to study. Maybe learning here involves just straight reading and note-taking or listening and reflecting. Maybe the process of learning is varied and different over time. Bottom line: develop means and methods (a system) for interacting with what you are studying.
> ➢ Consider an "application" project to test what it is you are learning. Maybe this is a paper that you write. Or, conceiving of a situation in your life that might benefit

from addressing it with the resources you are using for your learning. Try it out. Test it. Put it to work. Experiment with it.

➢ Take stock of what you want and need to continue to learn as a result of attempting to put it into practice.

Be earnest about being pro-growth; your growth in understanding and fruitful practice of what is being learned. I strongly recommend learning in the context of a small group of three to five people at most. See Appendix 1.

Second, *read it as a model.* This is not to say that you have to answer these questions in the same manner that Bill answered them in order to be effective. But wisdom would seem to dictate that it is for our benefit that we take stock of those who are exemplars in our midst. When approaching answers to the questions in this book, as earnest readers we should be asking something like, "Would I answer this question in this same way?" "What can I learn by how Bill answers this question?" In short, what is there to be gained by studying or paying attention to the manner in which these questions are answered? Here, I have tried throughout to note some "teaching-learning" examples, which are expressed in the parenthetical **Insight** boxes.

Third, *read it as a resource.* I decided to do theological and historical studies as an undergraduate, and then go on to do graduate work in philosophy, for one simple yet consequential reason: *I wanted to become a more resourceful person for the people I served and would likely serve through my vocations in our Father's world* (I say a little more about this in the Conclusion). Dear reader, may I suggest that you approach your reading of this book in a similar manner? Maybe even your own questions are not exactly or entirely surfaced in this book. But it's likely that you know someone who seeks an answer to some of these kinds of questions.

Read this book in order to benefit those you serve. This is an application of what I mean by saying, "becoming a more resourceful person." It is viewing the goods of your life—whether your gifting, skills, knowledge, education, social status, relationships, etc.—from the standpoint of how to help serve your neighbor who needs you to be you, in the full-service capacity of blessing them in Jesus' name. Here we now run into that perennial question, to which Jesus Himself gave due attention; the question of *who is my neighbor?* Philosopher and friend Dallas Willard has discerningly said that our neighbors are those "with whom we are in effectual contact."[38] What does that mean? It means that by virtue of your relationship

38. Dallas Willard, *Knowing Christ Today* (San Francisco, Calif.: HarperOne, 2009), 86ff.

with others you have the actual ability to do something for their good.

Thus, it is quite true to think that our neighbor is often within the sphere of our own vocation, whether our vocation be as parents, students, pastors, business leaders, etc. What a shame it would be to read—or even just consult—a book like this and not have our own attention drawn outside of ourselves toward our neighbor in need. Lance Pittluck, my pastor, says that the "poor in spirit are those who are needy and they know it." Could it be that there are "poor in spirit" in our midst wanting to receive a word of counsel, encouragement, and wisdom in light of this book? Yes, I think this is quite plausible, unless we live our life inattentive to other people's needs. But this would also seem to imply that we ought to read a book like this with *prayerful concern* for our neighbor.

Isn't it interesting that the ministry of answering other people's questions requires both attention to others *and* openness to them? (This is the point that the above Matthew Anderson quote addresses.) Simple or casual awareness is not enough. It's a start. Again, as Willard has said, "Attention is the first act toward loving someone." For what would it mean to have an inattentive love of our neighbor? So, we have to be open to listening to the needs of our neighbor. And, as philosopher Cliff Williams has shown, "need" comes in a variety of forms.[39] To be sure, intellectual needs tend to be the most closely associated with the work of "Christian apologetics." But even those can be colored by other needs of a more emotional, psychological, and relational variety. With Spirit-led discernment, we need to recognize where our neighbors are at—in the range of their needs—when they seek to have their questions taken seriously and answered effectually.

---

39. Clifford Williams, *Existential Reasons for Belief in God* (Downers Grove, Ill.: InterVarsity, 2011).

Part 1

QUESTIONS ON KNOWING
AND BELIEVING WHAT IS REAL

Coming to understand the nature, role, and value of how beliefs and knowledge—indeed, "worldview"—operate in life is one of the most consequential lessons to learn as a human being. It is often the case that the prevailing pressures and attitudes of our society frustrate and even war against such self-understanding; for we are pressured into becoming mostly mindless, sensate, desire-fulfilling creatures of instinct. That's how we are often expected to live and move and have our being. But one of the dignifying features of theism, and Christian theism specifically, is the acknowledgement that human beings are "more than" what our society pressures us into being. We have minds to know, hearts to grow in love and understanding, and beliefs to help order our ways in the world. Herein, the dignity of asking questions and discovering answers is given a hospitable home.

The seventeen questions in this part seek to reflect the value of knowing and believing what is real. Whether addressing the popular questions like "Does knowledge require certainty?" "Is there objective truth?" or topics that seek to grasp the role of the Holy Spirit in our belief formation and to understand how God is the basis for objective morality, this part offers a beneficial learning opportunity. In this part, questions regarding the authority of Scripture remind us of how all knowers and believers rely on testimony to some degree, but that the issue is whether such testimony is a reliable authority to trust. Many of the objections to the inspiration and inerrancy of Scripture are, ultimately, questions regarding authority.

By interacting with the questions and answers of Part One, you can benefit in the following ways.

In section 1, you can come to understand that
- "Certainty" is not a necessary condition in order to know something.
- It does matter whether someone does or does not believe in God, given the consequences of apathy and indifference.

47

- The distinction between *knowing* and *showing* is helpful for understanding how belief in God is "properly basic" and does not need to be swayed by merely changing evidences in order to be warranted.
- The Holy Spirit's self-authenticating witness has real power to shape and justify our beliefs in God in view of *de facto* vs. *de jure* objections.
- Trusting our "common sense" and intuitions has a valuable role to play in knowing reality and meaningfully resisting a knowledge-assaulting skepticism.

In section 2, you can come to grasp
- The value of helping people reason to a conclusion in light of their premises.
- How arguments function.
- How to avoid formal and informal logical fallacies.
- How to think about what it means to make a good (apologetics) argument.
- How "thinking logically" is not merely an academic exercise or a way to manipulate people.

In section 3, you can come to discern
- How you can know there is objective morality.
- The value of appealing to one's moral experience as a way of grasping objective moral values.
- How God is the basis for morality.
- Why it is important to distinguish between moral reality and *knowing* moral reality.
- Why atheism does not provide an adequate basis for objective moral values and duties.

In section 4, you can come to know
- How Scripture is a trustworthy source of knowledge of reality.
- The cost of "biblical errancy."
- How specific facts about Jesus can be established without assuming the general reliability of the gospels.
- Why it is significant to make a deductive instead of an inductive argument for biblical inerrancy.
- How God could inspire the content of Scripture's written text in light of human authors and human ways of communicating.

The above areas have a long history in the study of philosophy of religion, philosophical theology, natural theology, epistemology, metaphysics, systematic theology, apologetics, and ethics. You can discover further background to these issues, grow your understanding, and become even more skillful in your communication of what you learn by interacting with some of these valuable resources:

Dig Deeper into Dr. Craig's Work

BEGINNER

Craig, William Lane. *On Guard: Defending Your Faith with Reason and Precision.* Colorado Springs: David C. Cook Publishers, 2010. Chapters 1–2.

Craig, William Lane. "In Intellectual Neutral." Johnson Ferry Baptist Church, Marietta, Ga. January 3, 2010. http://bit.ly/IntellectuallyNeutral.

Craig, William Lane. "Apologetics in Pastoral Ministry," Pastors Conference in North Carolina (2006). http://bit.ly/ApologeticsPastors.

Craig, William Lane. "Advice to Christian Apologists." Calvin College, Grand Rapids (2004). http://bit.ly/ChristianApologistAdvice.

Craig, William Lane. "Advice to (European) Christian Apologists." Budapest, Hungary. http://bit.ly/EuroApologists

Craig, William Lane. See the col.lection of "One Minute Apologist" interviews at ReasonableFaith.org (http://bit.ly/RFInterviews).

INTERMEDIATE

Craig, William Lane. *Reasonable Faith: Christian Truth and Apologetics.* 3rd ed. Wheaton, Ill.: Crossway, 2008. Chapters 1–2.

Moreland, J. P. and William Lane Craig. *Philosophical Foundations for a Christian Worldview.* Downers Grove, Ill.: InterVarsity, 2003. Chapters 2–7, 19–22.

"Craig v. Harris: Is the Foundation of Morality Natural or Supernatural?" University of Notre Dame, Notre Dame, Ind., debate, April 7, 2011. http://bit.ly/HarrisDebate.

"Craig vs. Antony: Is God Necessary for Morality?" University of Massachusetts, Amherst, Mass., debate, April 10, 2008. http://bit.ly/CraigAntony.

ADVANCED

Craig, William Lane. "'Men Moved By The Holy Spirit Spoke From God' (2 Peter 1.21): A Middle Knowledge Perspective on Biblical Inspiration." *Philosophia Christi* 1:1 (1999): 45–82 (http://bit.ly/MolinismInspiration).

Craig, William Lane. "The Indispensability of Theological Meta-ethical Foundations for Morality." *Foundations* 5 (1997): 9–12 (http://bit.ly/FoundationsOfMorality).

Supplemental Recommended Resources

BEGINNER

Copan, Paul. *True for You, But Not for Me*. Minneapolis: Bethany, 1998.

Copan, Paul. *That's Just Your Interpretation*. Grand Rapids: Baker, 2001.

Morris, Thomas V. *Making Sense of It All: Pascal and the Meaning of Life*. Grand Rapids: Eerdmans, 1992.

INTERMEDIATE

Campbell-Jack, W. C. *New Dictionary of Christian Apologetics*. Downers Grove, Ill.: InterVarsity, 2006.

Copan, Paul and William Lane Craig, eds. *Come Let Us Reason: New Essays in Christian Apologetics*. Nashville: B&H Publishers, 2012. Chapters 1, 3.

Cowan, Steven. *Five Views on Apologetics*. Grand Rapids: Zondervan, 2000.

Craig, William Lane and Chad Meister, eds. *God Is Great, God Is Good: Why Believing in God Is Reasonable and Responsible*. Downers Grove, Ill.: InterVarsity, 2009. Chapters 11, 14.

Dulles, Avery. *A History of Apologetics*. London: Hutchinson, 1971.

Groothuis, Douglas. *Christian Apologetics*. Downers Grove, Ill.: InterVarsity, 2011. Chapters 1–3, 6, 8.

Sire, James W. *Habits of the Mind*. Downers Grove, Ill.: InterVarsity, 2000.

Sweis, Khaldoun A. and Chad V. Meister. *Christian Apologetics: An Anthology of Primary Sources*. Grand Rapids: Zondervan, 2012. Chapters 3, 29–32.

ADVANCED

Copan, Paul and Paul Moser. *The Rationality of Theism*. London: Routledge, 2003.

Garcia, Robert and Nathan King, eds. *Is Goodness without God Good Enough?* Lanham, Md.: Rowman & Littlefield, 2008.

Meister, Chad and James Stump, *Christian Thought: A Historical Introduction*. New York: Routledge, 2010.

Plantinga, Alvin. *Warranted Christian Belief*. New York: Oxford University Press, 2000.

Taliaferro, Charles. "The Project of Natural Theology." In *The Blackwell Companion to Natural Theology*. William Lane Craig and J. P. Moreland, eds. Malden, Mass.: Wiley-Blackwell Publishing, 2009. Chapter 1.

1

ON BELIEVING AND KNOWING

Does Knowledge Require Certainty?

Dear Dr. Craig,

I have been studying the defense of the Christian faith for the better part of six months now. I acknowledge that six months is not a vast amount of time; however there has been one idea that I have not been able to surmount or give a dispute when brought up in conversation or debate. Many people, some Christians included, plead intellectual ignorance as it applies to knowing anything about life, the universe, or logic. They state that since every possible option has not been explored that nothing can be said for certain. Since nothing can be said for certain, all of the premises that you pose may seem true to us, but we cannot say they are absolutely true. If they cannot be proven absolutely true, then there is no reason to believe them, and the argument dies right there.

It is becoming increasingly frustrating and disheartening to begin to speak to someone based on logic that is accepted and proven, and then be stopped before a discussion can even begin. For instance, in the Kalam cosmological argument, the first premise states: "Everything that begins to exist, has a cause." But many people question that premise due to the fact that we humans have not traveled the extent of the universe to conclude that premise. Because we have not explored the possibilities of the rest of the universe, it is impossible to base something off of an idea that may or may not be true in the whole universe.

I am sure that you have heard this before in debates, this idea of uncertainty of anything. I am very unsure of how to proceed in talking to people when they think this way. What advice would you give for responding to these objections?

Christopher

(country not specified)

53

Dr. Craig's Response

The folks you mention, Christopher, are victims of an unjustified and ultimately self-defeating skepticism.

Notice that they equate knowledge with certainty. If you're not certain that some proposition p is true, then you do not know that p. But what justification is there for that assumption? I know that I have a head, for example. But I could be a brain in a vat of chemicals being stimulated by a mad scientist to think that I have a body. Does this mere possibility imply that I do not know that I have a head? If your friends answer, "Yes," ask them for their justification for thinking that knowledge requires certainty. *Anything* they say, you can reply to by asking, "Are you certain of that?" If they say, "No," then they don't know that knowledge requires certainty. If they say, "Yes," then it's not true after all that we can't know anything about life, the universe, or logic.

Skepticism, ironically, draws its life's blood from claims to have a good deal of knowledge. For example, your friends claim to know, "Since every possible option has not been explored, nothing can be said for certain." That statement is itself a claim to knowledge! (A claim that is patently false, but never mind!) How do they know that? Or again, how do they know that "Since nothing can be said for certain, we cannot say that your premises are absolutely true"? This is a claim to knowledge (again, funnily enough, a false claim). Or how about the claim, "If the premises cannot be proven absolutely true, then there is no reason to believe them"? How do they know that? (Again, this seems patently false, but leave that aside.) Where do these skeptics come up with all this knowledge?

And if we cannot know anything about logic, how can they reason:

1. Since every possible option has not been explored, nothing can be said for certain.
2. Since nothing can be said for certain, all of the premises that you pose may seem true to us, but we cannot say they are absolutely true.

3. If they cannot be proven absolutely true, then there is no reason to believe them.

That looks to me for all the world like the premises for the logical inference form called Hypothetical Syllogism! But if that inference rule is not true, then no conclusion follows from (1-3) and we have no reason to doubt my original argument.

The fundamental problem with skepticism is that it presupposes that in order to know p, you must know that you know p. But if I can know some truth without knowing how it is that I know it, then the nerve of skepticism is severed. The skeptic actually is making a very radical claim, for which he cannot provide any justification without pulling the rug from beneath his own feet.

Skepticism is thus strangely presumptuous and self-defeating. It relies on our having knowledge of some very non-obvious claims. The skeptic cannot provide any justification of those claims, lest his view becomes self-referentially incoherent; yet without them his skepticism collapses, for then his lack of certainty does not imply that he has a lack of knowledge.

On How to Confront the Challenge of Apatheism

After just one visit to your fine *reasonablefaith.org*, I'm reasonably sure that I can demonstrate to the atheist that his position is untenable. However, I've recently come across a person who describes himself as an *apatheist.* After a little research, I find that all of the arguments that I can come up with will be responded by, "Your God's not relevant, and it doesn't matter to me."

This guy may be a lost cause; however, he has a large following. How can I confidently present the case for God any time a discussion that touches Christianity, or any other faith for that matter, on his site?

Thanks for your time.

Mike

Dr. Craig's Response

This is the second time this week that I've heard someone use this solecism to describe his views on the existence of God. Must be the newest trend among unbelievers!

"Apatheism" (presumably from "apathy" + "theism") characterizes people who just don't care whether or not God exists. As such, apatheism is not a truth claim and so can be neither true nor false. It asserts nothing and denies nothing. It is merely an attitude or a psychological state of indifference with respect to God's existence.

It follows that the apatheist has nothing to offer by way of refutation of your arguments for God's existence. In response to your case, he merely says, "I don't care." The soundness of your arguments remains unaffected by his lack of interest. So you can continue to present your arguments confidently, knowing that his apathy in no way calls into question the truth of your premises or the validity of your inferences.

In fact, it would be interesting to see what your friend would say if you were to respond to his apatheism by saying, "I realize that you don't care whether or not God exists. But do you think He does exist? Since it doesn't matter to you, you can be totally objective. So what do you think? Is there a God?" He may reveal that he's really an atheist or agnostic after all, and then you can ask him for his reasons for believing as he does.

On the other hand, if he merely continues to repeat that he just doesn't care, say to him, "Hmm, that's odd! Even most atheists recognize that God's existence would make a tremendous difference to mankind. Why don't you care?"

At this point he's got to say something like your friend's remark: "Your God's not relevant, and it doesn't matter to me." Now, this response is astonishing. To be relevant is to have practical consequences, to make a difference. To my mind, anybody who thinks Christianity is irrelevant either is using the word "irrelevant" in an idiosyncratic sense or else, frankly, is just not a very deep thinker. (Of course, if Christianity is not true, then it's not relevant. But then, presumably, the reason it doesn't matter to him is not because it's irrelevant but because it's not true. But I find it bewildering that anyone could think that Christianity might be true and yet be irrelevant.) To the superficial person Christianity may not *seem* relevant because he never thinks to ask the deep questions about life.

So invite him to think about the question, "*IF* Christianity were true, what consequences would it have for your life? What difference would it make?" I think that if Christianity is true, then it is hugely relevant to our lives. I've tried to deal with this question in my talks and writing on "The Absurdity of Life without God."[1] Let me, therefore, simply list six ways in which Christianity is relevant if true.

1. If Christianity is true, there is meaning to your life.
2. If Christianity is true, there are objective moral values and duties in life.
3. If Christianity is true, there is a purpose to your life.
4. If Christianity is true, there is hope for deliverance from the shortcomings of our finite existence, such as suffering, aging, and death.
5. If Christianity is true, there is forgiveness for all the wrong things you have done.
6. If Christianity is true, you have the opportunity of a personal relationship with God and eternal happiness.

Given all these wonderful benefits, it seems to me utterly imperative to find out whether Christianity is true. But that imperative is incompatible with an attitude of apatheism.

The challenge of apatheism, then, is not philosophical but psychological. The question is how we can get folks interested in the question of God. By showing them the stark contrast in the respective consequences of atheism and of Christianity for human beings, we perhaps motivate them to take seriously the question of whether or not the biblical God exists.

But since the challenge of apatheism is psychological, the best strategy for dealing with it is not intellectual but relational. Become a true friend to the apatheist, show that you care for him as an end in himself, and in time your genuine love for him will probably be more

INSIGHT

Notice the quotable wisdom here. It is reminiscent of what Joan Chittister says: "Superficial people are those who simply go along without a question in the world—asking nothing, troubled by nothing, examining nothing. Whatever people around them do, they do, too. That's a sad and plastic life—routine and comfortable maybe, but still sad" (*Seeing with Our Souls*, 79). One wonders if apatheism might very well be ripe for a kind of easy group think. Note Dr. Craig's wise advice at the end of his answer when he talks about the "best strategy" with the self-identified apatheist.

1. Readers can access Dr. Craig's article for free by visiting ReasonableFaith.org (http://bit.ly/lifewithoutgod).

effective than any rational apologetic you can give him. Remember: the challenge here is simply getting him to *care* about the question. That is more likely to occur as a result of your friendship than as a result of your arguments.

I strongly suspect that the self-styled apatheist is usually just a lazy atheist. He really thinks that there is no God but just can't be bothered to justify his viewpoint. He doesn't care because he thinks it isn't true.

On Common Sense, Intuitions, and the Limits of Reason

Dear Dr. Craig,

I am an atheist but still a big fan of yours. I always defend you against *dumb internet atheists* who never bother to read anything yet think they can ridicule a man with two PhDs and two dozen books.

You defend the classic God proofs so well. But I think you are relying on commonsense and intuition too much in this day and age. We are not in an age where we can be confident that the laws of reason are the same as the laws of reality, like people in the time of Aristotle believed. If that were the case, we would never have had to abandon Aristotelian physics. It sounded perfectly intuitive but turned out to be false even on the simple idea of inertia, which is a principle that our brains will just not accept because of how we are wired, apparently.

So we can just see how reason is limited in understanding physics, then how much more would it be limited in understanding the creation and God? When thinking about the beginning of time and about creation and God, our reason actually generates contradictory ideas. It is not satisfied with the idea that the past should be infinite, yet at the same time not with the idea that time has a beginning either. They both sound absurd and we are forced to believe the opposite, yet its opposite is also equally absurd. Furthermore reason demands that the causal chain to the past should not go on forever, but it cannot really make sense of the very idea of a "first cause" either. And also it demands that contingent things must ultimately be explained by a necessary being, but it finds the very idea of a "necessary being" incoherent at the same time. It wants to have God as the creator of time, yet it cannot comprehend the idea that there can be an agent that acts to create, yet has no time dimension of his own, while at the same time in our own experience we can act precisely because we are in time; it is what makes any action possible in the first place.

These examples should be an indicator that we shouldn't really pursue our intuitions to their logical conclusions beyond the limits of the natural world. Because reason wants to follow the train of thought to the end, but apparently it is trying to deal with a realm that doesn't work in human logic after a point. We may feel we are onto something, but that is just an illusion, and we shouldn't take such feelings seriously.

I will admit that atheism comes with its own problems. It is obvious from how we atheists have to either accept positivism or postmodernism and they both have fatal problems. Postmodernism is self-refuting as you explain in your great book *Philosophical Foundations for a Christian Worldview.* And positivism apparently is just logically immature and on its way to postmodernism if one has to be consistent. Wittgenstein matured and abandoned his positivism to become a postmodernist. And that is the end of the road.

So it seems the debate between atheism and theism is a stalemate. But if you still say that I must reject atheism because it ends up in the absurdity of postmodernism and I must, therefore, adopt its negation that is theism, well, then I will have to remind you of fatal problems in your worldview such as JEDP theories for the origin of Torah and the academic success of Darwinism which demands acceptance.

> Best Regards
> KS
> Turkey

Dr. Craig's Response

I really appreciate your interesting question, KS, and especially sticking up for me in your atheist forums!

As I read your letter, I thought, *Wow, this sounds just like a good Kantian!* (Have you read Kant's *Critique of Pure Reason* [1781]? Your arguments are echoes of his!) Now, scarcely any philosophers today are Kantians with respect to reason's ability to deliver to us important truths about reality. Since the demise of Verificationism in the mid-twentieth century, metaphysics, despite Kant's strictures, has been booming once again. That suggests that there must be something wrong with your argument. So let's talk about it.

INSIGHT

Notice what Dr. Craig is doing. He's contextualizing the perspective suggested by KS. This is important to do where possible in order to help people gain an appreciation of a broader discussion related to their questions. For this reason, knowing some history can be worthwhile for helping people understand what it is they are claiming.

First, it seems to me that we have no choice but to take common sense and intuition as our starting points. I very strongly suspect that even those who claim to place no stock in common sense and intuition in fact rely on them all the time with respect to unconscious metaphysical assumptions. So when a philosophical viewpoint flies in the face of common sense and intuition (e.g., that the external world does not exist), then we may justly demand a very powerful argument in favor of that viewpoint. In the absence of some defeater of what common sense and intuition tell us, we are rightly skeptical of that viewpoint and perfectly rational to reject it. So while the deliverances of common sense and intuition are certainly defeasible and may on occasion need revision, still they are an indispensable starting point that should not be lightly abandoned.

Are the laws of reason and the laws of reality the same, as people in Aristotle's time believed? Nothing has happened since the time of Aristotle that has undermined the truths of logic or logic's applicability to the world. Aristotle's logic is called syllogistic logic. He identified valid argument forms which are still recognized today, *e.g.*, All As are Bs; no Bs are Cs; therefore, no As are Cs. This is an undeniably valid pattern of reasoning. The principal advance of modern logic over Aristotle's is that modern logicians came to realize that the premises of syllogistic reasoning like "All As are Bs" have themselves a logical structure which Aristotle's logic failed to disclose. A statement like "All As are Bs" has in modern sentential logic (the logic of sentences) the structure of a conditional: "For any item *x*, if *x* is an *A*, then *x* is a *B*." This allows us to make inferences that Aristotle's syllogistic logic cannot express, e.g., "Whatever begins to exist has a cause; the universe began to exist; therefore, the universe has a cause."

Formal logic has become a discipline of incredible technical precision and rigor, akin to mathematics. Indeed, formal logic often goes by the name "mathematical logic." There is nothing in the advance of this discipline that should lead us to doubt reason's ability to make valid inferences about reality. Indeed, the development of subdisciplines like modal logic (the logic dealing with the necessary and the possible) and counterfactual logic (dealing with subjunctive conditional statements) has been a great asset in our being able to reason more carefully and rigorously when doing metaphysics.

Don't confuse Aristotelian logic with Aristotle's physics! Aristotle was not only a great philosopher but a natural scientist as well. As you might expect, his scientific work has been superseded by subsequent science, as most sophisticated instruments for probing the physical world have developed. As science advanced in our understanding of nature's laws, Aristotelian physics was replaced by Newtonian physics, which was in turn replaced by Einstein's physics, which will soon, we expect, be superseded by a quantum gravitational unified physics. In each successive scientific revolution, the earlier science is not simply abandoned; rather its truths are recast and preserved in the theory that supersedes it and its inaccuracies abandoned.

I hope you can see that none of this gives any cause to doubt the efficacy of human reason in knowing reality; quite the contrary, this is testimony to the incredible power of human reason!

The lesson here for the natural theologian is that he needs to be scientifically literate and to keep abreast of current discoveries and new theories in science. For that reason I have striven to be responsible in this regard. I want to have a theology that is scientifically informed and so to present an integrated perspective on reality.

Now, you remind us quite rightly that when it comes to subjects like God and creation, we are doing metaphysics, not physics (though physics may provide evidence in support of premises in a metaphysical argument leading logically to a conclusion which is of theological significance). So if we have plausibly true premises that imply by the standard rules of logic a conclusion of theological significance, why should we resist that conclusion?

Here's where your Kantianism enters the picture. You assert, *"When thinking about the beginning of time and about creation and God, our reason actually generates contradictory ideas."* You're claiming that reason leads us into antinomies and so cannot be trusted. I have responded to this Kantian claim.[2] KS, if you're serious about getting your reservations resolved,

---

2. See, for example, "Appendix 2: The Kalam Cosmological Argument and the Thesis of Kant's First Antinomy," in Dr. Craig's *The Kalam Cosmological Argument* (London: MacMillan, 1979).

please read that section. I show that there is no antinomy because there is nothing incoherent about a beginning of time. Kant thought that in order for time to have a beginning, there had to be a time before time during which nothing existed. That is a mistake. All that is required is that there was a time that was not preceded by any prior time. Far from being incomprehensible, this is precisely the concept of a beginning to time that is used in contemporary astrophysics. For example, the agnostic cosmologist Sean Carroll characterizes cosmological models that feature a beginning of the universe by saying, "there was a time such that there was no earlier time."[3]

Similarly, there's no problem about postulating a Creator or first cause who exists timelessly sans the universe. Again, Carroll uses precisely this notion with respect to a boundary condition on space-time: "There is no logical or metaphysical obstacle to completing the conventional temporal history of the universe by including an atemporal boundary condition at the beginning."[4] God's eternal, atemporal state is, as it were, such a boundary condition to time. God's act of creating the universe is simultaneous with the universe's coming into being. So God is atemporal sans creation and temporal since creation. So where's the problem?

As for the argument from contingent being to a metaphysically necessary being, what is the difficulty supposed to be? Many philosophers think that abstract objects like numbers and other mathematical objects exist necessarily. So where is the incoherence in the idea of a necessary being? It's a being that exists in every broadly logically possible world. (Here the advances in modal logic that I spoke of earlier actually help us to better understand this notion of a metaphysically necessary being.) So what's the objection?

These pseudo-antinomies thus do not support the radical conclusion that *"we shouldn't really pursue our intuitions to their logical conclusions beyond the limits of the natural world."* Indeed, when you assert, *"reason is trying to deal with a realm that doesn't work in human logic after a point. We may feel we are onto something, but that is just an illusion,"* we may justifiably turn the tables and ask you, "How do you know that? How, on your view, can you know anything about what that realm is like? How do you know human logic doesn't work there?

---

3. "Does the Universe Need God?" in *The Blackwell Companion to Science and Christianity*. James B. Stump and Alan G. Padgett, eds. (Wiley-Blackwell, 2012). For an audio discussion of Carroll's article listen to Dr. Craig's series of podcasts at ReasonableFaith.org (http://bit.ly/RFPodcasts). "Is Atheism Growing at the Expense of Theism" (7/16/2012), "Does Reason Lead to Atheism or Theism" (7/23/2012).

4. Ibid.

Indeed, how can logic 'not work'?" KS, you, like Kant before you, are in the self-refuting position of making metaphysical claims yourself!

The lesson here is not that we should just quit thinking but that we should think even harder. Listen, KS, you're not at the end of the road by a long shot. Even for an atheist, your choices are not limited to Positivism and Postmodernism. But why stick with atheism? Theism offers an intellectually expansive and richly rewarding view, not to speak of its spiritual benefits.

And, KS, what shall I say in response to your final paragraph? "C'mon Man!" You know better than that. You can be a theist and a Christian and accept the documentary hypothesis of the Pentateuch as well as a Darwinian theory of evolution, if you think that's where the evidence leads.[5]

How Is Belief in God Properly Basic?

Dr. Craig,

I have some questions about Reformed Epistemology and your view on the witness of the Holy Spirit.

Following the lead of Alvin Plantinga, you try to argue that classical foundationalism is self-refuting because the criterion used by classical foundationalism ("only propositions that are self-evident or incorrigible are properly basic") for discerning properly basic beliefs and beliefs derived from properly basic beliefs is itself neither properly basic nor derived. You say it is not properly basic because, using classical foundationalism's own criterion, it is neither self-evident nor incorrigible. But your assertion that the criterion cannot be demonstrated by using evidence is a bit hasty. After all, you have not shown that the criterion used in classical foundationalism is incoherent; all you've shown is that we simply lack any evidence for it at the moment, but as you know, absence of evidence is not evidence of absence. And unlike the self-refuting criterion used in logical positivism, the one in classical foundationalism can at least be verified in principle. Furthermore,

---

5. For more on this topic, see the questions on "Evolutionary Theory and Theism" and "Who Speaks for Science?" (pages 238–48.)

appealing to Reformed Epistemology to escape this does not help either because the criterion used by Reformed epistemologists ("only propositions that are self-evident, incorrigible, or appropriately grounded are properly basic") is itself not properly basic and, using Plantinga's hasty reasoning, is not evidentially supported either. So Reformed Epistemology does not do anything to alleviate the problem. Given this, should not one also reject Reformed Epistemology as self-refuting as well?

Second, there are better criteria available than the ones used either by the classical foundationalist or the Reformed epistemologist, particularly universal sanction. According to universal sanction, a belief is properly basic if it is pragmatically indispensable. The nice part about this criterion is that it allows for a type of evidentialism which avoids all of Plantinga's counterexamples. For instance, under universal sanction, memory beliefs, belief in the reality of the external world, belief in other minds, and so on, are properly basic because doubting or denying them would make living a normal human life impossible. We need these beliefs in order to live happy and fulfilling lives. Now, interestingly enough, universal sanction effectively prevents any theistic beliefs from being properly basic, for it is pragmatically conceivable that one lives a happy life without belief in God. I think Sennett is spot-on in his analysis here. The reason we accept belief in other minds, the external world, and our memories is not because we somehow "know" that they are true; it is all psychological, for we desperately want these beliefs to be true because we know that it would be impossible to live a fulfilling life without them. Now, Plantinga would probably say that universal sanction is self-refuting, but there are problems with that strategy as mentioned earlier. Would you now agree that universal sanction is superior to Plantinga's criterion?

Third, in the context of Plantinga's work, a properly basic belief is a basic belief that has not been attacked with any defeaters; once a defeater is given, though, the properly basic belief becomes simply a basic one. At this point, one can either relinquish the basic belief or hold on to it in the case that she can find arguments with which to defeat the original defeater, which would then restore the belief's proper basicality. On your view, though, the witness of the Holy Spirit is a properly basic belief AND an intrinsic defeater-defeater, so if someone were to offer a defeater to Christianity that you could not answer, would your belief in God be basic or properly basic?

Next, when you say that one is rational to believe in God on the basis of the witness of the Holy Spirit, do you mean rational in the sense pertaining to justification or warrant? If by "rational" you mean "justified," then you have really shown nothing. Muslims, Hindus, and atheists are all rational under this definition since they are within their epistemic rights. Nothing has been done to show that Christianity is true. On the other hand, if by "rational" you mean "warranted" in the Plantingian sense, then you need to explain why other properly basic beliefs that are warranted turn out to be false (like faulty memory beliefs).

It is worth noting that the relationship between properly basic non-theistic beliefs and their grounds are vastly different from the relationship between supposedly properly basic theistic beliefs and their grounds. There is always a certain correspondence between the content of an experience and the content of a belief grounded by that experience. For instance, my feeling of pain grounds the belief that I am in pain, not some unrelated belief like "evolution is true" or "a=a." However, according to Plantinga, experiencing guilt, happiness, and danger or reading the Bible serves as grounds for properly basic theistic belief. But surely you notice the disparity here, Dr. Craig! What Plantinga is asking us to do is to conclude, on the basis of a few emotions, that a necessary, eternal, self-existing, omnipotent, omniscient, omnibenevolent, omnipresent, omnitemporal, unembodied mind created the universe out of nothing and regularly interacts with humans and has revealed himself to man in the form of Jesus of Nazareth, who was born of a virgin, performed numerous miracles, was crucified, descended into hell, rose from the dead, ascended to heaven, and now sits at the right hand of God! The belief is so unrelated to its alleged grounds that one can only wonder how Plantinga gets away with this! Surely you don't believe that belief in the God mentioned above is solely grounded by a mere religious experience, right?

Finally, Plantinga's model presupposes that Christianity is true. Plantinga essentially is defending the proposition: If Christianity is true, then Christian belief is warranted (as explained by his model). But Plantinga never gives any support for the antecedent of that material conditional; he just says that demonstrating the antecedent is not his project. But if that is so, then Plantinga really has not shown much other than that *de jure* objections to Christianity fail. But I fail to see how his model shows how a Christian can rationally believe that Christianity is true. Do you hold to this view? You seem to argue in the opposite direction of Plantinga: If there is a witness of the Holy Spirit, then Christianity is true. Do you believe that THAT conditional is true?

Thank you,

Timaeus

(country not specified)

Dr. Craig's Response

In assessing Alvin Plantinga's theory of religious knowledge, it's important to keep clearly in mind what his aims are. As he describes his project, it is twofold: First, a public project aimed at showing that there is no objection to Christian belief unless Christian beliefs can be shown to be false and, second, a private project aimed to provide the Christian community with a plausible account of how Christian belief is warranted.

With regard to the public project, Plantinga wants to show that there is no good reason to think Christian belief is unjustified, irrational, or unwarranted unless it can be shown that Christian beliefs are false. Some readers might think, "Well, of course!" But they need to understand that at least until recently it has been argued that even if Christianity were true, we would not be justified in believing it. Usually this is because it is claimed that there is a lack of evidence for Christian beliefs such as the belief that God exists. Plantinga disagrees with that assertion; he thinks that the theistic arguments make it more probable than not that God exists. But he wants to defend the view that Christian belief can be justified, rational, and warranted even in the absence of evidence. In order to show this he develops a model for how one might be warranted in Christian belief on the basis of an innate cognitive faculty designed by God to produce belief in Him under certain circumstances and on the basis of the witness of the Holy Spirit to the great truths of the gospel contained in Scripture.

Plantinga doesn't claim to show that his model is true but merely that for all we know, it *may* be true, and, moreover, if Christianity *is* true, then something like the model is very likely to be true. If he succeeds in establishing these modest claims, he will have shown that there is no objection to Christian belief apart from demonstrating that Christianity is false, or, as he puts it, there is no *de jure* objection to Christian belief independent of a *de facto* objection.

So on Plantinga's view, belief in God can be (and he thinks should be) a properly basic belief not inferred on the basis of evidence. Now, as you note, Timaeus, the classical foundationalist has traditionally held that only self-evident or incorrigible beliefs are properly basic. Plantinga doesn't deny that such beliefs are properly basic, but he presents two considerations to prove that so restricting properly basic beliefs is untenable:

(i) If only self-evident and incorrigible propositions are properly basic, then we are all irrational, since we commonly accept numerous beliefs that are not based on evidence and that are neither self-evident nor incorrigible.

(ii) The proposition *Only beliefs that are self-evident or incorrigible are properly basic* is not itself properly basic, since it is neither self-evident nor incorrigible. Therefore, if we are to believe this proposition, we must have evidence that it is true. But there is no such evidence.

ANSWERING THREE OBJECTIONS TO BELIEF IN GOD AS PROPERLY BASIC

Now, your first objection is that perhaps the evidence justifying this belief will be found. It's very difficult to see how that could possibly happen, Timaeus. It's hard to see what sort of evidence *could* justify such a view, especially in light of (i). If we take an inductive survey of beliefs we think are properly basic, there will be no agreement that they are so restricted. But the more important point is that given the admitted *present* absence of such evidence, it is currently irrational to accept classical foundationalism. Therefore, it is impotent as an objection to including belief in God as properly basic.

You then assert that the criterion used by Reformed epistemologists is itself not properly basic or evidentially supported. But this is a misunderstanding. Reformed epistemologists like Plantinga don't offer any criterion of proper basicality. Plantinga eschews any search for such a criterion and suggests that if we want to see which beliefs are properly basic, the best we can do is just take an inductive survey of our beliefs, and he insists that the theist will include belief in God among such beliefs, even if unbelievers do not. So Reformed Epistemology is not self-refuting, since it doesn't offer any criterion of which beliefs are properly basic.

Your second objection is to offer another criterion for properly basic beliefs that would exclude belief in God as properly basic, namely, properly basic beliefs must be universally sanctioned. But this criterion falls prey to the same two objections raised by Plantinga. (i) There are a myriad of beliefs that we accept in a properly basic way that aren't universally sanctioned. For example, my belief that I had scrambled eggs for breakfast is not pragmatically indispensable. Even if it were for me (which it's not), it certainly isn't for someone else who isn't I and didn't eat scrambled eggs for breakfast. Most of our properly basic beliefs are highly individualized and, therefore, not universally sanctioned. (If you relativize your criterion to individual persons, then you'll have to allow that for some people belief in God might be pragmatically indispensable!) (ii) The belief that only universally sanctioned beliefs are properly basic is not itself universally sanctioned. But neither is there any evidence that only universally sanctioned beliefs are properly basic. So this objection doesn't exclude the proper basicality of belief in God. Universal sanction is not superior to Plantinga's criterion, first, because Plantinga doesn't have a criterion, and second, because universal sanction falls prey to the above objections. (Not to mention the fact that on your view, while our beliefs may be properly basic, they don't seem to be really warranted, leaving us in almost utter skepticism!)

Third, as to the role of defeaters of properly basic beliefs, the notion of an intrinsic defeater-defeater is not mine, but Plantinga's. An intrinsic defeater-defeater is a belief that is so powerfully warranted that it defeats the putative defeater brought against it without any need of additional beliefs to come to the rescue. Plantinga gives the charming illustration of someone accused of a crime that he knows he didn't commit even though all the evidence is stacked against him. He is rational in believing in his own innocence despite the evidence that would rightly convince someone else that he is guilty. In application to the witness of the Holy Spirit, my claim is that God can so powerfully warrant Christian beliefs that they become intrinsic defeaters of the defeaters lodged against them, so that, yes, they remain both properly basic and warranted.

THE RATIONALITY OF THEISTIC BELIEF

When I say that one is rational to believe in God on the basis of the witness of the Holy Spirit, do I mean rational in the sense pertaining to justification or warrant? Read what Plantinga says in response to the "Son of Great Pumpkin" objection in *Warranted Christian Belief*. He is emphatic that justification is easy to achieve (even Voodoo epistemologists can be justified in their beliefs!) and that what he's talking about is warrant, that which turns true belief into knowledge. You complain, "Nothing has been done to show that Christianity is true." Ah, but Timaeus, that's no part of Plantinga's project! His aim, remember, is merely to show that for all we know, his model may be true. When you assert, "you need to explain why other properly basic beliefs that are warranted turn out to be false (like faulty memory beliefs)," you err in thinking that such beliefs are warranted; they're not. They may be *justified* in the sense that the person holding them is within his rational rights or exhibits no cognitive defect, but he's not *warranted*.

As for the disparity of the conditions grounding properly basic beliefs, there's no reason to think there has to be uniformity here. In any case you misconstrue the model when you say that "on the basis of a few emotions" Plantinga is asking us "to conclude" that such and such a being exists. You're treating these experiences as something from which a belief is inferred, and that's not the model. Rather, these experiences serve as triggers for the operation of this innate, God-given faculty which forms belief in God (and even then not necessarily including all the superlative theological attributes you mention, of which very few people are even aware). As for the content of Christian beliefs, you're overlooking the role of Scripture in Plantinga's model: it is through Scripture that we learn of the great truths you mention, and then the Holy Spirit commends these truths to us. We don't just come up with them out of the blue; we read of them in Scripture. So, right, I and Plantinga do not think or propose that "belief in the God mentioned above is solely grounded by a mere religious experience."

Finally, you're correct that Plantinga claims that "if Christianity is true, then Christian belief is warranted." You're also correct that he "says that demonstrating the antecedent is not his project." You then complain, "But if that is so, then Plantinga really has not shown much other than that *de jure* objections to Christianity fail." Right, which is to admit that his public project has been a resounding success! No longer can unbelievers grumble that Christians are irrational, unjustified, or unwarranted in believing as they do in the absence of evidence. Unbelievers will have to come up with disproofs of Christian beliefs in order to show that such beliefs are irrational, unjustified, or unwarranted. So your next remark, Timaeus, just doesn't make sense: "I fail to see how his model shows how a Christian can rationally believe that Christianity is true." That's exactly what you just admitted it *does* show, unless you've got some arguments you've not yet shared to show that Christianity is false.

Do I hold Plantinga's view? That question takes us from his public project into his private project. Should I as a Christian adopt his model as a way of understanding how Christian beliefs are warranted? Here I do have some reservations. See my assessment in the chapter on Religious Epistemology in *Philosophical Foundations for a Christian Worldview*. I'm inclined to place more emphasis on the witness of the Holy Spirit rather than on some innate cognitive faculty. Still, at the end of the day I think that Plantinga is right that if Christianity is true, then *something like the model* is very likely to be true. I also think that "if there is a witness of the Holy Spirit, then Christianity is true." And I think Plantinga would agree.

On Question-Begging and Appealing to the Holy Spirit

Dear Dr. Craig,

I've found that the relationship between reason and faith is one of the less understood aspects of Christianity; especially the aspect related to if we know that Christianity is true. When pressed to explain how you know that your experience of the Holy Spirit is veridical and not false (like the experience of Mormons or Muslim), you have replied: "The experience of the Spirit's witness is self-authenticating for the person who really has it. The Spirit-filled Christian can know immediately that his claim to the Spirit's witness is true despite the false claims made by persons adhering to other religions."

It seems to me that your reply begs the question in favor of Christianity (or more specifically, in favor of Christians' claims of having veridical experiences of the Holy Spirit) and against other religious people's claims of having similar non-Christian experiences of God's Spirit.

In other words, your reply assumes:

1. That Christianity is true (hence, the Holy Spirit actually exists as experienced by Christians)
2. That Christians have access to that truth and, therefore, that other non-Christian claims about God's Spirit (or the claims of other religious people) are false.

But precisely what is at stake is whether Christianity is true or not (this is what we want to know) and, if it is the case, how could we KNOW it objectively (not purely through a subjective experience which, by itself, is equivalent to other subjective experiences of other non-Christian religious believers).

The question-begging nature of your explanation becomes more clear when you rhetorically ask: "How is the fact that other persons, like Muslims or Mormons, falsely claim to experience a self-authenticating witness of God's Spirit relevant to my knowing the truth of Christianity via the Spirit's witness?"

True, if Christianity is true and the Holy Spirit exists, then the fact that other people falsely claim to experience God's Spirit is irrelevant to my knowing of the truth of Christianity.

But the problem is that we don't know in advance if Christianity is true or not (this is what we are trying to know!), so I cannot assume that MY experience of the Holy Spirit is the veridical one, and the experience of other people is the false one.

Can you expand in more detail on these questions please?

Best regards,

Mary

Dr. Craig's Response

Mary, this is an objection that, though understandable, is based on a failure to grasp correctly Alvin Plantinga's project in religious epistemology. Plantinga distinguishes between what he calls *de facto* and *de jure* objections to Christian belief. A *de facto* objection is one aimed at the truth of the Christian faith; it attempts to show that Christian truth claims are false. By contrast a *de jure* objection attempts to undermine Christian belief even if Christianity is, in fact, true.

Plantinga identifies three versions of the *de jure* objection: that Christian belief is unjustified, that it is irrational, and that it is unwarranted. Plantinga's aim is to show that all such *de jure* objections to Christian belief are unsuccessful, or, in other words, that Christian belief can be shown to be unjustified, irrational, or unwarranted only if it is shown that Christian beliefs are false. There is thus no *de jure* objection to Christian belief independent of a *de facto* objection.

To show this, Plantinga develops a model or theory of warranted Christian belief, that is to say, an account of how it is that we know the truth of various Christian truth claims. On behalf of his model Plantinga claims, not that it is true, but that

(1) It is epistemically possible, that is to say, for all we know, it may be true;

(2) If Christianity is true, there are no philosophical objections to the model;

(3) If Christianity is true, then something like the model is very likely to be true.

71

According to Plantinga's model, God warrants to us the great truths of the gospel by means of the inner witness of the Holy Spirit. Such beliefs are for us properly basic beliefs grounded in (but not inferred from) the witness of the Holy Spirit.

Now, the point is, such a model may for all we know be true. Moreover, if Christianity is true, then, as you note, there is no problem with the model. Finally, I think that Plantinga is right that if Christianity is true, then something like his model is very likely to be true. So there is no *de jure* objection to Christian belief. The unbeliever who wants to argue that Christian belief is unjustified, irrational, or unwarranted has to present objections to the truth of the Christian faith. For if he doesn't, then for all he knows, Christianity may well be true, in which case there just is no problem with Christian belief.

None of this begs the question, I hope you can see. For the key claims are conditional. Neither of them assumes that Christianity actually is true.

Now, of course, a Muslim could make exactly similar claims about Islam, as Plantinga acknowledges. There is, therefore, no *de jure* objection to Muslim belief either.

INSIGHT

Notice the relevancy of *de jure* objections in an interreligious dialogue context. What can you appreciate about Dr. Craig's insight and its applicability to dialoguing with a very different religious and philosophical worldview?

So we'll naturally want to know, "Well, then, is Christianity true?" The Christian will say, "Yes." That raises a further question: "How do you know?" The Christian may answer, "Because I do experience the inner witness of the Holy Spirit." There's nothing circular here, anymore than in someone's reporting that he does experience the reality of the external world or the presence of other minds. If some solipsist said to me that he doesn't believe in the reality of the external world or other minds, that wouldn't do anything to defeat my beliefs. Even if he claimed that God was warranting to him his solipsistic beliefs in a properly basic way, that wouldn't do a thing to call my beliefs into question. He can claim what he wants; I know better.

Of course, the Muslim can say the same thing, and so we have a standoff. But here my distinction between knowing our faith to be true and showing it to be true becomes relevant. In order to show our Muslim friend that his beliefs are not properly basic, we can present *de facto* objections to the truth of Islam. Since he does not in fact have a genuine witness of the Holy Spirit to the truth of Islam, we can hope that his confidence will crack under the force of the evidence and that he will come to see that his experience was either non-veridical or misinterpreted.

Again, the Muslim can say the same thing and so engage in Muslim apologetics aimed at providing *de facto* objections to Christianity. Great! Bring on the debate!

2

ON ARGUMENTATION AND LOGIC 101

An Exercise in Argumentation and Logic

Hi Dr. Craig,

My question pertains to your work in *Philosophical Foundations for a Christian Worldview*. In Argumentation and Logic, I was confused by argument B in the first exercise set:[6]

The argument is as follows:

1. God is timeless only if he is immutable

2. God is immutable only if he does not know what time it is now

3. If God is omniscient, then he knows what time it is now

4. God is omnipotent and omniscient.

The assignment is to symbolize each argument and the draw the conclusion stating the rule and the justification of each step.

So, I think the argument should look like the following:

1. P → Q

2. Q → R (MP 1)

3. S → T

4. O & S (MP/Conj. 3)

I am confused by how the argument can go from God's immutability to his omniscience.

---

6. William Lane Craig and J. P. Moreland, *Philosophical Foundations for a Christian Worldview* (Downers Grove, Ill.: InterVarsity, 2003), 39.

I don't know what rule is being used and I was hoping you could help me think better about these nine rules of logic and which ones are used in this argument.

Thank you and God bless!

Daniel

Dr. Craig's Response

This is a good exercise for our readers. What mistake(s) has Daniel made? Has he correctly symbolized the four premises? What follows from them? Can you name the rules of inference that are used in this argument? Take a moment to work on this problem before reading on.

So, Daniel, where did you go wrong? First, a couple of minor points: (2) is not an inference from (1) using the rule MP (*modus ponens*) as your notation indicates. It's just a premise in its own right. *Modus ponens* is the rule that would allow you to infer from P ¬ Q and P that, therefore, Q. But in this argument P doesn't appear as a premise; it's just the antecedent clause of (1).

Second, premise (4) is similarly not an inference but just a premise in the argument. It is a conjunction, but it is not using the rule of inference called Conjunction to infer from O and S that therefore O & S. The argument doesn't "go from God's immutability to his omniscience."

Your main misstep, Daniel, occurs in your symbolization of premises (2) and (3). Look at the consequent clause of (2) and the consequent clause of (3). The consequent clause of (2) is just the negation of the consequent clause of (3)! So the clause should be symbolized by the same letter with a negation sign "¬" in front of it, so:

2. $Q \rightarrow \neg R$

So (3) should become:

3. $S \rightarrow R$

Our symbolization of the premises should now look like this:

1. $P \rightarrow Q$

2. $Q \rightarrow \neg R$

3. $S \rightarrow R$

4. $O \& S$

OK, now apply your rules of inference and what do you get?

5. S (Simplification, from 4)
6. R (*Modus ponens*, from 3, 5)
7. $\neg \neg R$ (Double negation, from 6)
8. $\neg Q$ (*Modus tollens*, from 2, 7)
9. $\neg P$ (*Modus tollens*, from 12, 8)

In English: we can infer that God is not timeless. Pretty nifty, eh? Now, all we have to do is assess the truth of the premises to see if we have a sound argument for God's temporality.[7]

What Is a Criterion for a Good (Apologetics) Argument?

Dear Dr. Craig,

    I have a question dealing with what constitutes a good argument. You frequently state in your popular work that a good argument must: be logically valid, be sound, and have premises more plausible than their negations. Now, I know you rightly ignore the popular objections to your work raised by Internet atheists, but regarding your third criterion, I think they raise a valid point. Several atheists and skeptics, both on YouTube and

7. For that discussion see Dr. Craig's book *Time and Eternity*.

elsewhere, have objected that there exist counterexamples to your third criterion that the premises must be more plausible than their negation. The first one proceeds as follows:

1. If (A & B), then C.
2. A.
3. B.
4. Therefore, C.

Now, suppose we learn that the credence (I'm using this term in a probabilistic sense) for believing (1) is 1, and the credence for believing (2) and (3) are each 0.6. Now, here is the problem: although all three premises are more plausible than their negations (all of them have a credence above 0.5), their conclusion is not, for when the probabilities of the premises are multiplied, the conclusion's credence is a mere 0.36! So something clearly went wrong, but what?

Another example proffered which does not use probability is as follows:

1. It is raining.
2. My neighbor's dog is outside.
3. Therefore, it is raining and my neighbor's dog is outside.

This is a logically valid argument, since the conclusion follows from an inference rule known as conjunction introduction.

So here's the problem with this argument: (1) might be more plausible than its negation because I might see rain falling through my window, whereas (2) might be more plausible than its negation since I know my neighbor's dog is always outside. Yet, I am nowhere near as certain about the conclusion! If my neighbor is a good owner, he would bring his dog in when it rains, meaning that the conclusion is less plausible than its negation! Moreover, one cannot say that (2) is implausible because it is raining, for he then is bringing (1) into consideration and is, therefore, commenting on the argument's conclusion.

So Dr. Craig, these are the main issues raised by atheists and skeptics on the Internet against your third criterion. Is there any way for one to answer them? And if they are right, then how should seekers of truth approach the premises of an argument and how much warrant should they demand of them?

Thank you and God bless,
Pranav
(country not specified)

Dr. Craig's Response

It's scary how really *desperate* these people are becoming! Far from raising valid points, Pranav, these objections are just worthless, based on fundamental misunderstandings of what makes good apologetics arguments. The people who posted these criticisms on YouTube, if they continue their study of philosophy, are going to be very embarrassed someday about these videos.

Let me back up and take a run at your question. What makes for a sound deductive argument? The answer is: true premises and valid logic. An argument is sound if the premises of the argument are true and the conclusion follows from the premises by the logical rules of inference. If these two conditions are met, then the conclusion of the argument is guaranteed to be true.

However, to be a good argument, an argument must be more than just sound. If the premises of an argument are true, but we have no evidence for the truth of those premises, then the argument will not be a good one. It may (unbeknownst to us) be sound, but in the absence of any evidence for its premises it won't, or at least shouldn't, convince anyone. The premises have to have some sort of epistemic warrant for us in order for a sound argument to be a good one.

INSIGHT

"Question-begging" is an informal fallacy that pertains to whether a person's *only reason* for believing in a premise is that he already believes in the conclusion. Notice one could believe in a premise because he believes in the conclusion and this would not be question-begging unless that reason for believing were the only reason. Bottom line: we want to learn to offer arguments that have reasons for a premise that are "independent" of a conclusion.

QUESTION-BEGGING

This is why question-begging arguments are not good arguments. A person is guilty of begging the question if his only reason for believing in a premise is that he already believes in the conclusion.

For example, suppose you were to present the following argument for the existence of God:
1. Either God exists or the moon is made of green cheese.
2. The moon is not made of green cheese.
3. Therefore, God exists.

Now, this is a sound argument for God's existence: its premises are both true and the conclusion follows from the premises by the rules of logic (specifically, disjunctive syllogism).

Nevertheless, the argument is not any good because the only reason for believing the first premise to be true is that you already believe that God exists (a disjunction is true if one of the disjuncts is true). But that's the argument's conclusion! Therefore, in putting forward this argument you're reasoning in a circle or begging the question. The only reason you believe (1) is because you believe (3).

So, soundness is not sufficient for making an argument a good one. Something more is needed concerning the warrant the premises have for us. Following the lead of George Mavrodes[8] and Steve Davis[9], I've argued that what is needed is that the premises be not only true but more plausible than their opposites or negations. If it is more plausible that a premise is, in light of the evidence, true rather than false, then we should believe the premise.

I trust that this clears up the gross misunderstanding propagated in a YouTube video that when I say that the premises of a good argument must be more plausibly true than their negations, I'm positing a range of additional truth values in between true and false. No, I presume the classical Principle of Bivalence, according to which there are only two truth values, *True* and *False*. There are different degrees of plausibility, not of truth, given the varying amounts of evidence in support of one's premises.

8. George I. Mavrodes, *Belief in God: A Study in the Epistemology of Religion* (New York: Random House, 1970).
9. Stephen T. Davis, *God, Reason and Theistic Proofs* (Grand Rapids: Eerdmans, 1997).

THE RELATION OF CONCLUSION TO PREMISES

Moreover, in a valid deductive argument, like the *kalam* cosmological argument, any probabilities assigned to the premises are not used to calculate the probability of the conclusion.[10] If the premises are true, then it follows necessarily that conclusion is true, period. It's logically fallacious to multiply the probabilities of the premises to try to calculate the probability of the conclusion. That's why you wind up with the clearly wrong results that you did. In a sound deductive argument the most we can say about the probability of the argument's conclusion is that it cannot be less than some lower bound; but it could be as high as 100 percent.

So with respect to your first example, we have here a valid deductive argument, since from (2) and (3), we may infer

3*. A&B

and from (1) and (3*) it follows logically that (4). All we need to find out is whether there are better reasons to believe (1), (2), and (3) rather than their opposites. If there are, then you have a good argument for (4). The probability of (4) doesn't even enter the picture.

As for your second example, this is also, as you note, a valid argument. So you just need to find out whether the evidence makes each premise more likely to be true than its negation. The misgiving you share is simply evidence that (2) may not be more plausible than its negation. You're entitled to look at all the evidence relevant to (2). If it's raining or 40 degrees below zero or you heard your wife say your neighbor was taking his dog to the vet today, etc., you may well have good grounds for thinking (2) is not true. You might know, *e.g.*, 1*. If it is raining, my neighbor takes his dog inside.

It follows from (1) and (1*) that (2) is false. But if, on balance, the evidence supports (1) and (2) rather than their opposites, then you've got a good argument for (3).

So you can see that good apologetics arguments are simply those which are sound and whose premises have more warrant than their negations. If these are really "the main issues raised by atheists and skeptics on the Internet against [my] third criterion," we're in great shape, and they are in deep trouble.

---

10. With Dr. Craig, it is preferable to speak of plausibility rather than probability to avoid the problem that it is often difficult to assign probability values to the premises.

Why "Soundness" Is Not Sufficient for Making a Good Argument

Hello,

My name is Manol. I am from Albania. I have just graduated in Medicine and Surgery in the University of Bologna in Italy. I am a Christian, and I have been using your arguments many times during evangelism. I am also preparing for teaching others in church about these arguments. I am writing because I have a question on the moral argument. The argument is:

1) If God does not exist then objective moral values do not exist.

2) Objective moral values do exist.

3) Therefore God exists.

I agree with all of that. The first premise seems very obvious to me. And I agree that in our moral experience we do discern a realm of objective moral truth.

But one day as I was thinking about it, considering what an atheist may answer to this argument, it came to my mind that he might answer that the argument is too "simplistic", or too "obvious".

Let me explain what I mean. Your argument in support of premise 2 is that in the same way the outer world is objective, in the same way moral values are objective. Our perception of objective moral values is on a par with our perception of the outer world with the five senses.

But if this parallelism between moral values and the outer world is true, then it means that the argument may be turned into something like this:

1) If God does not exist, then an objective outer world does not exist.

2) An objective outer world does exist.

3) Therefore God exists.

But as an argument it doesn't seem very convincing. Is the parallel correct? If yes, then why not using this second argument in the debates or talks? If this second argument is used and it is proven not convincing, why should the moral argument, which is a parallel argument, be convincing? Or, if you think this second argument is not convincing, why is it so?

Thanks for all you are doing and God bless,
Manol

Dr. Craig's Response

Manol, I can't tell you how thrilled I am to receive a question from so articulate and thoughtful a Christian in Albania, a traditionally Muslim and lately Marxist country! With your education and obvious language skills, you are well-prepared to be mightily used of God in your homeland.

I'm impressed that in contrast to so many native English speakers you have correctly grasped the moral argument which I defend. You are spot-on in thinking that the support for the second premise lies in the fact that "in our moral experience we do discern a realm of objective moral truth." You have correctly grasped the parallel between the deliverances of our five senses about the realm of physical objects and the deliverances of our moral sense about the realm of values and duties. Just as we cannot get outside our five senses to check their veridicality and so prove that we are not the proverbial "brain in a vat" being stimulated by a mad scientist to perceive an external world, so we cannot get outside our moral sense to check its veridicality. But in both cases we are perfectly rational, in the absence of any defeater of our beliefs, to believe that we do apprehend objective realities.

On this basis you construct a parallel argument, which, if dubious, ought to make us think that the moral argument is also dubious. Now, the parallel argument you construct is actually a sort of cosmological argument for God's existence. In fact, I think it is a sound argument! It is obviously valid, and both the premises seem to me to be true. For the objective outer world obviously exists, and if God did not exist, then no world at all would exist, including an objective outer world! It's not that if God did not exist, then the outer world would be merely a subjective illusion; rather it's that there wouldn't be anything at all!

So why not use this parallel argument in debates or talks? The answer to that question serves to highlight what makes for a good argument. Soundness is not sufficient to make an argument a good one. It's easy to construct sound arguments for God's existence. For example:

1. Either God exists or the moon is made of green cheese.
2. The moon is not made of green cheese.
3. Therefore, God exists.

This argument is logically valid, and both its premises are true (a disjunction like (1) is true if one of its disjuncts is true, and in this case the first disjunct "God exists" is true). But I'm sure you wouldn't recommend my using this argument in debates and talks! Why not? Simply, because no one would believe the first premise unless he already believed the conclusion to be true. The argument is thus circular or, as we say, begs the question.

So being sound is not sufficient to make an argument a good one. The argument must also not commit any informal logical fallacies like begging the question, and the premises must be more plausible than their negations. The first premise of your parallel argument threatens to beg the question and is not apt to appear more plausible than its negation to someone who is not already a theist. By contrast, as you know, the first premise of the moral argument is one that many atheists themselves believe and argue for. Thus, although the premises of your two arguments are parallel, the support for the premises is quite different.

In order to run a good cosmological argument, we need to provide some reason to think that if God did not exist, then the world would not exist. I, myself, like the following version of Leibniz's cosmological argument:

1. Anything that exists has an explanation of its existence, either in the necessity of its own nature or in an external cause.
2. If the universe has an explanation of its existence, that explanation is God.
3. The universe exists.
4. Therefore, the universe has an explanation of its existence. (from 1, 3)
5. Therefore, the explanation of the existence of the universe is God. (from 2, 4)

In this argument, premise (1) is a modest version of the Principle of Sufficient Reason and (2) is logically equivalent to the atheist's typical claim that if atheism is true, then there is no explanation of the universe's existence. This argument is, I think, a good one.[11]

11. For more on this, see the question in this book, "On Assessing the Argument from Contingency" (pages 148–53).

3

ON THE BASIS FOR OBJECTIVE MORALITY

Is There Objective Truth?

Dr. Craig,

Life has become absurd to me. Having had conversations with several individuals in my school years has taught me that most do not think that there is such a thing as truth, rather the word "truth" is only a matter of opinion and, therefore, has no absolute meaning. At the end of my conversations it has been revealed to me that anything that is not a scientific fact is false, and that this "truth" is only a coping mechanism that human beings have created to make it appear that life has meaning, but in reality it has none.

How do you as a philosopher/theologian deal with this? I am anxious for your response!

Steven

United States

Dr. Craig's Response

Steven, your despair is wholly unnecessary and even misconceived. The individuals who told you that "there is no such thing as truth" are not clear thinkers or reliable guides. The position that they espouse is self-referentially incoherent, that is to say, it is literally self-refuting.

Just ask yourself the question: is the statement "1. There is no such thing as truth" true? If not, then no need to worry, right? On the other hand if (1) is true, then it follows that (1) is not true, since there is no truth. So if (1) is false, it's false; and if (1) is true, it's false. So either way (1) is false. The position that your friends espoused is just incoherent.

Please don't dismiss this response as mere logic-chopping. The position your friends taught you is just self-refuting and silly.

Indeed, the rest of your letter reveals that you implicitly reject their self-defeating view, for you go on to affirm quite a number of alleged truths:

2. The word "truth" is only a matter of opinion and, therefore, has no absolute meaning.
3. Anything that is not a scientific fact is false.
4. Truth is only a coping mechanism that human beings have created.
5. Life really has no meaning.

If (1) is true, then (2)–(5) cannot be true. Now, since (1) is self-defeating, you'll have to abandon it and just assert the truth of (2)–(5).

But then the problem is that (1) was given as the *justification* for asserting (2)–(5). So if you give up (1), what warrant is there for (2)–(5)?

Indeed, (2)–(5) have self-referential problems of their own. Take (2). This statement is a real mess. Clearly the *word* "truth" is not a matter of opinion. The word "truth" is an English word with five letters. It doesn't assert anything and so can't be a matter of opinion. Similarly, what does it mean to say that "truth" has no absolute meaning? Clearly, this word has a meaning (look it up in any dictionary), as is evident from the fact that we are discussing it. If it has a meaning in English (unlike, say, "zliibckk"), I don't know what is meant by saying that the meaning isn't absolute. Of course, the meaning of "truth" is relative to the English language. It has no meaning in German, for example (as opposed to "*Wahrheit*"). Clearly, what is meant by (2) is something more like

2*. What is true is person-relative and only a matter of opinion.

"True for you," as they say, "but not true for me." But then the same self-referential problems arise again. If (2*) is true, then (2*) itself is just matter of opinion and is person-relative. But then it's not objectively true that truth is only a matter of opinion. It's just your opinion that truth is a matter of opinion, so who cares? The problem is that relativists want to assert that (2*) is *objectively* true; but in that case (2*) is false. So once more, it's self-defeating.

Or take (3). (3) is not itself a scientific fact. There are no experiments you could conduct to prove it, nor will you find it asserted in any science textbook. It is a philosophical statement about the nature of facts. But it states that anything that is not a scientific fact is false. But then it follows that (3) itself is false! Wake up, Steven! How could you have been blind to these incoherencies?

What about (4)? Truth and falsehood are properties of statements. A statement *S* is true if and only if what *S* says is the case really is the case. For example, "Snow is white" is true if, and only if, snow is white. Obviously, truth is not a coping mechanism, since coping mechanisms are not properties of statements. This is just muddled thinking. What is intended by (4) must be something like

4*. We think that *S* is true only because so thinking enables us to cope in life.

> **INSIGHT**
> We all are led by something or someone. If our "guides" cannot direct us to what is real and knowledge of it, (among other reasons) they should not be considered reliable. Dr. Craig's exhortation is authentic and important.

Now, on the face of it, (4*) strikes me as utterly implausible. Surely you can think of all sorts of statements you think are true quite independently of whether so thinking helps you to cope in life. Indeed, some of the things we think are true are positive impediments to our coping successfully with life! But let that pass. The more important thing is that if (4*) is true, then the only reason you believe (4*) is because it helps you to cope. In that case we might feel sorry for you, but we won't be worried about the objectivity of truth as a result.

As for (5), that is a coherent and important assertion. I agree with you that if God does not exist, then (5) is true. But if He does, then (5) is false. So what evidence do you have to support your view? It's going to be pretty tough for you to give any evidence for your view if you deny that truth is objective and can be objectively known!

The bottom line, Steven, is that it is a substantive claim to say that life is absurd, and these acquaintances of yours who have led you to embrace such a belief have deceived you through sophomoric arguments and self-refuting assertions. I urge you to shake off the stupor caused by such sophisms and come to think clearly about such matters!

On the Value of Appealing to One's Moral Experience

Dear Dr. Craig,

I asked my pastor if one could present your argument from the existence of objective moral values to the atheist as evidence of God's existence. The argument was:

1. If God does not exist, objective moral values do not exist.
2. Objective moral values do exist.
3. Therefore, God exists.

My pastor flat out deemed this as logically flawed, saying that we could not use it at all. He disagreed with premise 2, that objective moral values exist. He said that although we believe they exist, we cannot say they exist until we know that God exists. He also said that while we are tempted (probably by our social values) to say that objective moral values do exist, we cannot know that they do until there is a transcendent God to ground them in. I suspect his argument would go like this:

1. If God does not exist, objective moral values do not exist.
2. God exists.
3. Therefore, objective moral values do exist.

However this immediately raises the same question, namely, how do we know that the second premise (in each argument) is true?

How could I show him that objective moral values do exist? Is there any way apart from affirming them because we apprehend a realm of objective morality? Couldn't premises 2 and 3 just be circular?

Keep up the great work!

Yours In Christ,

Rohit

Dr. Craig's Response

I was disheartened to read your email, Rohit, because it illustrates so well the sloppy thinking that all too often characterizes pronouncements from evangelical ministers. (I'm assuming, of course, that you have accurately represented your pastor's views and that it is not you who are confused!) His muddled response to your argument underlines the importance of some philosophical training in the seminary studies of our future ministers.

His fundamental confusion concerns the difference between the *truth* of a premise and our *warrant* for it. I take it as obvious that a statement can be true even if we have no evidence at all for its truth; by the same token we can have pretty strong evidence for a statement that is, in fact, false. I'll leave it up to you to think of some examples.

Now, I don't think your pastor really denies the *truth* of premise (2) (if he did, you'd better look for another church!). Rather what he thinks is that we have no *warrant* for believing (2) independent of our belief in God. For he thinks that once we do know that a transcendent God exists, then we know that there is a ground for objective moral values. So he really does believe that objective moral values exist, and, therefore, he should agree that (2) is true. Moreover, (3) follows logically from (1) and (2) by the rule of inference called *modus tollens*. So your pastor shouldn't complain about the logic of the argument. (Your attempt to reconstruct his thinking presumably doesn't accurately represent his reasoning because it is just logically invalid: no rule of logic will permit you to infer (3´) from (1´) and (2´).)

Rather your pastor's complaint is best understood as the allegation that we can't use the moral argument, not because it is formally invalid or has a false premise, but because it is question-begging, that is to say, the only reason we have for believing (2) is that we already believe (3). So anyone who uses this argument is reasoning in a circle.

So understood, I think that he is clearly mistaken. People don't believe in (2) because they believe in God. They believe in (2) because of their moral experience, in which they apprehend certain values that impose themselves upon us and certain duties that lay claim upon us. That goes for atheists and agnostics as well as theists. Non-theists who accept (2) obviously do not do so in a question-begging way, and neither do theists, I should say.

Of course, your pastor may be skeptical of our moral experience, thinking that it is as plausibly attributed to social conditioning as to a genuine experience of moral values. But why agree with him about that? I am far more confident that I apprehend objective moral values and duties than I am of the premises in any argument for moral skepticism. And so are most nontheists, whom we are seeking to persuade.

Your pastor seems to be confusing the order of knowing (*ordo cognoscendi*) with the order of being (*ordo essendi*). In the order of knowing, we first apprehend a realm of objective moral values and then infer to God as their ground. But in the order of being, God is primary as the ground of objective moral values, and moral values depend for their objective reality upon Him. Just because God comes first in the order of being doesn't imply that He comes first in the order of knowing.

So in answer to your question, the best way to convince anyone of the objective reality of moral values is to appeal to his moral experience. Give some illustrations of moral outrages and ask people if they think such things are really evil or wrong. I think you'll find 98 percent of people will agree on the basis of their experience that we do apprehend at least some objective moral values and duties. With such persons your argument does not beg the question.

How Can God Be the Ground of Morality?

My question concerns the discussion of God as a logically necessary being in the book where you debate then atheist Antony Flew.[12] For clarification, you say that for God to be logically necessary, he must be all-powerful, all-knowing, and morally perfect in all possible worlds. You demonstrated these by the *kalam*, fine-tuning, and moral arguments respectively. Is this brief summary correct?

12. See *Does God Exist?* with Antony Flew. Responses by K. Yandell, P. Moser, D. Geivett, M. Martin, D. Yandell, W. Rowe, K. Parsons, and Wm. Wainwright. Ed. Stan Wallace (Aldershot: Ashgate, 2003).

My question regards Christian philosophers Keith Yandell's/Richard Swinburne's objection that God cannot explain the objectivity of morality. You argue that because God is logically necessary that thus (and among other reasons) He can explain morality. But it seems like a circular (I think) argument because you need the proof from the moral argument to prove that God is logically necessary so that you can counter Swinburne's objection. But you have to counter the objection before arguing that God is logically necessary. What is your reply? Have I understood this correctly?

Thomas

Dr. Craig's Response

Your question evinces some misunderstanding. So before I address your question directly, let me clarify what I said. First, God's existing necessarily is not related to His being all-powerful, all-knowing, and morally perfect, at least in any direct way. For God to be logically necessary He simply needs to exist in every logically possible world; indeed, to say that God is logically necessary just is to say that He exists in every possible world. Now, of course, since the attributes you mention are essential to God, it follows that He will have such attributes in every possible world. But I'm not suggesting that God exists in all possible worlds because He has these attributes.

Second, I did not attempt to demonstrate that God has these attributes by means of the three arguments you mention. The *kalam* and fine-tuning arguments imply the existence of an enormously powerful and intelligent being, but not an omnipotent or omniscient being. The moral argument can be augmented to lead to the conclusion that God, as the ground of objective moral value, is morally perfect, but that is not the conclusion of the argument itself.

Now, Yandell and Swinburne think that God cannot be the ground of moral value in part because they both think that God exists merely contingently rather than necessarily, whereas at least some moral values exist necessarily. So on their view there are possible worlds in which God does not exist and yet moral values exist. My point is that the classical theist faces no such problem, since he believes that God is a logically necessary being and so can ground moral values in every logically possible world. So the objection finds no purchase against the classical theist.

I think you can see now that there is no circularity involved. If God is a contingent being, He cannot ground moral values. Agreed! It is now up to Yandell or Swinburne to prove that God is a contingent being. Unless they do that, the conclusion does not follow that God cannot ground moral values.

Thus, it is really irrelevant *why* the classical theist believes that God is logically necessary. He might believe it on religious grounds or on the basis of the ontological argument or the argument from contingency. He might, as you suggest, believe it on moral grounds. For if objective moral values imply God's existence, this is plausibly not merely a contingent fact. Moral values cannot exist without God; they entail His existence. So if moral values exist necessarily, it follows that God exists necessarily.

So the argument looks like this:

1. Necessarily, if moral values exist, then God exists.
2. Necessarily, moral values exist.
3. Therefore, necessarily, God exists.

Yandell and Swinburne deny (1) because they think that God is contingent. But you can't just assume that God is contingent or else you're begging the question. For that just is to assume that the conclusion (3) is false, that God does *not* exist necessarily. So if anyone is in danger of circular reasoning, it is the objector to the moral argument.

So the classical theist who believes even on moral grounds that God is logically necessary is not reasoning in a circle. To the objector who denies (1) because God exists contingently, he replies, "Prove it (without begging the question)!" The ball is now in the objector's court.

The Importance of Distinguishing Between Moral Epistemology and Moral Ontology

Dr. Craig,

I have been debating several atheists regarding the existence of objective moral values being grounded in God. I have been doing quite well avoiding the red herring of moral epistemology and have managed to keep the debate to moral ontology. Now, I am stuck and need your help.

Quoting you in a debate with Dr. Harris you said, "Theism provides a sound foundation for objective moral duties. On a theistic view, objective moral duties are constituted by God's commands. God's moral nature is expressed in relation to us in the form of divine commandments. These constitute our moral obligations."[13]

By saying this, is not one already providing an argument for Revealed Theology and thus making an argument for moral epistemology? That is, unless divine commandments don't come through Revealed Theology.

Please help, I don't know how to wiggle out of this one. It seems I am trapped into having to discuss moral epistemology now.

Bethany Joy

Dr. Craig's Response

As I explain in *Philosophical Foundations for a Christian Worldview*, it is vitally important in discussing moral arguments for God's existence to distinguish clearly various areas of Moral Theory.[14]

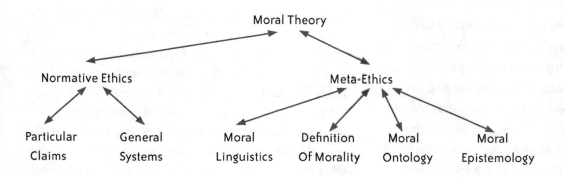

13. To view and read the whole debate, you can access it for free at ReasonableFaith.org (http://bit.ly/HarrisDebate).

14. See Walter Sinnott-Armstrong, "Moral Skepticism and Justification," in *Moral Knowledge?* Walter Sinnott-Armstrong and Mark Timmons, eds. (New York: Oxford University Press, 1996), 4–5.

The claim that moral values and duties are rooted in God is a Meta-Ethical claim about Moral Ontology, not about Moral Linguistics or Epistemology. It is fundamentally a claim about the objective status of moral properties, not a claim about the meaning of moral sentences or about the justification or knowledge of moral principles.

I'm convinced that keeping the distinction between moral epistemology and moral ontology clear is the most important task in formulating and defending a moral argument for God's existence of the type I defend. A proponent of that argument will agree quite readily (and even insist) that we do not need to know or even believe that God exists in order to discern objective moral values or to recognize our moral duties. Affirming the ontological foundations of objective moral values and duties in God similarly says nothing about how we come to know those values and duties. The theist can be genuinely open to whatever epistemological theories his secular counterpart proposes for how we come to know objective values and duties.

So I am delighted that you have been keeping the distinction between moral epistemology and moral ontology clear in your discussions with non-theists. If you maintain a firm grasp on that distinction, I think you can readily see the answer to your question: "By saying [that objective moral duties are constituted by God's commands], is not one already providing an argument for Revealed Theology and thus making an argument for moral epistemology?" So saying will, indeed, imply that one of the ways we could come to know our moral duties is via a (scriptural) revelation of God's commands. But that isn't to say that the *only* way of coming to know our moral duties is through such a means. As Paul says, "When Gentiles who have not the law do by nature what the law requires, they are a law to themselves, even though they do not have the law. They show that what the law requires is written on their hearts, while their conscience also bears witness and their conflicting thoughts accuse or perhaps excuse them" (Romans 2:14–15).

The salient point is that God's commands *constitute* our moral duties. That is a claim of moral ontology.

INSIGHT

By distinguishing between moral epistemology and moral ontology we can be in a better place to introduce Scripture's witness as an indispensable source of knowledge and wisdom about the moral life and its duties. We can do this by helping people pay attention to their moral experience and considering how Scripture has insight into questions like "how do I become moral?"

How we come to *know* our moral duties is a matter of moral epistemology and is irrelevant to the argument. There's nothing to wriggle out of.

Is It Arbitrary to Adopt God's Nature as the Good?

Dear Dr. Craig,

I thought you did very well in your debate with Sam Harris. Not only did you "knock down" his arguments but he knocked himself down by pretending that you weren't even on the stage with him!

However, something is troubling me about your Divine Command Theory. It takes the form of two questions, one simple and the other more complex:

1) Simple question: If Christianity were proven false, and Islam true, would you simply drop your current moral convictions and adopt those of Islam because you found you "had the wrong God"? Would there not be a part of you that may rebel, against Allah, when faced with certain scenarios concerning judgments on creaturely well-being?

2) Trickier question: you say that God is the Good, or that Goodness flows from God's nature. This is supposed to split the horns of the Euthyphro Dilemma: that God doesn't conform to external standards of morality, but neither does He subjectively decide them on a whim.

However, I genuinely am troubled by the thought that this only seems to push the problem back one notch, because we can then ask:

Is Goodness "good" because it is found in God's nature, or is God "good" because His nature necessarily matches Good?

Or, let's put it as conditional statements to choose from:

A) If (X) is to be found in God's nature, then (X) is good.

or:

B) If (X) is good, then (X) is to be found in God's nature.

These choices of contention, "A" and "B," seem to open up different possibilities when it comes to modal logic:

Consider "A," that if something just so happens to be in God's nature, then we must call it "good." The trouble is, we can conceive of different possible worlds where God values completely different things and holds a different moral nature. We could imagine a world where, frankly, the questioner who claimed homosexual love-making was good . . . is correct! Or, like my first question, we could imagine a God of an Islamic nature, or one that says, "rape is OK."

In this respect, we can imagine there are many different possible moralities that God could hold to, as if they were cards in a pack, and we have been "dealt" a particular "moral" card. God's moral values could have been a "King of Clubs" compared to the "Ace of Spades" or the "Six of Hearts" (to make an analogy) and we just so happen to live in a world where our God holds the nature of the "3 of Diamonds."

If we adopt "A" then we simply have to say, no matter what possible world we find ourselves in, that the mere fact that God's moral values just so happen to be a certain way, means that they are "The Good." We would be saying this of God no matter what His moral nature actually (and specifically) turned out to be. Potentially, you may even be saying this depending on your answer to the first question.

How, therefore, do we guarantee that something is truly "good" if it is entirely contingent upon our simply "waking up" in a possible world where God's nature swings one way, rather than the other?

As for "B" this would imply that "Goodness" is self-existent, independent of God, and that God's moral nature cannot vary, because He is necessarily "locked" into reflecting these external, necessary truths.

So, if we adopt "B" we don't have the problem of God's moral nature being free to vary—and our merely calling it "Good" because that's the way things are in this world. We'd end up with a God whose moral nature is necessarily fixed a certain way.

Trouble is, that's simply because His nature conforms to a standard which doesn't require Him in the first place ... and maybe some sort of "science" (better than Sam Harris', of course) could discover it? (i.e., the Euthyphro argument would succeed in showing that the Good is independent of God.)

I hope that made sense. It's a real brain teaser, and currently holds me back from adopting a DCT model. Many thanks again for your brilliant work, Dr. Craig!

Peter

United Kingdom

Dr. Craig's Response

Nice to hear from you, Peter! I look forward to meeting you in October during our U.K. visit.

Let's deal first with the simple question. "If Christianity were proven false, and Islam true, would you simply drop your current moral convictions and adopt those of Islam because you found you 'had the wrong God'?" This question is, I think, misphrased. The important question is not what I *would* do under the envisioned circumstances, but what I *should* do. What I would do is an autobiographical fact about my personal psychology, which is of little philosophical interest. Moreover, it would be presumptuous for me to make predictions about what I would do under different circumstances (remember the apostle Peter on the night of Jesus' betrayal?). What is of interest rather is what I should do under the envisioned circumstances. So stated, the question's answer is clear: if Islam were proven true and Christianity false, then Islam would be true, and so of course I should believe in it. The same answer would present itself to the atheist: if atheism were proven false and Islam true, then should you obey the commands of Allah? Of course, for then Islam is the truth, and you really do have those moral obligations, however difficult it might be for you to stomach them.

Let's turn, then, to the second question: "Is Goodness 'good' because it is found in God's nature, or is God 'good' because His nature necessarily matches Good?" Again, I think the wording of the question might be improved by selecting certain qualities like compassion, fairness, generosity, and so forth, and asking, "Are these qualities good because they are found in God's nature or are they good quite independently of God?" The answer to that question is obvious: the theistic view is that these qualities are good because they are found in God's nature. The alternative (that God is good because His nature matches the Good) is just Platonism all over again, which we've already rejected.[15]

So what's the problem supposed to be for the classical theist? The objection is that we can conceive of different possible worlds in which God's moral character is different. But, Peter, that isn't the model I defend! On most Divine Command theories God possesses His moral qualities essentially (indeed, that's just what it means to say they're part of His nature!). So there is no possible world in which God is not kind, impartial, gracious, loving, and so on. So I don't think it is possible that Allah is God, since Allah is not all-loving and impartial.

God's moral qualities are an essential part of His nature

Your deck of cards analogy presupposes that God's moral qualities are contingent properties of God. But classical theism holds these properties to be essential to God. So it's fundamentally mistaken to say that God's moral qualities "just so happen to be a certain way."

Let's think a minute as well about alternative B. Why think that the content of the Good is the same in every possible world? What about worlds in which the Good comprises different moral properties? And why think that God is necessarily locked into reflecting the Good? Why, on this view, couldn't it also be contingent that God is good? I think you'd rightly say that there are no such worlds. The content of the Good is essential to it, and God is necessarily good, so He could not have failed to reflect the Good. I agree; but then why isn't a similar answer available to the classical theist? The only difference between the Platonist and the classical theist on this score is that the theist identifies the Good with God Himself. Just as the Good could not have been different, so God could not have been different.

INSIGHT

Note this crucial point in Dr. Craig's reasoning: *God's moral qualities are an essential part of His nature.* It's a helpful condition for adjudicating between different "God-claims" and "God-talk" among different religions.

15. See Dr. Craig's three-pronged critique of "Platonism": "Why are (some) Platonists so insouciant?" *Philosophy* 86:2 (2011): 213–29. You can access this article for free by going to ReasonableFaith.org (http://bit.ly/Platonism).

I think that what this objection is really getting at is the claim that it's somehow arbitrary to adopt God's nature as the Good. But every moral realist theory has to have an explanatory stopping point at which one reaches the ultimate good. Anyone who broaches a moral theory is entitled to identify whatever he wants as his ultimate explanatory stopping point. The question then becomes, is the explanatory ultimate posited by some moral theory plausible? In the case of theism, taking God to be one's explanatory ultimate is, I think, eminently plausible. For the very concept of God is the concept of a necessary, metaphysically ultimate being, one, moreover, that is worthy of worship. Indeed, He is the greatest conceivable being, and it is greater to be the Good than merely to reflect it. So the theist's stopping point, in contrast to, say, the humanist's, is not at all arbitrary or premature.

4

ON THE AUTHORITY OF SCRIPTURE
Establishing the Gospels' Reliability

I noticed that in many of your debates and articles, you put a lot of stock and faith in the gospel narratives. I do consider myself a Christian but have a big doubt. How do we really know if those gospel narratives are really all that reliable? Sure, they are historical, but are they true or not? I could write a paper about how Bigfoot, the Easter bunny, and Santa Claus came to my house and watched TV with me, then thousands of years later people stumble upon my documents and consider them to be true. The discoverers of the Ancient Joe Documents then say, "Well, we consider it truthful because there are about 26,000 complete copies and fragments of these ancient documents that have been found in Europe, Asia, and Africa. Plus, there are only about 680 copies of the Odyssey by Homer, which makes the Joe narratives completely reliable." Sure, they are historical but definitely not true. What makes the gospel narratives truthful and not fake? If I can get this question answered, I can finally have faith that God has truly risen Jesus from the dead, and know that I will go to heaven. If you, or maybe one of your assistants, can answer this question, that would help me a lot. Thank you.

Joe

Dr. Craig's Response

I'm glad for your question, Joe, because it surfaces a number of misconceptions that are widely shared by Christians and non-Christians alike.

Your fundamental question is: how do we know that the gospel narratives are historically reliable? You correctly observe that that question is *not* to be answered by appeal to the abundance and age of the manuscripts of the gospels. The idea that the abundance and age of the manuscripts of the gospels is evidence for their historical reliability is a misconception fostered by popular Christian apologetics. It's true that the New Testament is the best attested book in ancient history, both in terms of the number of manuscripts and the nearness of those manuscripts to the date of the original. What that goes to prove is that the text of the New Testament that we have today is almost exactly the same as the text as it was originally written. Of the approximately 138,000 words in the New Testament only about 1,400 remain in doubt. The text of the New Testament is thus about 99 percent established. That means that when you pick up a (Greek) New Testament today, you can be confident that you are reading the text as it was originally written. Moreover, that 1 percent that remains uncertain has to do with trivial words on which nothing of importance hangs. This conclusion is important because it explodes the claims of Muslims, Mormons, and others that the text of the New Testament has been corrupted, so that we can no longer read the original text. It's awe-inspiring to think that we can know with confidence that when we pick up Paul's letter to the church in Rome, for example, we are reading the very words he wrote almost 2,000 years ago.

But, as you say, that doesn't prove that what these documents say is historically accurate. We could have the text of Aesop's fables established to 99 percent accuracy, and that would do nothing to show that they are true stories. After all, they are intended to be fables, not history. People in the future would say something similar about the Joe narratives, no matter how many copies existed.

Now, as you point out, the gospels are intended to be history. That is the import of your insight that the gospels "are historical" even if they are not true. That is to say, the gospels are of the literary genre of historical writing. They are not of the genre of mythology, fiction, or fable. This is an extremely important insight. Something of a consensus has developed within New Testament scholarship that the gospels are closest in genre to ancient biographies ("Lives," as they are called, as in Plutarch's *Lives of Noble Greeks and Romans*). Though differing in certain respects from modern biographies, such as lack of concern with strict chronology, ancient Lives did have a historical interest in presenting truthfully the life of the subject. That will make them very different from a deliberate fiction, such as you envision being written by yourself. The gospel writers were trying to write a historical account about real people, places, and events (just look at Luke 3:1–3).

So were they successful in getting the facts straight about Jesus of Nazareth? There are two ways to get at that question. One way would be by assessing the general credibility of the gospel accounts.[16] The other way, more influential in contemporary New Testament

16. Take a look at Dr. Craig's free article at ReasonableFaith.org titled, "The Evidence for Jesus" (http://bit.ly/
    EvidenceForJesus) for five lines of evidence supporting the general credibility of the gospel records of Jesus' life.

scholarship, is to establish specific facts about Jesus without assuming the general reliability of the gospels. The key here are the so-called "Criteria of Authenticity" which enable us to establish specific sayings or events in Jesus' life as historical. Scholars involved in the quest of the historical Jesus have enunciated a number of these criteria for detecting historically authentic features of Jesus, such as dissimilarity to Christian teaching, multiple attestation, linguistic semitisms, traces of Palestinian milieu, retention of embarrassing material, coherence with other authentic material, and so forth.

It is somewhat misleading to call these "criteria," for they aim at stating sufficient, not necessary, conditions of historicity. This is easy to see: suppose a saying is multiply attested and dissimilar but not embarrassing. If embarrassment were a necessary condition of authenticity, then the saying would have to be deemed inauthentic, which is wrong-headed, since its multiple attestation and dissimilarity are sufficient for authenticity. Of course, the criteria are defeasible, meaning that they are not infallible guides to authenticity. They might be better called "Indications of Authenticity" or "Signs of Credibility."

In point of fact, what the criteria really amount to are statements about the effect of certain types of evidence upon the probability of various sayings or events in Jesus' life. For some saying or event S and evidence of a certain type E, the criteria would state that, all things being equal, the probability of S given E is greater than the probability of S on our background knowledge alone. So, for example, all else being equal, the probability of some event or saying is greater given its multiple attestation than it would have been without it.

What are some of the factors that might serve the role of E in increasing the probability of some saying or event S? The following are some of the most important:

> **INSIGHT**
> Note the helpful suggestions on how to go about assessing whether the gospel accounts get the facts straight about the historical Jesus. This also reminds me of why we need not fear assessment or "critical scrutiny" about why we believe what we believe. If anything, assessing the credibility of the gospel accounts can show how our beliefs are rooted in knowledge of what is real.

(1) Historical congruence: S fits in with known historical facts concerning the context in which S is said to have occurred.

(2) Independent, early attestation: S appears in multiple sources which are near to the time at which S is alleged to have occurred and which depend neither upon each other nor a common source.

(3) Embarrassment: S is awkward or counter-productive for the persons who serve as the source of information for S.

(4) Dissimilarity: S is unlike antecedent Jewish thought-forms and/or unlike subsequent Christian thought-forms.

(5) Semitisms: traces in the narrative of Aramaic or Hebrew linguistic forms.

(6) Coherence: S is consistent with already established facts about Jesus.[17]

Notice that these "criteria" do not presuppose the general reliability of the gospels. Rather they focus on a particular saying or event and give evidence for thinking that specific element of Jesus' life to be historical, regardless of the general reliability of the document in which the particular saying or event is reported. These same "criteria" are thus applicable to reports of Jesus found in the apocryphal gospels, or rabbinical writings, or even the Qur'an. Of course, if the gospels can be shown to be generally reliable documents, so much the better! But the "criteria" do not depend on any such presupposition. They serve to help spot historical kernels even in the midst of historical chaff. Thus we need not concern ourselves with defending the gospels' every claim attributed to Jesus in the gospels; the question will be whether we can establish enough about Jesus to make faith in Him reasonable.

I'm convinced that we can. Indeed, it's shocking to me how much of Jesus' life can be established, including His radical personal claims, His crucifixion, His burial in a tomb, the discovery of His empty tomb, His post-mortem appearances, and His disciples' coming to believe suddenly and sincerely that God had raised Him from the dead. Take a look at my book *Reasonable Faith* for detailed argument. We, therefore, have quite solid reasons for believing in Christ on the basis of the historical facts preserved about Him in the gospels.

---

17. For a good discussion of these factors see Robert Stein, "The 'Criteria' for Authenticity," in *Gospel Perspectives I*, R. T. France and David Wenham, eds. (Sheffield, England: JSOT Press, 1980), 225–63.

Is the Price of "Biblical Errancy" Too High to Pay?

After re-evaluating my Christian faith and pruning it for two years, I can't shake what seem like two disparate conclusions. One is that the evidence for Jesus' resurrection is impeccable. But the other is that there seem to be some very awkward realities about the composition of Scripture (like errors or authors claiming to write by another name). Yet, the authors of the New Testament, including Jesus, seem to use Scripture in a way that assumes it is word for word from God.

While inductive logic is used to arrive at a strong historical case for the resurrection of Jesus, inductive logic can also be used to arrive at a strong case for many of the peculiarities about Scripture previously mentioned.

It seems that the approach that many apologists take at this point is that, having established the authority of Jesus by the resurrection, if the argument being raised against Scripture contradicts an opinion expressed by Jesus in the gospels, then the argument for a contradiction must have no possible harmonization for it to really stick. But I don't see how this is fair to say, since (1) it seems unfair to use inductive logic to evidence Jesus' resurrection but then not use it for criticisms against the Bible and (2) an inductive argument can be strong despite what Jesus, as recorded in the gospels, says, especially since we cannot assume the precision with which many of the sayings were recorded. And (3), anybody can cook up a harmonization of some verse that is possible but not plausible, which I am sure you have seen firsthand many times.

Yet, holding these two positions in tension tends to be corrosive to my faith and ultimately leads to a certain bitterness against God for allowing the biblical writers to play fast-and-loose with His words and for not providing a clarity that brings more certainty about what is from Him and what isn't. Any help you can give to relieve this tension would be greatly appreciated.

Thanks,

Joshua

Dr. Craig's Response

Your question is one that every Bible-believing Christian familiar with modern biblical criticism has had to wrestle with. There's much to be said here, so let me hit a few main points.

INSIGHT

Notice some of the factors involved in seeking an answer to these questions; namely, bitterness against God seems to be real and formational for how Joshua has come to view this tension. That's not to delegitimize Joshua's questions. Rather, it is to acknowledge that more than mere intellectual tensions are at play. For example, what if some of his presuppositions were rooted in recognizing that God is trustworthy because what He communicates is true? What difference would that make, even as a hypothesis, to inform even his "inductive" approach to the question?

To begin with, the doctrine of biblical inerrancy, as I learned it and, I think, as most of its adherents today would defend it, is not arrived at *inductively*, but *deductively*. Inerrantists freely admit that no one reading through the Bible and keeping a list of difficulties encountered along the way, whether inconsistencies or mistakes, would come to the conclusion at the end of his reading that the Bible is inerrant. He would likely conclude that the Bible, like almost every other book, has some errors in it. But inerrantists have maintained that belief in biblical inerrancy is justified as a deduction from other well-justified truths. For example, the late Kenneth Kantzer, Dean of the seminary I attended, argued for inerrancy by means of the following two syllogisms:

1. Whatever God teaches is true.
2. Historical, prophetic, and other evidences show that Jesus is God.
3. Therefore, whatever Jesus teaches is true.
4. Whatever Jesus teaches is true.
5. Jesus taught that the Scriptures are the inspired, inerrant Word of God.
6. Therefore, the Scriptures are the inspired, inerrant Word of God.

The claim here is that we have good reasons to think that the Bible, despite its difficulties, is the inerrant Word of God and, therefore, we should accept it as such. As Martin

Kahler once put it, "We do not believe in Christ because we believe in the Bible; we believe in the Bible because we believe in Christ."[18]

When confronted with biblical difficulties, the inerrantist will attempt to show that alleged mistakes are not really mistakes after all and to provide plausible harmonizations of apparent inconsistencies. Where this cannot be done, he will honestly admit that he doesn't know the solution to the difficulty but nonetheless insist that he has overriding reasons to think that the text is accurate and that were all the facts to be known the alleged difficulty would disappear. Such an approach has served the inerrantist well: example after example could be given of supposed biblical errors identified by previous generations which have now been resolved in light of more recent discoveries. One of my favorite examples is Sargon II, an Assyrian king mentioned in Isa. 20:1. Earlier critics claimed that the reference to Sargon was an error because there was absolutely no evidence that an Assyrian king named Sargon II ever even existed—until, that is, archaeologists digging in the region of Khorsabad unearthed the palace of one Sargon II! We now have more information about Sargon than about any other ancient Assyrian king.

Now, the question raised by your letter is what our reaction should be if we become convinced that there really is an error in the Bible. Won't such a conclusion have a kind of reverse effect along our chain of deductive reasoning, leading us to deny Jesus' resurrection and deity? This was apparently the conclusion of Bart Ehrman, who says he lost his faith in Christ because he discovered one minor error in the gospels.

Such a conclusion is unnecessary for two reasons. First, we may need instead to revise our understanding of what constitutes an error. Nobody thinks that when Jesus says that the mustard seed is the smallest of all seeds (Mark 4:31) this is an error, even though there are smaller seeds than mustard seeds. Why? Because Jesus is not teaching botany; He is trying to teach a lesson about the kingdom of God, and the illustration is incidental to this lesson.

Defenders of inerrancy claim that the Bible is authoritative and inerrant in *all that it teaches* or *all that it means to affirm*. This raises the huge question as to what the authors of Scripture intend to affirm or teach. Questions of genre will have a significant bearing on our answer to that question. Poetry obviously is not intended to be taken literally, for

18. Martin Kahler, *The So-called Historical Jesus and the Historic, Biblical Christ*, translated, edited, and with an introduction by Carl E. Braaten (Philadelphia: Fortress Press, 1964), 75. Readers may be interested to know that one of the best examples of the approach that the Kahler quote suggests to the doctrine of biblical inerrancy is John Wenham's *Christ and the Bible* (Downers Grove, Ill.: InterVarsity, 1972).

example. But then what about the gospels? What is their genre? Scholars have come to see that the genre to which the gospels most closely conform is ancient biography. This is important for our question because ancient biography does not have the intention of providing a chronological account of the hero's life from the cradle to the grave. Rather ancient biography relates anecdotes that serve to illustrate the hero's character qualities. What one might consider an error in a modern biography need not at all count as an error in an ancient biography. To illustrate, at one time in my Christian life I believed that Jesus actually cleansed the Temple in Jerusalem twice, once near the beginning of His ministry as John relates, and once near the end of His life, as we read in the Synoptic gospels. But an understanding of the gospels as ancient biographies relieves us of such a supposition, for an ancient biographer can relate incidents in a non-chronological way. Only an unsympathetic (and uncomprehending) reader would take John's moving the Temple cleansing to earlier in Jesus' life as an error on John's part.

We can extend the point by considering the proposal that the gospels should be understood as different performances, as it were, of orally transmitted tradition. The prominent New Testament scholar Jimmy Dunn, prompted by the work of Ken Bailey on the transmission of oral tradition in Middle Eastern cultures, has sharply criticized what he calls the "stratigraphic model" of the gospels, which views them as composed of different layers laid one upon another on top of a primitive tradition.[19] On the stratigraphic model each tiny deviation from the previous layer occasions speculations about the reasons for the change, sometimes leading to quite fanciful hypotheses about the theology of some redactor. But Dunn insists that oral tradition works quite differently. What matters is that the central idea is conveyed, often in some key words and climaxing in some saying which is repeated verbatim; but the surrounding details are fluid and incidental to the story.

Probably the closest example to this in our non-oral, Western culture is the telling of a joke. It's important that you get the structure and punch line right, but the rest is incidental. For example, many years ago I heard the following joke:

"What did the Calvinist say when he fell down the elevator shaft?"

"I don't know."

"He got up, dusted himself off, and said, 'Whew! I'm glad that's over!'"

Just recently someone else told me what was clearly the same joke. Only she told it as follows:

"Do you know what the Calvinist said when he fell down the stairs?"

19. See James D. G. Dunn, *Jesus Remembered* (Grand Rapids: Eerdmans, 2003).

"No."

"'Whew! I'm glad that's over!'"

Notice the differences in the telling of this joke; but observe how the central idea and especially the punch line are the same. Well, when you compare many of the stories told about Jesus in the gospels and identify the words they have in common, you find a pattern like this. There is variation in the secondary details, but very often the central saying is almost verbatim the same. And remember, this is in a culture where they didn't even have the device of quotation marks! (Those are added in translation to indicate direct speech; to get an idea of how difficult it can be to determine exactly where direct speech ends, just read Paul's account of his argument with Peter in Galatians 2 or Jesus' interview with Nicodemus in John 3.) So the stories in the gospels should not be understood as evolutions of some prior primitive tradition but as different performances of the same oral story.

Now, if Dunn is right, this has enormous implications for one's doctrine of biblical inerrancy, for it means that the evangelists had no intention that their stories should be taken like police reports, accurate in every detail. What we in a non-oral culture might regard as an error would not be taken by them to be erroneous at all.

I was struck by your insight that you feel "a certain bitterness against God for allowing the biblical writers to play fast-and-loose with His words and for not providing a clarity that brings more certainty about what is from Him and what isn't." Joshua, you are imposing upon God what you think ought to be the standards of inerrancy rather than coming to the Scriptures and learning from them what inerrancy means. The biblical writers aren't playing fast and loose with His words if God never intended His words to be taken in the way you suggest. A Bible that employs a rich variety of genres should not be treated like a flat, monotone book. We need to come to God's Word with humility and learn from it what it intends to teach and affirm.[20]

INSIGHT
Note that how or why Joshua imposes what he does may very well relate to whether he actually trusts that God is actually a good and credible authority on what He says.

20. For further study, see Dr. Craig's article "'Men Moved by the Holy Spirit Spoke from God' (2 Peter 1:21): A Middle Knowledge Perspective on Biblical Inspiration," *Philosophia Christi* 1:1 (1999): 45–82, for a proposal on how to conceive of verbal, plenary, congruent inspiration of Scripture. This article can be accessed for free at ReasonableFaith.org (http://bit.ly/MolinismInspiration). To subscribe to *Philosophia Christi*, the journal of the Evangelical Philosophical Society and where many of Dr. Craig's scholarly articles first appear, please visit www.epsociety.org/philchristi for more info, or to purchase, www.epsociety.org/store.

So if we are confronted with what appears to be an error in Scripture, *we should first ask whether we're not imposing on Scripture a standard of inerrancy that is foreign to the genre of the writing and the intent of its author.* I remember Dr. Kantzer once remarking that many of his constituents would be shocked if they knew what he was willing to allow in Scripture and not call it an error. He understood that we must put ourselves within the horizon of the original authors before we ask if they have erred.

But secondly, suppose you've done all that and are still convinced that Scripture is not inerrant. Does that mean that the deity and resurrection of Christ go down the drain? No, not at all. For the far weaker premise in the above two syllogisms will be premise (5), rather than premise (2). As you recognize, we have a very strong case for the resurrection of Jesus. That case in no way depends on the Bible's being inerrant. This became very clear to me during my doctoral studies in Munich with Wolfhart Pannenberg. Pannenberg had rocked German theology by maintaining that a sound historical case can be made for the resurrection of Jesus. Yet he also believed that the gospel resurrection appearances stories are so legendary that they have scarcely a historical kernel in them! He did not even trust the Markan account of the discovery of the empty tomb. Rather his argument was founded on the early pre-Pauline tradition about the appearances in 1 Cor. 15:3–5 and on the consideration that a movement based on the resurrection of a dead man would have been impossible in Jerusalem in the face of a tomb containing his corpse.

Evangelicals sometimes give lip service to the claim that the gospels are historically reliable, even when examined by the canons of ordinary historical research; but I wonder if they really believe this. It *really is true* that a solid, persuasive case for Jesus' resurrection can be made without any assumption of the gospels' inerrancy.

By contrast, the case for Jesus' belief that the Old Testament Scriptures are inerrant is much weaker. I think there's no doubt that (5) is the premise that would have to go if biblical inerrancy were to be abandoned. We should have to re-think our doctrine of inspiration in that case, but we needn't give up belief in God or in Jesus, as Bart Ehrman did. Ehrman had, it seems to me, a flawed theological system of beliefs as a Christian. It seems that at the center of his web of theological beliefs was biblical inerrancy, and everything else, like the beliefs in the deity of Christ and in His resurrection, depended on that. Once the center was gone, the whole web soon collapsed. But when you think about it, such a structure is deeply flawed.

At the center of our web of beliefs ought to be some core belief like the belief that God exists, with the deity and resurrection of Christ somewhere near the center. The doctrine of inspiration of Scripture will be somewhere further out and inerrancy even farther toward the periphery as a corollary of inspiration. If inerrancy goes, the web will feel the reverberations of that loss, as we adjust our doctrine of inspiration accordingly, but the web will not collapse because belief in God and Christ and His resurrection and so on don't depend upon the doctrine of biblical inerrancy.

So rather than be corrosive to your faith, I hope that biblical studies can become for you, as they have for me, a source of novelty, excitement, and encouragement.

A Middle Knowledge Perspective on Biblical Inspiration

I have been listening to Series 2 of your Defenders Class and just finished the one on the doctrine of Revelation.[21] In this recording, you defend the Middle Knowledge perspective of the verbal, plenary, and confluent view of revelation.

My question is: If we invoke middle knowledge to describe inspiration, how do we avoid saying that all writings in history are inspired? Wouldn't God know exactly what type of book any author, say Christopher Hitchens, would freely write given their particular set of circumstances? Therefore, all writings, including Christopher Hitchens', are inspired.

Aaron

United States

Dr. Craig's Response

For those who are not familiar with the background of this question, let me explain that it concerns my defense of verbal, plenary, confluent inspiration of the Bible in my *Philosophia Christi* article, "'Men Moved by the Holy Spirit Spoke from God' (2 Peter 1:21), A Middle Knowledge Perspective on Biblical Inspiration."[22] In that piece, I argue that

21. This audio is accessible for free at ReasonableFaith.org (http://bit.ly/DoctrineOfRevelation).
22. This article can be accessed for free at ReasonableFaith.org (http://bit.ly/MolinismInspiration).

divine middle knowledge enables us to affirm the verbal, plenary inspiration of Scripture without divine dictation. For God knows under just what circumstances Paul would, for example, freely write his letter to the Romans. By placing Paul in those circumstances, God can bring it about that Romans is just the message He wants to convey to us.

Now, your question, Aaron, is a good one. Since God is omniscient, He knows what any human author would freely write in whatever circumstances He might place him. By placing Christopher Hitchens in the circumstances he has been in, God sovereignly brought it about that Christopher Hitchens freely wrote just what he did. So what makes the one God's Word to us and the other not?

The essential difference lies not in the mode of God's action. Remember that inspiration is a property of the written text, not the mode of its production (though I am entirely open to the idea that the circumstances surrounding Paul's freely writing Romans may have included certain promptings of the Holy Spirit absent from Hitchens' circumstances). Rather, the essential difference lies in God's attitude toward what is written. In the one case, God wills to communicate via the author His message to us.

INSIGHT
Note that Dr. Craig raises some important nuances here. (1) Inspiration is a property of the written text, not the mode of its production; and (2) what matters significantly is God's attitude toward what is written. Does it reflect His character, for example?

He intends that the letter to the Romans be His Word to us. Romans is, therefore, a case of appropriated or delegated speech, much as a boss makes a letter composed by his secretary his own by affixing his signature to it. By contrast, God merely allows Hitchens to write what he does without endorsing its truth or adopting it as His own. God lets Hitchens put forth his falsehoods because in His providence Hitchens' books have their part to play in God's overall plan for human history. But God does not see Hitchens' books as His Word to us, to be trusted and obeyed. Therein lies the essential difference between the Bible and every other literary product of free human activity.

On Inerrancy and the Resurrection

I was reading a debate between William Lane Craig and Bart Ehrman. Craig refuses to answer whether or not the Bible is inerrant when directly asked it by an audience member. He merely sidesteps the question and responds that this is not what they are debating.

1) What outside sources (outside of the Canon) are there that support Jesus' death, burial, and resurrection in bodily form, and ascension into heaven?

2) The message of Jesus was spread by word of mouth until the gospels were written. How do we know legend wasn't developed, such as Jesus being buried by Joseph of Arimathea?

3) What about other pagan miracle workers such as Honi the Circle-Drawer, Hanina ben Dosa, and Apollonius of Tyana (p 27). Doesn't the fact that these pagan people doing miracles similar to Jesus discredit Jesus as a miracle worker?

4) What about the seeming contradictions in the different gospel accounts? Please give me a different answer other than, "These are only secondary details and do not lie at the heart of the matter." If we go to a university that declares the Bible is inerrant, then shouldn't we be able to explain these? I quote from Mr. Ehrman in his debate vs. Craig on p. 11:

"What day did Jesus die on and what time of day? Did he die on the day before the Passover meal was eaten, as John explicitly says, or did he die after it was eaten, as Mark explicitly says? Did he die at noon, as in John, or at 9 a.m., as in Mark? Did Jesus carry his cross the entire way himself or did Simon of Cyrene carry his cross? It depends which gospel you read. Did both robbers mock Jesus on the cross or did only one of them mock him and the other come to his defense? It depends which gospel you read. Did the curtain in the temple rip in half before Jesus died or after he died? It depends which gospel you read. Or take the accounts of the resurrection. Who went to the tomb on the third day? Was it Mary alone or was it Mary with other women? If it was Mary with other women, how many other women were there, which ones were they, and what were their names? Was the stone rolled away before they got there or not? What did they see in the tomb? Did they see a man, did they see two men, or did they see an angel? It depends which account you read. What were they told to tell the disciples? Were the disciples supposed to stay in Jerusalem and see Jesus there or were they to go to Galilee and see Jesus there? Did the women tell anyone or not? It depends which gospel

113

you read. Did the disciples never leave Jerusalem or did they immediately leave Jerusalem and go to Galilee? All of these depend on which account you read."

Well, thanks for any help. Please don't refer me to some book or website as I am reading these debates, *Evidence that Demands a Verdict* by McDowell and *The Case for Christ* by Strobel. Can I get a straight answer to each question from one of the top Christian Apologetic Centers in the world?

Thanks,

Grant

Dr. Craig's Response

INSIGHT

Note this important insight into the consequence of one's belief formation and how certain beliefs have "place" in one's "web of beliefs." It seems that part of our job when answering people's questions is to help them discern whether what is at the very center of their web of beliefs in fact merits such attention. We can help people come to see how these beliefs can form people's decisions.

Can you get straight answers to your questions? You betcha! Read on.

First, to set the context, you put it rather tendentiously when you say that I "merely sidestepped" the question of biblical inerrancy in my debate with Bart Ehrman over whether there is historical evidence for the resurrection of Jesus. A more sympathetic and, I think, more accurate way of putting it would be to say, "Craig refused to let Ehrman derail the debate into a discussion of biblical inerrancy but kept the debate on track." Or an even more accurate reading of the situation would be: "Ehrman tried to goad Craig into an affirmation of biblical inerrancy so that he could impugn Craig's objectivity and, hence, integrity as a historian; but Craig, knowing that his case for Jesus' resurrection didn't presuppose biblical inerrancy, refused to take the bait."

As I explain elsewhere,[23] Ehrman, when he was a Christian, had a flawed theological system in which

23. See Dr. Craig's reply to the question above, "Is the Price of 'Biblical Errancy' Too High to Pay?" pages 105–11.

inerrancy lay at the very center of his web of beliefs, so that once he became convinced of a single error in Scripture the whole web collapsed. As a result, the doctrine of inerrancy looms abnormally large in his thinking. But the case for Jesus' resurrection that I presented doesn't in any way presuppose the inerrancy of the documents, so that the doctrine becomes irrelevant so far as belief in the resurrection goes.

Now to your questions:

1. WHAT SOURCES OUTSIDE OF THE CANON ARE THERE THAT SUPPORT JESUS' DEATH, BURIAL, AND RESURRECTION IN BODILY FORM, AND ASCENSION INTO HEAVEN?

Actually, there are lots of extra-canonical sources that support Jesus' death, burial, and resurrection, sources which I suspect you've never thought of. You're thinking of *later* extra-canonical sources like Josephus and Tacitus. But the really interesting extra-canonical sources are the *earlier* ones, that is to say, the sources used by the New Testament writers themselves. Now, before you cry foul, you need to reflect that these sources are not themselves in the Canon but go back even closer to the events than the canonical books. These are, therefore, the center of historical Jesus study today, not the later extra-canonical sources. Honestly, if you're focused on what later extra-canonical sources there are for Jesus, you're really missing the boat.

What are some of these sources? The Passion story used by Mark, the formula cited by Paul in 1 Cor. 1:3–5, Matthew's special source called M, Luke's special source called L, and so forth. Some of these are incredibly early sources (which helps to answer your second question). The pre-Markan Passion story probably dates from the 30s AD and is based on eyewitness testimony, and the pre-Pauline formula in 1 Cor. 15:3–5 has been dated within a couple of years or *even months* of Jesus' death. I think you can see why these are the really interesting sources, not some later report by Josephus.

Now, these sources provide abundant, independent testimony to the death, burial, and resurrection of Jesus. Later references to Jesus by the Roman historian Tacitus, the Jewish historian Josephus, the Syrian writer Mara bar Serapion, rabbinical writings, and extra-biblical Christian authors confirm what the New Testament documents tell us about Jesus but don't really give us anything new. You can find such sources cited and discussed in R. T. France's very fine book *The Evidence for Jesus*[24] or in Robert Van Voorst's definitive *Jesus*

---

24. R. T. France, *The Evidence for Jesus* (Downers Grove, Ill.: InterVarsity, 1986).

Outside the New Testament.[25] What is key for the historian, however, will be not these later sources, but the New Testament documents themselves and their sources.

Which leads to my question to you: why are you interested in extra-canonical sources rather than the primary source documents themselves? Doesn't your very question betray the prejudice that the New Testament documents are historically unreliable? But if there are sources outside the New Testament that speak of Jesus, ah, that's *real* evidence!

You need to keep in mind that originally there wasn't any such book called "The New Testament." There were just these separate documents handed down from the first century, things like the Gospel of Luke, the Gospel of John, the Acts of the Apostles, Paul's letter to the church in Corinth, and so on. It wasn't until a couple of centuries later that the church officially collected all these documents under one cover, which came to be known as the New Testament. The church only included the earliest sources that were closest to Jesus and the original disciples and left out the later, secondary accounts like the forged apocryphal gospels, which everyone knew were fakes. So from the very nature of the case, the best historical sources were included in the New Testament. People who insist on evidence taken only from writings outside the New Testament don't understand what they're asking for. They're demanding that we ignore the earliest, primary sources about Jesus in favor of sources that are later, secondary, and less reliable, which is just nuts as historical methodology.

The real question is, how reliable are the documents for the life of Jesus that came to be incorporated into the book we now call the New Testament? That leads to your second question.

2. THE MESSAGE OF JESUS WAS SPREAD BY WORD OF MOUTH UNTIL THE GOSPELS WERE WRITTEN. HOW DO WE KNOW LEGEND WASN'T DEVELOPED, SUCH AS JESUS BEING BURIED BY JOSEPH OF ARIMATHEA?

In my article "Rediscovering the Historical Jesus,"[26] I discuss five reasons why we can have confidence in the general reliability of the gospels:

1. There was insufficient time for legendary influences to expunge the hard core of historical facts.

---

25. Robert E. Van Voorst, *Jesus Outside the New Testament* (Grand Rapids: Eerdmans, 2000).

26. "Rediscovering the Historical Jesus: The Evidence for Jesus," *Faith and Mission* 15 (1998): 16–26. This article can be freely accessed at ReasonableFaith.org (http://bit.ly/RediscoveringHistoricalJesus).

2. The gospels are not analogous to folk tales or contemporary "urban legends."
3. The Jewish transmission of sacred traditions was highly developed and reliable.
4. There were significant restraints on the embellishment of traditions about Jesus, such as the presence of eyewitnesses and the apostles' supervision.
5. The gospel writers have a proven track record of historical reliability.

I won't repeat here what I already develop there.

In addition to these general considerations, scholars have enunciated certain "criteria of authenticity" to help detect historically reliable information about Jesus even in a document which may not be generally reliable. What the criteria really amount to are statements about the effect of certain types of evidence upon the probability of various sayings or events narrated in the sources. For some saying or event S, evidence of a certain type E, and our background information B, the criteria would state that, all things being equal, Pr (S|E&B) > Pr (S|B). In other words, all else being equal, the probability of some event or saying is greater given, for example, its early, independent attestation than it would have been without it.[27]

Now, specifically with respect to Jesus' burial by Joseph of Arimathea, this is one of the best-established facts about Jesus. Space doesn't permit me to go into all the details of the evidence for the burial. But let me just mention a couple of points: First, *Jesus' burial is multiply attested in extremely early, independent sources.* The account of Jesus' burial in a tomb by Joseph of Arimathea is part of Mark's source material for the Passion story. Moreover, the formula cited by Paul in 1 Cor. 15:3–5 refers to Jesus' burial:

> . . . that Christ died for our sins in accordance with the Scriptures,
> and that He was buried,
> and that He was raised on the third day in accordance with the Scriptures,
> and that He appeared to Cephas, then to the Twelve.

27. As the reader may recall, the "criteria" mentioned has already been discussed in the question on "Establishing the Gospel's Reliability" (pages 101–4). The important point to recall is that these criteria do not presuppose the general reliability of the gospels. Rather, they focus on a particular saying or event and give evidence for thinking that specific element of Jesus' life to be historical, regardless of the general reliability of the document in which the particular saying or event is reported.

But, we might wonder, was the burial mentioned by the formula the same event as the burial by Joseph of Arimathea? The answer to that question is made clear by a comparison of the four-line formula with the gospel narratives on the one hand and the sermons in the Acts of the Apostles on the other:

1 Cor. 15:3–5	Acts 13:28–31	Mark 15:37–16:7
Christ died . . .	Though they could charge him with nothing deserving death, yet they asked Pilate to have him killed.	And Jesus uttered a loud cry and breathed his last.
he was buried . . .	they took him down from the tree and laid him in a tomb.	And he (Joseph) bought a linen shroud, and taking him down, wrapped him in the linen shroud and laid him in a tomb.
he was raised . . .	But God raised him from the dead. . . .	"He has risen, he is not here; see the place where they laid him."
he appeared . . .	. . . and for many days he appeared to those who came up with him from Galilee to Jerusalem, who are now his witnesses to the people.	"But go, tell his disciples and Peter that he is going before you to Galilee; there you will see him."

This remarkable correspondence of independent traditions is convincing proof that the four-line formula is a summary in outline form of the basic events of Jesus' passion and resurrection, including His burial in the tomb. We thus have evidence from two of the earliest, independent sources of the New Testament for the burial of Jesus in the tomb.

But that's not all! For further independent testimony to Jesus' burial by Joseph is also found in the sources behind Matthew and Luke and the Gospel of John, not to mention the extra-biblical Gospel of Peter. The differences between Mark's account and those of Matthew and Luke suggest that the latter had sources other than Mark alone. These differences are not plausibly explained as Matthew's and Luke's editorial changes of Mark because of their sporadic and uneven nature, the inexplicable omission of events like Pilate's interrogation of the centurion, and the agreements in wording between Matthew and Luke in contrast to Mark.

Moreover, we have another independent source for the burial in John's gospel. Finally we have the early apostolic sermons in the book of Acts, which are probably not wholly Luke's creation but preserve the early preaching of the apostles. These also make mention of Jesus' interment in a tomb. Thus, we have the remarkable number of at least four and perhaps more independent sources for Jesus' burial, some of which are extraordinarily early.

Second, *as a member of the Jewish Sanhedrin that condemned Jesus, Joseph of Arimathea is unlikely to be a Christian creation.* Joseph is described as a rich man, a member of the Jewish Sanhedrin. The Sanhedrin was a sort of Jewish high court made up of seventy of the leading men of Judaism, which presided in Jerusalem. There was an understandable hostility in the early church toward the Jewish Sanhedrists. In Christian eyes, they had engineered a judicial murder of Jesus. The sermons in Acts, for example, go so far as to say that the Jewish leaders crucified Jesus (Acts 2:23, 36; 4:10)! Given his status as a Sanhedrist—all of whom, Mark reports, voted to condemn Jesus—Joseph is the last person one would expect to care properly for Jesus. Thus, in the words of the late New Testament scholar Raymond Brown, Jesus' burial by Joseph is "very probable," since it is "almost inexplicable" why Christians would make up a story about a Jewish Sanhedrist who does what is right by Jesus.

For these and other reasons, the wide majority of New Testament critics concur that Jesus was buried in a tomb by Joseph of Arimathea. Since even Ehrman affirms this, along with most scholars, why don't you?

3. What about other pagan miracle workers such as Honi the Circle-Drawer, Hanina ben Dosa, and Apollonius of Tyana? Doesn't the fact that these pagan people doing miracles similar to Jesus discredit Jesus as a miracle worker?

First of all, these aren't pagan miracle workers. Honi and Hanina ben Dosa were Jewish holy men who also were reputed as miracle workers. Far from undermining the historicity of the gospel accounts, the existence of such figures supports the credibility of the gospel accounts of Jesus' ministry as a miracle worker, since it shows that such activity was at home in first-century Judaism and was not ascribed to Jesus as a result of the influence of so-called "divine men" of pagan mythology.

The stories of Jesus' miracles are so widely represented in all strata of the gospel traditions that it would be fanciful to regard them as not rooted in the life of Jesus. Thus, the consensus of New Testament scholarship is that Jesus did carry out a ministry of "miracle" working—however one might want to interpret or explain these. At the end of his long and detailed study of Jesus' miracles John Meier concludes:

> The overall attestation of the figure of Jesus as healer of physical infirmities and illnesses is thus even stronger than the attestation of his activity as an exorcist. . . . In sum, the statement that Jesus acted as and was viewed as an exorcist and healer during his public ministry has as much historical corroboration as almost any other statement we can make about the Jesus of history.[28]

The miracles of Jesus, like His exorcisms, were taken to be signs of the in-breaking of the kingdom of God. As such, they functioned fundamentally differently from the wonders performed by Hellenistic magicians or Jewish holy men. Moreover, Jesus' miracles differed from those of Honi and Hanina in that Jesus never prays for a miracle to be done; He may first express thanks to the Father, but then He effects it Himself. And He does so in His own name, not God's. Moreover, neither Honi nor Hanina carried out a prophetic ministry, made messianic claims, or brought any new teaching in conjunction with their miracles. Thus, Jesus is more than just another charismatic Jewish holy man.

As for Apollonius of Tyana, this is a figure constructed in large part by Philostratus centuries later as a deliberate counterpoint to Christianity. The church had grown quite large and influential by that time, so Philostratus constructed Apollonius as a pagan alternative to Jesus. How does this in any way undermine the historical credibility of the gospel accounts of Jesus' miracles?

4. WHAT ABOUT THE SEEMING CONTRADICTIONS IN THE DIFFERENT GOSPEL ACCOUNTS?

Here's your straight answer, Grant: *they don't matter*. I could accept that all of these apparent discrepancies are irresolvable, and it wouldn't affect my historical argument one wit. Don't believe me? Then let's let Bart Ehrman speak for himself. Does he think that the seeming contradictions he lists undermine the historical credibility of the facts upon which my argument is based? No! He says:

---

28. John Meier, *A Marginal Jew*, vol. 2 (New York: Doubleday, 1994), 969–70 (Dr. Craig's emphasis).

The resurrection of Jesus lies at the heart of Christian faith. Unfortunately, it also is a tradition about Jesus that historians have difficulty dealing with. As I said, there are a couple of things that we can say for certain about Jesus after his death. We can say with relative certainty, for example, that he was buried . . .

Some scholars have argued that it's more plausible that in fact Jesus was placed in a common burial plot, which sometimes happened, or was, as many other crucified people, simply left to be eaten by scavenging animals (which also happened commonly for crucified persons in the Roman Empire). But the accounts are fairly unanimous in saying (the earliest accounts we have are unanimous in saying) that Jesus was, in fact, buried by this fellow, Joseph of Arimathea, and so it's relatively reliable that that's what happened.

We also have solid traditions to indicate that women found this tomb empty three days later. This is attested in all of our gospel sources, early and late, and so it appears to be a historical datum. As so I think we can say that after Jesus' death, with some certainty, that He was buried, possibly by this fellow, Joseph of Arimathea, and that three days later He appeared not to have been in His tomb.[29]

The same goes double—well, many times more than double—for Jesus' crucifixion. This event is widely recognized as the most solidly established fact about the historical Jesus, denied only by kooks and Muslim true believers. Yet Ehrman's first five discrepancies are all connected, not with the burial and empty tomb narratives, but with the crucifixion accounts! So are you going to deny that Jesus of Nazareth was crucified under Roman authority at the time of the Jewish Passover feast in 30 AD because of these differences in the narratives? If so, Grant, then you will have not only intellectually marginalized yourself but also shown that you are not a sincere seeker after truth.

Do you see now, Grant, why I refused to be drawn into a dispute about how many angels there were at the tomb? Insofar as the historicity of the empty tomb is concerned, it just doesn't matter. You say those who go to a university committed to biblical inerrancy should be able to explain these discrepancies. That's silly, Grant. Why think that Coach Holmquist should be able to explain these discrepancies? Why think that even someone in the New Testament department should be able to explain these? Maybe there just isn't the

---

29. See Ehrman's "From Jesus to Constantine: A History of Early Christianity," Lecture 4: "Oral and Written Traditions about Jesus," The Great Courses, at http://www.thegreatcourses.com/tgc/Courses/course_detail.aspx?cid=6577.

historical information available to resolve every discrepancy. It seems to me that you must think that the belief in biblical inerrancy is arrived at inductively, but that is problematic.[30]

I think what you really want to say is that those affiliated with such a university ought to be interested in explaining these discrepancies and, therefore, should not "sidestep" them, as you accuse me of doing. Yes, I'd agree with you that we inerrantists ought to be interested in explaining such discrepancies. But there's a time and place for everything. A debate on the historical evidence for the resurrection of Jesus, where time is limited and the central facts of the case are agreed upon by the majority of scholars in the field, is not the time for being diverted into such a discussion. That discussion can be profitably pursued and is being pursued elsewhere.

So let's take them one at a time:

Date and time of the crucifixion: All the sources agree that Jesus was crucified on Friday. What is in dispute is whether Passover was on Thursday or Friday. The Synoptics seem to suggest that Jesus' Last Supper with the disciples on Thursday night was a Passover meal. John agrees that Jesus did share a Last Supper with His disciples on Thursday night in the upper room prior to His betrayal and arrest. But John says that the Jewish leaders wanted to eliminate Jesus *before* the Passover meal began Friday night. So was Passover on Thursday or Friday? That's the whole dispute! (I hope this puts the issue in perspective for you.)

One possibility is that John has moved the Passover to Friday to make Jesus' death coincide with the slaughter of the Passover lambs in the Temple. But maybe not: since there were competing calendars in use in first-century Palestine, the sacrifices may have been made on more than one day. The Pharisees and people from Galilee reckoned days as beginning at sunrise and ending at the following sunrise. But Sadducees and people from Judea reckoned days as beginning at sunset and ending with the next sunset. In our modern age, we adopt what I think is the rather weird convention that the day begins in the middle of the night at midnight and goes until the next midnight. Well, this difference in reckoning days completely throws off the dating of certain events.

Passover lambs were offered on the 14th of the month of Nisan. According to the Galilean reckoning, the 14th of Nisan begins about 6:00 a.m. on the day we call Thursday. But for the Judean, 14 Nisan doesn't begin until 12 hours later, about 6:00 p.m. on our Thursday. So when the Galilean, following Jewish regulations, slays the Passover lamb on

---

30. To learn more, see Dr. Craig's answer to the question, "Is the Price of 'Biblical Errancy' Too High to Pay?" (pages 105-11).

the afternoon of 14 Nisan, what day does he do it on? Thursday. But when the Judean offers his lamb in sacrifice on the afternoon of the 14th of Nisan, what day is that? Friday! When night falls, he then feasts on the lamb, by his reckoning, on 15 Nisan. Thus, in order to meet the demands of both Galilean-Pharisaical sensibilities and of Judean-Sadducean sensibilities, the Temple priesthood would have to have made Passover sacrifices on both Thursday and Friday. Jesus, as a Galilean and knowing of His impending arrest, chose to celebrate the Passover Thursday night, whereas the chief priests and scribes responsible for Jesus' arrest went by the Judean calendar, as John says. Although we have no evidence that Passover sacrifices were made on both days, such a solution is very plausible. The population of Jerusalem swelled to around 125,000 people during the Passover festival. It would be logistically impossible for the Temple priesthood to sacrifice enough lambs for that many people between 3:00 and 6:00 on one afternoon. They must have sacrificed on more than one day, which makes it entirely possible for Jesus and His disciples to celebrate the Passover Thursday night prior to His arrest.

Similarly for the time of Jesus' crucifixion: Mark says the crucifixion was at the third hour, that is, 9:00 a.m., but John says Jesus was condemned "about the sixth hour," that is, around noon. Again, maybe John has moved the time until later. But maybe not: in the Synoptic gospels and Acts the *only* times of day ever referred to (with one exception) are the third, sixth, and ninth hours. Obviously in an age without modern time-keeping devices, round numbers or quarters of the day are being used. The third hour could refer to any time between 9:00 a.m. and noon.

Did Jesus carry His cross the entire way? No, Simon of Cyrene was a historical person, whose role in the narrative John simply chooses to omit. Simon was probably impressed into service by the soldiers when Jesus proved too weak to carry the crossbeam all the way to Golgotha.

Did the robbers rail against Jesus? Mark says merely that those who were crucified with Jesus reviled Him. No details are given. But Luke tells of how one of the criminals expressed faith in Jesus. You could just write off Luke's story as a pious development of the crucifixion narrative. But how do we know that Luke is not working with an independent source here that remembers this man's repentance, whereas Mark passes over it? I don't have any confidence that we have a real contradiction here.

When did the veil of the Temple tear? This alleged discrepancy is purely imaginary, since Mark and Luke mention the rending of the Temple curtain but don't pretend to specify its timing. Luke would have been amazed had some modern reader accused him of contradicting

Mark when he groups together the supernatural signs occurring at Christ's death.

Who went to the tomb? A group of women, including Mary Magdalene, who is always named. John focuses on her for dramatic effect, but he knows of other women, as is evident in Mary's words, "They have taken the Lord out of the tomb, and *we* do not know where they have laid him" (John 20:2; cf. 20:13). We don't know all the names of the other women, but they included another Mary, who was the mother of James and Joses, and Salome. The fact that women, rather than men, appear in the narrative as the discoverers of Jesus' empty tomb is, by the way, one of the most convincing factors leading most scholars to accept the historicity of the narrative.

Was the stone rolled away before they got there and what did they see? Yes, it was; there's no discrepancy here. They saw one or two angels. Mark's "young man" is clearly an angelic figure, as evident from his white robe, his revelatory message, and the women's response of fear and trembling. Moreover, Mark's earliest interpreters (Matthew and Luke) understood the young man to be an angel.

What were they told? They were told to go to Galilee, where they would see Jesus. Since Luke doesn't plan on narrating any Galilean appearances, he alters Mark's wording of the angel's message for literary purposes. The tradition of appearances in Galilee is very old and virtually universally accepted.

Did the women tell anyone? Of course, they did! When Mark says that they said nothing to anyone, he obviously means *as they fled back to the disciples.* Mark foreshadows the appearances in Galilee, so obviously he didn't mean that the women failed to give the angel's message to the disciples. This discrepancy is purely imaginary.

Did the disciples leave Jerusalem for Galilee? Of course, as indicated above. Luke just chooses not to narrate any Galilean appearances because he wants to show how the gospel became established in the holiest city of the Jews, Jerusalem.

So some of these alleged discrepancies are easy to answer and are what we should expect from independent accounts of the same event. Others are more difficult but are in the end not of great consequence. Historians expect to find inconsistencies like these even in the most reliable sources. No historian simply throws out a source because it has inconsistencies. Moreover, the inconsistencies Ehrman is talking about aren't within a single source; they're between *independent* sources. But obviously, it doesn't follow from an inconsistency between two independent sources that *both* sources are wrong. At worst, one is wrong if they can't be harmonized.

The problem with focusing on discrepancies is that we tend to lose the forest for the trees. The overriding fact is that the gospels are remarkably harmonious in what they relate. The discrepancies between them are in the secondary details. *All* four gospels agree: Jesus of Nazareth was crucified in Jerusalem by Roman authority during the Passover Feast, having been arrested and convicted on charges of blasphemy by the Jewish Sanhedrin and then slandered before the governor Pilate on charges of treason. He died within several hours and was buried Friday afternoon by Joseph of Arimathea in a tomb, which was sealed with a stone. Certain women followers of Jesus, including Mary Magdalene, having observed His interment, visited His tomb early on Sunday morning, only to find it empty. Thereafter, Jesus appeared alive from the dead to the disciples, including Peter, who then became proclaimers of the message of His resurrection.

All four gospels attest to these facts. Many more details can be supplied by adding facts which are attested by three out of four. So don't be misled by the minor discrepancies. Otherwise you're going to have to be skeptical about all secular historical narratives that also contain such inconsistencies, which is quite unreasonable.

Part 2

QUESTIONS ABOUT GOD

Questions about the nature, existence, value, and implications of God's existence have not only shaped humanity but entire conditions and institutions of human society. As you discover from Part One, if God exists there is great reason to think that objective moral values and duties exist. And, in turn, we humans bank on their existence for our everyday life and interactions. At the very least, we live as if it is true. Thus, lawless societies are not generally regarded as theistic-like societies. The very institution of the "rule of law," as Harvard historian Niall Ferguson has observed in his 2011 book, *Civilization*, has its basis in a Judeo-Christian framework. Is that coincidental? Probably not. So, the questions of God's existence are as relevant for the "City of Man" as they are for the "City of God," a point which atheist-turned-Christian Peter Hitchens also acknowledges in his 2011 book *Rage Against God: How Atheism Led Me to Faith* (Peter is the brother of the late "new atheist" Christopher Hitchens, who debated Dr. Craig in 2009).

The questions in this part seek to get at the "God Question," but not merely the generic God question, but questions about the Trinitarian God and His attributes as revealed in Scripture. Whether popular questions regarding if "God's existence can be evident to every sincere seeker," or deep questions regarding the meaning of the Incarnation in light of the Trinity, these questions will surely challenge and provoke thought.

By interacting with the questions and answers of Part Two, you can benefit in the following ways.

In section 1, you can come to understand that
- God has necessary existence.
- God is a maximally great being.
- Theistic arguments do provide positive evidence for God's existence in non-question-begging ways.

In section 2, you can come to grapple with
- How God is a "simple" being.
- Why God's infinite personhood does not imply pantheism.
- The meaning of God's "omni-attributes" among the persons of the Trinity.
- How the persons of the Trinity are interrelated with each other.

In section 3, you can come to appreciate
- Why "perfect being theology" is significant.
- Why the attributes of God are reason for us to be morally obligated to worship God.
- Why a doctrine of divine impassibility creates problems for what it means for God to be compassionate.
- How Reformed theology's conception of God and creation is problematic.

The above areas have a long history in the study of philosophy of religion, philosophical theology, "natural" and "revealed" theology, and Christian apologetics. You can discover further background to these issues, grow your understanding, and become even more skillful in your communication of what you learn by interacting with some of these valuable resources:

Dig Deeper into Dr. Craig's Work

BEGINNER

Craig, William Lane. *On Guard: Defending Your Faith with Reason and Precision.* Colorado Springs: David C. Cook Publishers, 2010. Chapter 3.

Craig, William Lane. *Defenders Podcast: Series 2.* ReasonableFaith.org. http://bit.ly/ DefendersPodcast.

Craig, William Lane. "The Arguments for God's Existence and Critique of New Atheists." GracePoint Church, Berkeley, Calif., April 17, 2010. http://bit.ly/ GodsExistenceGracePoint.

INTERMEDIATE

Craig, William Lane and Walter Sinnott-Armstrong. *God? A Debate between a Christian and an Atheist.* Oxford: Oxford University Press, 2004.

Craig, William Lane and J. P. Moreland. *Philosophical Foundations for a Christian Worldview*. Downers Grove, Ill.: InterVarsity, 2003. Chapters 8–10, 23–26, 29.

Craig, William Lane. *Reasonable Faith: Christian Truth and Apologetics*. 3rd ed. Wheaton: Crossway, 2008. Chapters 3–4.

Craig, William Lane. "Is God a Delusion?" Lecture on Richard Dawkins' argument. Sheldon Ian Theatre, Oxford, UK, October 24, 2011. http://bit.ly/GodADelusion.

Craig, William Lane and Antony Flew. "Craig v. Flew: Does God Exist?" University of Wisconsin, Madison, Wisc., 1998. http://bit.ly/CraigFlew.

Craig, William Lane and Peter Atkins. "Craig v. Atkins: What Is the Evidence for/ against the Existence of God." Carter Presidential Center, Atlanta, April 3, 1998. http://bit.ly/CraigAtkins.

Craig, William Lane and Austin Dacey. "Craig v. Dacey: Does God Exist?" Purdue University, West Lafayette, Ind., 2004. http://bit.ly/CraigDacey.

ADVANCED

Craig, William Lane and J. P. Sinclair. "The Kalam Cosmological Argument." *The Blackwell Companion to Natural Theology*, William Lane Craig and J. P. Moreland, eds. Malden, Mass.: Wiley-Blackwell Publishing, 2009. Chapter 3.

Flint, Thomas and Michael Rea, eds. "Divine Eternity." *The Oxford Handbook of Philosophical Theology*. Oxford: Oxford University Press, 2009. 145–66. http://bit.ly/DivineEternity.

Supplemental Recommended Resources

BEGINNER

Strobel, Lee. *The Case for a Creator*. Grand Rapids: Zondervan, 2004.

Zacharias, Ravi. *Can Man Live Without God?* Nashville: Word Publishing Group, 1994, 2002.

INTERMEDIATE

Copan, Paul and William Lane Craig, eds. *Come Let Us Reason: New Essays in Christian Apologetics*. Nashville: B&H, 2012. Chapters 4–6.

Copan, Paul and William Lane Craig, eds. *Contending with Christianity's Critics*. Nashville: Broadman and Holman, 2009. Chapters 1, 4, 6, 13–16, 18.

Craig, William Lane and Chad Meister, eds. *God Is Great, God Is Good: Why Believing in God Is Reasonable and Responsible.* Downers Grove, Ill.: InterVarsity, 2009. Chapters 1–3.

Groothuis, Douglas. *Christian Apologetics: A Comprehensive Case for Biblical Faith.* Downers Grove, Ill.: InterVarsity, 2011. Chapters 9–12, 15–16.

Sweis, Khaldoun A. and Chad V. Meister. *Christian Apologetics: An Anthology of Primary Sources.* Grand Rapids: Zondervan, 2012. Chapters 7–25.

Williams, Clifford. *Existential Reasons for Belief in God: A Defense of Desires and Emotions for Faith.* Downers Grove, Ill.: InterVarsity, 2011.

ADVANCED

Craig, William Lane and J. P. Moreland, eds. *The Blackwell Companion to Natural Theology.* Malden, Mass.: Wiley-Blackwell Publishing, 2009. Chapters 2–7, 10.

Meister, Chad and Paul Copan. *Routledge Companion to Philosophy of Religion.* New York: Routledge, 2009. Parts 4–8.

Wallace, Stan, ed. *Does God Exist?* Aldershot, England: Ashgate, 2003.

1

ON THE EXISTENCE OF GOD

On Whether God's Existence Can Be Evident to Every Sincere Seeker

This is an argument I read on the ReasonableFaith.org forum, and I'm wondering how you would respond. In my opinion, it's not a very strong argument. But here it is:

1. If God exists, then His existence would be evident to anyone who sincerely seeks God.
2. God's existence is not evident to everyone who sincerely seeks God.
3. Therefore, God doesn't exist.

I take it that most Christians accept (1)—I know William Lane Craig does. Hence, to deny the conclusion, Christians must reject (2), but (2) is evidently obvious to anyone who sincerely gave Christianity a chance and yet is not convinced of God's existence. To me, the truth of (2) is far more plausible than its denial: if (2) were false, then it would have to be true that every person who claims to have sincerely sought God, but couldn't find Him, must be lying, either to others or themselves.

Do Christians really believe this?

As expected, most who resist the argument claim that premise (2) is false, which I find extraordinary. To hold that (2) is false, one would have to believe that every non-Christian is lying, either about God's existence being evident or about being sincere. Compare premise (2) with the following:

1. Allah's existence is not evident to everyone who sincerely seeks Allah.
2. Brahman's existence is not evident to everyone who sincerely seeks Brahman.

3. Bigfoot's existence is not evident to everyone who sincerely seeks Bigfoot.

4. Santa's existence is not evident to everyone who sincerely seeks Santa.

And so on.

Most of us would not doubt these statements, since we generally take people at their word about what they believe. Why, then, shouldn't we generally take the word of non-Christians who claim they sincerely sought to find God? Without an adequate answer to this question, those who reject premise (2) are just guilty of special pleading.

Sorry if it's a little bit long. Look forward to hearing from you.

Sincerely,

Tapji

Canada

Dr. Craig's Response

I believe that God's existence—that is to say, the existence of the God described in the Bible—is or will become evident in this lifetime to anyone who sincerely seeks Him. Now, by "evident" I don't mean obvious or certain. I mean that the sincere seeker will come to saving faith in God; his search will be successful; he will not only come to believe that God exists but will come to know God.

Why do I believe such a thing? Well, primarily because that is what Jesus taught, and I have good reasons for believing that Jesus is the revelation of God to mankind and, therefore, to be believed in what He taught. You can find my reasons for so thinking in *Reasonable Faith*. As for Jesus' teaching, consider this saying from His Sermon on the Mount:

Ask, and it shall be given you; seek, and you shall find; knock, and it shall be opened to you. For every one that asks receives; and he that seeks finds; and to him that knocks it shall be opened. (Matt. 7:7–8)

By "seeking," Jesus obviously didn't mean a merely intellectual inquiry but a genuine search of the soul, a spiritual quest in humility and with a contrite heart. This teaching comports well with the universal salvific will of God (1 Tim. 2:3–4; 2 Peter 3:9).

Of course, God's providence in each person's life plays itself out over time. God's existence may not be evident to someone at certain stages of his life but may become evident when and through what means God chooses. If a person is truly seeking God, he will persist in his search and will eventually find God.

So I would replace premise (1) with

1´. **If God exists, then His existence will become evident to anyone who sincerely seeks God.**

So to those who say, "I've sincerely sought God and haven't found Him," I say, "Don't give up! Keep searching, and you will find God."

If we have, as I think we do, good reasons to believe that Jesus was who He claimed to be, then we have good reasons to believe that what He taught is true. So what defeater is offered by the detractor of this doctrine?

It's the claim that

2. **God's existence is not evident to everyone who sincerely seeks God.**

But (2), even if true, is not incompatible with (1´). From (1´) it follows only that God's existence will become evident to a sincere seeker after God. Of course, (2) is easily adjusted to the claim that

2´. **God's existence never becomes evident to some people who sincerely seek God.**

But why should we think that (2´) is true? How do we know that? It's obviously inadequate to say that (2´) "is evidently obvious to anyone who sincerely gave Christianity a chance and yet is not convinced of God's existence." For perhaps his lack of persistence is an indication that his search was not as earnest as he imagines (he gave Christianity "a chance"?) or

> **INSIGHT**
> Note this important distinction between "seeking" as mere intellectual inquiry vs. seeking as a genuine search of the soul. Our apologetics endeavors should seek to be mindful of this distinction in order to avoid the distraction of merely entertaining people's intellectual curiosities.

perhaps that person will yet find God.

To establish (2′) it seems we'd have to appeal to cases in which a person was a sincere seeker but at the end of his life failed to come to faith in God. The problem with such an argument, however, is that we're just not in a position to look into the human heart and judge a person's sincerity in this regard. This would require a kind of psychological insight that is not available to us. Only God is capable of doing the spiritual cardiogram necessary for answering this question.

Your "Edit" tries to support (2′) by saying that "we generally take people at their word about what they believe. Why, then, shouldn't we generally take the word of non-Christians who claim they sincerely sought to find God?" I've already answered that question: if a person persists in unbelief until his death, then the evidence for Jesus' identity and the truth of His claims gives us reason to think that that person was not as sincere as he imagined himself to be.

Notice that in so saying, we do not presume to have the sort of psychological insight that the atheist claims to have. Notice as well that this answer is not to say that "every non-Christian [who persists until death in unbelief] is lying, either about God's existence being evident or about being sincere." Rather such a person may be self-deceived. He imagines himself to be sincere and earnest in seeking God, when in truth he may not be.

There is a large amount of literature on the incredible human capacity for rationalization and self-deception that is relevant here. We all see the remarkable blind spots in others; but of course we do not see our own. Pride, the desire to be right, and the wish for self-autonomy all conspire to subvert our vaunted sincerity. It is not at all implausible that those who persist in unbelief until their deaths have not truly sought God.[1]

As for the four examples of other things whose existence is not evident to every sincere seeker, the last two are just silly, and there is every reason to think that the existence of Bigfoot and Santa Claus should not be self-evident. By contrast, the first two examples, especially the first, deserve to be taken very seriously. A Muslim might well claim that Allah will make his existence evident to anyone who sincerely seeks him. I don't find that claim at all implausible, given that Allah exists. The problem is, we have good reasons to think

---

1. Readers might be interested in such books as Gregg A. Ten Elshof, *I Told Me So: Self-Deception and the Christian Life* (Grand Rapids: Eerdmans, 2009); James S. Spiegel, *The Making of an Atheist: How Immorality Leads to Unbelief* (Chicago: Moody, 2010); James R. Peters, *The Logic of the Heart: Augustine, Pascal, and the Rationality of Faith* (Grand Rapids: Baker, 2009); Patrick Downey, *Desperately Wicked: Philosophy, Christianity and the Human Heart* (Downers Grove, Ill.: InterVarsity, 2009).

that the God described in the Qur'an does not exist. We have good reasons to think that the God revealed by Jesus of Nazareth does exist. So in contrast with the four examples, we have good reason to believe that (1′) is true and no comparably good reasons to think that the claims offered on behalf of Allah, Brahman, Bigfoot, or Santa Claus are true.

Now, I realize that my saying these things makes atheists see red! But that is no argument, and they need to ask themselves honestly whether their anger and indignance at Jesus' wonderful promise that everyone who sincerely seeks God will find Him may not be an indication of just where their hearts really are in regard to God.

What Does It Mean to Define "God"?

I recently posted a YouTube video respectfully asking atheists to comment with what their strongest argument in favor of atheism was. Then, atheists could vote on the comment they felt was their strongest argument. After 1,000 views, the current #1 argument is:

"God" is not meaningfully defined, ergo, by simple tautology, it is 100 percent certain that "God" does not refer to anything that exists (or that does not).

I don't even understand what this means. I have never heard this argument before. Please help!

Michael

United States

Dr. Craig's Response

Wow, wow, wow, wow! Positivism lives! I just shake my head in disbelief when I see how pervasive this old-line positivistic philosophy still is in popular culture despite its demise among philosophers fifty years ago. Those who roundly proclaim that we live in a postmodernist culture need to reflect long and hard on data like this.

INSIGHT

Interested readers may also wish to see Dr. Craig's comments on whether we live in a postmodern society in Part Six of this book.

The reason you haven't heard of this objection, Michael, is probably because no philosopher presses it anymore. During the positivist era back in the 1920s and '30s, it was widely thought among philosophers that "metaphysical" notions like God were meaningless. Why? Because no empirical content could be given to such notions. To be meaningful an informative sentence had to be empirically verifiable. Since it was thought that sentences like "God exists" could not be verified through the five senses, they were dismissed as meaningless. The so-called verification principle of meaning, however, was soon found to be unduly restrictive, rendering even some sentences of science meaningless, and in the end self-defeating. With the abandonment of the verification principle of meaning, the vital nerve of positivism was severed, and so it sank into the grave it so richly deserved. A new era then dawned in Anglo-American philosophy, ushering in a renaissance of metaphysics, ethics, and philosophy of religion, which the positivists had suppressed.

It would be very interesting to learn what undergirds the YouTube atheists' conviction that "God" is a meaningless word. Is it verificationism? If so, then the foundations of their conviction have, unbeknownst to them, already collapsed long ago.

It's easy to give content to the word "God." This word can be taken either as a common noun, so that one could speak of "a god," or it can be used as a proper name like "George" or "Suzanne." Richard Swinburne, a prominent Christian philosopher, treats "God" as a proper name of the person referred to by the following description:

> a person without a body (*i.e.*, a spirit) who necessarily is eternal, perfectly free, omnipotent, omniscient, perfectly good, and the creator of all things.

This description expresses the traditional concept of God in Western philosophy and theology. Now, the YouTube atheist might protest, "But how do you know God has those properties?" The question is misplaced. "God" has been stipulated to be the person, if any, referred to by that description. The real question is whether there is anything answering to that description, that is to say, does such a person exist? The whole burden of Swinburne's natural theology is to present arguments that there is such a person. You can reject his arguments, but there's no disputing the meaningfulness of his claim.

The best definition of God as a descriptive term is, I think, St. Anselm's: the greatest conceivable being. As Anselm observed, if you could think of anything greater than God, then *that* would be God! The very idea of God is of a being than which there cannot be a greater.

This question has relevance to my recent debate with Sam Harris on whether the foundations of morality are natural or supernatural. Following the debate my friend John wrote:

> Bill, in your debate with Sam Harris you claimed God was the grounding of objective morality. That word "God" is problematic though. Until that word is defined, or until you tell us how we know what this "God" wants us to do, or what it is, what you end up saying is that there is an objective grounding to morality, and that's it. But then Sam Harris agreed with you on that score.

If you'll look at the text of my opening statement in the debate, which I've posted on our Reasonable Faith Facebook page,[2] you'll see that I did define what I mean by "God." I stated: "On the theistic view objective moral values are grounded in God. As St. Anselm saw, God is by definition the greatest conceivable being and, therefore, the highest Good. Indeed, He is not merely perfectly good; He is the locus and paradigm of moral value."

Since moral goodness is a great-making property, the greatest conceivable being must be morally perfect (as well as have the other superlative properties listed by Swinburne). Indeed, the greatest conceivable being will be the paradigm of moral value. Of course, it remains to be asked whether such a being actually exists. But the contentions I laid out for defense in our debate were conditional: If such a being exists, then . . . That's why I think my first contention is almost obviously true. Of course, if such a greatest conceivable being exists, objective moral values and duties exist! How could they not?

The real question was whether Harris could provide an ontological foundation for objective moral values and duties in the absence of such a being. I presented what I take to be a decisive argument against his solution to what he calls "the Value Problem" as well as powerful objections to his attempt to derive objective moral duties from science and his desire to affirm objective moral duties in the absence of any sort of free will.

Finally, let me say again what I said previously: I do not need to provide an account of "how we know what this 'God' wants us to do," since that is a question, not of moral ontology, but of moral epistemology.[3] My concern is with the reality of objective moral values and duties; I'm open to any epistemological theories anyone wants to suggest for how we come to know the values and duties that there are.

---

2. For those interested, here is the text of Dr. Craig's opening remarks: http://bit.ly/HarrisOpening.

3. For more on this matter, see the question above, "The Importance of Distinguishing Between Moral Epistemology and Moral Ontology" (pages 92–95).

What Does It Mean for God to Have Necessary Existence?

Dr. Craig,

I really want to learn more about theism but I have hit an intellectual roadblock with God's necessary existence. I understand what it means for an entity to necessarily exist in a logical sense. Yet when you attribute metaphysical necessity to God (de re necessity) my brain gets muddled.

As I understand it, to say that God necessarily exists in the metaphysical (de re) sense, you mean to state that in every world in which God exists, God must exist. Other scholars of a theistic persuasion reinterpret the same point as proclaiming that God's existence is part of His essence. But what in the world does that mean? How should I contrast it to logically necessary existence? Moreover, assuming that existence is a property, isn't it the case that you, me, and everyone else has existence as part of his or her essence? After all, it seems plausible that there is no possible world wherein I reside and do not exist. Hence, the property of existence is part of my essence.

Finally, do you believe it is logically possible that God does not exist? Please explain your answer.

Mikhal

Dr. Craig's Response

Understanding God's necessity is fundamental to our grasping *who* God is, so your question is a vital one, Mikhal. I think some of your confusion may be due simply to terminological muddles, so let's try to clear them up.

When philosophers speak of metaphysical necessity/possibility, they are thinking in terms of a modality that lies somewhere in between the strict logical modality that characterizes the laws of logic and the broader physical modality that characterizes what is permitted by nature's laws and boundary conditions. Metaphysical possibility has to do with what is actualizable or realizable, what can actually be. So, for example, I would say that it is metaphysically possible that I might have had an alligator body, even though such a thing is not physically possible. But it is metaphysically impossible that I could have actually been an alligator rather than a human being. Metaphysical necessity has to do with what must be the case, even though its denial does not involve a contradiction. For example, I think it is metaphysically necessary that everything that begins to exist has a cause, even though there is no logical inconsistency in saying that a certain thing came into being without a cause. If this metaphysical modality strikes you as rather vague, you're right! What we take to be metaphysically necessary/possible depends on our intuitions about such matters.

Now, *de re* (from the Latin, meaning *pertaining to a thing*) modality has to do with a thing's essential properties. When it is said that a property belongs to a thing's essence or is essential to it, that means that the thing could not have lacked that property and still remained itself. If something loses one of its essential properties, then that thing ceases to exist. A cow, for example, has the essential property of being an animal. If it were slaughtered and ground up into hamburger, then it would cease to be a cow. Properties that a thing has which are not essential to it are called contingent properties.

So metaphysical necessity and *de re* necessity aren't the same thing. When we say that God is metaphysically necessary, we mean that it is impossible that He fail to exist. This is a much more far-reaching claim than the claim that "in every world in which God exists, God must exist." When you think about it, anything that exists must have the property of existing in every world in which it exists! So you're right that you, I, and everyone else has existence as part of his or her essence in that sense. Rather, the claim here is that God exists in every possible world. What God has that we don't, then, is the property of *necessary existence*. And He has that property *de re*, as part of His essence. God cannot lack the property of necessary existence and be God. Of course, if something has the property of necessary existence, it can't lose

> **INSIGHT**
> Even though this can feel a little "heady," the distinctions that Dr. Craig articulates are important for clearly thinking about a whole range of issues in philosophy, theology, and apologetics. Try to cultivate your intuitions about what things are metaphysically necessary/possible. You can do this by taking stock of what you already know to be real, for example.

that property, since if it did, there would be a possible world in which it lacked necessary existence and so it was never necessarily existing in the first place![4]

So is it logically possible that God not exist? Not in the sense of metaphysical possibility! There is no strict logical contradiction in the statement "God does not exist," just as there is not a strict logical contradiction in saying "Jones is a married bachelor," but both are unactualizable states of affairs. Thus, it is metaphysically necessary that God exists.

We have here the germ of the ontological argument for God's existence. For if it is possible that God exists, there is a possible world in which God has necessary existence. But then He exists in every world, including this one. Thus, the atheist is thrust into the awkward position of having to say that God's existence is impossible. It is not enough to say that in fact God does not exist; the atheist must hold that it is *impossible* that God exists—a much more radical claim!

Is a Maximally Great Being Possible?

Dear Dr. Craig,

My first question concerns the soundness of the argument in general. The second, however, concerns its theological implications.

Firstly, then, the soundness of the argument. I'm thinking particularly about the version of the OA you propose in *To Everyone an Answer* (InterVarsity, 2004) together with what you write about the argument in *Philosophical Foundations* (InterVarsity, 2003) (though my rendering of the argument below isn't an exact quote),

(OA1) It's possible that an all-surpassingly great being exists (i.e., a being greater than which nothing can be conceived). In other words, an all-surpassingly great being exists in some possible world.

4. It is important to note that when medieval theologians spoke of existence as uniquely part of God's essence, they were using the word "essence" in a different way. For them a thing's essence defined what it is. In their view only God has existence essentially, since every other being is contingent and so is not defined as something existing.

(OA2) If an all-surpassingly great being exists in some possible world, then it exists in every possible world.

(OA3) If an all-surpassingly great being exists in every possible world, then it exists in the actual world (since the actual world is clearly a possible world).

(OA4) If an all-surpassingly great being exists in the actual world, then an all-surpassingly great being actually exists.

The problem I have with this argument is that we seem able to take the general form of the key premise (i.e., it's possible that X exists) and then plug in various different definitions of X in order to arrive at absurd answers.

Obviously, defining X as something like an all-surpassingly great island doesn't work, since, as you and others rightly point out, islands are, amongst other things, inherently material (and are, therefore, contingent on the existence of space and time); moreover, it's far from clear as to what properties make an island great (for some it might involve plenty of palm trees; for others, it might involve no palm trees at all). So defining X in such a way doesn't seem to work.

But what if we define X as a being that necessarily exists but isn't, say, necessarily all-knowing? The argument you give against this idea (if I understand you correctly) is that God must be such that nothing can exist independently of His power, meaning there must be a possible world where God alone exists. You then argue that the existence of God is therefore logically incompatible with the existence of X, meaning X is an incoherent concept.

But I have two problems with this argument. Firstly, for God to be able to actualize a world where X doesn't exist seems to be asking God to do the logically impossible (since X exists necessarily). So why should we think God must be capable of doing such a thing? Secondly, even if we grant that the existence of God is incompatible with the existence of X, why should it follow that GOD exists as opposed to X? That is, if the proponent of the OA in its original form can argue that, since God's existence entails there being possible worlds where God alone exists, the concept of X is incoherent, why can't the skeptic argue that, since X's existence entails there being NO possible worlds where God alone exists, the concept of God is incoherent? This looks like a "Mexican stand-off" to me.

I've considered appealing to factors like simplicity or likeliness at this point; but this seems misguided. Simplicity can be important in deciding on the most likely explanation for a given body of facts. But I'm not sure this is relevant here, since the OA isn't an inference to the most likely explanation. Rather, the OA starts from the premise that God's existence is either possible or it isn't, and then tells us what logically follows as a result. If God's existence is possible, then it's necessary, meaning God exists; if it isn't, God obviously doesn't exist.

The OA is, therefore, different from something like the teleological argument, where we might want to argue that God is a simpler and more elegant explanation for the universe's apparent fine-tuning than the extravagant ontologies posited by many-worlds-hypotheses. The OA is a question of metaphysical fact. From what we have said about X, it, therefore, seems to follow that either God exists or X exists (together with any number of other necessarily-existent beings; for if a modified OA works for X, why can't it work for any other similarly-defined X? It might, I guess, be argued that to simply tack 'necessarily-existing' onto a being is somewhat gratuitous. But I don't see why this would be any more gratuitous than tacking 'all-surpassingly great' onto a being, or why gratuity would even be important here. In any case, couldn't X be a necessarily-existing number or a necessarily-existing set or something like that? Granted, the existence of such entities is problematic for the same reasons Platonism as a whole is problematic. But the existence of such entities doesn't seem logically impossible; nor do the entities in question seem conceptually gratuitous or incoherent.

I, therefore, have concerns about the soundness of the OA.

But I also have concerns about its theological implications. For, in light of the OA, doesn't it follow that God's actions are a necessary consequence of His nature, since, given any set of conditions, an all-surpassingly great being will necessarily react in the "greatest" possible way? Creating the universe, for instance, gives God opportunity to lavish His love and grace on other creatures, meaning only a lesser being would choose not to create the universe. It, therefore, follows that God's creating the universe is necessary—which logic can be extended to God's answering of prayers, and, worse still, Christ's dying on the cross. In fact, on this view, the only thing that makes our world contingent is man's free will; and, while this may be so, it seems wrong to me, since it leaves so little scope for the action of

God's grace and freedom and sovereignty. The OA, therefore, appears to eliminate God's free will in the same way physicalism eliminates man's free will.

As always, I'd be extremely grateful if you could spare the time to address these issues. (Though I don't have a philosophical background, so I'd be grateful if you could assume a low level of technical knowledge as your starting point—especially when it comes to the nature of necessity!).

Thanks,

James

Dr. Craig's Response

Let's deal with the soundness objection to the ontological argument for the existence of God first, James. What you're really objecting to is not the soundness of the argument. An argument is sound if it is logically valid and has true premises. Since this argument is logically valid, your objecting to the argument's soundness would require you to think that (OA1) is false. But the parodies of the argument you mention don't show that it's impossible that there be a maximally great being, or, as you put it, an all-surpassingly great being. Rather the point of such parodies is that there is no good reason to think that (OA1) is true. For any reason for thinking that premise to be true would also be a reason for accepting an obviously false premise in one of the parodies of the argument. So the argument, even if sound, is not a good argument because there's no non-circular reason to think that (OA1) is true.

Now, as you note, some of the parodies, like arguments for an unsurpassingly great island or a necessarily existent lion, are not well thought-out. We have good grounds for thinking that such concoctions are impossible, in contrast to the apparently coherent idea of a maximally great being. More difficult to assess is the notion of what I called a quasi-maximally great being: a being which is just like a maximally great being except that it lacks, for example, complete omniscience (like the God of so-called Open Theism, who lacks knowledge of future free acts of men).

My argument against such a parody is that any reason for thinking a quasi-maximally great being is possible also warrants belief in the possibility of a maximally great being, but if we think that a maximally great being is possible, then we must say that a quasi-maximally great being is impossible after all, since it's impossible for the two to coexist in the same world.

Now, you object, why should we think that God must be capable of refraining from creating a quasi-maximally great being, since His refraining from creating it would be logically impossible?

I think your question highlights the inadequacy of a definition of omnipotence simply in terms of what is logically possible for someone to do. To borrow a famous example, on this definition a person who is essentially capable of only scratching his ear could count as omnipotent since other actions are logically impossible for him to do! That is surely an inadequate concept of omnipotence! Similarly, if there exists another being outside God's creative power, then this is plausibly not consistent with God's being omnipotent. I'd say the same with respect to numbers and other allegedly necessarily existing abstract objects: given God's necessary existence, they are broadly logically impossible.[5]

Is a Maximally Great Being Possible?

Your second objection to the ontological argument for the existence of God is the more difficult of the two: even if we grant that the existence of God is incompatible with the existence of a quasi-maximally great being, why should it follow that *God's* existence is possible as opposed to the existence of a quasi-maximally great being? My answer here is that there's an asymmetry between our intuitions about the possibility of such beings. Any intuition for thinking a quasi-maximally great being to be possible also warrants belief in the possibility of a maximally great being; indeed, the way we came to form the idea of the former was by diminution of the idea of the latter. But our intuition of the possibility of a maximally great being, once we understand its implications, tends to undermine our intuition of the possibility of a quasi-maximally great being. We begin to suspect that despite appearances, it's not really possible after all.

INSIGHT

Note what Dr. Craig highlights here. It is a helpful example of adequate vs. inadequate conceptualization of God's attributes.

Notice that all this is said solely on the basis of appeal to modal intuitions alone (*i.e.*, our intuitions about what is possible or necessary). But one of the significant new wrinkles

---

5. For a brilliant yet technical discussion of an adequate definition of omnipotence, see Thomas Flint and Alfred Freddoso, "Maximal Power," in *The Existence and Nature of God*, Alfred Freddoso, ed. Notre Dame, Ind.: University of Notre Dame Press, 1983, 81–113.

in discussions of the ontological argument is support for (OA1) which goes beyond mere modal intuitions. Here, considerations of simplicity may indeed have a role to play. By appealing to such factors, one is not altering the form of the ontological argument for the existence of God but marshaling reasons in addition to modal intuitions for the truth of (OA1).

Now, concerning your theological misgiving: I don't see that this has anything to do with God's being metaphysically necessary. Even if God exists contingently, so long as He is essentially morally perfect you can run your argument that He is morally obligated to do the best and, therefore, must create the best possible world. So this is a problem that faces any theist who thinks that God is morally perfect.

The misgiving is to be met, I think, by questioning the assumption that there is a best of all possible worlds. Worlds may just get better and better without limit. For any world God chooses to create there will always be a better one that He could have created. God must at most create a good world, not the best world (since there is no such thing). Moreover, there's no reason to think that God must create anything at all. In a possible world in which God creates nothing, there is only He Himself, the paradigm and locus of goodness—the *summum bonum*. That's a pretty good world, to say the least!

Naturalistic Appeal to Ignorance

Dr. Craig,

To say that I appreciate your work would be an understatement. I'll spare you a paragraph or two elaborating on that subject but I do want to take the opportunity to express my sincere gratitude both to you and all the people who work behind the scenes in order to make your work available to people such as myself. May God truly bless your work and allow it to have an impact for Christ all over the world. For my part, I'm getting ready to teach a class using *On Guard* in a town called Hovd in western Mongolia. A place, I'm sure, you never would have imagined your books working their way to Mongolia.

At any rate, due to the miracles of modern technology also working their way to our corner of the world, I just finished watching your debate with Christopher Hitchens and the City of Ideas debate and I think that it is fairly clear that these popular type "new atheists" are unable to, or unwilling to, interact in any kind of detail with your arguments.

However, the kind of umbrella argument they do give to superficially cover your points seems to run along the lines of the following:

> We are only beginning to understand the universe and all that is contained in it. Our current knowledge is very limited right now; we are only beginning to discover the questions, let alone the answers. However, this is the job of science and someday, as science progresses, all of these unanswered questions will in fact be answered. In other words, yes, there are mysteries in the universe which may give the appearance of a transcendent being, but, as experience has shown us already with other things that were thought to be of divine origin, these mysteries will eventually be solved and there will be no place for any kind of a "God hypothesis." In short, God is not necessary and science will eventually explain everything in a naturalistic way given enough time.

I don't doubt that you did respond to this line of thinking which they throw out there, seemingly, to avoid having to interact with your premises in any kind of detail but I don't remember hearing a definitive response on your part—maybe I missed it. Would you mind responding to the above "argument" now?

Thank you once again,

Craig

Mongolia

Dr. Craig's Response

Craig, your letter made my day! I was just reading the brand-new edition of *Operation World* and was struck by the following sentence:

Patrick Johnstone, when queried in 1979 about the most difficult places for gospel breakthrough, named Mongolia and Albania. Today, there are at least 40,000 Mongolian believers. Albania is open and churches are growing. (p. 4)

I praise God and thank you for your pioneering work! Folks, if you don't know where western Mongolia is, take a look at a globe or world map. It may not be the end of the world, but you can see it from there!

As for your question, I, too, hear the naturalistic appeal to ignorance all the time. I think the fallacy of this reasoning is that it assumes that I'm appealing to a sort of "God of the gaps" to plug up the gaps in our scientific knowledge of the world. But I'm not. In fact, I'm not even offering scientific evidence for God. Rather here is how I put it:

1. Scientific evidence can support a premise in an argument leading to a conclusion having theological significance.

Reflect for a moment on that statement. The scientific evidence I offer is for premises which are religiously neutral statements that can be found in any science textbook. Take, for example, the *kalam* cosmological argument. My claim is that we have good scientific evidence in support of the premise

2. The universe began to exist.

There's nothing about this statement that would make it incapable of being supported by the scientific evidence. Whether the universe began to exist is precisely one of those questions which science seeks to answer. Are we to think that science is incapable of returning an affirmative answer to this question? Why? That would be to impose some sort of philosophical constraint on what answers science is capable of giving to this question.

INSIGHT
This is indeed worth pondering. For it offers insight not only into how to think about the role of scientific evidence in arguments for God's existence but how science and theology can converge or integrate in relevant ways in order to grasp an understanding of the world. This is not the only way they can converge, but it is a significant way.

Similarly, the second premise of the teleological argument from fine-tuning is a religiously neutral statement to which scientific evidence can in principle give an answer:

3. The fine-tuning is not due to physical necessity or chance.

Richard Dawkins, following Sir Martin Rees, rejects the hypothesis of physical necessity as a scientifically plausible explanation of the fine-tuning, and Roger Penrose similarly rejects chance as a reasonable explanation. Neither of these non-theists appeals to theological grounds for rejecting these options; their reasons are strictly scientific. So are we to say that they cannot be correct, that science cannot return a negative verdict on these hypotheses? Why? These are strictly scientific statements that must be open to support by the empirical evidence.

Now, of course, the naturalist may claim that the scientific evidence doesn't in fact support either of these two premises. But then you've got him right where you want him: namely, a discussion of how good the evidence for these two statements is! That's just what we want to discuss.

Now, it should go without saying that scientific evidence is by the very nature of the case always provisional and open to revision. But that's no special liability of the scientific statements that constitute these two premises. The question will always be, what does our best evidence indicate is true? For example, is the evidence of contemporary cosmology more probable given the beginning of the universe or more probable given that the universe is beginningless?

Notice, too, that it would be hypocritical to demand evidence for these two premises, which is in excess of that which is assumed to constitute adequate support for the acceptance of other scientific hypotheses. If one is rational to accept the neo-Darwinian theory of biological evolution by random mutation and natural selection, for example, then why is it not equally rational to accept that the universe began to exist?

Note, finally, that some of the theistic arguments are philosophical, for example, the moral argument and the ontological argument, or have premises that are supportable not just scientifically but philosophically, and are, therefore, immune to the objection based on scientific ignorance.

On Assessing the Argument from Contingency

Dr. Craig,

I want to say that I am in favor of the Kalam cosmological argument. But, I was wondering what is your opinion of the cosmological argument from contingent being?

William

Dr. Craig's Response

I've briefly defended the cosmological argument from contingent being in my and J. P. Moreland's *Philosophical Foundations for a Christian Worldview* (InterVarsity, 2003) and expand my treatment in the third edition of *Reasonable Faith* (Crossway, 2008).

There are three premises in the argument:

1. Everything that exists has an explanation of its existence (either in the necessity of its own nature or in an external cause).
2. If the universe has an explanation of its existence, that explanation is God.
3. The universe exists.

Now, what follows logically from these three premises?

From 1 and 3 it logically follows that:

4. The universe has an explanation of its existence.

And from 2 and 4 the conclusion logically follows:

5. Therefore, the explanation of the universe's existence is God.

Now, this is a logically airtight argument. So if the atheist wants to deny the conclusion, he has to say that one of the three premises is false.

But which one will he reject? Premise 3 is undeniable for any sincere seeker after truth. So the atheist is going to have to deny either 1 or 2 if he wants to remain an atheist and be rational. So the whole question comes down to this: are premises 1 and 2 true, or are they false? Well, let's look at them.

According to premise 1 there are two kinds of things: (a) things that exist necessarily and (b) things that exist contingently. Things that exist necessarily exist by a necessity of their own nature. Many mathematicians think that numbers, sets, and other mathematical entities exist in this way. They're not caused to exist by something else; they just exist by the necessity of their own nature. By contrast, contingent things are caused to exist by something else. They exist because something else has produced them. Familiar physical objects like people, planets, and galaxies belong in this category.

So what reason might be offered for thinking that premise 1 is true? Well, when you reflect on it, premise 1 has a sort of self-evidence about it. Imagine that you're hiking through the woods one day and you come across a translucent ball lying on the forest floor. You would naturally wonder how it came to be there. If one of your hiking partners said to you, "It just exists inexplicably. Don't worry about it!" you'd either think that he was crazy or figure that he just wanted you to keep moving. No one would take seriously the suggestion that the ball existed there with literally no explanation.

Now, suppose you increase the size of the ball in this story so that it's the size of a car. That wouldn't do anything to satisfy or remove the demand for an explanation. Suppose it were the size of a house. Same problem. Suppose it were the size of a continent or a planet. Same problem. Suppose it were the size of the entire universe. Same problem. Merely increasing the size of the ball does nothing to affect the need of an explanation.

Premise 1 is the premise that the atheist typically rejects. Sometimes atheists will respond to premise 1 by saying that it is true of everything *in* the universe but not *of* the universe itself. But this response commits what has been aptly called "the taxicab fallacy." For as the nineteenth-century atheist philosopher Arthur Schopenhauer quipped, premise 1 can't be dismissed like a hack once you've arrived at your desired destination!

It would be arbitrary for the atheist to claim that the universe is the exception to the rule. The illustration of the ball in the woods showed that merely increasing the size of the object to be explained, even until it becomes the universe itself, does nothing to remove the need for some explanation of its existence.

Notice, too, how unscientific this atheist response is. For modern cosmology is devoted to the search for an explanation of the universe's existence. The atheist attitude would cripple science.

Some atheists have tried to justify making the universe an exception to premise 1 by saying that it's *impossible* for the universe to have an explanation of its existence. For the explanation of the universe would have to be some prior state of affairs in which the universe did not yet exist. But that would be nothingness, and nothingness cannot be the explanation of anything. So the universe must just exist inexplicably.

This line of reasoning is obviously fallacious. For it assumes that the universe is all there is, so that if there were no universe there would be nothing. In other words, the objection assumes that atheism is true! The atheist is thus begging the question, arguing in a circle. I agree that the explanation of the universe must be a prior state of affairs in which the universe did not exist. But I contend that that state of affairs is God and His will, not nothingness.

So it seems to me that premise 1 is more plausibly true than false, which is all we need for a good argument.

What, then, about premise 2? Is it more plausibly true than false?

What's really awkward for the atheist at this point is that premise 2 is logically equivalent to the typical atheist response to the contingency argument. Two statements are logically equivalent if it is impossible for one to be true and the other one false. They stand or fall together. So what does the atheist almost always say in response to the argument from contingency? The atheist typically asserts the following:

A. If atheism is true, the universe has no explanation of its existence.

This is precisely what the atheist says in response to premise 1. The universe just exists inexplicably. But this is logically equivalent to saying:

B. If the universe has an explanation of its existence, then atheism is not true.

So you can't affirm (A) and deny (B).

But (B) is virtually synonymous with premise 2! So by saying in response to premise 1 that, given atheism, the universe has no explanation, the atheist is implicitly admitting premise 2, that if the universe does have an explanation, then God exists.

Besides that, premise 2 is very plausible in its own right. For think of what the universe is: *all* of space-time reality, including *all* matter and energy. It follows that if the universe has a cause of its existence, that cause must be a non-physical, immaterial being beyond space and time. Now, there are only two sorts of things that could fit that description: either an abstract object like a number or else an unembodied mind. But abstract objects can't cause anything. That's part of what it means to be abstract. The number 7, for example, can't cause any effects. So the cause of the existence of the universe must be a transcendent Mind, which is what believers understand God to be.

The argument thus proves the existence of a necessary, uncaused, timeless, spaceless, immaterial, personal Creator of the universe. This is truly mind-blowing!

The atheist has one alternative open to him at this point. He can retrace his steps, withdraw his objection to premise 1, and say instead that, yes, the universe *does* have an explanation of its existence. But that explanation is: the universe exists by a necessity of its own nature. For the atheist, the universe could serve as a sort of God-substitute which exists necessarily.

Now, this would be a very radical step for the atheist to take, and I can't think of any contemporary atheist who has in fact adopted this line. A few years ago at a Philosophy of Time conference at City College in Santa Barbara, it seemed to me that Professor Adolf Grünbaum, a vociferous atheistic philosopher of science from the University of Pittsburgh, was flirting with this idea. But when I raised the question from the floor whether he thought the universe existed necessarily, he was quite indignant at the suggestion. "Of course not!" he snapped and went on to say that the universe just exists without any explanation.

The reason atheists are not eager to embrace this alternative is clear. As we look about the universe, none of the things that make it up, whether stars, planets, galaxies, dust, radiation, or what have you, seems to exist necessarily. They could all fail to exist; indeed, at some point in the past, when the universe was very dense, none of them did exist.

But, you might say, what about the matter out of which these things are made? Maybe the matter exists necessarily, and all these things are just different contingent configurations of matter. The problem with this suggestion is that, according to the standard model of subatomic physics, matter itself is composed of tiny particles called "quarks." The universe is just the collection of all these quarks arranged in different ways. But now the question arises: couldn't a different collection of quarks have existed instead of this one? Does each and every one of these quarks exist necessarily?

Notice what the atheist cannot say at this point. He cannot say that the quarks are just configurations of matter which could have been different, even though the matter of which the quarks are composed exists necessarily. He can't say this because quarks aren't composed of anything! They just *are* the basic units of matter. So if a quark doesn't exist, the matter doesn't exist.

Now, it seems obvious that a different collection of quarks could have existed instead of the collection that does exist. But if that were the case, then a different universe would have existed. To see the point, think about your desk. Could your desk have been made of ice? Notice that I'm not asking if you could have had an ice desk in the place of your wooden desk that had the same size and structure. Rather I'm asking if your very desk, the one made of wood, if *that* desk could have been made of ice. The answer is obviously, no. The ice desk would be a different desk, not the same desk.

Similarly, a universe made up of different quarks, even if identically arranged as in this universe, would be a different universe. It follows, then, that the universe does not exist by a necessity of its own nature.

So atheists have not been so bold as to deny premise 2 and say that the universe exists necessarily. Premise 2 also seems to be plausibly true.

But given the truth of the three premises the conclusion is logically inescapable: *God is the explanation of the existence of the universe.* Moreover, the argument implies that God is an uncaused, unembodied Mind who transcends the physical universe and even space and time themselves and who exists necessarily. What a great argument!

Justification of the Moral Argument's Second Premise

Dear Dr. Craig,

I have recently been working through your book *On Guard*, and have a question concerning the Moral Argument (which I have also heard you use in several of your debates). I have seen it most commonly set up as:

1. If God does not exist, objective moral values and duties do not exist.
2. Objective moral values and duties do exist.
3. Therefore, God exists.

Essentially, I find that although the moral argument has a role in our discussions with atheist and other worldviews, it does not seem to be actual evidence for God's existence, but rather an implication of His existence. An atheist can say that morality (although subjective) has developed from biological and sociological influences evolving into what we now consider to be "right and wrong."

Although discussing how we come to know morality says nothing about the ontology of morality, it would seem that the only way a theist can show that an objective moral stand exists is by proving (or providing a greater probability through evidence) that God exists. This is due to the fact that the conversation almost always moves from the ontology of morality to the epistemology of morality. It would seem the only way to clear the air is to determine which worldview is true. My concern may be founded on my own ignorance, but the moral argument would seem to be a one-way street in that by showing God to exist, objective morality exists. However, following this line of thought in its reverse proves increasingly difficult without pointing to God, since either side can offer an explanation of how we come to an understanding of morality—which again, says nothing about the subjective or objective nature of morality.

I do find that the moral argument helps to count the cost of either ideology or as you said in your book, "what is at stake." But I do not find that the "cost" should be a reason to accept something as true, since our like or dislike of a truth has no effect on that truth. I guess my point is using objective values to show that God exists and then using God to show that objective values exist would seem to be circular reasoning to me. Can we use the moral argument, as given above, as actual evidence for God's existence and if so, how do we "prove" or give evidence for objective morality apart from pointing to God?

Corey
United States

Dr. Craig's Response

Corey, your question asks, in effect, whether the moral argument, as I have framed it, is not question-begging, since the only justification for believing premise (2) to be true is believing that God exists, which is the argument's conclusion, so that one is reasoning in a circle.

I reply that the argument is not question-begging, since the warrant I offer for belief in objective moral values and duties is not God but moral experience.[6] That such an appeal is not question-begging should be evident from the fact that the majority of non-theists, including atheists, believe in the truth of premise (2) precisely on this basis.

Louise Antony, herself a non-theist, put it so well in our debate a few years ago at U Mass, Amherst[7]: *Any argument for moral skepticism will be based upon premises which are less*

6. William Lane Craig, *On Guard: Defending Your Faith with Reason and Precision* (Colorado Springs: David C. Cook, 2010), 141–43.
7. You can access this debate for free by visiting ReasonableFaith.org (http://bit.ly/CraigAntony).

obvious than the existence of objective moral values themselves. That seems to me quite right. Therefore, moral skepticism is unjustifiable.

The humanist philosopher Peter Cave gives the following example:

> Whatever skeptical arguments may be brought against our belief that killing the innocent is morally wrong, we are more certain that the killing is morally wrong than that the argument is sound. . . . Torturing an innocent child for the sheer fun of it is morally wrong.[8]

In moral experience we encounter objective moral values and duties, and so, in the absence of some sort of defeater of that belief, we are perfectly rational to hold to it. Moral realism is the default position, and the moral skeptic needs to provide some powerful defeater to overcome it.

One can make the same point another way by comparing, as William Sorley does[9], our apprehension of the moral realm with our apprehension of the physical realm. Just as we can't get outside our moral perceptions to try to justify them, so we cannot get outside our sensory perceptions to try to justify them. Just as, in the absence of some defeater, we trust our sense perceptions

INSIGHT

This is an insightful admission from Antony. It is not only valuable when considering objections against the moral argument for God's existence, but it is also useful for weighing a skepticism, in general, which tends to proffer assumptions that are "less obvious" than the existence of x. Bottom line: moral skepticism fails to attend to our direct acquaintance with reality even though this is how our moral experience encounters objective moral values and duties.

that there is a realm of objectively existing physical objects around us, so we trust our moral perceptions that there is an objectively existing realm of moral values and duties. For any argument for skepticism about our moral perceptions we could run a parallel argument for skepticism about our sensory perceptions. But you'd have to be crazy to doubt the veridicality of your sense perceptions of a realm of objectively existing physical objects. Similarly, until we are given a defeater, we ought to trust our moral perception of a realm of objectively existing values and duties.

8. Peter Cave, *Humanism* (Oxford: OneWorld, 2009), 146. Thanks to Peter S. Williams for this reference.
9. See Craig, *On Guard*, 128.

Now, as I say, this is not a theistic justification of belief in objective moral values and duties; this is the way almost every moral realist justifies his belief in the objectivity of values and duties. There is no circularity here.

In any case, I'd encourage you to simply ask your conversation partner whether he believes in some objective moral values and duties. Ask what he thinks of examples of moral atrocities. Even if the unbeliever has no justification for believing in premise (2), so long as he *does* believe in premise (2), the argument goes through. Since almost everyone does believe that (2) is true, the debate really comes down to (1). The unbeliever will have to explain how objective moral values and duties can exist in a world without God as an absolute standard and law-giver.

You must resist resolutely the tendency to conflate moral ontology with moral epistemology. If the unbeliever tries to steer the conversation toward epistemology, you must bring the conversation back on track. It is just irrelevant that, as you put it, *"either side can offer an explanation of how we come to an understanding of morality."* You could agree with everything the unbeliever says about that: we come to an understanding of morality through biological evolution, societal conditioning, parental influences, etc. All of that is irrelevant to the question of whether objective moral values and duties exist, as you, yourself, observe. Of course, the unbeliever might present the socio-biological account as a putative defeater of (2), in which case you've got to deal with it.[10]

Finally, when I talk about the cost of denying the premises of a theistic argument, I'm talking about the *intellectual* cost. A determined skeptic can always deny the conclusion of one's argument simply by denying one of the premises. (This calls to mind an observation by Alvin Plantinga that one can reduce someone from knowledge to ignorance by offering him a valid argument based on premises he knows to be true for a conclusion he simply will not accept!) You want to make the intellectual price tag of atheism as high as you can, in hopes that the unbeliever will come to see that the price is simply too high, that to maintain his atheism in the face of the argument would compromise his intellectual integrity. That is the method of good argumentation.

---

10. Dr. Craig does deal with two versions of this objection in *On Guard*, pp. 142–44. We invite you to reflect on what he says there.

2

ON THE TRINITY

Is Trinity Monotheism Orthodox?

Dear Dr. Craig,

I've been listening to your Defenders podcast since it restarted in December of '09 and have greatly benefited from the content. I'd like to thank you for your continuous love for God and His truths; your work is a real blessing. Recently, in your Defenders class, you have been discussing the doctrine of the Trinity. The most recent two podcasts have been on an attempt to understand the relationship between the diverse members of the Trinity and their unity. You have been forming and defending the model that is in *Philosophical Foundations for a Christian Worldview* in chapter 29 in your podcasts where you use the analogy of Cerberus in Greek mythology.

My question has to do with your model of the Trinity and a recent article that I've read which disagrees with your formulation. In Thomas Flint and Michael Rea's *The Oxford Handbook of Philosophical Theology*, specifically in chapter 18, Michael Rea argues against your formulation starting on page 415. He labels the model you are defending a part-whole Trinitarianism. He writes, "... Moreland and Craig want to preserve the view that God is divine while denying that that God is a fourth divine thing on a par with the persons. Thus, they distinguish two kinds of divinity: the full divine nature, which is possessed by God and implies tri-unity; and a derivative divine nature, possessed by each person."

Rea then objects by raising two problems, which he thinks are "devastating" to your model. First he argues that you are unable to affirm the opening line of the Nicene Creed. Rae writes, "... Moreland and Craig cannot affirm the opening line of the Nicene Creed: 'We believe in one God, the Father, almighty.' For, on their view, God is a fundamentally different thing from the Father" (p. 416).

Second, Rea argues that the model you defend cannot affirm the crucial *homoousion* clause in the same creed "unless they reject the idea that there is exactly one divine nature." Rea unpacks this when he writes, ". . . the only viable interpretations of the creedal claim that the Son is *homoousion* with the Father have it that the Son is either numerically the same substance as the Father or of the same nature as the Father. (Natures were also referred to as 'substances'; hence, being consubstantial with something might just mean having the same nature.) The former, of course, they reject. The latter they accept; but in accepting it, they posit, effectively, two divine natures, one 'genuine', possessed only by God; the other derivative, but still divine, possessed by the two persons. Of course, they could deny that the derivative nature is a divine nature. But in so doing, they seem to strip the persons of their divinity, which would conflict with other parts of the Nicene and Constantinopolitan creeds. If all this is right, then, part-whole Trinitarianism is in serious trouble . . ." (p. 416).

I'm curious how you would respond to Michael Rea as I value both of your contributions to theology in particular, and the advancement of the kingdom of God in general. I'm not sure if you have interacted with Rea on these points before, but I'd love to hear a response to these objections. Thanks again for all that you do.

Jeff

United States

Dr. Craig's Response

Thank you, Jeff, for drawing my attention to these criticisms! Are they as devastating as Michael thinks?

(1) Does the opening line of the Creed affirm that God just *is* the Father? I think Michael fails to take into account the New Testament background of the phrase "We believe in one God, the Father, almighty." The creedal context of that phrase is:

We believe in one God, the Father, almighty . . . ;
And in one Lord Jesus Christ, the Son of God . . . ;
And in the Holy Spirit.

The confession is drawn from 1 Cor. 8:6: "For us there is one God, the Father, from whom are all things and for whom we exist, and one Lord, Jesus Christ, through whom are all things and through whom we exist." The creed lifts Paul's key phrase "one God, the Father . . . and one Lord, Jesus Christ" and then tacks on for Trinitarian purposes the terse mention of the Holy Spirit. As Murray Harris explains in his fine book *Jesus as God*,[11] the reason one finds relatively few references in the New Testament to Jesus as *ho theos* (God) is because that term was reserved for the Father. When the New Testament writers use the word "God," they are typically referring to the Father. Since the New Testament writers didn't believe that Jesus was the Father, they had to find other expressions to indicate His deity, such as *ho kyrios* (Lord). The creed follows this idiom. So when it refers to "one God, the Father," that needn't be taken to mean that the Father is the whole of who God is. To talk of *ho theos* is just to talk about the Father. Thus, when Jesus is confessed to be "the Son of God," this is taken to mean "begotten from the Father."

> **INSIGHT**
> Note these valuable distinctions and emphases in Dr. Craig's answer. They will shape not only our theology of the Trinity but our relationship with the Trinity. For example, if the Father is the whole of who God is, think of the implications of that for not only personal interaction with the members of the Trinity but for understanding God's actions in His world. For more on this, see Fred Sanders' book *The Deep Things of God.*

(2) Being *homoousion* (consubstantial) with the Father is then not problematic because the Father isn't taken to be the whole being God is. The Father and the Son share the same derivative nature (as Michael puts it; I'm not altogether happy with this way of making the distinction). We shouldn't think of the divine persons as instances of God's nature, lest we have a quaternity instead of a Trinity. There is just one being which is the Triune God. The Father, Son, and Spirit share the same essential properties that make them count as divine, like omnipotence, omniscience, moral perfection, necessity, etc. It is misleading to contrast the persons' nature with the "genuine" nature of

11. Murray J. Harris, *Jesus as God* (Grand Rapids: Baker, 1992). This has now been reprinted by Wipf and Stock (2008).

God, as though their divinity were somehow second-rate or counterfeit. A cat's skeleton and DNA are fully and genuinely feline even if they are not themselves cats, that is, instances of the cat nature. Similarly, the Father, Son, and Spirit are genuinely divine, though they are not each a Trinity, that is, an instance of God's nature.

Does Infinite Personhood Imply Pantheism?

Dear Dr. Craig,

My name is Nathan. I am 17 and live in Birmingham, United Kingdom. After reading Spinoza's *Ethics*, I am now in a philosophical conflict between what seems to be rational in pantheism and my religious views of Calvinism. I was wondering if you could help.

My question is regarding whether the concept of an "infinite person" makes sense if you believe in the theist conception of God. As God is infinitely powerful, wise, and loving, if an infinite person as a concept makes no logical sense, then neither does the idea of God.

First, we must identify what it means to be a person. A person is to be a particular person, distinct from others and with our own boundaries. The interaction between two people is only possible due to them having their own border, for otherwise they would not be a distinct person. Thus, we arrive at our first premise: "Personhood is finite."

If personhood is finite then it follows, "Infinite beings are not persons."

Then we come to the idea of God. God is by definition an infinite being. This entails He has no boundaries, and He is not distinct from other beings. Therefore, "God is infinite, and thus is not a person."

We can summarize the argument as the following:

1) Personhood is finite
2) Infinite beings are not persons
3) God is infinite, and thus is not a person

This argument does not have implications for a pantheist, for it shows that if God is infinite, He is not distinct from anything. However, a monotheist will have to reject this argument, for they believe that one can have a personal relationship with God, which is only possible if He is a distinct being from the believer. Therefore, my question Dr. Craig is how would you respond to this pantheistic argument?

Nathan

United Kingdom

Dr. Craig's Response

I was intrigued by your question, Nathan, because it mirrors so closely the argument of three theologians that I criticize in my article "Pantheists In Spite of Themselves?"[12] in which I argue that these theologians, in endorsing your sort of argument, are implicitly embracing pantheism! The article appears on our site, and I'd commend it to you.

The problem with the argument, it seems to me, is that the first premise is false. The justification given for the first premise is that persons have "borders" or "boundaries" and are, therefore, finite. The assumption is that anything that is bounded is finite. That is demonstrably false. The natural number series 0, 1, 2, 3, . . . is bounded by 0 but is not, therefore, finite. To give a physical example, a wall of bricks with an infinite number of bricks in it may stretch to infinity to one's right but may have a front edge and be, say, only three bricks in height. Persons have "boundaries" in a metaphorical sense: you are not I. God is not Gordon Brown. But the fact that two persons are distinct doesn't imply that one of them can't be infinite. Of course, God's infinity isn't really a quantitative concept but has reference to His superlative attributes. But then there's no reason to think that one person could not be omniscient, omnipotent, omnipresent, morally perfect,

> **INSIGHT**
> Note the important distinction between infinity as a qualitative concept vs. infinity as a reference to God's superlative attributes.

12. William Lane Craig, "Pantheists in Spite of Themselves? Pannenberg, Clayton, and Shults on Divine Infinity," *American Theological Inquiry* 5:1 (2012): 3–23.

eternal, etc., and the other limited in these same respects. None of those attributes excludes the existence of a distinct person who has limited knowledge, goodness, power, etc.

By the way, why not explore Wesleyan theology as an alternative to Calvinism? That's a far better alternative than Spinozism!

Trinity and Incarnation

Dr. Craig,

First let me start by saying that your Defenders class has become part of my daily routine. I use part of my lunch hour (about 45 minutes) to listen on my iPod and take notes.

While listening to the Doctrine of Christ series, which I've completed by the way, only one question had me on the edge of my seat and I was burning hoping someone in the class would ask! You were giving a plausible theory on how to reconcile the fact that the Trinity consists of 3 persons, yet Jesus, to qualify as fully God and fully human, might pose the problem of adding a "4th" person to the Godhead. You then went on to discuss that it was possible that all the attributes of the Logos were kept in the subconscious of Jesus' mind. What about the attribute of omnipresence? Omnipresence doesn't have the quality of being conscious or unconscious no more than my hair color being so whether I recognize it or not.

So in short, how to you reconcile the divine attribute of omnipresence in the Logos and the limited physical body of Jesus?

Aaron

Dr. Craig,

Thank you for your ministry. Your work and your example are a real inspiration.

I've been studying the Trinity, and I have a question about how the Trinity and the Incarnation relate to each other. As I understand it, in the Incarnation a human nature was added to and united with the eternal divine nature of the Son. As I understand the Trinity, the divine nature is one, a unity in which the three divine persons subsist. So the question is, if the divine nature of the Son is conjoined to a human nature, doesn't that affect the divine nature of the Father and the Spirit as well, since they share the same, undivided divine nature with the Son? I struggle to understand how the union of two natures in Christ is "compartmentalized" in the Son, without in some way "adulterating" the divine nature in the other two persons. True, the Person of Christ is distinct from the Father and Spirit, but all three share in the one divine nature, which now seems to include the human nature of Christ.

I hope this question is clear. Trying to understand the Trinity can be confusing at times. Thank you for any help you can provide on this issue.

Clark

Bronx

Dr. Craig's Response

As both of you discern, the doctrines of the Trinity and the Incarnation are closely connected in very interesting ways. Let's take your question first, Clark. Yes, God's nature is one both in the sense that there is an essence of God comprised of certain properties which all of the members of the Trinity share, such as aseity, necessity, eternity, omnipotence, omniscience, etc., and in the sense that there is just one concrete entity that is God.[13] I think that the persons of the Trinity, who are distinct from one another, also have contingent properties that are not shared by all three persons. For example, only the Son has the property of having a human as well as a divine nature.

Now, your question is how the Son can assume a human nature without the nature of the other two persons being affected. I take it that you think that if the Son is incarnate, then it follows that the Father and the Spirit must become incarnate, too, since they all share the same nature. The mistaken assumption behind your question, I think, is that it is the *nature* rather than the *person* of the Son that becomes incarnate. The doctrine of the Incarnation is not that the Son's divine nature somehow took on a human nature. Rather the claim is that the Second Person of the Trinity, who has a divine nature, took on in addition to His divine nature a human nature as well. So you shouldn't think of the Incarnation

13. For more on this, see "In What Sense Is God a 'Simple Being'?" below regarding individual natures, pages 172–74.

in terms of two natures somehow blending together; indeed, the classical formulation is that the natures remain unchanged and distinct in the Incarnation. They are united only in the sense that there is one person who comes to have them both.

So it's quite mistaken to say that "the one divine nature . . . now seems to include the human nature of Christ." *Au contraire*, the natures remain distinct even for the Son. This is evident in the fact that the Son's having a human nature is a *contingent* fact about Him; in possible worlds in which God refrains from creation altogether, the Second Person of the Trinity has no human nature. So His humanity cannot be part of His divine nature or essence.

INSIGHT

Note the important distinction between nature and person with respect to which becomes incarnate. This allows us not only to better understand the omnipresence of the Logos during His "state of humiliation" but it also allows us to appreciate how the Son genuinely and consciously experienced His earthly life.

Since neither the Father nor the Spirit took on a human body, they do not have human natures in addition to the divine nature. Only the Son assumed flesh and so took on a human nature.

Now, in answer to your question, Aaron, my goal was to find a biblically faithful and logically coherent account of the Incarnation that ascribes to Christ two complete natures, human and divine, but does not postulate two persons in Christ, a human person and a divine person (a heresy known as Nestorianism). I do this by postulating that the soul of Jesus of Nazareth was the divine Logos. In order to make such an account biblically adequate, I differentiate in a theologically significant way between Jesus' conscious life and His subconscious during His earthly sojourn (His so-called state of humiliation).

Now, you want to know how such an account deals with the omnipresence of the Logos during His state of humiliation. If you'll listen to the Defenders podcasts on the doctrine of God, you'll find that when it comes to omnipresence, I take this attribute to mean not that God is spread out like ether throughout space but that He is cognizant of and causally active at every point in space. That can still hold for the Logos during His state of humiliation. It just wasn't part of Jesus' conscious life.

I suspect your difficulty is that you're thinking of the Incarnation as the Logos' somehow shrinking Himself down to the size of a human body. But then you're making the same mistake as Clark: thinking of the Incarnation as something the divine nature does rather than something a divine person does. The Logos takes on a human body as His own; but He does not cease to be cognizant of and causally active at every point in space.

The Trinity and God's Omni-Attributes

Dear Dr. Craig,

I have been diligently listening to your podcasts. You are doing an amazing work for the kingdom. I am keeping you in my prayers for wisdom, purity, and strength. You mentioned the Trinity may be explained by three personalities in one being, kind of like a multiple personality disorder, but in this case, it would be very ordered. I found that very helpful.

The question is if each personality is omniscient, omnipresent, and omnipotent that would mean that three different persons would have these properties. But these properties are things only one person can have, necessarily so. That is one of the arguments given to why there can only be one God.

I look forward to reading, or hearing your response.

Under His Mercy,

Khaldoun

Dr. Craig's Response

It's great to hear from a philosophy colleague, Khaldoun! Thank you for your prayers! I trust you're doing well.

It doesn't seem to me that either omnipresence or omniscience presents even a *prima facie* problem for a plurality of persons in the Godhead. Omnipresence is, in God's case, the property of transcending space (*i.e.*, existing but not existing in space) but being cognizant of and causally active at every point in space. There's just no apparent reason why several persons could not be omnipresent in this sense. So I see no argument for monotheism based on the attribute of omnipresence (any more than timelessness).

The property of omniscience is the property of knowing that *p*, for any true proposition *p*, and not believing not –*p*, or, in other words, the property of knowing only and all true propositions. Again, this definition seems to pose no difficulty for a plurality of omniscient persons. It would occasion difficulty only if you held that there are purely private propositions, like "I am J. P. Moreland," which could not be truly believed by anyone other than J. P. Moreland. If you held to that, you would have to hold, not merely that there can be only one omniscient person, but that if such a person exists, there are no other persons at all! For if Jones, say, existed, God could not Himself know "I am Jones" (only Jones knows that!) and so He would not be omniscient after all. But virtually all philosophers hold that the propositional content of sentences containing what are called personal indexical terms (like "I," "you," "we," etc., is universally accessible. When I say, "I'm hungry," and you say to me, "You're hungry," we express the same proposition, namely, that *Bill Craig is hungry*, from our different standpoints. If this is correct, then there is no difficulty with the three Trinitarian persons' each having complete propositional knowledge.

Rather, the only possible difficulty is occasioned by omnipotence. Philosophers like Richard Swinburne have, indeed, argued for monotheism on the grounds that there cannot be a plurality of omnipotent beings because they could come into conflict with each other and so would limit each other's power. But suppose that it is logically impossible for the persons to come into conflict because they are essentially harmonious and so always will the same thing. Then the argument would fall to the ground. And it is part of the classical doctrine of the Trinity that the persons of the Godhead all share the same knowledge, love, and volition, making conflict impossible.

INSIGHT

Note how this concept of "essentially harmonious" is crucial for understanding how the attribute of omnipotence is shared by the persons of the Godhead.

A better argument for there being at most one omnipotent God is that any other being that exists must be within the power of God to create or not. But then the existence of that being depends asymmetrically upon God. So God has power over it, while it lacks this power over God. So there can be at most one omnipotent God.

This conclusion will, however, be welcomed by the Trinitarian theist, since he believes that there is in fact only one God! Perhaps we should say that omnipotence is, like necessity and timelessness, primarily a property of the Godhead and only derivatively of its members. So while there can be at most one omnipotent God, there is no problem with that God's being tri-personal.

3

ON DIVINE ATTRIBUTES

On Appraising Perfect Being Theology

Dr. Craig,

I first would like to thank you for your work. Although I am an agnostic with theistic leanings, I was first directed to your website by a persistent friend of mine who has gotten me to consider the deep questions of life. I find what you have to say about the existence of God clear and stimulating in helping me formulate my views on this most important of questions. That being said, I do take issue with one aspect of your theological views, as I am somewhat puzzled by your tacit endorsement of Anselmian perfect being theology (APBT), which attempts to describe God as "the greatest conceivable being" or "that which no greater can be conceived." I have noticed that you use APBT quite a bit in your debates and publications to argue against the Islamic conception of God, defend the Divine Command Theory of ethics, and establish God as a necessary being. Nevertheless, in spite of its advantages, I am convinced that APBT is an untenable Christian theological doctrine for three reasons.

First, the concept of a greatest conceivable being which is central to APBT is inherently subjective, for what seems great to one person might not be great at all to another. To illustrate, consider a moral realist and an "enchanted" moral nihilist, who relishes the destruction of all objective moral value, duty, and accountability. To the moral realist, the property of being omnibenevolent might be conducive to being a greatest conceivable being. However, to the enchanted nihilist, omnibenevolence might be seen as a crutch which limits God's omnipotence; hence, he does not think that omnibenevolence is a great-making property. Another example would be God's being a concrete object rather than an abstract object. While most of us today agree that being concrete is greater than being abstract, for a follower of Platonism living 2,200 years ago, it would be the opposite.

Thus, many of the intuitions people appeal to in order to justify their conception of God under APBT are unreliable because they conflict with one another and are largely shaped by the surrounding culture.

Second, even if the problem mentioned before can be answered, APBT makes theism impossible. One of the benefits of APBT is that it can be used to silence the atheist who thinks that he can conceive of a greater being than God. For if he is telling the truth, then that being would be God, not that to which he was originally referring. To see why this is problematic for theism, consider two people A and B, who both have conceptions of the greatest conceivable being. However, B has a greater imagination than A and conceives of a greater greatest conceivable being than A. Under APBT, B, by definition, has the correct conception of God. Now, suppose C enters the picture and has a greater imagination than either A or B. As such, his conception of God is the correct one under APBT, and A's and B's are false. This process can be repeated until we arrive at a being who has the greatest imagination possible. However, such a being is God Himself! Only God can correctly conceive of God under APBT! This makes theism impossible since in order to believe in x, one must first be able to conceive of x, which cannot happen since every human's conception of God would be false.

Finally, APBT is not only problematic, but also contrary to what Christianity teaches. As Greg Bahnsen and others have pointed out, APBT undermines the glory and might of God by limiting His power and attributes to what we humans think of Him. If Christianity is really true, then God is not simply a being whose properties are contingent upon human cognition; rather, He, as the Creator of the world, is entirely independent in both existence and essence from what we as humans think of Him.

So, because of these problems, I believe that Christians should abandon APBT, regardless of its assets. Instead, they should move towards something akin to Plantinga's maximally great being theology, which describes God by attributing to Him a set of clearly-defined properties. But what are your thoughts on this? Do you think that these problems with APBT can be surmounted?

Thanks,
Aditya
(country not specified)

Dr. Craig's Response

To say that I tacitly endorse Anselmian Perfect Being Theology is an understatement, Aditya. I am an enthusiastic proponent. As I explain in *Philosophical Foundations for a Christian Worldview*, I see the conception of God as the greatest conceivable being as one of the guides for systematic theology's formulation of the doctrine of God:

Two controls have tended to guide this inquiry into the divine nature: Scripture and Perfect Being Theology. For thinkers in the Judeo-Christian tradition, God's self-revelation in Scripture is obviously paramount in understanding what God is like. In addition, the Anselmian conception of God as the greatest conceivable being or most perfect being has guided philosophical speculation on the raw data of Scripture, so that God's biblical attributes are to be conceived in ways that would serve to exalt God's greatness. Since the concept of God is underdetermined by the biblical data and since what constitutes a 'great-making' property is to some degree debatable, philosophers working within the Judeo-Christian tradition enjoy considerable latitude in formulating a philosophically coherent and biblically faithful doctrine of God.[14]

It seems to me that your questions evince some confusions about Perfect Being Theology and that once these are cleared up your misgivings will be allayed. Indeed, Perfect Being Theology includes among its advocates Alvin Plantinga, whose view you endorse. So let's look at each of your three misgivings.

First, the concept of a greatest conceivable being is inherently subjective, for what seems great to one person might not be great at all to another. This objection seems to confuse *God's being* the greatest conceivable being with *our discerning* what properties a greatest conceivable being must possess. I've already acknowledged a degree of play in the notion of a great-making property. For example, is it greater to be timeless or omnitemporal? The answer

INSIGHT
Note this important distinction. It also underscores how "conceivability" is not the same as "imaginability," which Dr. Craig develops later on in his answer.

14. Craig and Moreland, *Philosophical Foundations for a Christian Worldview*, 501.

169

is not clear. But our uncertainty as to what properties the greatest conceivable being must have does nothing to invalidate the definition of "God" as "the greatest conceivable being." Here Anselm's intuition which you mention seems on target: there cannot by definition be anything greater than God.

Now, you might think, "But what good is it defining God as the greatest conceivable being if we have no idea what such a being would be like?" The answer to that question will depend on what project you're engaged in. If you're doing systematic theology, then you have that other control, namely, Scripture, which supplies considerable information about God, for example, that He is eternal, almighty, good, personal, and so on. Perfect Being Theology will aid in the formulation of a doctrine of God by construing those attributes in as great a way as possible. On the other hand, if your project is natural theology, which makes no appeal to Scripture, then you will present arguments that God must have certain properties. Note that mere disagreement about whether a property is great-making does not imply that there is no objective truth about the matter. When we have a disagreement, then we may present arguments why we think it is greater to have some property than to lack it. The fact that some properties (like timelessness) are not clearly great-making does not imply that no properties are great-making or that the concept of a greatest conceivable being is wholly subjective.

Consider your two examples. First, is it greater to be omnibenevolent rather than not? If omnibenevolence really is a moral property, then it seems morally better to be all-loving than partially loving. The problem with your moral nihilist is that he denies that such a property as omnibenevolence has any moral value! That strikes me, along with most ethicists, as incredible, since love is one of the clearest examples of a moral virtue. On the nihilist's view the concept of God, who is by definition a being worthy of worship, is incoherent. So the moral nihilist must be an atheist. If we believe that there are objective moral values, then we shall reject moral nihilism and along with it the nihilist's claim that the concept of God is incoherent.

So suppose someone is not a moral nihilist and thinks that omnibenevolence is a moral property but denies that God has it because it infringes on His omnipotence (I can imagine a Muslim arguing in this way). In that case, one has two strategies to pursue in response. One would be to hold that any increase in power enjoyed by a non-omnibenevolent being is offset by such a being's inferiority in moral worth and that on balance a being is greater if He is morally perfect even if unable to do certain (immoral) acts which a less than omnibenevolent being could do. The other strategy would be to show that omnipotence does not entail the ability to do just anything.[15] In fact, I think Anselm and others argued plausibly that the ability to do evil acts actually evinces weakness not power. So there is no inconsistency between omnipotence and omnibenevolence.

Next, is it greater to be concrete rather than abstract? What you need to understand here is that the modern conception of abstract objects is quite different than the ancient conception. In the contemporary sense, abstract objects are essentially causally effete. They can't do anything or cause anything. But for Plato and the ancients, the Forms were causally potent and affected the world. They were really more like concrete objects. Now, I take it to be clear that it is greater to be causally potent than impotent and that God, therefore, cannot be an abstract object in the modern sense. Moreover, God is personal and, therefore, cannot be an abstract object, since persons are concrete objects.

The point is that the attributes of God can be debated: there is no reason to think that we are utterly in the dark about the matter. Contrary to your claim, I think it is demonstrable that people's conception of what a greatest conceivable being would be like has a core that has not varied much over history and culture since Anselm.

Second, APBT makes theism impossible, since only God can correctly conceive of God under APBT. Ironically, the medieval proponents of Perfect Being Theology would have heartily agreed that God alone has a perfect comprehension of His essence! In fact, that's why Thomas Aquinas rejected Anselm's ontological argument. But they would rightly respond that your conclusion that theism is impossible does not follow. First, it at most follows from your argument that theistic *belief* would not be warranted, not that *theism* would be false. Second, a partial grasp of God's essential properties does not entail that one's conception of God is false, but merely incomplete—especially if one is aware that one grasps only a glimmer of God's greatness. Third, one can believe in *x* without being able to grasp *x*'s essence. For example, one could believe in God as the Creator and Designer of the universe.

But there is a more fundamental confusion underlying the second question, and that is the confusion of *conceivability* with *imaginability*. These are not the same. A thousand-sided polygon is unimaginable, but it is hardly inconceivable. Conceivability is taken to be co-extensive with metaphysical possibility. So the greatest conceivable being is the same thing as the greatest possible being. It is, as Plantinga says, a maximally great being, the greatest being possible. True, Plantinga does give content to this notion in terms of specific properties, but

15. See, for example, Flint and Freddoso's article "Maximal Power" in Dr. Craig's anthology *Philosophy of Religion: A Reader and Guide* (New Brunswick, N.J.: Rutgers University Press, 2002), 265–83.

those properties are obviously chosen because he thinks of them as great-making properties, which a maximally great being cannot lack. Maximal greatness is doubtless not exhausted by the properties he mentions. His version of the ontological argument is based, in effect, on one of those incomplete, inadequate conceptions of God that you mention in this question.

Third, APBT undermines the glory and might of God by limiting His power and attributes to what we humans think of Him. The two confusions underlying the first two questions come together in this terribly misconceived objection. Of course, God "is entirely independent in both existence and essence from what we as humans think of Him." To think otherwise is to confuse once again God's being the greatest conceivable being with our discerning what properties a greatest conceivable being must possess. Moreover, the concept of the greatest conceivable being is not the same as the concept of the greatest imaginable being. No advocate of Perfect Being Theology thinks that God is "a being whose properties are contingent upon human cognition." The very absurdity of such an allegation should have led you to suspect that something was very much amiss with the argument leading to such a conclusion.

So these objections are, I think, far from insurmountable. Notice that if you do think that Plantinga's conception of God as a maximally great being is a metaphysically possible concept—as your advocating it for the task of Christian theology seems to suggest—then it follows that God exists.

In What Sense Is God a "Simple Being"?

Dear Dr. Craig,

I've been using *On Guard* to facilitate our adult Sunday school class. This is the second question that's come up as I read and study the book. In the chapter on Fine-Tuning, you make the statement, ". . . God is a remarkably simple entity." And, further, "a divine mind is startlingly simple." I have to admit I've never thought of God as being "simple." And the concept seems to be at odds with how I've always interpreted Scripture, where we read, for example, Paul's rhetorical question in 1 Corinthians and Romans (quoting Isaiah), "Who has known the mind of God?"

I wonder if describing God as a "simple entity" isn't perhaps an unnecessary attempt to align the steps of the Design or Cosmological arguments with Occam's razor. At any rate, if you could shed any additional light on this, I'd greatly appreciate it. Thanks!

Tom

United States

Dr. Craig's Response

The problem here, I'm sure, is that the word "simple" in English can mean "easy" or even "dumb," so that to call God simple sounds rather like an insult. But "simple" can also mean "non-composite," that is to say, not composed of parts, and this is the relevant sense here. An electron, for example, is a simple particle, whereas a proton is not, the latter being composed of quarks. The degree to which an entity is simple is the degree to which it is made up of potentially separable parts.

Far from being a misguided attempt to save the cosmological and design arguments, simplicity is one of the classic attributes of God! For example, the very first attribute of God, which is discussed by Thomas Aquinas following his five proofs of God's existence, is God's simplicity.[16]

Thomas upholds an extraordinarily strong doctrine of divine simplicity, arguing that God is utterly without composition of any sort. In my discussion of this divine attribute[17], I reject Thomas's very strong view in favor of a weaker form of divine simplicity. I see no reason, for example, to think that God's essence and existence are the same.

Still, as a mind without a body, God is amazingly simple. Being immaterial, He has no physical parts. Therefore to postulate a pure Mind as the explanation of fine-tuning is the height of simplicity!

If you doubt this, then I invite you to explain the sense in which a pure mind is complex. What Richard Dawkins does is to confuse the mind itself with a mind's thoughts. Certainly a mind's thoughts can be complex, but a mind's thoughts are not the mind itself (for a mind can cease to think its complex thoughts and contemplate something else instead).

So even if we accept the (erroneous) principle that an explanation, in order to be a

16. See, for example, Aquinas's Summa Theological, pt. 1, q. 3.
17. See the discussion in *Philosophical Foundations for a Christian Worldview*, 524–26.

good one, must be simpler than the thing to be explained, postulating a mind behind the universe, with all its variegated and contingent constants and quantities, does represent an advance in simplicity.

On Problems with "Reformed" Theology's Conception of God and Creation

Dr. Craig,

I am troubled at the mass amount of Calvinists I see who are incredibly intelligent and trustworthy Christian leaders yet seem to stick their head in the sand when it comes to the problem of evil. If they don't, then they tend to make God a self-contradicting being. Why do you think this is so?

I'm also personally troubled at how few leaders I see subscribing to Molinism. It seems to me that it answers the most questions and creates the least problems. I understand it can be complex, but I wouldn't think we would just rest with the problem of evil not being satisfied. I don't base what I believe on the beliefs of others, but we can't ignore the influence others have in our lives, or the desire to have a home with others when it comes to these thoughts.

Anyway, I would enjoy your thoughts . . . as I always do.

Thanks,

Gordon

Dr. Craig's Response

I think you're right, Gordon, that a great many intelligent and godly Christian leaders are Reformed, or followers of John Calvin, in their theology. I'm currently participating in a four-views book on divine providence along with a pair of Reformed theologians. It is evident from their contributions that, despite the intellectual puzzles raised by the Reformed view, they both embrace it because they are convinced that it most faithfully represents the teaching of Scripture on the subject, Scripture being the only authoritative rule of faith.

Actually, I have no problem with certain classic statements of the Reformed view. For example, the Westminster Confession (Sect. III) declares that:

> God from all eternity did by the most wise and holy counsel of his own will, freely and unchangeably ordain whatsoever comes to pass; yet so as thereby neither is God the author of sin; nor is violence offered to the will of creatures, nor is the liberty or contingency of second causes taken away, but rather established.

Now, this is *precisely* what the Molinist believes! The Confession affirms God's preordination of everything that comes to pass as well as the liberty and contingency of the creaturely will, so that God is not the author of sin. It is a tragedy that in rejecting middle knowledge Reformed divines have cut themselves off from the most perspicuous explanation of the coherence of this wonderful confession.

Accepting a Solution or a Mystery

By rejecting a doctrine of divine providence based on God's middle knowledge, Reformed theologians are simply self-confessedly left with a mystery. The great seventeenth-century Reformed theologian Francis Turretin held that a careful analysis of Scripture leads to two indubitable conclusions, both of which must be held in tension without compromising either one: that God on the one hand by His providence not only decreed, but most certainly secures, the event of all things, whether free or contingent; on the other hand, however, man is always free in acting and many effects are contingent. Although I cannot understand how these can be mutually connected together, yet (on account of ignorance of the mode) the thing itself is (which is certain from another source, i.e., from the Word) not either to be called in question or wholly denied.[18]

Here Turretin affirms without compromise both the sovereignty of God and human freedom and contingency; he just doesn't know how to put them together. Molinism offers a solution. By rejecting that solution, the Reformed theologian is left with a mystery. There's nothing wrong with mystery *per se* (the correct physical interpretation of quantum mechanics is a mystery!); the problem is that some Reformed theologians, like my two

---

18. See, for example, Turretin's *Institutes of Elenctic Theology*, 1: 512.

collaborators in the four-views book, try to resolve the mystery by holding to universal, divine, causal determinism and a compatibilist view of human freedom. According to this view, the way in which God sovereignly controls everything that happens is by causing it to happen, and freedom is reinterpreted to be consistent with being causally determined by factors outside oneself.

It is this view, which affirms universal determinism and compatibilism, that runs into the problems you mention. Making God the author of evil is just one of the problems this neo-Reformed view faces. At least five come immediately to mind:

1. UNIVERSAL, DIVINE, CAUSAL DETERMINISM CANNOT OFFER A COHERENT INTERPRETATION OF SCRIPTURE.

The classical Reformed divines recognized this. They acknowledge that the reconciliation of scriptural texts affirming human freedom and contingency with scriptural texts affirming divine sovereignty is inscrutable. D. A. Carson identifies nine streams of texts affirming human freedom: (1) People face a multitude of divine exhortations and commands, (2) people are said to obey, believe, and choose God, (3) people sin and rebel against God, (4) people's sins are judged by God, (5) people are tested by God, (6) people receive divine rewards, (7) the elect are responsible to respond to God's initiative, (8) prayers are not mere showpieces scripted by God, and (9) God literally pleads with sinners to repent and be saved.[19] These passages rule out a deterministic understanding of divine providence, which would preclude human freedom. Determinists reconcile universal, divine, causal determinism with human freedom by re-interpreting freedom in compatibilist terms. Compatibilism entails determinism, so there's no mystery here. The problem is that adopting compatibilism achieves reconciliation only at the expense of denying what various scriptural texts seem clearly to affirm: genuine indeterminacy and contingency.

2. UNIVERSAL CAUSAL DETERMINISM CANNOT BE RATIONALLY AFFIRMED.

There is a sort of dizzying, self-defeating character to determinism. For if one comes to believe that determinism is true, one has to believe that the reason he has come to believe it is simply that he was determined to do so. One has not in fact been able to weigh the arguments pro and con and freely make up one's mind on that basis. The difference between the person who weighs the arguments for determinism and rejects them and the person who

19. See Carson's *Divine Sovereignty and Human Responsibility: Biblical Perspectives in Tension* (Eugene, Oreg.: Wipf & Stock, 2002), 18–22.

weighs them and accepts them is wholly that one was determined by causal factors outside himself to believe and the other not to believe. When you come to realize that your decision to believe in determinism was itself determined and that even your present realization of that fact right now is likewise determined, a sort of vertigo sets in, for everything that you think, even this very thought itself, is outside your control. Determinism could be true; but it is very hard to see how it could ever be rationally affirmed, since its affirmation undermines the rationality of its affirmation.

3. UNIVERSAL, DIVINE DETERMINISM MAKES GOD THE AUTHOR OF SIN AND PRECLUDES HUMAN RESPONSIBILITY.

In contrast to the Molinist view, on the deterministic view even the movement of the human will is caused by God. God moves people to choose evil, and they cannot do otherwise. God determines their choices and makes them do wrong. If it is evil to make another person do wrong, then on this view God is not only the cause of sin and evil, but becomes evil Himself, which is absurd. By the same token, all human responsibility for sin has been removed. For our choices are not really up to us: God causes us to make them. We cannot be responsible for our actions, for nothing we think or do is up to us.

4. UNIVERSAL, DIVINE DETERMINISM NULLIFIES HUMAN AGENCY.

Since our choices are not up to us but are caused by God, human beings cannot be said to be real agents. They are mere instruments by means of which God acts to produce some effect, much like a man using a stick to move a stone. Of course, secondary causes retain all their properties and powers as intermediate causes, as the Reformed divines remind us, just as a stick retains its properties and powers, which make it suitable for the purposes of the one who uses it. Reformed thinkers need not be occasionalists like Nicolas Malebranche, who held that God is the only cause there is. But these intermediate causes are not agents themselves but mere instrumental causes, for they have no power to initiate action. Hence, it's dubious that on divine determinism there really is more than one agent in the world, namely, God. This conclusion not only flies in the face of our knowledge of ourselves as agents but also makes it inexplicable why God then treats us as agents, holding us responsible for what He caused us and used us to do.

5. UNIVERSAL, DIVINE DETERMINISM MAKES REALITY INTO A FARCE.

On the deterministic view, the whole world becomes a vain and empty spectacle. There are no free agents in rebellion against God, whom God seeks to win through His love, and no one who freely responds to that love and freely gives his love and praise to God in return. The whole spectacle is a charade whose only real actor is God Himself. Far from glorifying God, the deterministic view, I'm convinced, denigrates God for engaging in such a farcical charade. It is deeply insulting to God to think that He would create beings which are in every respect causally determined by Him and then treat them as though they were free agents, punishing them for the wrong actions He made them do or loving them as though they were freely responding agents. God would be like a child who sets up his toy soldiers and moves them about his play world, pretending that they are real persons whose every motion is not in fact of his own doing and pretending that they merit praise or blame. I'm certain that Reformed determinists, in contrast to classical Reformed divines, will bristle at such a comparison. But why it's inapt for the doctrine of universal, divine, causal determinism is a mystery to me.

INFORMING THEOLOGIANS MAY INCREASE MOLINISM'S ACCEPTANCE

So why do so many intelligent and faithful Christian leaders buy into Calvinism? I think that the sort of Calvinism represented by the statement quoted above from the Westminster Confession is a fair summary of Scripture's teaching and, therefore, should be believed. It's only when one goes beyond it to try to resolve the mystery by embracing determinism and compatibilism that one gets into trouble. So insofar as these Christian leaders are content to remain with the mystery, I think theirs is a reasonable position. The vast majority of them have probably little understanding of Molinism and so are just insufficiently informed to make a decision.

A few years ago, I spoke at Westminster Seminary in San Diego on middle knowledge, and halfway through

INSIGHT

As simple as this advice is, it may actually have a lot going for it, as Dr. Craig's anecdote suggests. One way to further suggest "something better" is to consider whether the God and human relationship, let alone God and people of God relationship, is in fact *livable* if the Reformed assumption (*universal, divine, causal determinism*), is true. That is, what are the existential reasons for living a meaningful life entailed by that assumption? Is it compelling? Is it hopeful? Does it seem to reflect people's experience (historically speaking, let alone your own experience) in relationship to God?

the Q&A period following my talk, one of the faculty said, "I'm embarrassed to say, Dr. Craig, that we aren't even able to discuss this with you because we just are completely unfamiliar with what you're talking about." He was embarrassed that as a professional theologian he was so ignorant of these debates. By contrast, some theologians who belong to the Reformed tradition have moved toward Molinism. When I gave the Stob lectures at Calvin College and Seminary, I was shocked when the theologians at the seminary told me that they were all Molinists! I increasingly encounter people who are moving in the Molinist direction (both from the Calvinistic end and the open theist end of the spectrum!).

So don't be too hard on our Calvinist brethren. Offer them something better, and hope that they will embrace it.

Divine Impassibility and the Crucifixion

Sir,

First of all, thank you very much for your lectures. Although I am a Muslim, they are very informative and helped me reason in my belief in God. (Even though sometimes, all that philosophy talk was too much for me!)

I have two questions:

1. In saying that God felt pain that mankind had sinned (and, therefore, sent Jesus as a lamb for their sins), or that Christ's soul suffered, or that Christ cried out to God for help when He was on the Cross, are we not degrading God's nature? Because if God is able to be hurt (not physically, but spiritually) by mankind, isn't it a weakness of character and shows that we are able to harm Him? In fact, that would mean that when God created Adam, He created within Himself a weakness because the sons of Adam would cause Him grievance. At least, that is my understanding of it.

2. I know that you tend to answer questions based on theism and not specifically on Christianity, but please bear with me here. As I understand the Trinity, each part of the Trinity is fully God. Jesus had to die because He was devoid of any sins (because He was divine). So, when He was crucified, the part of Him that had to die was not merely His human body, but the sinless soul, in order for the sacrifice

to mean anything. So, OK, He died and then was resurrected three days later. Does that mean that for that portion of three days, God had died? Because Jesus is fully God, right? Or, if He is not, does it mean that God was one-third less divine? And, if Jesus died (part of the triune), does that mean that part of God is not eternal?

Thank you very much for reading this (and possibly answering it).

Sincerely,

Mun

Canada

Dr. Craig's Response

Having an avid interest in medieval Islamic philosophy and having chosen Islam as my side area of specialization in my doctoral work in theology, I very much enjoy talking with Muslims about these important questions, Mun. Thanks for writing! Your question will help Muslim readers of our website all around the world to understand better what Christians believe.

1. Since Muslims and Christians alike accept Genesis as God's revealed Word, we all must deal with the question of what the text means when it says that when God saw the pervasive sin of mankind "it grieved Him to His heart" (Gen. 6:6). Is this to be taken literally, or is this just an anthropomorphic way of speaking of God (that is, speaking of God in human terms)? The biblical narrative is indisputably filled with anthropomorphic descriptions of God, describing Him as "seeing" and "hearing" things, and so on. But should we understand God to be literally without emotions?

The view that God is in no way affected by creatures is called the *impassibility* of God. This seems to be the view that you favor. God cannot suffer emotional pain. Divine impassibility was thought by medieval Christian theologians to be one of the attributes of God. So you would find many Christians historically who would agree with your view. But on the contemporary scene there are very few theologians who would defend such a doctrine. There seems to be no good reason for taking the biblical descriptions of God's emotions non-literally. Far from seeing susceptibility to emotional pain as a weakness, most contemporary Christian philosophers and theologians would say quite the opposite: that it is a weakness for a person to be unmoved by human suffering and a strength to feel emotions, including pain, indignation, compassion, etc. In fact, think of the etymology of the word "compassion": to suffer along with. As the greatest conceivable being, God must be compassionate and share our sorrows and joys. Impassibility is actually a weakness, whereas compassion redounds to God's greatness.

Alvin Plantinga speaks for many Christian thinkers when he writes:

> As the Christian sees things, God does not stand idly by, cooly observing the suffering of his creatures. He enters into and shares our suffering. He endures the anguish of seeing his son, the second person of the Trinity, consigned to the bitterly cruel and shameful death of the cross. Some theologians claim that God cannot suffer. I believe they are wrong. God's capacity for suffering, I believe, is proportional to his greatness; it exceeds our capacity for suffering in the same measure as his capacity for knowledge exceeds ours. Christ was prepared to endure the agonies of hell itself; and God, the Lord of the universe, was prepared to endure the suffering consequent upon his son's humiliation and death. He was prepared to accept this suffering in order to overcome sin, and death, and the evils that afflict our world, and to confer on us a life more glorious than we can imagine. So we don't know why God permits evil; we do know, however, that he was prepared to suffer on our behalf, to accept suffering of which we can form no conception.[20]

INSIGHT

Reflect on the spirituality that might follow if God is impassible or not. If God is in no way affected by creatures, in what sense can we meaningfully experience God's authentic compassion toward us? If we cannot receive this because He does not actually give it, why would we be compelled to give compassion to others? Theology affects our ethics. Consider this: If God's compassion is a way for Him to enter into and share our suffering, it is evidence of how He is acquainted with us and knows how to wisely love even at our deepest point of need.

---

20. Alvin Plantinga, "Self-Profile," *Alvin Plantinga*, Jas. Tomberlin, ed. (Dordrecht: Reidel, 1985), 36.

Defenders of divine impassibility will say that when Christ suffered on the cross, He did so only in His human nature, not in His divine nature. I find that Muslims frequently fail to understand that on the Christian view Christ has two natures: His divine nature which He has possessed from all eternity and His human nature which He assumed at the moment of Mary's conceiving Jesus in her womb. Defenders of divine impassibility say that Christ's human nature has both a human soul and a human body, and it was in these that He suffered, not in His divine nature, which was and is impassible. If you want to hold on to divine impassibility, Mun, you can take that route and be a Christian. But like Prof. Plantinga, I think God is greater if He is not impassible.

2. What I have just said bears on your second question, too. The Christian view is that Christ died in His human nature, that is to say, Christ's human nature died. He obviously did not die in His divine nature. The person who was from all eternity the Second Person of the Trinity didn't cease to exist between the crucifixion and resurrection. God is, after all, a necessary being and so cannot cease to exist.

In fact, neither did Christ's human soul or body cease to exist. What is human death, after all? It is the separation of the soul from the body. It is not the annihilation of the soul. Persons who die are in an intermediate, unembodied state until the day of the resurrection, when their souls will be reunited with their renewed bodies.

So it's a mistake to think either that one member of the Trinity was somehow deleted when Christ died or that Christ's human soul ceased to exist when He died. What happened is that His soul was separated from His body. The difference between what happened to Christ's human nature and what will happen to ours someday is that God the Father reunited Christ's soul with His body in advance of the general resurrection and raised Jesus to glory and immortality as the harbinger and guarantor of our own resurrection.

Part 3

QUESTIONS ABOUT ORIGINS
AND THE MEANING OF LIFE

It is not accidental that questions of origin are integral to questions about the meaning of life. One might say that it is by intelligent design that these areas are interrelated. Like questions about God and His attributes, concerns about origins are as old as humanity itself. With German philosopher, mathematician, and logician Gottfried Wilhelm Leibniz (1646–1716), humans have attempted for thousands of years to reason about origins along these similar ways:

1. Everything that exists has an explanation of its existence.
2. If the universe has an explanation of its existence, that explanation is God.
3. The universe exists.
4. Therefore, the universe has an explanation of its existence.
5. Therefore, the explanation of the universe's existence is God.

Leibniz's reasoning has an intuitional quality to it; it rings true about the meaning of something that contingently exists. Something exists; it must have an explanation of its existence, right? Moreover, major areas of the history of human thought are associated with any of these points, including major questions and topics in metaphysics, cosmology, epistemology, and philosophy of religion.

The questions in this part deal with evidence for and objections against many of the points above and beyond. Whether Dr. Craig is engaging contemporary scientists like Stephen Hawking or he is exposing weak objections to a theistic cosmology, experiencing his answers in this part is like being a fly on a wall in a classroom, picking up tidbits of insight in philosophy of time, cosmology, and philosophy of religion.

By interacting with the questions and answers of Part Three, you can benefit in the following ways.

In section 1, you can come to understand
- How God is the cause of the universe.
- What it means to bring into being that which does not exist.
- How Stephen Hawking and other atheists fail to think clearly about the philosophical implications of cosmology.
- Why the ultimate cause of the universe must be a personal being and not an impersonal force.

In section 2, you can come to discover
- Why the universe is not eternal but temporal and contingent.
- Why it is a mistake to speak of "a moment before creation," since time only exists with creation.
- The difference between tensed vs. tenseless views of time.
- How a tenseless view of time creates problems for personal identity over time.
- How God exists timelessly without creation but becomes temporal at the moment of creation.

In section 3, you can come to discern
- How life is absurd if God does not exist.
- Why meaning, value, and purpose should not be separated from each other.
- How unbelief is morally culpable before God, given our moral duty as humans to worship God.
- Why deism is a better alternative to atheism.

In section 4, you can recognize
- Why scientism is self-refuting.
- How terms like "undirected" and "purposeless" do not often mean the same things for theists and evolutionary biologists.
- How theism is not at war with evolution but in conflict with naturalism.
- Why a theist does not need to know exactly when humans emerged in the evolutionary process in order for theism to be rational to hold.
- How science sometimes masquerades as philosophy or theology.

You can discover further background to these issues, grow your understanding, and become even more skillful in your communication of what you learn by interacting with some of these valuable resources:

Dig Deeper into Dr. Craig's Work

BEGINNER

Craig, William Lane. "The Absurdity of Life without God." The Veritas Forum. Chicago, 2001. http://bit.ly/AbsurdityVF.

Craig, William Lane. "Has Science Made Faith in God Impossible?" The Veritas Forum. College Station, Tex., 1997. http://bit.ly/VeritasWLC.

Craig, William Lane. *On Guard: Defending Your Faith with Reason and Precision.* Colorado Springs: David C. Cook Publishers, 2010. Chapters 4–5.

Craig, William Lane. "Why Does Anything at All Exist." Carswell Lecture, Winston-Salem, N.C., 2008. http://bit.ly/WhyExist.

INTERMEDIATE

Craig, William Lane. *Reasonable Faith: Christian Truth and Apologetics.* 3rd ed. Wheaton: Crossway, 2008. Chapters 3–4.

Craig, William Lane. "Origins of the Universe: Has Stephen Hawking Eliminated God?" Lecture at St. Andrew the Great Church, Cambridge, UK, October 1, 2011. http://bit.ly/HawkingsOrigins.

Craig, William Lane and J. P. Moreland. *Philosophical Foundations for a Christian Worldview.* Downers Grove, Ill.: InterVarsity, 2003. Chapters 15–18, 28.

Craig, William Lane. "What Is the Relation between Science and Religion?" *Reasonable Faith.* http://bit.ly/ScienceReligionRelation.

ADVANCED

Craig, William Lane. "Much Ado about Nothing: A Review Essay on *The Grand Design.*" *Philosophia Christi* 12 (2): 409–18. Winter, 2010.

Craig, William Lane. "Theistic Critiques of Atheism." *The Cambridge Companion to Atheism*, M. Martin, ed. Cambridge: Cambridge University Press, 2007. 69–85. http://bit.ly/CritiquesOfAtheism.

Supplemental Recommended Resources

BEGINNER

Hitchens, Peter. *The Rage Against God: How Atheism Led Me to Faith.* Grand Rapids: Zondervan, 2010.

Moreland, J. P. *The God Question: An Invitation to a Life of Meaning.* Eugene, Oreg.: Harvest House, 2009.

Ordway, Holly. *Not God's Type: A Rational Academic Finds a Rational Faith.* Chicago: Moody, 2010.

Zacharias, Ravi K. *The End of Reason: A Response to the New Atheists.* Grand Rapids: Zondervan, 2008.

INTERMEDIATE

Copan, Paul and William Lane Craig, eds. *Contending with Christianity's Critics.* Nashville: Broadman and Holman, 2009. Chapters 1–6.

Craig, William Lane and Chad Meister, eds. *God Is Great, God Is Good: Why Believing in God Is Reasonable and Responsible.* Downers Grove, Ill.: InterVarsity, 2009. Chapters 1–2, 4–6, Postscript, and the Appendix.

Groothuis, Douglas. *Christian Apologetics: A Comprehensive Case for Biblical Faith.* Downers Grove, Ill.: InterVarsity, 2011. Chapters 13–14.

Sweis, Khaldoun A. and Chad V. Meister. *Christian Apologetics: An Anthology of Primary Sources.* Grand Rapids: Zondervan, 2012. Chapters 48–50.

ADVANCED

Craig, William Lane and J. P. Moreland, eds. *The Blackwell Companion to Natural Theology.* Malden, Mass.: Wiley-Blackwell Publishing, 2009. Chapters 2, 4.

1

ON THE ORIGINS OF THE UNIVERSE

"God" and "the Cause of the Universe"

Dr. Craig,

I was wondering what the relationship between the proper name "God" and the definite description "The cause of the universe" is. A widely held belief amongst philosophers of language is that definite descriptions do not have the same referent in every possible world. For example, "The man who won the election in 2008" is not necessarily Barack Obama. It may have been the case that John McCain won. So what about the definite description "The cause of the universe"? If this doesn't have God as a referent in all possible worlds, then there is a possible world in which God is not the cause of the universe. Does this entail that there is no God? If God exists, does He have to be the cause of the universe out of necessity?

Haigen
United States

Dr. Craig's Response

This is an interesting question, Haigen. To answer it straightforwardly, I'd say that God is the cause of the universe, where "is" is to be understood here, not as the "is" of identity (as in "Mark Twain is Samuel Clemens"), but as the "is" of predication (as in "Mark Twain is the most famous American humorist"). "God" is, in this case, a proper name that we use to refer to God, and the definite description "the cause of the universe" is a predicate which takes "God" as its subject.

So is there a possible world in which God is not the cause of the universe? Yes, indeed! Since creation is a freely willed act of God, God could have refrained from creation and

INSIGHT

Note the distinction between "is" of identity vs. of predication. A failure to grasp that in application to Dr. Craig's point could result in a pantheistic view of the universe, where the universe stands in an identity relation to the cause of the universe.

so existed alone without a universe. In such possible worlds, God is not the cause of the universe because there is no universe! So God is not the cause of the universe out of necessity. He has this property contingently.

A more interesting question is whether there is a possible world in which the cause of the universe is something other than God. Traditionally, Christian theology has taken *creatio ex nihilo* to be exclusively the prerogative of God. No finite creature has the power to create a material thing from nothing.[1] So there is no possible world in which something other than God is the cause of the universe.

Obviously the possibility of a world in which God is not the cause of the universe doesn't entail that God does not exist. On the contrary, in such worlds He's the only thing that exists! On the other hand, if you think there is a world in which something other than God is the cause of the universe, then you should give up the principle that only God can create a material thing *ex nihilo*. In such worlds, God would be the cause of the cause of the universe (e.g., a super-powerful angel to whom God delegated the task of creation). But there is no reason to think that there are worlds like that.

On Bringing into Being Things Which Do Not Exist

Hey there Dr. Craig!

I've been talking with an atheist friend of mine who has issues with *creatio ex nihilo*.

He claims that *creatio ex nihilo* is logically incoherent since things that exist have no causal

---

1. With Dr. Craig, that's why, by the way, we find no instances, apart from divine acts of creation, of material things beginning to exist without material causes. For a material thing to come into being without a material cause requires an efficient cause of infinite power. It follows that the cause of the universe must be a being of infinite power.

power over things that don't exist. In other words, how does God cause something that doesn't exist to do anything? How exactly would God *bring* something that doesn't exist into existence? He insists that that would imply that something can simultaneously exist and not exist at the same time. Therefore, it's logically incoherent. Doesn't it seem that for causality to work, existent things can only act on existing things?

What say you?

Thanks Doc!
John
United States

Dr. Craig's Response

Your question, John, reminds me of an objection another reader recently sent in from an atheist website. It goes like this:

The Kalam Argument AGAINST God:

P1: Nothing which exists can cause something which does not exist to begin existing.
P2: Given (1), anything which begins to exist was not caused to do so by something which exists.
P3: The universe began to exist.
P4: Given (2) and (3), the universe was not caused to exist by anything which exists.
P5: God caused the universe to begin to exist.
C1: Given (4) and (5), God does not exist.

The obvious mistake in both these objections is the assumption that creation or beginning to exist is a sort of change in a thing from being nonexistent to being existent, much as a thing might change color from being green to being red. Thus, (P1) seems to assume that there are things that do not exist, which most philosophers would regard as absurd. As your friend says, "that would imply that something can simultaneously exist and not exist at the same time." So it is trivially true that no existent thing can cause a non-existent thing to begin to exist or that, in your friend's words, "things which exist have no causal power over things which don't exist," since there are no non-existent things! (If you do think that there really are non-existent things, then (P1) is no longer clearly true. Why couldn't an existent thing cause one of these non-existent things to begin to exist?)

But neither *creatio ex nihilo* nor *beginning to exist* implies that something undergoes a change from non-existence to existence. As C. D. Broad put it, absolute becoming is not a case of becoming this or that but just of becoming, period, just beginning to be. But then your friend's questions, "How does God cause something which doesn't exist to do anything? How exactly would God *bring* something that doesn't exist, into existence?" are misconceived. God doesn't do that. Your friend's objection to *creatio ex nihilo* thus falls to the ground. No reason has been given why God cannot just create the matter and energy that constitute the universe.

Moreover, (P2) wouldn't follow from (P1). For things that begin to exist are not non-existent things that became existent. If it's to follow from (P1), (P2) requires a different interpretation of (P1),

(P1*) Nothing can cause something that exists but did not formerly exist to begin existing.

The problem is that (P1*) is patently false. I, for example, began to exist. Did I do so without a cause? According to (P2), which follows from (P1*), everything that begins to exist just pops into being uncaused. Not only is that patently false, but so believing would make science and life itself impossible. No need to learn about the birds and the bees! Do Internet atheists really expect people to swallow poppycock like this in order to avoid theism?

But it gets worse! For (P5) is taken by our atheist to be true! So the argument concludes that God is a non-existent object that caused the universe to begin to exist! Indeed, if we're to avoid the above conclusion that everything that begins to exist does so without a cause, it seems we have to say that everything that begins to exist is caused by non-existent objects to come into being. How they pull off that metaphysical trick our intrepid atheist does not tell us.

Stephen Hawking and Leonard Mlodinow: Philosophical Undertakers

Hi Dr. Craig,

Can you give your response to the following from Stephen Hawking who is quoted from his 2010 book, *The Grand Design*?

"Because there is a law such as gravity, the universe can and will create itself from nothing. Spontaneous creation is the reason there is something rather than nothing, why the universe exists, why we exist," and "It is not necessary to invoke God to light the blue touch paper and set the universe going."

If there is such a revolution in theistic philosophy, such as arguments for the origin of the universe as you maintain, how can physicists make these statements? Doesn't this show that theistic arguments don't hold much weight with current paradigm in physics?

Thanks!

Matthew

Australia

Dr. Craig's Response

Your question is just one of many such questions we've received concerning Stephen Hawking and Leonard Mlodinow's new book *The Grand Design*. In an earlier question, I addressed the implications of their theories for the *kalam* cosmological argument and the fine-tuning argument for a Creator and Designer of the universe. Here I want to use your question, Matthew, "If there is such a revolution in theistic philosophy, such as arguments for the origin of the universe as you maintain, how can physicists make these statements?" as a springboard for addressing an underlying issue raised in the book.

Hawking and Mlodinow open *The Grand Design* with a series of profound philosophical questions: *What is the nature of reality? Where did all this come from? Did the universe need a creator?* Then they say this:

Traditionally these are questions for philosophy, but philosophy is dead. Philosophy has not kept up with modern developments in science, particularly physics. Scientists have become the bearers of the torch of discovery in our quest for knowledge. (p. 5)

The professional philosopher can only roll his eyes at the effrontery and condescension of such a statement. Two scientists who have, to all appearances, little acquaintance with philosophy are prepared to pronounce an entire discipline dead and to insult their own faculty colleagues in philosophy at Cal Tech and Cambridge University, many of whom, like Michael Redhead and D. H. Mellor, are eminent philosophers of science, for supposedly failing to keep up. I couldn't help but wonder what evidence our intrepid authors have of Mr. Redhead's laggard scholarship? What recent works in philosophy have they read that form the basis for their verdict? Alas, they do not say.

The professional philosopher will regard their verdict as not merely condescending but also as outrageously naïve. The man who claims to have no need of philosophy is the one most apt to be fooled by it. One might, therefore, anticipate that Mlodinow and Hawking's subsequent exposition of their favored theories will be underpinned by a host of unexamined philosophical presuppositions. That expectation is, in fact, borne out. Like their claims about the origin of the universe from "nothing" or about the Many Worlds Hypothesis to explain fine-tuning, their claims about laws of nature, the possibility of miracles, scientific determinism, and the illusion of free will are asserted with only the thinnest of justification and little understanding of the philosophical issues involved.

Take, for example, their ruminations on laws of nature (pp. 27–34). After admitting the philosophical difficulty of defining just what a law of nature is, they proceed to ask three questions about natural laws: (i) What is the origin of the laws? (ii) Are there any exceptions to the laws, that is, miracles? (iii) Is there only one set of possible laws?

With respect to (i) they note that the traditional answer is that God established na-

INSIGHT

Notice what Dr. Craig is describing and the difference it makes in one's evaluation of the authors' ideas. He exposes their naïve disdain for philosophy. This attitude is to their detriment, since philosophy is unavoidable. Such an attitude also precludes any fruitful interdisciplinary discussion between science and philosophy.

ture's laws. But Hawking and Mlodinow complain than unless one invests God with certain attributes, this answer amounts to no more than defining God as the embodiment of the laws of nature. I find this complaint perplexing. Since the classical theists they have in mind (including Descartes, whose views they misrepresent) thought that nature's laws were freely willed by God, God could not be just the embodiment of those laws, since God could have established quite different laws. What Mlodinow and Hawking are describing is the view of Spinoza, a pantheist who regarded "God" and "nature" as synonyms. Of course, classical theists regarded God as having certain attributes, which distinguished Him from nature; that is simply entailed in the answer that God established the laws.

Hawking and Mlodinow seem prepared to acknowledge the coherence of this answer, but they think the "real crunch" then comes with (ii), Are there miracles? Hawking and Mlodinow apparently think that answering (ii) negatively casts doubt on a theistic answer to (i). If so, this claim is baffling. Suppose one is a deist who thinks that God, having established the clockwork universe, chooses not to intervene in it? In that case, there is no "crunch" at all in answering (i) by "God" and (ii) by "No."

In any case, why answer (ii) negatively? Incredibly, Hawking and Mlodinow think that science requires it:

The scientific determinism that Laplace formulated is the modern scientist's answer to question two. It is, in fact, the basis of all modern science, and a principle that is important throughout this book. A scientific law is not a scientific law if it holds only when some supernatural being decides not to intervene. (p. 30)

This argument is multiply confused. First, it is false that Laplacean determinism[2] is the basis of modern science. Never mind the hordes of theistic scientists who affirm the reality of miracles; there are plenty of scientists, including Hawking and Mlodinow themselves (p. 72), who regard the indeterminism characteristic of quantum physics as ontic, not

---

2. Pierre Simon de Laplace was an eighteenth-century Newtonian physicist who boasted that armed with Newton's laws of motion, along with the knowledge of the present position of every particle in the universe, he could predict the exact description of the universe at any other time in its history. Story has it that when the Emperor Napoleon asked him what place God has in his system, the laconic Laplace replied, "Sire, I have no need of that hypothesis."

merely epistemic.[3] If nature itself is indeterministic, then the determinism of Laplace, a Newtonian, does not hold. Even a complete set of nature's laws will not fully determine the future. It's easy to imagine all sorts of ways in which indeterminacy on the quantum level can be amplified so as to issue in macroscopic changes in the world. (I recall the amusing illustration of a grad student who is delayed in leaving the lab while waiting for the decay of a radioactive isotope and who, as a result, meets a girl in the hallway whom he falls in love with and eventually marries!) It's puzzling that Hawking and Mlodinow are oblivious to the contradiction between their affirmation of both Laplacean determinism and quantum indeterminacy.

Second, Hawking and Mlodinow confuse *determinism* with *naturalism*. Quantum indeterminacy is the proof positive that modern science is not based on determinism. Their argument against the intervention of a supernatural being is an argument for naturalism, not determinism. Quantum indeterminacy is acceptable because it is naturalistic, whereas miracles involve supernatural agency. But then their claim that scientific laws would not be laws if they hold only when a supernatural being decides not to intervene is clearly false. The laws of nature describe the behavior of physical systems in the absence of any supernatural intervention. Were a supernatural agent to intervene, the predictions based on the laws would not hold precisely because non-natural factors, not envisioned by the laws, have entered the picture. The laws thus have implicit *ceteris paribus* ("all things being equal") conditions: they describe the behavior of physical systems given that no supernatural agent intervenes. If such a being does intervene, the natural law is not abrogated, since it describes the behavior of the system only under the assumption that such a being does not intervene.

Perhaps what Hawking and Mlodinow really mean to say is that science must presuppose naturalism in order to be a viable enterprise. But in that case, they have failed to distinguish *methodological* naturalism from *metaphysical* naturalism.[4] Their argument at best

---

3. That is to say, real, not just a matter of our limited knowledge. It is an unresolved debate whether the indeterminacy characterizing quantum physics is just a matter of our ignorance or is a mind-independent reality. For example, do sub-atomic particles really lack a precise location at a specific time, or is it just that we cannot simultaneously measure a particle's precise location and motion? Many, if not most, scientists take quantum indeterminacy to be ontic, not merely epistemic, in which case Laplace's boast noted above falls to the ground.

4. Metaphysical naturalism is the view that no supernatural entities exist. Usually, this is taken to imply that nothing other than space-time and its contents exists. Methodological naturalism makes no such claim. It holds that science only seeks for natural explanations of natural phenomena. There may be supernatural entities, but they're not the concern of science.

would show that science is methodologically committed to entertaining only hypotheses positing natural causes; but that would do nothing to justify a negative answer to (ii), that there are no miracles. And even the question of science's commitment to methodological naturalism is not itself a scientific question but a philosophical question about the nature of science.

Hawking and Mlodinow plunge into still deeper philosophical waters when they proceed to argue that because people live in the universe and interact with other objects in it, "scientific determinism must hold for people as well" (p. 30). Therefore, "we are no more than biological machines and . . . free will is just an illusion" (p. 32). This is very weak. I see no reason to think that a creature endowed with freedom of the will could not exist spatio-temporally and act upon and be acted upon by other objects; so what's the argument against such a thing? Hawking and Mlodinow ask, "If we have free will, where in the evolutionary tree did it develop?" If this is supposed to be an argument, there are at least two things wrong with it. First, my having free will does not depend upon my being able to specify where in the evolutionary process organisms first acquired it. Second, free will presumably arose as soon as the human brain evolved sufficient complexity to support self-conscious, rational reflection. So what's the problem?

> **INSIGHT**
> Notice what Dr. Craig is doing. He is trying to offer a clearer read of the authors' own meaning for the sake of understanding what is being claimed. Note the important distinction between "methodological naturalism" and "metaphysical naturalism" in this discussion.

Mlodinow and Hawking also argue that free will is illusory because neurosurgeons can stimulate a person's brain in such a way as to create the desire to move his limbs or lips. The fallacy here is thinking that because one can intervene to deterministically produce an effect, therefore, the effect occurs deterministically in the absence of such intervention. Just because a neurosurgeon can stimulate my brain to make me want to move my arm obviously does not imply that on other occasions I do not or cannot move my arm freely.

Those are the only arguments for determinism that Mlodinow and Hawking present, and they do not consider any of the arguments against determinism. I wonder, for example, why they think that anything they've said in their book is true, since, on their view, they were determined to write it. Everything they say is the product of blind physical causes, like water's gushing from a pipe or a tree's growing a branch. What confidence can they have that anything they have said is true—including their assertion that determinism is true?

Mlodinow and Hawking reserve discussion of question (iii) about the uniqueness of nature's laws until their treatment of the design argument from the fine-tuning of the universe for intelligent life. Since I commented on their discussion of (iii) elsewhere, I'll refrain from repeating myself here. But I trust that it is clear that, as one might expect, Mlodinow and Hawking are up to their necks in philosophical questions.

What one might not expect is that, after pronouncing the death of philosophy, Hawking and Mlodinow should themselves jump immediately into a *philosophical* discussion of scientific realism vs. anti-realism! The first third of their book is not about current scientific theories at all but is a disquisition on the history and philosophy of science. I found this section to be the most interesting and mind-boggling of the whole book.

Let me explain. Having set aside a Monday afternoon to read Hawking and Mlodinow's book, I spent that morning working through a scholarly article from Blackwell's *Contemporary Debates in Metaphysics* on a philosophical viewpoint known as *ontological pluralism*. Ontological pluralism is a view in a sub-discipline of philosophy whose name sounds like stuttering: meta-metaphysics, or, as it's sometimes called, meta-ontology. This is philosophy at its most ethereal. Ontology is the study of being or of what exists, the nature of reality. Meta-ontology is one notch higher: it inquires whether ontological disputes are meaningful and how best to resolve them.

Ontological pluralism holds that there really is no right answer to many ontological questions (such as, "Do composite objects exist?"). According to the ontological pluralist there are just different ways of describing reality, and none of these is more correct or accurate than another. There literally is no fact of the matter at all in answer to these questions. So if you were to ask, "Is there such a thing as the Moon?" the ontological pluralist would say that the question has no objective answer. It's not true that the Moon exists, and it's not true that the Moon does not exist. There just is no fact of the matter about whether there is such a thing as the Moon. Ontological pluralism is thus a radical view that is defended by a handful of philosophers.

Imagine my utter astonishment, therefore, to find Hawking and Mlodinow espousing ontological pluralism (without being aware of the name) as their philosophy of science! They call their view "model-dependent realism." Their view is actually even more radical than ontological pluralism, for Hawking and Mlodinow take it to hold, not merely for high-level ontological disputes, but for our entire apprehension of the world. They explain,

. . . our brains interpret the input from our sensory organs by making a model of the world. When such a model is successful at explaining events, we tend to attribute to it, and to the elements and concepts that constitute it, the quality of reality or absolute truth. But there may be different ways in which one could model the same physical situation, with each employing different fundamental elements and concepts. If two such physical theories or models accurately predict the same events, one cannot be said to be more real than the other; rather, we are free to use whichever model is most convenient. (p. 7)

On this view, a model seems to be an (at least in part) unconscious way of organizing sense perceptions, which can be refined by scientific theorizing. We never come to know the way the world is; all we achieve are more or less convenient ways of organizing our perceptions. Such skepticism would be bad enough; but the situation is even worse. For these various models are not, *even unbeknownst to us*, more or less accurate approximations of reality. Rather there is no objective reality to which our models more or less accurately correspond. This is full-blown ontological pluralism.

Mlodinow and Hawking are thus extreme anti-realists. Now, they try to distinguish their view from scientific anti-realism by defining the latter as the view that "observation and experiment are meaningful but that theories are no more than useful instruments that do not embody any deeper truths underlying the observed phenomena" (p. 44). What Hawking and Mlodinow are describing here, however, is not scientific anti-realism but positivism, a philosophy of science popular in the 1930s and '40s. Positivism proved to be untenable in part because of its artificial distinction between observation statements and theoretical statements. But anti-realism does not depend on positivism. Hawking and Mlodinow are *more* anti-realist than the positivists, for they not only deny that theoretical statements express objective truths about the world, but they deny this of observation statements as well, since even observation is model-dependent. Again, what they're denying is not just knowledge of the way the world is, but that there even *is* an objective world to be known.

Just how serious they are about their anti-realism is evident from their examples. If a goldfish viewing the world through a curved bowl could formulate a model that enabled it to make successful predictions, then "we would have to admit the goldfish's view as a valid picture of reality" (p. 39). Ptolemy's geocentric model of the world was just as adequate as Copernicus' heliocentric model. "So which is real, the Ptolemaic or Copernican system?

Although it is not uncommon for people to say that Copernicus proved Ptolemy wrong, that is not true" (p. 41). This point is not that Copernicus' evidence was insufficient, but that neither theory is objectively true. Contrasting young earth creationism and the big bang theory, Hawking and Mlodinow claim that while the big bang theory is "more useful," nevertheless, "neither model can be said to be more real than the other" (p. 51)!

One cannot help but wonder what sort of *argument* would justify adopting so radical an ontological pluralism. All that Mlodinow and Hawking have to offer is the fact that if we were, say, inhabitants of a virtual reality controlled by alien beings, then there would be no way for us to *tell* that we were in the simulated world and so would have no reason to doubt its reality (p. 42). The trouble with this sort of argument is that it does not exclude the possibility that we have in such a case two competing theories of the world, one the aliens' and one ours, and one of the theories is true and one false, even if we cannot tell which is which.

Moreover, the fact that our observations are model-dependent or theory-laden doesn't imply that we cannot have knowledge of the way the world is (much less that there is no way the world is!). For example, a layman entering a scientific laboratory might see that there is a piece of machinery on the lab table, but he would not see that there is an interferometer on the lab table, since he lacks the theoretical knowledge to recognize it as such. A caveman entering the laboratory would not even see that there is a piece of machinery on the table, since he lacks the concept of a machine. But that does nothing to undermine the objective truth of the lab technician's observation that there is an interferometer on the table.

Mlodinow and Hawking, not content with ontological pluralism, really go off the deep end when they assert, "There is no model-independent test of reality. It follows that a well-constructed model creates a reality of its own" (p. 172). This is an assertion of *ontological relativity*, the view that reality itself is different for persons having different models. If you are Fred Hoyle, the universe *really* has existed eternally in a steady state; but if you are Stephen Hawking, the universe *really* began with a big bang. If you are the ancient physician Galen, blood *really* does not circulate through the human body, but if you are William Harvey, it does! Such a view seems crazy and is made only more so by Mlodinow and Hawking's claim that the model itself is responsible for creating its respective reality. It hardly needs to be said that no such conclusion follows from there being no model-independent test of the way the world is.

Whatever verdict we make on their arguments, the point is that despite their claim to speak as scientific torchbearers of knowledge, what Hawking and Mlodinow are engaged in is *philosophy*. The most important conclusions drawn in their book are philosophical, not scientific. Why, then, do they pronounce philosophy dead and claim as scientists to be bearing the torch of discovery? Simply because that enables them to cloak their amateurish philosophizing with the mantle of scientific authority and so avoid the hard work of actually arguing for, rather than merely asserting, their philosophical viewpoints.

The answer to your question, Matthew—"how can physicists make these statements?"—was given long ago by Albert Einstein, when he remarked, "The man of science is a poor philosopher." Hawking and Mlodinow's book bears witness to Einstein's sagacity.

INSIGHT

Notice what Dr. Craig observes here and with the Einstein quotation. Philosophy is unavoidable. Hiding one's philosophical assumptions, viewpoints, and commitments behind the cloak of another discipline only disadvantages both authors and readers.

On Whether the Universe Must Have a Material Cause

Dear Professor Craig,

To start, I would like to thank you for your service to the Christian community, and for guiding me in my quest to understand Christian theology.

Likewise, my question deals with the doctrine of creation, which you (and mainstream Christianity) hold to. That doctrine is that God created the world *ex nihilo*, and the universe (by which I mean, all of reality) was created literally out of nothing. The problem with this concept, which I just can't seem to shake off, is that it seems to violate a basic principle of causation. So for a casual event to occur, you would need potentiality and an agent or object to actualize it.

For example, a block of wood has the potentiality to be carved into a wooden train, and a skilled worker would be the agent, which actualizes the possibility of a wooden train carved from said block of wood.

However, according to you, God's initial act of causation was different than the example provided above, as it did not involve a material cause, but only an efficient cause. But here comes the problem, by taking out the material cause from the initial act of creation, aren't you taking out the potentiality of God creating anything. The material cause seems to be the carrier of the potential in the act of causation. So when you rule out a material cause, you are simultaneously ruling out the potentiality of an agent causing anything. So to clarify and conclude:

- A casual event requires an agent to actualize an event (or an object), and the potentiality of the event to occur.
- "Nothingness" contains no potentiality, or else it would be "something" (which would completely undermine Judeo-Christian theology, as something cannot exist alongside God eternally).
- Therefore, since creation *ex nihilo* tries to bring an object/agent out of nothing (with no potentiality), it is logically impossible.

I have tried to find ways out of this conundrum, but all of them have failed. For example, if you believe that you do not need potentiality for a casual event to occur, you end up with a logical contradiction. So for example:

A block of wood does not have the potentiality to become the number 3; however, a skilled worker can still actualize a non-potentiality, and make a block of wood the number 3. Obviously, this leads to metaphysical absurdities, which cannot possibly exist.

The other solution, which I have thought of is for God to also serve as the "potentiality," however this would no longer be creation *ex nihilo* (from nothing) but creation ex-deli-ho (out of God) as God would be using himself and his existing potential to create the universe. However, this would be an appeal to pantheism, and would no longer serve as a viable option for a Christian theist. This has forced me into concluding God created the universe from forms already existing in his mind (which still seems to be an appeal to pantheism, and conceptualism). I would like to ask what your solution to the problem is that I have presented and whether I have made any fallacies in my train of thought. Basically, how do you overcome this hurdle in creation *ex nihilo*. Sorry for the very long question, and thank you for your time.

God Bless,
Richard
United States

Dr. Craig's Response

I've addressed this issue before in one of its many guises. But since you present the question in yet another form and it seems to be of interest, let me take it up again.

Let me begin by affirming that Christian theology is committed to *creatio ex nihilo*, that is to say, the doctrine that God created the universe without any material cause. God is the efficient cause that produced the universe, and there was no material cause. He, Himself, created the matter and energy. When we say that the matter and energy were created out of nothing, we mean merely that, although created, they were not created out of anything.

Let me also affirm that, as you put it, "for a casual event to occur, you would need potentiality and an agent or object to actualize it." For that reason, something's coming into being spontaneously from nothing is metaphysically impossible. For, as you say, non-being has no potentialities, no powers, no properties—it is not anything. That's why being comes only from being. *Ex nihilo nihil fit*—out of nothing, nothing comes. So if something has an absolute beginning of existence, there must exist an actual being which produces the thing in existence.

The question, then, is whether there is a conflict between the principle *Ex nihilo nihil fit* and *creatio ex nihilo*. Clearly not! For in *creatio ex nihilo* there is an efficient cause of the effect, whereas the principle *Ex nihilo nihil fit* concerns something's beginning to be in the absence of any sort of cause.

> **INSIGHT**
> Notice what this affirmation of *creatio ex nihilo* articulates about the difference between a material vs. efficient cause. The difference will help avoid confusions and mistaken views about the God-creation relationship.

But is there a problem with *creatio ex nihilo*? I agree with your premise: *A causal event requires an agent to actualize an event (or an object), and the potentiality of the event to occur.* Moreover, I also agree with your second premise: "Nothingness" contains no potentiality, or else it would be "something."

But your conclusion just doesn't follow from (1) and (2). Your conclusion assumes that in *creatio ex nihilo*, the potentiality of the universe's existence must lie (impossibly) in the nothingness that preceded it. But, as Thomas Aquinas pointed out, in *creatio ex nihilo* the potentiality of the universe lay in the power of God to create it. Since God has the power to create the universe, then even in the state of affairs of God's existing alone, there is the potential for a universe to exist. That potential resides, not in some non-existent object or in nothing, but in God Himself and His ability to cause the universe.

This solution is very different from the panentheistic solution you mention and rightly reject, that the universe is made out of God's own being. Rather, the idea is that God has causal powers and, therefore, there is a potential for the universe to be actualized.

This account underlines the fact that *creatio ex nihilo* is not a type of change. For in creation there is no enduring subject that goes from non-being into being. It is an absolute beginning of existence. It is not as though there were something with a passive potentiality to be actualized and God acts on that potentiality to actualize it. Rather the potentiality lies wholly in God's power to create.

Must the Cause of the Universe Be Personal?

Dr. Craig,

There has been considerable discussion on your ReasonableFaith.org forum about your response to the question about whether the "Cause of the Universe must be Personal . . ." Particularly, I have some concerns with your response that mainly center around your use of the Islamic principle of determination. I am asking on behalf of Cyrus, with some of my own inquiries added.

Our first question is: what exactly do you mean by "eternal" in the argument from the principle of determination and in the general context of the kalam cosmological argument? In the *Blackwell Companion to Natural Theology*, you write:

> The cause [of the universe] is in some sense eternal, and yet the effect which it produced is not eternal but began to exist a finite time ago. How can this be? If the necessary and sufficient conditions for the production of the effect are eternal, then why is not the effect eternal?

As Cyrus pointed out, if one takes "eternal" to mean "existing at all moments of time" and interprets the question as asking "If the cause of the universe is existing at all

moments of time, then why did the universe come into existence only a finite time ago?,"
then this question cannot be used with the KCA. If the cause existed "at all moments
of time," then it would be temporal, which would imply a Newtonian view of time. The
second premise of the argument, though, guarantees that no time exists before the
universe and that the cause must be timeless. You replied:

> This surprised me, since I thought my position has always been that that question
> is meaningless, since I hold to a relational view of time. In the passage you cite, the
> point was to prove precisely that the big bang did not occur in a super dense pellet
> existing from eternity! Time (and space) came into being with the big bang, and so it's
> meaningless to ask why it didn't happen earlier.

But notice that if this is correct, then the principle of determination no longer works.

According to the principle of determination, the creation of the universe requires a
particularizer (a being with free will who decides the course of an action between various
choices) to will the universe into existence at a particular moment. But if you are right
there is no time before the big bang, then it makes no sense to rhetorically ask why the
cause of the universe, if a mechanical one, did not create the universe an infinite time
earlier, because there was no time earlier. The principle of determination only, then,
works within time. This is most evident with your examples of the freezing water and the
seated man; both instances are not timeless like God, but are in fact temporal and have
existed beginninglessly for an infinite time, (which the KCA says is impossible)! Only in a
temporal framework is the principle of determination meaningful.

To illustrate, suppose that the cause of the universe was in fact mechanically
operating, with all of the necessary and sufficient conditions in place to create the
universe. You say that this would not work because this mechanical cause would have
created the universe an infinite time earlier, making the universe also as eternal and
beginningless as the cause. But is it clear now where the error is? To object by saying that
a mechanical cause would have created the universe an infinite time earlier assumes that
time existed before the universe, which you argue is impossible. If you do not mean this
when you state the principle of determination, then I think you will need to clarify then
in a way that does not suggest time before the universe. Now, if you define "eternal" as

"timeless," it does not make sense either to ask why the effect is not eternal (timeless), since the universe in the KCA is by definition the totality of all of space-time and is by definition temporal.

Our second question is: why could not the cause of the universe be indeterministic yet impersonal? Such a cause could escape the alleged problems with a mechanical cause just as well as a personal cause could. The indeterministic, impersonal cause of the universe could have generated an indeterministically produced creation event that caused the universe and was simultaneous with it as well. You state that because Cyrus has not given a detailed explanation of what such an indeterministic, impersonal cause could be, such an explanation is not valid or worth considering. But in your outline of the KCA, you explicate in argument 4.1 that:

4.11 The universe was brought into being either by a mechanically operating set of necessary and sufficient conditions or by a personal, free agent.

4.12 The universe could not have been brought into being by a mechanically operating set of necessary and sufficient conditions.

4.13 Therefore, the universe was brought into being by a personal, free agent.

Since this is a deductive argument, the mere possibility of an indeterministic, impersonal cause shows this argument to be a false dilemma, meaning that you can neither use the argument to show the personhood of the cause of the universe nor use it as a deductive proof against the inductive evidence against the existence of an unembodied mind. But furthermore, an atemporal initial singularity could be a plausible candidate for this cause, for the singularity is lawless, indeterministic, and impersonal, and, due to its atemporality, is timeless, meaning that it did not begin to exist. Because the singularity did not begin to exist, it would not need to have a cause.

Now, I see that you have responded to similar questions by saying that the singularity, though out of physical time, comes into being with time and, therefore, needs a cause. But this appears to contradict your analysis of what it means to begin to exist. One of the conditions for x to begin to exist is that there is no state of affairs in which x exists timelessly. But, if the singularity is atemporal, then it would exist in a timeless state of affairs and, therefore, would not have begun to exist under your analysis. These, Cyrus and

I feel, are the biggest flaws in the KCA that we think you have not adequately addressed, and we would be happy to see them given justice.

Shah

(country not specified)

Dr. Craig's Response

These are important questions, Shah, so I'll try to clarify my positions in response.

1. WHAT DO I MEAN BY "ETERNAL" IN THE ARGUMENT FROM THE PRINCIPLE OF DETERMINATION?

In a word, *permanent*. Something is eternal if it exists permanently, or without beginning or end. But eternal existence can take two forms: timelessness or infinite omnitemporal existence (sometimes called sempiternity). God is essentially eternal, but on my view whether He is timeless or omnitemporal is contingent, depending on His will.

So the reason for my gloss "in some sense eternal" is precisely to indicate that the argument for the cause's being personal works on *either* construal of eternity.

Recall that by this point we've already proved that the first cause exists beginninglessly and changelessly without creation. That is the key to the argument, not whether this cause is timeless or in a sort of eventless, undifferentiated time before creation. (You know my own view is the former, though I'm prepared to fall back to the latter if my preferred position is shown to be untenable.) The point is that if the causal conditions sufficient for the universe were permanently present (whether timelessly or sempiternally), then the universe should exist as permanently as the cause. Here's how I put it in *Reasonable Faith*:

One way to see the difficulty is by reflecting on the different types of causal relations. In event/event causation, one event causes another. For example, the brick's striking the window pane causes the pane to shatter. This kind of causal relation clearly involves a beginning of the effect in time, since it is a relation between events which occur at specific times. In state/state causation one state of affairs causes another state of affairs to exist. For example, the water's having a certain density is the cause of the wood's floating on the water. In this sort of causal relation, the effect need not have a beginning: the wood could theoretically be floating eternally on the water. . . . Now, the difficulty that arises in the case of the cause of the beginning of the universe is that we seem to have a peculiar case of state/event causation: the cause is a timeless state but the effect is an event that occurred at a specific moment in the finite past. Such state/event causation doesn't seem to make sense, since a state sufficient for the existence of its effect should have a state as its effect.[5]

There seems to be only one way out of this dilemma, and that is to say that the cause of the universe's beginning is a personal agent who freely chooses to create a universe in time. Philosophers call this type of causation "agent causation," and because the agent is free, he can initiate new effects by freely bringing about conditions which were not previously present.

Now, you object that "saying that a mechanical cause would have created the universe an infinite time earlier assumes that time existed before the universe, which you argue is impossible." Be careful here, Shah. The question is not why the universe wasn't created earlier (regardless of how much earlier). I agree that it makes no sense to ask why the universe didn't begin at an earlier point of time. But it doesn't follow from that that it is meaningless to ask why a universe with a beginning exists rather than an eternal universe with no beginning. Nor is it meaningless to ask how an effect with a beginning can originate from a changeless, permanent cause. That's the real head-scratcher! I think al-Ghazali and those medieval Muslim theologians were dead-on concerning this argument for a free agent as the cause of the universe.

2. WHY COULD NOT THE CAUSE OF THE UNIVERSE BE INDETERMINISTIC YET IMPERSONAL?

Again, you need to recall what has already been established prior to this point. If the argument so far is correct, then we have proved that there exists an uncaused, beginningless, changeless, immaterial, timeless, spaceless, enormously powerful, indeterministic cause of the universe. Now, the question is, what is it? What entity fits this description? The answer, it seems to me, is clear: a person, an unembodied mind.

We can think of this conclusion as an inference to the best explanation. In inference to the best explanation, we ask ourselves, what hypothesis, if true, would provide the best

---

5. William Lane Craig, *Reasonable Faith*, 3rd ed. (Wheaton, Ill.: Crossway, 2008), 153–54.

explanation of the data? The hypothesis that there is a personal Creator of the universe explains wonderfully all the data. By contrast, as I said, there's nothing like this in a naturalistic worldview. Even given quantum indeterminism (itself a moot point), such indeterminacy is a property of changing, spatiotemporal, physical systems. I don't know of any competing explanation to, much less better explanation than, the hypothesis of a personal Creator.

Notice that it is not legitimate to offer as an explanation a hypothesis which simply repeats the data to be explained—for example, explaining that opium induces sleep because it has "dormitive powers." Saying that the cause of the universe is an uncaused . . . indeterministic, impersonal being is like that. It is not to offer an explanation at all. Therefore, it could never be the better explanation. Similarly, it is no good appealing to unknown entities. That just is to admit that one has no explanation, no alternative hypothesis to offer. It would be like saying that fossils are not best explained as the vestiges of organisms that once lived on Earth but were instead the effect of some mysterious, unknown fossil-forming power in the rocks. Again, that could never count as the best explanation.

There are two ways to defeat such an inference to the best explanation: (i) provide an equally good explanation that does not involve the existence of a personal Creator; or (ii) provide overriding reasons to think that a personal Creator does not exist. The arguments against the coherence of an unembodied mind would be examples of strategy (ii), while our present discussion concerning an alternative explanation is an example of strategy (i). It remains to be seen whether either strategy can be successfully carried out. We've yet to see any evidence that the notion of an unembodied mind is incoherent or even any evidence against mind-body dualism in human beings. On the contrary I think that we have good reason to think that anthropological dualism is true; but that's another story, since it's the atheist who bears the burden of proof here.

Now, as to the formulation of my dilemma, remember that in order for a disjunction to be true all that is required is that one of the disjuncts be true. So long as the true disjunct is included, you don't need to include all the other logical possibilities as well. So, for example, a political observer might justifiably reason, "Either Cuomo or Paladino will win the New York governor's race. But Paladino's negatives are too high. Therefore, Cuomo will win." The argument is a good one, despite the fact that the major premise ignores all of the other fringe candidates on the ballot in New York! Their winning is so improbable that the premise as the pundit states it is very likely true.

Similarly, think of (4.11) as drawing from the pool of live explanatory options those candidates for the best explanation of the cause of the universe. Since I'm not aware of any candidate at all for an impersonal, indeterministic cause of the universe that fits all the other properties already proved thus far, I just ignored that idea.[6] Indeed, the lack of any such candidate is what led to my abbreviated argument that the cause of the universe is either a mind or an abstract object. Now, of course, if someone adds to the pool of live options another explanation (see below on the initial cosmological singularity), then we'll have to consider it.

In any case, Shah, don't get hung up over the mere *form* of the argument. One can always reformulate it inductively. For example, we could say that the probability that the cause of the universe is personal (P) is much higher given the evidence (E) for the deduced cause of the universe than it is on our background information (B) alone, that is, $\Pr(P|E\ \&\ B) \rightarrowtail \Pr(P|B)$, which cannot be said of the probability that the cause is impersonal $(\neg P)$. This is, in large part, because the probability that there should be a cause of the universe such as we have described is so much higher given the hypothesis that the cause is personal than it is if the cause is impersonal, that is, $\Pr(E|P\ \&\ B) \rightarrowtail \Pr E|(\neg P\ \&\ B)$.

Finally, as for the suggestion that the singularity is the cause of the universe, this has the merit of at least positing some explanatory entity. But in my original response to Cyrus, I explained why the initial cosmological singularity cannot be the ultimate cause of the universe, since it is either unreal or else part of the universe and, therefore, itself in need of explanation of its coming into being. The sense in which the singularity is "timeless," Shah, is a highly technical sense in that in the General Theory of Relativity, it is not a point *in* space-time. Rather it is a point on the boundary of space-time. But it is not eternal in the ordinary sense of the term; namely, it is not permanent. On the contrary, it is fleetingly evanescent. It is, therefore, temporal and began to exist and, therefore, requires a cause.

---

6. Dr. Craig has, by contrast, discussed at some length the hypothesis that the cause of the universe might have been an indeterministic, quantum mechanical, physical cause. See, for example, his contribution to the volume *Mere Creation: Science, Faith and Intelligent Design* (Downers Grove, Ill.: InterVarsity, 1998), 332–59.

2

GOD AND TIME

On a Framework for Thinking about God, Creation, and Time

In Lee Strobel's interview with you in his book *The Case for a Creator* (Chapter 5, in the subsection "Pathway of Mathematics") you stated:

Time and space are creations of God that began at the big bang. If you go back beyond the beginning of time itself, there is simply eternity. By that, I mean eternity in the sense of timelessness. God, the eternal, is timeless in His being. God did not endure through an infinite amount of time up to the moment of creation; that would be absurd. God transcends time. He's beyond time. Once God creates the universe, He could enter time, but that's a different topic altogether.

Also, in your book *Reasonable Faith* (p. 117) you wrote:

For example, a man sitting from eternity could will to stand up; thus, a temporal effect arises from an eternally existing agent. Similarly, a finite time ago a Creator endowed with free will could have willed to bring the world into being at that moment. In this way, God could exist changelessly and eternally but choose to create the world in time. By "choose" one need not mean that the Creator changes His mind but that He freely and eternally intends to create a world with a beginning.

This is all hard for me to comprehend.

1) I am having trouble comprehending the difference between a Creator who endured through an infinite amount of time up to the moment of creation and a timeless

Creator who, a finite time ago, willed to bring the world into being at that moment? Could you elaborate please?

2) Doesn't speaking of before "the moment of creation" imply that there was time before creation? Please explain.

3) I don't understand how "a man sitting from eternity could will to stand up." Again, wouldn't that imply that he endured through a period of time before standing up? Similarly, if "a finite time ago a Creator endowed with free will could have willed to bring the world into being at that moment," wouldn't that imply that the Creator endured through a period of time before bringing the world into being?

4) I don't understand how anyone could do anything if there was no time?

5) I am having trouble comprehending "By 'choose' one need not mean that the Creator changes His mind but that He freely and eternally intends to create a world with a beginning." Do you mean that by "choose" all that is meant is "intend"? That God always wanted to create a world with a beginning and never changed his mind about this? If so, why wasn't the world created from an infinite time ago? I know this sentence is precisely meant to answer this problem (why the world wasn't created an infinite time ago), but I am still having trouble understanding how this sentence answers this problem.

Sincerely,
Paul

Hello, Dr. Craig,

When studying systematic theology, and specifically the doctrine of God, I have come to God's relation to time and eternity and I want to see if you could address a few concerns that are popping up. I have come across an excerpt from a certain systematic theology book that affirms

> It is . . . worthy of note that it is . . . incoherent to speak of God being eternal before creation and temporal after creation. For a theist, creating the world does not change the nature of God. The world is not created *ex deo* ('out of God'); that is pantheism. And for theism, the world is created *ex nihilo* ('out of nothing'). Consequently, God does not change 'internally,' that is, in His essence, by creating something else. The

only thing that changes is 'external,' the relationship of the world to Him. Prior to creation, the world has no relationship to God, since it did not exist. At creation and after, God became 'Creator' for the first time.... Prior to creation, He was God, but not Creator. That is, at creation God gained a new relationship, but not any new attributes. He did not change in His essence, but in His external activity.... [The divine temporality argument] assumes that to act in time is to be temporal. It does not demonstrate that the Actor is temporal; only that His acts are temporal. Classical theists do not deny that God's actions are temporal—they only insist that God's attributes are not temporal.

From listening and reading your work I understand that you hold to the position that God is eternal without creation and temporal subsequent to creation. My question is, "Is it not possible that God can remain eternal while His *acts* are seen temporally?" Why assume that by simply acting that He must becoming "wholly" spatially and temporally located?

An example of what I am trying to get across: A person could take a stamp with a date and press it on a piece of paper. While the stamped date is fixed with that specific date—we have a time at which something occurred—the stamper is not necessarily contained (trying not to use emotionally laden terms like "trapped") to that stamped time. Right?

I am trying to make sense of this. Why would God simply acting in time fix Him to time? Further is it not even possible or probable that a model of some divine hyper time could not actually be (even possibly formulated in the future) and we are simply limited in fully grasping a concept like eternity?

Sincerely,
Michael

Dr. Craig's Response

These *are* difficult issues to understand, Paul! Next to God Himself, I know of no subject so baffling, so mind-expanding, as the concept of time. Try to put God and time together and you've got something that you could spend a lifetime studying! I hope that your puzzlement is due simply to the difficulty of the subject rather than to any incoherence on my part.

INSIGHT

This really is one of the most succinct statements of Dr. Craig's view of time. It is worth returning to in the midst of all the interesting, stimulating, and challenging questions regarding God's relationship to time and creation.

Before I consider your several questions, allow me to state succinctly my understanding of God's relationship to time. I argue that God, existing changelessly alone without the universe, is timeless. Time comes into existence at creation and so has a beginning and is finite in the past. God, in virtue of His real relation to the temporal world, becomes temporal at the moment of creation. So God exists timelessly without creation and temporally since the moment of creation.

(1) If I am right, then there is no moment prior to creation. Rather, time begins at creation. This is the classical Christian view, as defended, for example, by Augustine. On this view, it is logically incoherent to ask, "What was God doing prior to creation?" because "prior to creation" implies a moment before creation, which the view denies. So the question is asking, "What happened at a moment of time before the first moment of time?" which makes no sense. It's like asking, "What is the name of that bachelor's wife?"

Now, some theists have disagreed with the classical view. Isaac Newton, the founder of modern physics, for example, believed that time is infinite in the past and never had a beginning. For Newton absolute time just is God's duration. Because God has always existed, time goes back and back and never had a beginning. So on Newton's view, it makes perfect sense to ask, "What was God doing prior to creation?" In fact, the philosopher G. W. Leibniz, who held to the Augustinian view, tormented Newton's follower Samuel Clarke in their celebrated correspondence with the question, "Why [on Newton's view] didn't God create the world sooner?" This question is very difficult to answer from a Newtonian point of view.[7]

Whichever view you take, I think you can see that there's a huge difference between holding that God exists timelessly without creation and holding that He has endured through an infinite past time prior to the moment of creation. For a lively and interesting

---

7. See Dr. Craig's discussion in *Time and Eternity* (Wheaton, Ill.: Crossway, 2001).

discussion of the alternatives, see the book *God and Time*,[8] featuring an exchange between me, Alan Padgett, Nicholas Wolterstorff, and Paul Helm on such questions.

(2) Yes, speaking of a moment "before" the moment of creation does imply time before time, which is incoherent on the Augustinian view I defend. But notice that I don't use that word in your quotation from my interview with Lee. In my early work, I thought people would understand, once I explained my view, that the expression "before creation" is just a harmless *façon de parler* (manner of speaking), not to be taken literally. But in light of the confusion engendered by the phrase, I have since been very careful to avoid it, speaking rather of God's existing without (or sans) creation or existing beyond, though not before, the big bang. One nice way of expressing God's priority to creation is to say that God is causally but not temporally prior to the beginning of the universe.

(3) Obviously a man sitting "from eternity" doesn't exist timelessly. But my thought experiment is meant to illustrate a point about freedom of the will. A person can exist changelessly and then freely execute a certain intention because free will doesn't require any antecedent determining conditions. The very nature of free will is the absence of causal determinants. So a free choice has the appearance of a purely spontaneous event. The man can simply freely will to stand up. Thus, you can get a temporal effect from a changeless cause, if that cause is a free agent. Now, in God's case, God exists changelessly without the universe. Creation is a freely willed act of God that, when it occurs, brings time into being along with the universe. Thus, to say that "a finite time ago a Creator endowed with free will could have willed to bring the world into being at that moment" does not imply that there was time prior to that moment.

(4) What timelessness entails is that one doesn't do anything *different*, that is, that one does not *change*. Timelessness implies an unchanging state of being. Now, some activities don't require change and time. For example, knowing something doesn't require change or time. God can know all truths in that timeless state without any change. Similarly, one can have unchanging intentions. So long as one's intentions don't change they can be timelessly held. That's why I said that God can exist without the universe with a timeless intention to create a world with a beginning. One can love someone else without change. Here we have insight into the nature of the love relationship among the three persons of the Trinity in that timeless state without creation. There exists a perfect, changeless state of mutual knowledge, will, and love among the persons of the Trinity without the creation. (The wonder

8. Greg Ganssle, ed., *God & Time: Four Views* (Downers Grove, Ill.: InterVarsity, 2001).

of creation is that God would bother to create a world of creatures and invite them to freely enter the joy of that fellowship as adopted children!)

(5) Yes, by "choose" I mean that God has a free intention of His will. Its timelessness does not negate that this is, indeed, a choice. For one can conceive of possible worlds in which God has a quite different intention, namely, to refrain from creating a world at all. Initially, I thought that this was all that was needed to explain the origin of the world; but reflecting on agent causation leads me to think that in addition to that timeless intention there must also be an exercise of causal power on God's part. That act is simultaneous with the moment of creation—indeed, it just *is* the act of creating—and brings God into time. If you ask, "But why didn't God execute His intention sooner?" you've fallen back into the Newtonian view of thinking of God as existing temporally prior to creation. On the Augustinian view, the question is unintelligible.

Now, Michael, to your questions, I think an answer (which you might be already anticipating based on the above) will depend on which view of time you adopt: a tensed view (A-theory) or a tenseless view (B-theory). According to the B-theory of time, there is no mind-independent temporal becoming; all events in time are equally real, just as every inch on a yardstick is equally real. On this view, it's easy to see how God can exist outside of time and His acts be located at various points in time. Or maybe it would be more accurate to say that God has just one multifaceted timeless action and its effects occur at various points in time. It would be like a three-dimensional person's simultaneously producing effects at various places in two-dimensional flatland. Since the whole four-dimensional space-time "block" co-exists tenselessly with God, God never comes into a new relation to it, and His effects in it need not be produced by successive actions on His part.

Contrast the A-theory. According to this view, temporal becoming is real, and events in time are not all on an ontological par. God cannot be tenselessly causing future events or else they would exist at their future coordinates, which on an A-theory they do not. Your analogy of the stamper is not really relevant. It just amounts to saying that someone can stamp a false date. The relevant point is that God cannot tenselessly produce an event at a future date without the event's existing tenselessly at that date.

The theologian you cite actually gives his case away by admitting that at creation God comes into a new relation to the universe. If something changes in relation to other things, then it has undergone an extrinsic change and so must be in time. For example, if I change in relation to my son from standing in the *taller than* relation to standing in the *shorter than* relation, I have not changed intrinsically. Nevertheless, in order to undergo such a relational change, I must be in time. There was a time when I stood in one relation and then another time at which I stood in the other relation.

Thomas Aquinas recognized that God's undergoing even such an extrinsic change would be sufficient to render God temporal, and he avoided this conclusion only by adopting the very problematic doctrine that while creatures are really related to God, God is not really related to creatures.

So it is not quite right to say that "[The divine temporality argument] assumes that to act in time is to be temporal." Rather it holds that if an A-theory of time is true, then to act in time is to be temporal.

It is futile to try to avoid this argument by positing a higher hyper-time in which God produces all events in our time. For then the whole debate just replays itself on the hyper-level. Is hyper-time a tensed time or is it a tenseless time? The same conclusions will follow, and nothing has been gained by kicking the debate upstairs.

Is There a Contradiction in God's Creation of Time?

The Law of Contradiction states that two mutually exclusive statements cannot both be true at the same time and in the same respect.

The statements "God exists and the universe does not exist" and "God exists and the universe exists" are mutually exclusive statements and do not differ in respect. The only way to avoid a contradiction, if both are to be asserted, is to assert that each is true at a different time.

But if we take the word "universe" to mean both space and time, and affirm that time itself had a beginning, then time only exists provided that the statement "God exists and the universe exists" is true, and time does not exist provided that the statement "God exists and the universe does not exist" is true. And if time does not exist, provided that the statement "God exists and the universe does not exist" is true, then there is no time at which that statement is true. But if that is the case, then must we not conclude that each of these statements cannot be true at different times, and so that to maintain that God existed at a time before the universe existed is self-contradictory? Would it not also lead to the conclusion that if God is the cause of the universe, the universe must co-exist eternally with Him and, therefore, has no beginning? Or would that only lead one to the bizarre, but not necessarily self-contradictory, conclusion that the universe had a beginning and yet there was no time at which the universe did not exist?

Travis

United States

Dr. Craig's Response

This is a delightful brainteaser, Travis! Your informal statement of the Law of Contradiction is, "Two mutually exclusive statements cannot both be true at the same time and in the same respect." Let's accept that statement. So consider the two statements:

1. God exists and the universe does not exist.

and

2. God exists and the universe exists.

These are, as you put it, mutually exclusive, that is to say, they cannot both be true without qualification. But why is that? Each statement is a conjunction, and there is obviously no incompatibility between their initial conjuncts—indeed, they are the same: "God exists." So any incompatibility between (1) and (2) has to be between their second conjuncts. Adding God to the picture does nothing to generate a contradiction, any more than if we were to add "Obama exists" as a conjunct to each. The real problem, then, is how

1*. The universe does not exist.

and

2*. The universe exists.

can both be true, since they are logically contradictory. The theist who believes that God created time and the universe believes that (1*) and (2*) are, indeed, both true in the actual world. But how can he avoid running afoul of the Law of Contradiction?

You say, "The only way to avoid a contradiction, if both are to be asserted, is to assert that each is true at a different time." But, as you point out, that is impossible, given that God created time. For at no time is (1*) true. To think that there was once such a time is to postulate a time before time began, which is logically incoherent. So you are quite right to conclude that "each of these statements cannot be true at different times, and so . . . to maintain that God existed at a time before the universe existed is self-contradictory."

Is the defender of *creatio ex nihilo* thus trapped in self-contradiction? Not at all! For it does not follow from the Law of Contradiction that "the only way to avoid a contradiction, if both are to be asserted, is to assert that each is true at a different time." For the Law states merely that the two mutually exclusive statements "cannot both be true *at the same time*," not that they must be true *at different times*. And even though (1*) and (2*) are not true at different times, still they are not true at the same time. (2*) is true at every time (assuming that time begins at creation); but (1*) is true but not true at any time. (1*) is true relative to the state of affairs of the actual world, which is God, existing timelessly sans the universe. This state of affairs is causally prior to the universe but not temporally prior to the universe.

So it does not then follow that "if God is the cause of the universe, the universe must co-exist eternally with Him and, therefore, has no beginning." God existing alone sans the universe is simply timeless, and time comes into being with the universe at the moment of creation. Hence (1) and (2) do not violate the Law of Contradiction: they are not true at the same time.

So I agree with and wholeheartedly endorse "the bizarre but not necessarily self-contradictory conclusion that the universe had a beginning and yet there was no time at which the universe did not exist." (This conclusion is actually an implication of the standard model of big bang cosmology!) What I would add is the even stranger, but non-contradictory, conclusion that God exists timelessly without the universe and that (1) is true relative to that state of affairs.

Tenseless Time and Identity over Time

Hi, Dr. Craig, I'm from Brazil. I watched your interview with Robert Lawrence Kuhn (host of PBS' "Closer to Truth"),[9] in which you distinguished two philosophical views of time. The first one is the tensed view of time.

9. You can watch this for free at ReasonableFaith.org (http://bit.ly/KuhnGodTime).

But I have wondered deeply about the tenseless one. In this view, the past, the present and the future are equally real and the observed "tenseness" of time is just an illusion of our minds.

Here is the problem: if the positions (a) and (b) of an observed electron (x) are simultaneously real, then the statement "electron (x) is electron (x)" would be false, which means that the principle of identity would be false too. Is that right?

The tenseless model has some other absurd implications:

- If all the states of my mind are simultaneously real, why in the world do I have this dynamic illusion?
- Am I already dead but not aware of it?
- Moreover, I think that it entails that the nature of our minds isn't material.

If this model of time is indeed so absurd, why does Stephen Hawking embrace it despite all odds? Is modern science that much incompatible with our awareness of the world? Or is Hawking just making the same mistake as Einstein did regarding the expansion of space just to avoid the beginning of the Cosmos?

I'm not an English native writer, but I did my best. God bless you Dr. Craig!

Daniel

Brazil

Dr. Craig's Response

I'm so encouraged by the number of astute Christians in Brazil whom we are encountering through Reasonable Faith. As Brazil emerges to superpower status during this century and as the Christian church there continues to burgeon, it gives grounds for great optimism about the future.

Your perceptive question, Daniel, is one that I've addressed in my essay "McTaggart's Paradox and the Problem of Temporary Intrinsics."[10] For those who are unfamiliar with the background of Daniel's question, let me explain that, broadly speaking, there are two

10. Published in *Analysis* 58 (1998): 122–27.

competing views of the nature of time: the tensed view, which holds that temporal becoming is a real, objective feature of the world, and the tenseless view, which holds that all moments of time, whether past, present, or future, are equally real and existent, so that temporal becoming is an illusion of human consciousness. Philosophers are deeply divided as to which view is correct.

Now, what Daniel has noticed is that the tenseless view has a very strange implication. Consider some entity *x* that exists at two different moments of time. Rather than an electron, let *x* be you yourself, to sharpen the paradox. It follows from the Principle of the Indiscernibility of Identicals that you are not the same person who existed just one minute ago! For on the tenseless theory of time, these are two distinct objects occupying different locations in space-time. Moreover, they have different properties: the later person may have a slightly different shape or a few less molecules. So they cannot be identical, since they have discernible properties.

What this implies is not that the tenseless time theorist must abandon the principle of identity, since that is a necessary truth of logic, but rather that the tenseless time theorist must hold that intrinsic change is impossible and that nothing actually endures through time! These consequences are generally acknowledged by tenseless time theorists. They hold that what we call persons are just three-dimensional slices of four-dimensional space-time "worms." The various slices are different objects, just as the different slices of a loaf of bread are. One slice does not turn into another, nor does any undergo intrinsic change. The appearance of change arises because the various temporal slices have different intrinsic properties. There is no more intrinsic change in objects over time than in a loaf of bread that tapers from large slices at one end to small slices at the other.

I agree with you, Daniel, that this seems really crazy. I have every reason to believe that there is at least one thing that endures through intrinsic change, namely, I myself. I existed a second ago, and despite the changes which have taken place in me, I still exist now. No sane person really believes that he is not the same person who existed a minute ago. Moreover, the tenseless view is incompatible with moral responsibility, praise, and blame. The non-conscious, four-dimensional object of which I am a part cannot be regarded as a moral agent and is, therefore, not morally responsible for anything. One might say that the spatio-temporal slices or parts of such objects are moral agents. But then it becomes impossible to hold one slice responsible for what another slice has done. How can one person be blamed and punished for what an entirely distinct, different person did? Why should I be punished for his crimes? By the same token, how can moral praise be given to a person for what some other, no longer existent person did? Why should I, who have done nothing, get the credit for the heroism of some other person?

This argument has serious theological ramifications, for Christian theism affirms not only that people are responsible moral agents but also that God is just in holding them responsible for their deeds.

Your second objection about the explanation of the illusion of temporal becoming is also a pressing problem. On the tenseless view, mental events themselves are strung out in a tenseless series just as physical events are and are all equally real. My now-awareness of tomorrow is just as real as my now-awareness of today. The experience of the successive becoming of experiences is illusory. Experiences do not really come to be and pass away. But that flies in the face of the phenomenology of time consciousness. It denies that we experience the becoming of our experiences. For if we do have such an experience, then we must ask all over again whether that experience is mind-dependent or not, and so on. To halt a vicious infinite regress, the tenseless time theorist must deny that we do experience the becoming of experiences. But such a phenomenology is obviously inaccurate.

I'm not sure why you say that the tenseless view implies materialism with respect to human beings; but tenseless time theorists are for the most part wedded to naturalistic epistemology and so would in any case be ill-disposed to any mind-body dualism.

So why does someone like Stephen Hawking espouse a tenseless view of time? I think that the main reason is that physics finds it useful to treat time and space as a four-dimensional entity called space-time in which temporal becoming plays no part. Relativity Theory in particular becomes perspicuous in such a context. Unfortunately, far too many physicists, having never studied philosophy, naively take this geometrical representation as a piece of metaphysics rather than as a merely heuristic device. One, therefore, has to be very cautious about the statements of physicists when it comes to the nature of time.

3

ON ATHEISM AND MEANING IN LIFE

Is Life Absurd without God?

Dr. Craig,

Though I respect you as one of today's most rational Christian thinkers, I passionately disagree with your assertion that life without God is absurd. The arguments you proffer to support this are quite superficial, and it is unfortunate that intelligent philosophers like yourself have fallen prey to accepting these monstrosities. In your work on the subject, you seem to put forth two basic contentions,

(1) that life without God is devoid of ultimate meaning, purpose, and value and
(2) that theism can provide ultimate meaning, purpose, and value.

Now, I think that the issue of human value can be considered separately from the other two (none of which you bother defining first); but regarding the meaning and purpose of life, I believe that Thomas Nagel has eloquently refuted (1) and (2) in his paper "The Absurd."

In defense of (1), you appear to argue that life on atheism is absurd because God and immortality conditions you declare are necessary for an objectively meaningful life are absent on such a view. You give some informal quasi-arguments for this grand claim, namely by contending that (a) life is absurd on atheism because of the man's inability to evade the heat death of the universe, (b) his insignificance in the cosmos, and (c) his ultimate death. Regarding (a), you ask, "Suppose the universe had never existed. What ultimate difference would that make? The universe is doomed to die anyway." Nagel poignantly replies in his paper as follows:

It is often remarked that nothing we do now will matter in a million years. But if that is true, then by the same token, nothing that will be the case in a million years matters now. In particular, it does not matter now that in a million years nothing we do now will matter. Moreover, even if what we did now were going to matter in a million years, how could that keep out present concerns from being absurd? If their mattering now is not enough to accomplish that, how would it help if they mattered a million years from now?

Whether what we do now will matter in a million years could make the crucial difference only if its mattering in a million years depended on its mattering, period. But then to deny that whatever happens now will matter in a million years is to beg the question against its mattering, period; for in that sense one cannot know that it will not matter in a million years whether (for example) someone now is happy or miserable, without knowing that it does not matter, period.

It is also worth noting that your entire argument is a non sequitur, for even if one concedes that our actions will lose their meaning, it is undeniable that they will always have had meaning in the past; facts about the past like these cannot be obliterated with the passage of time. Moreover, one could go even further and adopt the mainstream B-theory of time, in which the past is as real as the present, meaning that human actions will always have meaning!

On (b), you suggest man's spatial and temporal insignificance with the universe, which is far larger and older than humanity, stating that "[m]ankind is thus no more significant than a swarm of mosquitoes or a barnyard of pigs." Again, Nagel argues that such egocentric notions are false:

What we say to convey the absurdity of our lives often has to do with space or time: we are tiny specks in the infinite vastness of the universe; our lives are mere instants even on a geological time scale, let alone a cosmic one; we will all be dead any minute. But of course none of these evident facts can be what makes life absurd, if it is absurd. For suppose we lived forever; would not a life that is absurd if it lasts seventy years be infinitely absurd if it lasted through eternity? And if our lives are absurd given our present size, why would they be any less absurd if we filled the universe?

Finally, concerning (c), you allege that atheism teaches that: "You are the accidental by-product of nature, a result of matter plus time plus chance. There is no reason for your existence. All you face is death." Nagel responds admirably:

> Another inadequate argument is that because we are going to die, all chains of justification [of meaning] must leave off in mid-air ... All of it is an elaborate journey leading nowhere ...
>
> There are several replies to this argument. First, life does not consist of a sequence of activities each of which has as its purpose some later member of the sequence ... No further justification is needed to make it reasonable to take aspirin for a headache, attend an exhibit of the work a painter one admires, or stop a child from putting his hand on a hot stove ...
>
> Even if someone wishes to supply a further justification for [things], that justification would have to end somewhere too. If nothing can justify unless it is justified in terms of something outside itself, which is also justified, then an infinite regress results, and no chain of justification can be complete. Moreover, if a finite chain of reasons cannot justify anything, what could be accomplished by an infinite chain, each link of which must be justified by something outside itself? [Note: you ought to believe that such a regress is impossible, given your stance on actual infinites in the context of the Kalam cosmological argument.]
>
> Since justifications must come to an end somewhere, nothing is gained by denying that they end where they appear to, within life or by trying to subsume the multiple, often trivial ordinary justifications of action under a single, controlling life scheme. We can be satisfied more easily than that. In fact, through its misrepresentation of the process of justification, the argument makes a vacuous demand. It insists that the reasons available within life are incomplete, but suggests thereby that all reasons that come to an end are incomplete. This makes it impossible to supply any reasons at all.

For these reasons raised in Nagel's paper, then, I cannot bring myself to rationally accept your arguments for the supposed absurdity of life sans God.

Now, concerning (2), Nagel offers a brilliant argument against a theistic foundation for the meaning of life. First, he defines absurdity as the conspicuous discrepancy between pretension or aspiration and reality (e.g., as you are being knighted, your pants fall down). According to Nagel, the absurdity of life arises from the clash "between the seriousness with which we take our lives and the perpetual possibility of regarding everything about which we are serious as arbitrary, or open to doubt." To understand this, it first helps to distinguish between the engaged and detached perspectives of life. In the engaged perspective, we assume that life is meaningful as we strive to survive, reproduce, and enjoy ourselves. However, according to Nagel, one can always step back "out of life" and examine it from the third person viewpoint, entering the detached perspective. From there, he can then ask, "Why is this meaningful?," and if he receives an answer to that, he can continually step back, enter the detached perspective, and repeat the process infinitely.

Now, suppose that theism is true and God created man to glorify him and enjoy him forever. While this first might sound meaningful from the engaged perspective, one can always step back into the detached perspective and ask, "Why is glorifying and enjoying God meaningful? Is this really it?" In other words, (2) is incoherent; the desire for an ultimate meaning to life might be just as irrational as the desire for married bachelors. Moreover, following the orders of God does not seem like a very fulfilling or satisfying meaning to life. If instead God was simply bored and decided to create humans to watch them mercilessly slaughter one another for his pleasure, I would do everything I could to promote peace and love to actively stop this evil being's capricious demands. That would be my meaning of life in such a world. [Note: you cannot appeal to God's omnibenevolence to dismiss this issue, since you say in your article on the Canaanites that God does not have moral duties since he cannot command himself.] Nagel further adds:

> But a role in some larger enterprise cannot confer significance unless that enterprise is itself significant . . . If we learned that we were being raised to provide food for other creatures fond of human flesh [then] even if we learned that the human race had been developed by animal breeders precisely for this purpose, that would still not give our lives meaning, for two reasons. First, we would still be in the dark

as to the significance of the lives of those other beings; second, although we might acknowledge that this culinary role would make our lives meaningful to them, it is not clear how it would make them meaningful to us.

But finally, even if you think these unanswerable problems can be resolved, I think it's a bit disingenuous to argue in this fashion, for even if you're right that life really is absurd without God, that does not imply in the slightest that God exists. One cannot simply change reality by wishing something to be the case; propositions must be supported by epistemic arguments, not pragmatic ones.

So, ultimately, do you think Nagel's response succeeds? Or it is absurd? And in either case, why?

Best,
Bennington
Ireland

Dr. Craig's Response

Thank you for your comments, Bennington! These are questions to be passionate about, for they touch us at the core of our being. I felt deeply the absurdity of life and its attendant despair during my non-Christian years. When I later encountered the French existentialists, their message struck a chord in me. It does seem to me that if atheism is true, then life is, in the final analysis, absurd.

I've tried to analyze the absurdity of life in terms of life's lacking ultimate meaning, value, and purpose. The word "ultimate" is important here, for obviously we can have subsidiary purposes and conditional values without God, but my claim is that ultimately nothing really matters if there is no God. It seems to me that there are two prerequisites to an ultimately meaningful, valuable, and purposeful life, namely, God and immortality, and if God does not exist, then we have neither.

By "meaning" I mean something like significance or importance. By "purpose" I mean a *telos* or goal of life. By "value" I mean objective moral values and duties. We mustn't separate off the question of value from meaning and purpose, as you try to do in your question, for if there are objective moral values and duties, then life is likely to be meaningful. So the atheist can't say that life can be ultimately meaningful in the absence of God because there are truly valuable things in life, since if I'm right, there aren't any objective moral values in the absence of God. These three elements, while distinct, are interrelated and hang together.

Now, in your question you tend to run my arguments together and omit others. With respect to (a) what I claim is that without personal immortality our lives ultimately have no meaning or purpose. (I also argue that the same would be the case without God, even given immortality.) I find Nagel's response to this point to be confused. He seems to be using the phrase "does not matter" equivocally, to mean either "is ultimately insignificant" or "makes no difference." When we clarify the meanings, then his argument makes no sense: "If what we do now is ultimately insignificant because it will make no difference in a million years, then what happens in a million years is also ultimately insignificant because it makes no difference to what we do now." That doesn't make sense because the arrow of time is from past to future. To see if what happens in a million years makes any difference, you don't look to its impact on today but to its impact on the future, and there isn't any in the end. So, of course, in the absence of backward causation, it makes no difference now what will happen in a million years. The point is that what happens now or in a million years makes no ultimate difference on the outcome of the universe.

So, in a sense, Nagel is right that what happens a million years from now is ultimately meaningless and so never matters and so doesn't matter now. But the point remains that without immortality nothing we do makes any ultimate difference. Maybe Nagel's claim is that it doesn't matter that nothing matters; but that doesn't deny my point that it doesn't matter, that there is no ultimate meaning. I agree with him that immortality alone is not sufficient for ultimate meaning: mere prolongation of existence isn't enough. But it is a necessary condition.

As for your point that past facts always remain past facts, that does not invest those facts with any ultimate importance in the grand scheme of things. It will always be the case that the Third Reich went down to defeat in World War II, but so what? Everything is doomed to end up in the same lifeless, featureless condition of the cold heat death of the universe. It is ultimately insignificant who won the Second World War (don't say that it mattered because good triumphed over evil, for then you're assuming the reality of objective moral values without God).

As for (b), my point in the passage you quote was rather that in the absence of God we were not created with a purpose in mind; we are the blind by-product of the evolutionary process. That seems to me undeniable on atheism. I do also make the point that we are insignificant specks and so it is hard to see why our lives have any ultimate importance (again, you can't say that our moral worth overcomes our insignificance). Here, Nagel misses my point entirely. He asserts that if we were extended throughout all space and time, that would not invest our lives with ultimate significance. But I agree with that! He's confusing necessary with sufficient conditions. Immortality is a necessary but not a sufficient condition for ultimate meaning; we also need God, as I have argued.

As for (c), this is again the point that in the absence of God we are blind products of the evolutionary process and, therefore, have not been created with any purpose in view. But I do also make the point that in the absence of immortality there is no ultimate purpose for our lives, since whatever we do, we end up the same: utter extinction. I don't see the relevance of Nagel's first point. How does my claim require that everything we do is done purposefully? That doesn't show that on atheism life has an ultimate purpose. Nor am I advocating an infinite chain of justifying purposes. Rather the chain ends in God. We were made to know God, and our ultimate fulfillment is found in being properly related to Him, the source of infinite goodness and love. I obviously don't hold that "all reasons that come to an end are incomplete." Rather the key question for us here is whether there is an adequate end for bringing the chain to completion. On atheism there is no such end. There is no reason for which we exist.

So, Bennington, it seems to me that these aren't very good responses. They confuse necessary and sufficient conditions and don't even take account of my arguments that God, as well as immortality, is a necessary condition for ultimate meaning, value, and purpose.

Turn now to point (2), that on biblical theism life does have ultimate meaning, value, and purpose. Look at theism from a detached perspective. Does it supply conditions sufficient for ultimate meaning, value, and purpose? Well, it certainly seems to, and a good many atheists ruefully admit that it does. It invests our lives with eternal significance: by our free choices we determine our eternal destiny. Moreover, we come into personal relation with the supreme good, God Himself. Moreover, God supplies the basis for objective moral values and duties, as I've argued elsewhere. Finally, God created us for the purpose of knowing Him and His love forever. So from the most detached, philosophical perspective you can take, biblical theism supplies the conditions for a meaningful and valuable life. If you ask, "Is this really it?" the answer is "Yes, it can't get any better than this!"

Now, if you say that there cannot be a self-justifying end, then it is you who are assuming that the chain of justifications must be infinite and cannot be complete—a position you earlier rightly rejected. The point is that with God we have reached an end that is truly worthy and capable of being an intrinsically good and meaningful stopping point.

If you think the theistic answer is incoherent, like desiring a married bachelor, then you need to show some logical incompatibility in what I've said, which, so far as I can tell, you haven't tried to do.

Now, you say, "Moreover, following the orders of God does not seem like a very fulfilling or satisfying meaning to life." Ah, ah, Bennington, you've left the detached perspective and lapsed back into the engaged perspective. From the detached perspective the theistic answer is entirely adequate, whether or not you find it satisfying or fulfilling yourself.

Besides, your engaged judgment is spoken as a true non-Christian. As someone whose life has been transformed by the love of God, I, by contrast, find from the engaged perspective nothing more fulfilling than knowing Him. Obedience to His commands comes, not grudgingly, but gratefully and eagerly from a willing heart.

Your hypothesis about God's character is impossible, so it is pointless. Remember that on my view, although God does not act *from* duty He nonetheless acts *in accordance* with duty because of His essentially kind and just character. Therefore, His commands are not capricious but necessary reflections of His nature. When you say that the meaning of your life would be to oppose a capricious God, you have lapsed into thinking of meaning not objectively but subjectively. I've never denied we can invent subjective meanings for our lives (like hitting 60 home runs in a season). What I claim is that on atheism our lives would have no objective meaning.

Finally, as to Nagel's point about humans being raised for food, that only reinforces my point that the end for which we exist must be adequate for the purpose. That is why I argue that God is necessary, as well as immortality. As the highest good, the greatest conceivable being, God furnishes an adequate ending point to our quest.

As for your final point, if you've read my work, you know that I never argue for God's existence on the basis of the absurdity of life without God. I'm very explicit about this. Rather the purpose of this exercise is to arouse apathetic people from their stupor and get them to think about the importance of the question of God's existence, to get them to be as passionate as you are! Then, perhaps, they will be interested to hear my arguments for the existence of God.

No, I do not think Nagel's rejoinders are absurd. They are thoughtful, and worth considering. But in the end, I think they misfire and do nothing to show that on atheism life is not ultimately meaningless, valueless, and purposeless, nor that biblical theism fails to provide a framework for the affirmation of these same goods.

Is Unbelief Culpable?

Dear Dr. Craig,

I am a Brazilian Christian. Your work for the kingdom has been a tremendous help to me in my spiritual life.

I believe God exists, but I am troubled with a question. Christians are supposed to think that God will punish atheists for choosing not to believe. But how can a sincere atheist be blamed for not believing? I don't think belief is a choice.

Suppose your friends push you to believe in Santa Claus. Could you force yourself to believe in Santa? At most you can act like a believer, but you will never be a sincere believer. Therefore, you will be a hypocrite!

Now, suppose Santa Claus "asks" you to suffer for him. If you do not believe in Santa, will you have enough motivation to endure suffering for him? Can you be blamed for giving up suffering for Santa?

Jesus asks the believer to do more than suffer for Him. Christ asks the believer to hate his own life in this world (John 12:25). Now, how can an atheist have enough motivation for obeying Christ if he even not believes in Jesus?

If a sincere atheist thinks God is a fairy tale, how can he be blamed? If belief is not a choice, no one can be blamed for not believing. It seems absurd to punish an atheist for being an atheist like it is absurd to punish a dog for being a dog.

How should we respond to this objection?

Thank you!

Wagner

Brazil

Dr. Craig's Response

I find that contemporary atheists take great umbrage at the biblical claim that God holds people to be morally culpable for their unbelief. They want to maintain their unbelief in God without accepting the responsibility for it. This attitude enables them to reject God with impunity.

Now, we can agree that a person cannot be held morally responsible for failing to discharge a duty of which he is uninformed. So the entire question is: are people sufficiently informed to be held morally responsible for failing to believe in God? The biblical answer to that question is unequivocal. First, God has provided a revelation of Himself in nature that is sufficiently clear for all cognitively normal persons to know that God exists. Paul writes to the Roman church:

> The wrath of God is being revealed from heaven against all the godlessness and wickedness of men, who suppress the truth by their wickedness, since what may be known about God is plain to them, because God has made it plain to them. For since the creation of the world God's invisible qualities—his eternal power and divine nature—have been clearly seen, being understood from what has been made, so that men are without excuse.
>
> For although they knew God, they neither glorified him as God nor gave thanks to him, but their thinking became futile and their foolish hearts were darkened. (Rom. 1:18–21)

In Paul's view, God's properties, His eternal power and deity, are clearly revealed in creation, so that people who fail to believe in an eternal, powerful Creator of the world are without excuse. Indeed, Paul says that they actually *do* know that God exists, but they suppress this truth because of their unrighteousness. As a result they become so clouded in their thinking that they may actually deceive themselves into thinking that they are open-minded inquirers honestly pursuing the truth. The human capacity for rationalization and self-deception, I'm sure we've all observed, is very great indeed, and in the biblical view, atheists are prey to it.

Second, wholly apart from God's revelation in nature is the inner witness which the Holy Spirit bears to the great truths of the gospel, including, I should say, the fact that God exists. Anyone who fails to believe in God by the end of his lifetime does so only by a stubborn resistance to the work of the Holy Spirit in drawing that person to a knowledge of God. On the biblical view, people are not like innocent, lost lambs wandering helplessly without a guide. Rather they are determined rebels whose wills are set against God and who must be subdued by God's Spirit.

The difference, then, between God and Santa Claus is that (i) there is good evidence in support of God's existence that is evident to all, and (ii) there is an objective witness of God's Spirit that warrants belief in Christian truths. Of course, the unbeliever will deny that there is such evidence and such a witness of the Spirit. Fine; we Christians disagree with them about that. We think they're mistaken. That's why we engage them in dialogue, to show them that the evidence is sufficient and that their objections are weak.

Contrary to what you say, Wagner, on the biblical view, unbelief is a choice. It is a choice to resist the force of the evidence and the drawing of God's Holy Spirit. The unbeliever is like someone dying of a fatal disease who refuses to believe the medical evidence concerning the efficacy of a proffered cure and who rejects the testimony of his doctor to it and who, as a result, suffers the consequence of his own stubbornness. He has no one to blame but himself.

INSIGHT
Note how the final paragraph summarizes the relevant claims of Dr. Craig's answer. His two main reasons for the culpability of unbelief are salient.

Atheists and agnostics are not like dogs. They are persons created in the image of God, endowed with freedom of the will, and pursued by a loving heavenly Father who yearns to reconcile them with Himself. Their unbelief is culpable because it is maintained in the face of the evidence and in defiance of the Holy Spirit.

Deism and Christian Theism

I am a former Christian. Through deep soul-searching and intellectual honesty, I have come to be skeptical of the so-called truths of the Christian doctrines, and have rejected "revealed" religion altogether. I think it violates the free will argument for one, and I am also aware of the eager human proclivity to make claims of divine inspiration, especially in biblical times. I have also become convinced of our evolutionary history, yet unable to reach perfect harmony in theistic evolution (a la Miller and Collins).

231

I am, however, unconvinced of materialist assertions that we arrived here spontaneously by mere chance. I find the kalam cosmological argument intellectually/logically compelling. This has led me in the direction of deism (a la Thomas Paine). This has been an internally painful and lonely journey for me (losing my Christian roots); but I feel like I'm being honest with myself, and am better able to defend my belief system. Am I wrong?

Paul

Canada

Dr. Craig's Response

Yeah, I think you are, Paul. But I'm not discouraged! The Grand Canyon separating deism from atheism is vastly greater than the gulch between deism and Christian theism. Once you've got a robust theism in place, it's not too hard to bridge the gap to Christian theism.

So let's begin where you are.

INSIGHT

Note Dr. Craig's approach, beginning the discussion where Paul is at in his beliefs.

You're skeptical of materialist claims that we arrived here by chance. That implies, given your commitment to our evolutionary history, that you think that the evolution of intelligent life must be superintended in some way by a guiding intelligence. That puts you in the same camp as Michael Behe, whose book *The Edge of Evolution* I recommend, if you don't already know it. You may also want to watch my debate with evolutionary biologist Francisco Ayala[11] on the viability of intelligent design as a hypothesis concerning biological complexity. Ayala, though an ardent Darwinian, is very candid that when biologists affirm that "evolution is a fact," what they are talking about is common descent. But he says that "evolution," when defined as either a reconstruction of the evolutionary tree of life or as an account of the mechanisms that explain evolutionary change, is very uncertain and a matter of ongoing study. So your position on intelligent design is

11. You can access this debate for free by going to ReasonableFaith.org (http://bit.ly/CraigAuala).

eminently defensible. You don't say enough to explain your reservations with Kenneth Miller's or Francis Collins' views on theistic evolution for me to comment; but your deism suggests that you do hold to some sort of theistic evolutionary account.

Moreover, you're persuaded by the *kalam* cosmological argument for a personal Creator of the universe. This argument gives us an uncaused, beginningless, timeless, spaceless, immaterial, enormously powerful, personal Creator of the universe, who, as we may infer from the design argument above, designed the universe and the Earth to bring forth intelligent beings like ourselves.

Now, if such a Creator and Designer exists and has brought us into existence, doesn't that suggest to you that He would have some purpose in mind which He would want us to know so that we might achieve the ends for which He created us? This consideration ought to make us take the claims of revealed religion, or at least the claims of the great monotheistic faiths that are consistent with the existence of such a transcendent Creator and Designer, very seriously.

Your misgivings about revealed religion are too vaguely expressed for me to know exactly what the obstacle is for you. You say it "violates the free will argument." I'm not sure what you mean. Are you equating Christianity with that minority of Christian denominations that deny human free will? If so, why not go with the majority? I think that the biblical view that people sin against God is proof positive that in the biblical view human beings are free agents before God, since God is not the author of sin.

You also express misgivings about "the eager human proclivity to make claims of divine inspiration, especially in biblical times." I'm not sure that such a proclivity existed in biblical times. Take the New Testament books, for example. Where will you find in the gospels or Acts any claim to be writing by divine inspiration? There is none. Instead, we find claims to have looked into eyewitnesses testimony about the events of Jesus' life (Luke 1:1–4; John 21:24). There just is no appeal to divine inspiration on the part of Jesus' biographers.

So why don't you do what most New Testament scholars do: set aside the theological conviction that the gospels are inspired and look at them as ordinary historical documents about the life of this remarkable man, Jesus of Nazareth? What you'll find, Paul, is that we have more information about this relatively obscure man than we do about most *major* figures of antiquity! It's really quite amazing when you think about it.

So what do we learn about the historical Jesus when we examine these documents critically, as we would other ancient biographical works? As I have sought to show in my published work, we discover a man who had a radical self-consciousness of being the unique

Son of God and eschatological Son of Man prophesied by the prophet Daniel. Moreover, and most surprisingly, we have very good grounds for affirming that this man, after being executed by crucifixion, was buried in a tomb by a named individual, that His tomb was then found empty by a group of His women followers, that various individuals and groups on multiple occasions and under different circumstances saw appearances of Him alive, and that His disciples, against every predisposition to the contrary, suddenly and sincerely began to proclaim that God had raised Him from the dead. I can think of no better explanation for these facts than the one the disciples gave. But if God has raised Jesus from the dead, then we have very good grounds for thinking that the God of Israel revealed by Jesus of Nazareth is the true God.

None of this depends on divine inspiration. Whether, having come to believe in the claims of the religion revealed by Jesus, you take the logically subsequent step of regarding the gospels as divinely inspired is a secondary question. As you consider whether the Creator and Designer of the world has revealed Himself in some way that we can know Him more fully, why not look into Jesus?

4

ON THEOLOGY AND SCIENCE

Is Scientism Self-Refuting?

Dear Dr. Craig,

How would you reply to this argument that scientism is not self-refuting: Scientism has always been successful in the past; any supernaturalistic explanations used by our progenitors have been replaced by naturalistic explanations. Never has a supernaturalistic explanation superseded a naturalistic one. Since the predictions of scientism have always been later confirmed directly by the evidence, this amounts to a good inductive argument for scientism. So Craig is wrong that scientism cannot be scientifically proven because scientism's own success and adoption by scientists serves as evidence for its truth.

Basically, the person I quoted is a friend of mine who treats scientism itself as a scientific theory and argues that it is inductively warranted and evidenced. Hence, he alleges that it is not self-refuting. He also thinks that this strategy can be extended to evidentialism (I found this out when I tried explaining Reformed Epistemology to him). He rejects your other argument against scientism that science cannot account for mathematical truths (because he is an empiricist about mathematics and logic), morality (he is a nihilist), and aesthetics (he is a nihilist about that, too). The most disturbing thing is that I have seen other self-styled empiricists on the Internet run similar arguments to these. How should I respond to these types of assertions?

Thank you,

Neel

United States

Dr. Craig's Response

Neel, your friend is confusing *scientism* (an epistemological thesis) with *naturalism* (an ontological thesis). Scientism is the view that we should believe only what can be proven scientifically. In other words, science is the sole source of knowledge and the sole arbiter of truth. Naturalism is the view that physical events have only physical causes. In other words, miracles do not happen; there are no supernatural causes.

These theses are obviously different. A person could accept other sources of knowledge besides science, such as rational intuition, and still be a naturalist. Similarly, one could hold to an epistemology of scientism and yet be a non-naturalist. For example, the late W. V. O. Quine, who held that physical science is our only basic source of knowledge, freely admitted, "If I saw indirect explanatory benefit in positing *sensibilia*, *possibilia*, spirits, a Creator, I would joyfully accord them scientific status too, on a par with such avowedly scientific posits as quarks and black holes."[12] Thus, scientism does not imply naturalism, nor does naturalism imply scientism.

So leaving aside for the moment the question of naturalism, what problems are there with scientism? There are two that are especially significant. First, *scientism is too restrictive a theory of knowledge.* It would, if adopted, compel us to abandon wide swaths of what most of us take to be fields of human knowledge. Your friend admits this with regard to moral and aesthetic truths. On his view there is nothing good or evil, right or wrong, beautiful or ugly. But is it plausible to think that there are no aesthetic or moral truths? On your friend's view there's nothing wrong with torturing a little girl to death. Why should we accept such a conclusion simply because of a epistemological restriction? Isn't this a signal that we need rather to broaden the scope of our theory so as to encompass other types of knowledge? Your friend says he will treat logical and mathematical truths as merely empirical truths. Good luck! Truths like "If p implies q, and p, then q" or "2 + 2 = 4" are to all appearances necessary truths, not merely empirical generalizations. And what about science itself? Science is permeated with assumptions that cannot be scientifically proven, so that an epistemology of scientism would destroy science itself. For example, the principle of induction cannot be scientifically justified. Just because A has always been succeeded by B in the past provides no warrant for inferring that the next A will be followed by B. For we could be at the beginning

12. W. V. Quine, "Naturalism; or, Living within One's Means," *Dialectica* 49 (1995), 252.

of a chaotic series of As and Bs whose initial segment is ordered ABABAB. So trying to provide "a good inductive argument for scientism" is hopeless, since it must presuppose the validity of inductive reasoning.

Secondly, *scientism is self-refuting*. Scientism tells us that we should not believe any proposition that cannot be scientifically proven. But what about that very proposition itself? It cannot itself be scientifically proven. Therefore we should not believe it. Scientism thus defeats itself. Your friend's proffered argument for scientism is not an argument for *scientism* but for *naturalism*. He's arguing that the assumption that there are only natural causes operative in the world has achieved extraordinary success in contrast to the assumption that there are supernatural causes as well. That has no relevance to the epistemological question before us. It is at best an argument against miracles. Actually, it's much weaker than that: it is at best an argument for *methodological* naturalism, that is to say, the view that in doing natural science we should assume that all physical events have only natural causes. The methodological naturalist needn't be a metaphysical naturalist, that is to say, he needn't deny that miracles occur or that supernatural entities exist. He contends merely that they are not the concern of science. Science just *is* the search for natural causes or explanations of phenomena. This methodological thesis is one that a great many, if not most, Christian scientists agree with. So your friend's argument really doesn't amount to much.

As Michael Rea has shown in his incisive book *World without Design*[13] the only defensible form of epistemological naturalism (a.k.a. scientism) is that it is a methodological decision to follow a research program that takes the physical sciences to be the only basic source of knowledge. As such it cannot be justified. It just represents the naturalist's personal decision to adopt a certain research program. Anyone else can with equal right adopt a different research program that may accept additional sources of knowledge in addition to the physical sciences.

One final note about your friend's argument for naturalism: *of course*, no supernaturalistic explanation has ever superseded a naturalistic one! That's guaranteed by science's assumption of methodological naturalism. It prohibits supernatural explanations from even being included in the pool of live explanatory options. Thus it's impossible for a supernaturalistic explanation to supersede a naturalistic one! Only for theorists who are willing to challenge the assumption of methodological naturalism, like creation scientists

---

13. Michael C. Rea, *World without Design: The Ontological Consequences of Naturalism* (Oxford: Clarendon Press, 2002).

or advocates of intelligent design, is there the possibility that a naturalistic explanation might give way to a supernaturalistic explanation. They argue that it should in the case of biological complexity. But because they are working with a conception of science outside the mainstream (namely, they reject methodological naturalism), it's highly unlikely that their view will ever become the paradigmatic view of science, no matter what the evidence.

I note as well that in nearly two thousand years no naturalistic explanation has managed to supersede the resurrection of Jesus, a supernaturalistic explanation if there ever was one, of the facts concerning the fate of Jesus of Nazareth.

On Evolutionary Theory and Theism

Dear Dr. Craig

I want to start off by thanking you for what you've done for Christianity and for Jesus both in your written work and all throughout your career.

However, I do still have two questions regarding the nature of evolution and God's role to play.

1) Stephen Meyer, who is an American scholar, philosopher of biology, and advocate for intelligent design says, "Evolution is a purposeless, undirected process. No one, not even God, can direct an undirected process or give purpose to a purposeless process." He also has called theistic evolution an oxymoron. And yet he is not alone among many biologists. There's a trend to think like this in the United States. A 2009 poll by Pew Research Center found that 87 percent of scientists say evolution is due to natural processes, such as natural selection, genetic drift, and random mutation. So, does that really bother your theism?

2) If you do accept evolution, at what point did humans become human?

Did God sort of intervene in this point of history when He decided this creature is special? Because in evolution, a species is always the same as its parent; there is no one time in the history of any species where you can say "that's a new species." Why did God favor this one creature as opposed to the very similar

Homo heidelbergensis,

Homo neanderthalensis,

Homo floresiensis,

Homo habilis,

Homo georgicus,

Homo erectus,

Homo ergaster,

Homo antecessor, etc.

Many of these displayed human-like behavior and may have asked the "why" question also. So, does that bother your theism either?

Andrew

United Kingdom

Dr. Craig's Response

No, Andrew, neither point is bothersome for theism, it seems to me.

(1) I disagree with Steve Meyer's statement because the terms "undirected" and "purposeless" are not being used univocally by the theist and the evolutionary biologist.

If they were, then evolutionary theory would be enormously presumptuous, since science is just not in a position to say with any justification that there is no divinely intended direction or goal of the evolutionary process. How could anyone say on the basis of scientific evidence that the whole scheme was not set up by a provident God to arrive at *homo sapiens* on planet Earth? How could a scientist know that God did not

INSIGHT

As simple as this comment may be, it is important to recognize in a debate or discussion whether the same terms are being used univocally or equivocally. Failure to attend to that question can (re)shape the trajectory of an interaction between two competing perspectives that use the same terms.

supernaturally intervene to cause the crucial mutations that led to important evolutionary transitions, for example, the reptile to bird transition? Indeed, given divine middle knowledge, not even such supernatural interventions are necessary, for God could have known that were certain initial conditions in place, then, given the laws of nature, certain life forms would evolve through random mutation and natural selection, and so He put such laws and initial conditions in place. Obviously, science is in no position whatsoever to say justifiably that the evolutionary process was not under the providence of a God endowed with middle knowledge who determined to create biological complexity by such means. So if the evolutionary biologist were using words like "undirected" and "purposeless" in the sense that the theist is using those words, evolutionary theory would be philosophy, not science (which is precisely what some theists allege).

But the evolutionary biologist is *not* using those words in the same sense as the theist. This fact, unacknowledged by both critics of theistic evolution and apologists for naturalistic evolution, became clear to me in the course of my preparation for my debate with Francisco Ayala on the tenability of Intelligent Design in biology.[14] According to Ayala, when the evolutionary biologist says that the mutations that lead to evolutionary development are random, the meaning of the word "random" is *not* "occurring by chance." Rather it means "irrespective of their usefulness to the organism."

Now, this is hugely significant! The scientist is not, despite the impression given by popularizers on both sides of the divide, making the presumptuous philosophical claim that biological mutations occur by chance and, hence, that the evolutionary process is undirected or purposeless. Rather he means that mutations do not occur for the benefit of the host organism. If we take "random" to mean "irrespective of usefulness to the organism," then randomness is not incompatible with direction or purpose. For example, suppose that God in His providence causes a mutation to occur in an organism, not for the benefit of the organism, but for some other reason (say, because it will produce easy prey for other organisms that He wants to flourish or even because it will eventually produce a fossil that I will someday find, which stimulates my interest in paleontology, so that I embark upon the career God had in mind for me). In such a case, the mutation is both purposeful and random.

By contrast, when an intelligent design theorist like Michael Behe uses the word "random," he means "not oriented to any goal." He says, "if 'random' is defined as 'not

14. You can access this debate for free by going to ReasonableFaith.org (http://bit.ly/CraigAyala).

oriented to any goal', then I think the ambiguities disappear and it does clearly conflict with intelligent design" (personal communication). Right! But that's *not* the sense in which evolutionary biologists (at least when they are being careful rather than sloppy) are using the word. Meyer and Behe are right that not only the theist but scientists in general should correct naturalists who assert, on the supposed authority of science, that the evolutionary process is "not oriented toward any goal," but such a correction is relevant, not to evolutionary theory, but to the philosophy of naturalism which tries to piggyback on legitimate science.

As for the Pew survey, I think you can now see why it is irrelevant to theism that "evolution is due to natural processes, such as natural selection, genetic drift, and random mutation." Of course, it is! The statement as you give it doesn't even say that it is due *only* to such factors. Many evolutionary biologists think that additional non-genetic factors also play a role as well. In fact, I'm shocked that only 87 percent of scientists think that evolution is due to the three factors you mention.

In a recent report from the National Center for Science Education, which self-advertises as "the premier institution dedicated to keeping evolution in the science classroom and creationism out," Daryl Domning writes:

> In truth, many (perhaps most!) evolutionists *are* theists of one sort or another. Their views are as sincerely and validly held as those of the atheists and have as much (perhaps more!) claim to be representative of evolutionist thinking. Atheists have every right to believe that theists are woefully misguided in failing to see the obsolescence of religion after Darwin; but that is their philosophical opinion, not an infallibly proven proposition of science or logic.[15]

That puts a very different face on the matter, doesn't it?

Regardless of the numbers, however, the point remains that non-univocal use of words has misled many people into thinking that evolutionary theory presents some sort of challenge to teleology and, hence, to theism. I tell you, Andrew, this is just one more of those cases that illustrate so powerfully the importance of careful *philosophical* thinking about science.[16]

---

15. Daryl P. Domning, "Winning Their Hearts and Minds: Who Should Speak for Evolution?" *Reports of the National Center for Science Education* 29:2 (March-April 2009), accessed online: http://bit.ly/Domning.

16. See Dr. Craig's "Naturalism and Intelligent Design," in *Intelligent Design*, Robert Stewart, ed. (Minneapolis: Fortress Press, 2007), 58–71.

(2) As an anthropological dualist who thinks that human beings are body/soul composites, I think that a hominid animal, however advanced, which lacks a human soul is not a human being. So it really doesn't matter whether or not there was a sharp dividing line biologically between pre-human hominids and human beings. In any case, anthropologists to my knowledge have not been able to come to any sort of consensus on the tree of human ancestry, so that all the hominids you mention may simply be dead ends on the tree of primate evolution which never led to man.

Were Neanderthals truly human? God knows! I don't need to know exactly when humans emerged in the evolutionary process in order to maintain that in God's providence a first human being did arrive on the scene. So while your question poses an intriguing puzzle, I don't see that a theist needs to be able to answer it in order for theism to be rational to hold. Indeed, the existence of so improbable a biological organism as man is perhaps itself evidence that the evolutionary process, if it led to human beings, is under the supervision of a provident Designer.

Who Speaks for Science?

Dear Bill:

I hope you're doing well. A couple of people forwarded me (in distress) your response to "Evolutionary Theory and Theism."

As you no doubt know, your answer is similar to the one that Al Plantinga gives in his important book *Where the Conflict Really Lies*. Unfortunately, I think you're making the same mistake that Al makes. (I still love his book and have made it required reading for our summer seminars). You and Al are two of the most prominent and able defenders of the faith on the planet. So a mistake on this point is profoundly consequential.

Of course you're right that scientists are not *justified* in claiming that the history of life is the result of a purposeless process—that is, the empirical evidence doesn't establish anything like that (quite the contrary, in my opinion). The question, however, is what Darwinists typically claim for their theory and for the evidence. I think you're confusing what evolutionary biologists are *justified* in saying with what they typically are saying.

It's true that if the word "random" in evolutionary theory, Neo-Darwinism, etc., means merely something like "irrespective of their usefulness to the organism," then it's logically compatible with theism and teleology (though even this definition clearly excludes all sorts of possible divine activity and goes far beyond the empirical evidence). In your post, you quote Francisco Ayala to establish the official definition of "random" in biology. But why would you trust Francisco Ayala on something of this nature? He has devoted much of his career since he lost his faith by studying (Darwinian) evolutionary theory, trying to convince Christians that they have nothing to worry about (he had been a Dominican priest). He tells Christians that there's no conflict between Darwinism and Christianity, but if that is so, one might wonder why Ayala lost his faith once he came to identify with Darwinism.

But that's a tangential issue. The crucial question is this: Do evolutionary biologists, Neo-Darwinists, etc., consistently and representatively restrict their explanations in this way? Absolutely not. Biologists in general, and most presentations of (Neo-Darwinian) biological evolution, are not careful to circumscribe the meaning of "random" or "chance." One can construct an ideal form of the theory that avoids the metaphysical pretentions, but that's a private language game.

In fact, if one reads for long in the relevant literature, one discovers a common *bait-and-switch strategy* used by Darwinists, which is to present a metaphysically minimal definition of the word/theory in contexts such as "Debating William Lane Craig in public," and quite another definition in, well, every other context. Their equivocation is often coordinated and intentional. Other times, it's simply the Darwinian default. Surely one of the important services of "careful philosophical thinking about science" is to identify and expose this equivocation, rather than to obscure it or miss it.

The distinction between "popularizers" and scientists is common but artificial. The problem started with Darwin, who relied heavily on the argument form, *God wouldn't do X that way, so X must have evolved by selection and variation*, and it persists across the discipline to this day. If you doubt that the theory is normally and pervasively defined in a-teleological ways, I'm happy to send you quotes from scores of biology textbooks and official statements making it quite clear that the theory is intended to explain biological adaptation as an *alternative* to design. Words such as "blind" and "purposeless" turn up *everywhere*. This practice has been ubiquitous since Darwin wrote *On the Origin of*

Species. In the quote from Steve Meyer that you discuss, Steve is paraphrasing the famous quote from G.G. Simpson: "Man is the result of a purposeless and natural process that did not have him in mind." Simpson was hardly a "popularizer." It's inaccurate to treat the a-teleological part of the Darwinian theory as an accidental but easily detachable piggybacker.

I have a hard time understanding the wisdom of defining a theory in a way that fails to accommodate the language and explanations of the theory's founder and defenders. Surely they have a privileged claim on the question of what they mean by the theory.

Ayala himself often slides into anti-teleological language when talking about evolution even when he's trying to give a more nuanced definition of the theory. See, for instance, his "Darwin's greatest discovery: Design without designer," published in *Proceedings of the National Academy of Sciences USA* in 2007 (Vol. 104:8567-8573, May 15, 2007). PNAS isn't exactly a populist publication. He provides some nuanced definitions of "random" and "chance" there as well, and yet notice the *very title of the article*. He even uses "natural processes" in a teleological way, as if natural processes by definition exclude divine activity. He says that by finding that "the design of living organisms can be accounted for as the result of natural processes," Darwin completed a "conceptual revolution" that "is nothing if not a fundamental vision that has forever changed how mankind perceives itself and its place in the universe." Now, why would that be?

He claims that the Darwinian revolution, like the Copernican Revolution, brought a part of nature under the explanation of "natural laws." One of many problems with this common claim: the selection/mutation "mechanism," unlike natural laws in physics and chemistry, has no predictive power or mathematical expression, and no significant evidence in its favor apart from some trivial examples within species that no one has ever doubted. He also endorses the old historical myth about Copernicus "displacing the Earth from its previously accepted locus as the center of the universe and moving it to a subordinate place as just one more planet revolving around the sun. In congruous manner, the Darwinian Revolution is viewed as consisting of the displacement of humans from their exalted position as the center of life on earth, with all other species created for the service of humankind." Notice the metaphysical water that Darwin is carrying here. It is ever thus.

He then goes on to explain: "Biological evolution differs from a painting or an artifact in that it is not the outcome of preconceived design. The design of organisms is not intelligent but imperfect and, at times, outright dysfunctional." (This doesn't make sense, since a design could be both intelligent and imperfect. This mistake is ubiquitous with Darwinists but isn't central to my point here.) He also explains: "The design of organisms as they exist in nature, however, is not 'intelligent design,' imposed by God as a Supreme Engineer or by humans; rather, it is the result of a natural process of selection, promoting the adaptation of organisms to their environments." Notice the word "rather." He concludes the article by saying that "[n]atural selection does not have foresight; it does not anticipate the environments of the future," and thus "in evolution, there is no entity or person who is selecting adaptive combinations." This is how Darwinian Theory is *usually explained by its proponents*. The entire point of Ayala's article is to argue that the Darwinian process provides "some appearance of purposefulness" without actual purposefulness. Notice the explicitly theological language, in an article in the *Proceedings of the Natural Academy of Sciences.*

The Meyer quote, incidentally, looks like a garbled quote from a transcript of an extemporaneous speech. I know it's not from anything he's written, and it doesn't come up on an Internet search. In any case, Steve obviously wouldn't argue that "evolution" is by definition purposeless. His point, no doubt, was something like this: *If evolution is a blind and purposeless process, then, by definition, not even God could guide it. If He guided it, then, by definition, it wouldn't be purposeless.* Do you think it's plausible that Mike Behe and Steve Meyer, after all these years of studying, reading, writing, and debating on the subject, have failed to understand what Darwinian theorists are saying, and that no one had bothered simply to explain to them that the word "random" has a specialized, metaphysically neutral meaning when biologists use it? On the contrary, I can assure you that Steve, Mike, and every other prominent [intelligent design] advocate is intimately familiar with this Darwinian language game.

Although it's a separate issue, I'm surprised you would cite a report by Darrell Domning at the National Center for Science Education to the effect that "most evolutionists are theists of some sort." The NCSE, like Ayala, works to persuade religious people that there's nothing metaphysically problematic about Darwinian theory, and so has every motivation to misrepresent the facts here. It's headed by Eugenie Scott—a signer of the third humanist manifesto—and employs several village atheists. This is not exactly an organization we should trust to represent the subject under dispute.

In any event, in most polls, biologists are consistently identified as one of the most atheistic of the scientific disciplines (mathematicians and physicists tend to be the most theist-friendly). And in polls of biologists who are members of the NAS, 95 percent say they are atheists. In a well-crafted 2003 survey, Gregory Graffin and Will Provine polled 149 elite evolutionary biologists and found that 78 percent were "pure naturalists." Strikingly, "[o]nly two out of 149 described themselves as full theists." (*See* http://bit.ly/ AmericanScoemtost).

In short, Darwinism as it is taught, explained and understood by most of its proponents, and as it is identified with evolutionary biology itself, is not captured by Ayala's stipulated definition of "random," which you focused on in your response. In fact, by following Ayala in this way, I fear that you've taken the Darwinian bait but missed the switch.

All the best regards,

Jay

United States

Dr. Craig's Response

Thanks for these trenchant insights, Jay! Lest distressed readers miss the forest for the trees, we agree on the central point: that insofar as a person claims that the evidence of evolutionary biology has shown that the evolutionary process, based as it is on genetic mutations and natural selection, is undirected, purposeless, or non-teleological, he is making a claim that hopelessly outstrips the scientific evidence and so is unjustified. The remaining question is: is this vaunted claim, as I suspect, really philosophical, though masquerading as science, or is it, as you believe, in fact part and parcel of the scientific theory itself? If I am right, we should chastise biologists who transgress the bounds of science in making such a philosophical claim; whereas if you are right, we should reject the scientific theory that makes such a claim. In either case, the claim itself is rejected as unjustified; but are we rejecting a philosophical claim or a scientific claim?

The fundamental question, then, is, who determines the content of a scientific theory? Who speaks for science? Now, at one level the answer to that question is easy: the expert practitioners of a theory tell us what the content of that theory is. In practice, however, things are not so easy. For scientists, being philosophically untrained, may be blind to the philosophical assumptions and ramifications of their views, so that careless statements are often made, especially by those who have a philosophical or theological agenda, that are not really part of the theory itself. So when we find the expert practitioners disagreeing amongst themselves about the proper content of a scientific theory, that raises suspicions that extra-theoretical assertions are being made by some of them.

INSIGHT
Note how Dr. Craig summarizes the discussion and characterizes this as an endeavor to reject a philosophical vs. scientific claim. This, along with Dr. Craig's answer, is a helpful reminder to think about the role of philosophy (and even theology) in relationship to a scientific theory.

This is precisely the situation we confront concerning the definition of the word "random" as applied to genetic mutations. It is baffling when we hear so many expert biologists asserting that these occur wholly by chance or are wholly purposeless, since such claims could not be established scientifically. For that reason, Ayala's explication of randomness as "irrespective of their usefulness to the organism" is so stunning. It makes sense of the theory as science.

You ask, "*Why would you trust Francisco Ayala on something of this nature?*" Two reasons, I think. First, he is an expert practitioner of the theory, with more decorations than an Argentine general! Second, the principle of charity demands it. On Ayala's understanding, the theory makes sense as science. But on the non-teleological understanding, the theory turns into metaphysics, making claims that could not be established by empirical evidence. We should charitably interpret people's views in a way that makes the best sense of them, rather than construct straw men.

So I don't agree with you that "*the crucial question is this: Do evolutionary biologists, Neo-Darwinists, etc., consistently and representatively restrict their explanations in this way?*" Rather, the question is, when evolutionary biologists engage in making inflated claims about the absence of teleology, have they begun to philosophize about a theory that, strictly speaking, makes no such inflated claims? The very bait and switch strategy that you describe makes me suspect that they are, indeed, making philosophical claims on behalf of the theory which the theory itself does not make.

It's important to understand that it is not just popularizers who make such philosophical assertions on behalf of a scientific theory. Expert practitioners, especially in statements for popular audiences, will often make such claims. I see this happen all the time in an area of science with which I have more familiarity: cosmology. Expert physicists like Stephen Hawking and Lawrence Krauss have made outrageous claims on behalf of certain theories of the origin of the universe. The statement you quote from G. G. Simpson is similarly reckless and is a philosophical inference from evolutionary theory rather than a sober statement of it.

As for Ayala's seemingly inconsistent statements, you need to understand that he has *other* reasons for thinking that organisms are not designed in the form in which we find them, namely, the problem of natural evil and examples of poor design. This fact is alluded to in the remark you quote: "*The design of organisms is not intelligent but imperfect and, at times, outright dysfunctional.*" Debating Ayala on the viability of intelligent design, therefore, required me to prepare briefs on the subjects of animal pain and instances of non-optimal design. Those are very different issues than just the definition of "randomness"! Here are philosophical arguments against design. Indeed, Jay, how can you be sure that the authorities you mention are not saying that the evolutionary process is non-teleological, not simply by definition of randomness, but on the basis of arguments from evil and dysteleology?

So in my view, if there is a bait and switch going on here, it is the switch from doing empirically based science to making philosophical claims which far exceed the science. Rather than missing or ignoring the switch from science to philosophy, we need to spotlight it and call naturalists on it.

Part 4

QUESTIONS ABOUT THE AFTERLIFE AND EVIL

Questions related to the problem of evil and the eternal damnation of the unevange-lized consist of some of the most serious challenges against Christian theism. But so often objections in these areas are extracted and isolated from broader theological and philosophical considerations related to one's view of human nature and evil, the intent and scope of God's salvation in Christ, and one's view of the afterlife and eternity. The problem of the "problem of evil" is not merely a philosophical issue; it is as much a theological issue—specifically, a theological anthropology issue. With that in mind, it is important to recognize whose problem is the "problem of evil." Does the burden of proof fall only on the theist, specifically, the Christian theist? Or, is it mostly a burden on the atheist? Even if it does not fall to the theist, the theist does have a responsibility to offer intelligible reasons to both the emotional and intellectual aspects of the problem of evil to anyone who is willing to receive.

The eight questions posed in this part address both felt needs in this area and also developed objections against reasonable belief in God. In many ways, the discussion in this part can be read as an extension and application of topics in Part One, section 3 regarding how God is the basis of morality. One can come away with a sober-minded attitude as a result of studying the issues raised in this part. Perhaps one of the most intense questions is this one: "Was the slaughter of the Canaanites an act of 'Divine Genocide'?" This has become a popular issue in apologetics, if for no other reason than the amount of airplay it receives by the so-called New Atheists. Dr. Craig's steadfast answer shows us how the tough-minded questions can be frankly confronted. To readers "who have ears to hear, and eyes to see," you can experience a renewed, holy attentiveness for the justice and mercy of God when facing this issue.

By interacting with the questions and answers of Part Four, you can benefit in the following ways.

249

In section 1, you can come to discern
- How a middle knowledge view of God's sovereignty helps us better understand why some are eternally damned.
- How creation benefits the lost.
- How to understand nature's flaws and cruelties in light of God's providence.
- Why people in heaven won't sin.
- Why it is not an act of "cultural chauvinism" for some to be saved and for others not to be saved.

In section 2, you can come to understand
- How the burden of proof for the problem of evil is on the atheist, not the theist.
- Why it is important to distinguish between the emotional and intellectual problem of evil.
- Why the slaughter of the Old Testament Canaanites was not an act of divine genocide.
- Why skeptical theism is not a helpful descriptor for addressing the problem of evil.

You can discover further background to these issues, grow your understanding, and become even more skillful in your communication of what you learn by interacting with some of these valuable resources:

Dig Deeper into Dr. Craig's Work

BEGINNER

Craig, William Lane. *On Guard: Defending Your Faith with Reason and Precision.* Colorado Springs: David C. Cook Publishers, 2010. Chapters 6–7.

Craig, William Lane. *Hard Questions, Real Answers.* Wheaton: Crossway, 2003. Chapters 4–5.

INTERMEDIATE

Craig, William Lane and J. P. Moreland. *Philosophical Foundations for a Christian Worldview.* Downers Grove, Ill.: InterVarsity, 2003. Chapters 27–28.

Craig, William Lane and Ray Bradley. "Craig v. Bradley: Can a Loving God Send People to Hell?" Simon Frasier University, Vancouver, B.C., January 1994. http://bit.ly/CraigBradley.

Craig, William Lane. "How Can Christ Be the Only Way to God?" *Reasonable Faith*. http://bit.ly/OnlyWayToGod.

ADVANCED

Craig, William Lane. "'No Other Name': A Middle Knowledge Perspective on the Exclusivity of Salvation through Christ." *Faith and Philosophy* 6 (1989): 172–88.

Supplemental Recommended Resources

BEGINNER

Tada, Joni Eareckson. *A Place of Healing: Wrestling with the Mysteries of Suffering, Pain, and God's Sovereignty*. Colorado Springs: David C. Cook Publishers, 2010.

Zacharias, Ravi. *Cries of the Heart*. Nashville: Word Publishers, 1998.

INTERMEDIATE

Copan, Paul and William Lane Craig, eds. *Come Let Us Reason: New Essays in Christian Apologetics*. Nashville: B&H, 2012. Chapters 13–14.

Copan, Paul. *Is God a Moral Monster?* Grand Rapids: Baker, 2010.

Copan, Paul and William Lane Craig, eds. *Contending with Christianity's Critics*. Nashville: Broadman and Holman, 2009. Chapters 16–18.

Craig, William Lane and Chad Meister, eds. *God Is Great, God Is Good: Why Believing in God Is Reasonable and Responsible*. Downers Grove, Ill.: InterVarsity, 2009. Chapters 7–10.

Groothuis, Douglas. *Christian Apologetics*. Downers Grove, Ill.: InterVarsity, 2011. Chapter 25, Appendix 1–2.

Sweis, Khaldoun A. and Chad V. Meister. *Christian Apologetics: An Anthology of Primary Sources*. Grand Rapids: Zondervan, 2012. Chapters 43–47.

ADVANCED

Goetz, Stewart. "The Argument from Evil." In William Lane Craig and J. P. Moreland, eds. *The Blackwell Companion to Natural Theology*. Malden, Mass.: Wiley-Blackwell Publishing, 2009. Chapter 8.

Murray, Michael. *Nature Red in Tooth and Claw*. Oxford: Oxford University Press, 2008.

Plantinga, Alvin. *God, Freedom, and Evil*. Grand Rapids: Eerdmans, 1974.

1

ON THE AFTERLIFE, HELL, AND THE UNEVANGELIZED

On a Molinist View of Sovereignty, Hell, and Salvation

Dear Dr. Craig,

In your debate with Bradley on hell,[1] you allude to the possibility of individual "S" being saved in one feasible world, but not another—even that you yourself might not have been saved had God placed you in Nazi Germany or some other set of circumstances. Ultimately, given middle knowledge, it seems to become somewhat arbitrary (or predetermined) that God afforded me the appropriate circumstances to come under saving grace, but not my friend "S" while knowing all along that "S" would have been saved had he been born elsewhere or at a different time in history while I, or you, would not have been saved had God varied the circumstances in any number of ways.

Note, despite the notion of compossibility where the variable influence of rearranging individuals in feasible worlds changes things to some degree, we are left with nothing more than God deciding on some so-called optimal feasible world with the best balance of saved and damned. Of course, that is merely a numbers game. There is still the possibility of the feasible 10 person world where all might be saved, but so few overall, or a world with just a few more saved than the actual world, even if just that many more damned? God had to make a cut at some level of relatively more good and evil, saved and damned.

---

1. This is available for free at ReasonableFaith.org (http://bit.ly/CraigBradley).

I've always felt God yearned equally for all individuals, the notion of leaving even the 99 for the one. Middle knowledge solved the problem of someone receiving less than their fair share of info assuming God knew they would not have responded had they heard it. But, if I would have been damned in feasible world #2 for God (which He did not create and which had 10 more folks than the actual), but my friend "S" would have been saved, then there is nothing unique about me that affords the true libertarian freedom to enjoy saving grace.

That brings me to the final question. What then is different or unique about each soul placed into a body, time, and set of circumstances? Are all souls equivalent and then the circumstances take over, or does God create (you favor soul *creation ex nihilo,* as do I, not Oregon-ism or Traducianism) souls with unique properties, intrinsic or otherwise? It amounts to God's putting in certain soul qualities—plus or minus—coupled to a certain body, time, and set of circumstances, all of which equal whether in that situation any given individual would be saved. Had I been born better looking or more athletic, given the same intrinsic soul, perhaps I would have gone astray. Basically, I feel lucky, and as we often say in surgery, "better lucky than good", though I've always disliked that statement. Any thoughts on how to reconcile these things would be appreciated.

Sincerely,

Kevin

United States

Dr. Craig's Response

The question you're raising, Kevin, concerns God's sovereignty with respect to election of the saved. Molinism, like Calvinism, has a very strong doctrine of divine sovereignty but differs in that it also affirms libertarian freedom.

The Calvinist thinks that God unilaterally elects and causally determines who will be saved. The Molinist also affirms God's sovereign election of the saved but denies that people are causally determined by God to respond to His grace. Rather, God's saving grace is extended to every human being with the desire that he respond freely to it and be saved but with the knowledge that certain persons will freely reject God's grace and so damn themselves, contrary to God's perfect will. People in any possible world freely determine their own destiny by how they respond to God's saving grace, but it is God who decides which possible world to actualize. He doesn't simply "roll the dice" to see which world comes up (a gamble that might prove disastrous). Rather, He sovereignly chooses a world. As one French Molinist nicely put it, "It is up to God whether I find myself in a world in which I am predestined; but it is up to me whether I am predestined in the world in which I find myself."[2]

It's sobering to think that had God chosen some other world, I might have been born in Nazi Germany and become a member of the Hitler Youth Corps or been born in Afghanistan and joined the Taliban. Not that I would have been determined to do those things; but I would have perhaps freely chosen to do those things under those circumstances. Whether you're a theist or an atheist, we all face the realization that had circumstances been different, we might have been guilty of all sorts of horrors. Philosophers sometimes refer to this as "moral luck." Calvinists and Molinists attribute moral luck ultimately to God's free and sovereign choice. Lucky for you, God chose a world in which you were born in the USA; Heinrich was not so lucky.

The great thing is that on Molinism, God loves Heinrich just as much as He loves you and so accords him sufficient grace for salvation and seeks to draw him to Himself. Indeed, God may have known that through the guilt and shame of what Heinrich did under the Third Reich, he would eventually come to repent and find salvation and eternal life. Paradoxically, being a Nazi may have been the best thing that happened to Heinrich, since it led to his salvation. Of course, one may wonder about those poor people who suffered in the death camps because of Heinrich. But God has a plan for their lives, too, that includes their salvation and He accords them, like Heinrich, sufficient grace for salvation. Moreover, He knows what impact these events will have upon their children's lives and their children's children's lives and the lives of those with whom they come into contact. You can see that in no time we spiral into a complexity that only an infinite mind could encompass.

I've suggested, based on my reading of the New Testament, that God would choose a world having an overall optimal balance between saved and lost. This is far from just a numbers game. God wants as many people as possible to be freely saved and as few as possible to be freely damned. It's possible that the actual world is such a world. God wills the salvation of every person He creates and accords to each one sufficient grace for salvation. Whether they are saved or damned is up to them.

2. Theodore Regnon, *Bannesianisme et Molinisme* (Paris: Retaux-Bray, 1890), 48.

Of course, there is the sobering thought once more that had I been created under different circumstances then perhaps I would have freely rejected God's grace and been damned. But I see no problem in saying that had God actualized a different world, then I or any other saved person would have freely rejected His grace and been damned. For since God has chosen to actualize this world, in which we are freely saved, that counterfactual truth is of no consequence. The more difficult question is whether there are persons who freely reject God's grace and are damned but who would have freely been saved had God chosen to actualize some other world. On the one hand, that may just seem to be inevitable moral luck; the point remains that God strives to save them, and they freely spurn Him. They and they alone are responsible for their damnation.

But I have suggested that there is another possibility. Maybe God has so providentially ordered the world that all those who freely reject His grace and are lost are persons who would have freely rejected His grace under any circumstances and so been lost in any world feasible for God. We could say that such persons are trans-worldly damned. These would be incredibly reprobate people. If they do not appear so bad in this world, that may be because the actual world is one of the worlds in which they come closest to salvation, though in the end they freely thrust it from them. Thus, it's possible that there just are no such people as "S," as you've envisioned.

I don't understand, Kevin, why you think such a view denies your uniqueness or your libertarian freedom. Quite the contrary, the view wouldn't make sense without those elements. The idea is that God has selected a world containing just those persons in just those circumstances so as to maximize the number of those who would freely respond to His grace and be saved, while minimizing the number of those who would freely reject His grace and damn themselves and that, moreover, He has ensured that anyone in the world who would under any circumstances be freely saved is freely saved. You can't do any better than that!

INSIGHT

Note Dr. Craig's other possibility articulated in these paragraphs. What do you think? How might it be apropos (compared to the alternatives) to some of Kevin's questions/objections? It seems that there is some intentional emphasis on Dr. Craig's part to apply the insights of Molinism to this question in order to help Kevin see a context for his questions.

Does Creation Benefit the Lost?

Dear Dr. Craig,

Although I'm an atheist, I have a deep respect for you and other Christian philosophers, and I must thank you personally for forcing me to abandon my position of arrogant atheism (that of Dawkins, Hitchens, and Harris) and adopt the position of friendly atheism. It was a major revelation to me that someone defending Christianity could sound so rational, and even beat atheists in debates. (For the record, I think you have only possibly lost two or three debates, and none of those were on the existence of God, though I think some are too close to call.)

Now, on to my question. In your debate with Victor Stenger, he advanced the argument that God could not logically be a perfect being and creator of the universe. In response you stated that God does not create because of anything lacking in Himself, but because the creation of the universe benefits man, because he can come to know God and have a loving relationship with Him. I was just wondering, how does this square with the Christian doctrine of Hell? If Christ is the only way to God, and unbelief is punished by eternity in hell, it seems likely that the vast majority of people, or at least a good number, will end up in hell. In what way could we say that creation benefited these people? The doctrine of hell has always been one of my major problems with Christianity, and it was my main reason for becoming an atheist.

Thank you for your time.

Sincerely,
Mark

Dr. Craig's Response

Thanks so much for your kind letter, Mark! As one who has been privileged to have experienced firsthand the ongoing revolution in Anglo-American philosophy since the late 1960s, it often pains me to see how desperately ignorant many young atheists and agnostics are. Often as arrogant as they are ignorant, they just have no inkling of the incredible intellectual resources contemporary Christian philosophers have provided for the formulation and defense of basic Christian doctrines. I'm so glad that you've escaped from that unhappy subculture.

As for your question, my point in response to Stenger was that because God is a perfect being, complete in Himself with no need of anything, creation cannot have been motivated by any need or deficit in Himself. Creation, then, must be an act of grace, something done not for God's sake but for the sake of those created; namely, they are given the unspeakable opportunity to be personally related to the locus and source of infinite goodness and love. We were made to know God, and this is, in view of its object, an incommensurable good, incomparable to anything else, to any finite goods. It really is an amazing privilege when you think about it.

Now, the tragedy is that the unbeliever freely rejects this incomparable good that God offers him. So in that sense he does not benefit from being created. Nonetheless, it remains true that the reason God created him was for his own benefit, that is, for his own good, and every created person has the incredible benefit of the opportunity of knowing God, a benefit not enjoyed by persons whom God did not create (obviously!).

INSIGHT

There are some interesting nuggets of insight and wisdom in these comments. One important one is that if creation is a gift, it is to be received with gratitude. For gratitude, and even ingratitude, can shape our epistemology and view of ourselves in relationship to each other before God.

Think of it this way: if someone offered you a great gift with no strings attached simply because that person loved you, and you freely rejected the gift, then you wouldn't in the end have the benefit of the gift. But still the person offered it to you for your own benefit. And even having the opportunity to have such a great gift was itself a tremendous benefit that you were fortunate to have.

It can't be overemphasized that according to the Bible God desires every human being to be saved and find eternal life (1 Tim. 2:4), and He takes no pleasure whatsoever in the death of the wicked (Ezek. 33:11).

God created us for our benefit, not His, and every created person has the benefit of the opportunity to know God and His love forever, if only he will accept it. If he chooses to repulse God and His every effort to save him, the life of the unbeliever is ultimately tragic because he has freely rejected the benefit that God offers him.

Can People in Heaven Sin?

Dear Dr. Craig,

I was in attendance at one of your lectures in Baltimore around two years ago at the "Two Tasks" conference. I appreciate the tireless work you are doing. May God continue to strengthen you, while deepening your personal relationship with Him.

There is one question that is related to the problem of evil that has not been resolved in my mind. This question has chronically baffled me, and I feel leaves me intellectually vulnerable in defending Christianity.

One way to open up the issue is with the following question:

How does God guarantee that there will be no evil among the saved in heaven?

Some possible answers are sketched below. This is a product of my own thinking, influenced by lay research into the subject. Skeptics have posed the problem as well. Please help me decide which is the best, most biblical, most philosophically coherent answer, or point out an alternative that I have not thought through.

Note: Below, I use the pronoun "we" as a short-hand for the saved/elect.

Answer 1: There is *no* free will heaven. The saved are immutably good and have neither choice nor temptation to sin.

Rebuttal: Can lack of free will coexist with love of the saved towards God? (If answered yes, the free will defense of evil crumbles.) How would love not be diminished or extinguished without free will?

Answer 2: There *is* free will in heaven—we have the capacity to choose evil. But in our glorified body and regenerated nature, we abhor evil (no evil desire), and, therefore, never choose it. To back this up, consider God, who is free, despises evil, and is one of supreme love. Perhaps free will must be narrowly defined as having the ability to choose something, but not whether one would ever choose it because of one's nature.

Rebuttal: If this is the case, why does God not create Adam such that he has no desire towards evil in the first place? Also, how is Adam's pre-fall nature different from the one characterized in answer 2?

Answer 3: There is *no* free will in heaven. However, we cannot consider heaven in isolation from the earthly decision that led to eternal life. We had free will on earth, and God simply permanently cemented that freely chosen (salvifically efficacious) decision to accept Christ upon mortal death. Love still exists in heaven because God affirms the free-willed decision to follow God while on earth. (This is a tenuous underdeveloped train of thought).

Thank you very much.

Gary

Dr. Craig's Response

We're simply speculating when it comes to questions like this, so there may be more than one plausible answer. Insofar as skeptics are concerned, it's up to them to prove some sort of incoherence here, which would be very difficult to do.

My own inclination is for a view along the lines of (3). God has created us at an "epistemic distance," so to speak, which allows us the freedom to rebel against Him and separate ourselves from Him. This world is a vale of decision-making during which we decide whether we want to live with God forever or reject Him and so irrevocably separate ourselves from Him. As discussions of the so-called "Hiddenness of God" have emphasized, God could have made His existence overwhelmingly obvious, had He wanted to. During this life, we "see in a glass darkly," as St. Paul put it; but someday we shall see "face to face" (1 Cor. 13:12). Medieval theologians liked to talk of the "Beatific Vision" which the blessed in heaven will receive. There, the veil will be removed, and we shall see Christ in all of His loveliness and majesty. The vision of Christ, the source of infinite goodness and love, will be so overwhelming as to remove all freedom to sin. I like to think of it like iron filings in the presence of an enormously powerful electromagnet. They would be so powerfully attracted to the magnet that there is simply no possibility of their falling away. So with the blessed in heaven.

Something like this may have already occurred with angelic beings. Originally created "at arm's length" from God epistemically, they had a time to choose either for or against God. Those who chose for God were then sealed with the Beatific Vision, so that no further fall is possible. Fallen angels are Satan and his minions.

I find this a satisfying account of the matter. But the doctrine of middle knowledge affords a version of (2) that is viable as well. One could hold that God via His middle knowledge knew exactly which persons, if saved and glorified in heaven, would freely persevere in grace, even though they would retain the freedom to sin. It's not that they have a different nature than others; it's just that this is how they would freely choose. God has chosen to create a world in which all the saved are precisely such persons. Hence, everyone in heaven will freely persevere. They could fall away but they just won't. Interestingly, creating a world like this could involve God's having to put up with a lot of otherwise undesirable features of the world, such as vast amounts of natural and moral evil. Perhaps only in a world like that would all those who come freely to know God and His salvation be persons who would freely persevere in heaven. This view would have obvious relevance to the problem of evil.

My own preference remains for (3) simply because it seems right to think that the unalloyed vision of Christ would be something so overwhelmingly attractive that freedom to resist it would be utterly removed.

Do the Damned in Hell Accrue Further Punishment?

I have a concern with something I read from your article database. I find your explanation about sinning in the afterlife and what you believe that entails something of an oddity given the gulf between death and life and based upon the finality of judgment expressed in the Judeo-Christian heritage.

In your article "How Can Christ Be the Only Way to God?"[3] you mention that those who have been damned to hell continue to sin. This seems to fail on three levels:

1. Sin appears to be an earthly predisposition, not one that follows into eternity. The Greek "hamartia" implies "missing the mark." So as Christians, if we believe the "mark" is God or is righteous perfection, isn't that something that is achieved or absolutely not achieved in the afterlife? It would seem that if we leave open the possibility that a person continues "missing the mark" then we must also assume that the antithesis of this is that the saved somehow keep "gaining the mark"

3. You can access this article for free by visiting ReasonableFaith.org (http://bit.ly/OnlyWayToGod).

261

whether this be God or righteous perfection. Now, while I'm aware that we will continue in our knowledge of God throughout eternity (as Paul mentions), I don't see this as being the opposite of those who are damned. For their knowledge of God doesn't fail or diminish either it seems.

2. The idea of continuing to sin in eternity seems inadequate by way of analogy. Once a criminal is judged and sentenced for his crimes, he goes to prison. Let's say he gets life with no parole. Now, even while he may do deeds in prison that are abominable, say he kills another man in a fight, because he's lost all hope, can we really say it has any bearing on the judgment that has already been passed? There are some cases where that person might get another one hundred years slapped on, but we all know this is only a formality. He's not leaving his prison. There is no real hope of him achieving release.

3. The idea of continuing in sin is not wholly endorsed in Scripture. The real inadequacy I find in this example is the possibility it leaves open. Namely, if sin is what a person is judged upon in eternity, their rejection of Christ being the sum total of the individual sins, the possibility that a person (and not everyone damned) can go on sinning in hell implies the possibility that a person can also have a change of heart. And I think we see evidence of this in the example of Lazarus speaking to Abraham. Not everyone in hell, given this example in Scripture, seems to go on sinning. Some seem genuinely disturbed by their earthly decisions and want out. And when Lazarus speaks to Abraham, Abraham doesn't rebuke him for not accepting God's revelation in nature or through the law. He merely tells him there is a gulf between them. So saying that it's still a heart condition in Lazarus who is merely just trying to avoid the pains of hell is an inference that doesn't bear out in the dialogue.

So on the basis of these three objections, I'm wondering how adequate the idea of an eternal place of torment is?

In His Grace,

Trey

Dr. Craig's Response

Thanks for your thoughtful question, Trey! It's important that we first set the context for my proposal. I'm attempting to deal with the objection, urged not only by unbelievers but also by annihilationists, to the doctrine of hell, that hell is incompatible with the justice of God because the punishment doesn't fit the crime. Even sins like murder and cruelty, it is alleged, don't merit everlasting punishment, for these sins are of finite significance, whereas everlasting punishment is infinite in severity.

Now, my response to this objection is twofold, having the form "Even if . . . but in fact . . ." That is to say, I first argue *ex concessionis*, conceding the assumption made by the objector that no sin that human beings commit deserves an infinite punishment and trying to show that even on that assumption, the objection does not go through. Then I argue that we don't need to make the assumption presupposed by the objector and propose a quite different solution to the problem, which I, in fact, find preferable. So you mustn't take the first part of my response out of context, as though I did not offer the second part of the response.

Concerning, then, the first part of my response, what struck me as I thought about this problem is that it doesn't follow that because every sin that we commit deserves only a finite punishment, therefore no one merits infinite punishment. For if one commits an infinite number of sins, the sum total of sins would, indeed, merit infinite punishment. Of course, no one commits an infinite number of sins in his earthly life. But it occurred to me that in the afterlife one could commit at least potentially infinitely many sins, if one just keeps on sinning forever. And when one thinks of the damned in hell, it is not at all implausible to think that they do, indeed, continue to sin. Rather than repent, they grow only more implacable in their hatred and rejection of God.

I find it striking that when in the book of Revelation the bowls of God's wrath are poured out in judgment upon mankind, those judged are not repentant but curse God all the more: "men were scorched by the fierce heat, and they cursed the name of God who had power over these plagues, and they did not repent and give him glory . . . men gnawed their tongues in anguish and cursed the God of heaven for their pain and sores, and did not repent of their deeds . . . and great hailstones, heavy as a hundredweight, dropped on men from heaven, till men cursed God for the plague of hail, so fearful was that plague" (Rev. 16:9–11, 21 RSV). Whether in this life or the next, to hate and reject God is to sin, for we are morally obligated to worship and love God. Sin cannot go unpunished, since God is perfectly just, and so these sins in the afterlife must also be punished. Hence, because sinning goes on forever, so does the punishment. So even if we concede that every sin deserves only a finite punishment, hell is unceasingly self-perpetuating.

Let's consider, then, your objections. First, can or does sinning continue on in the afterlife? Well, why not? Men are morally obligated to worship God, and to fail to do so is, as you put it, to fall short of the mark. The damned surely fail to fulfill their moral obligations toward God. You say, "But then we must also assume that the saved somehow keep 'gaining the mark,' whether this be God or righteous perfection." Well, certainly we must say that the blessed no longer sin and in that sense continue to hit the mark, though we needn't think that they attain moral perfection, a property which plausibly belongs to God alone. Far from failing or diminishing, I should think that the blessed knowledge of God would grow without limit. So I don't see any problem here.[4]

Your second objection is based on an analogy to someone sentenced to prison. Now, I don't know much about criminal jurisprudence, but I really doubt that if someone in prison murders another prisoner (or a guard!) that he gets away scot-free in the eyes of the law. Surely he will be prosecuted and held responsible for such a crime—at least, I hope so! You say that if he's already received a severe sentence, then an additional one hundred years is a mere formality. Ah, but you're forgetting that we're granting the assumption made by the objector that our sins deserve only a limited punishment. A proper analogy would be someone who has to serve only a brief sentence but who continually keeps committing petty crimes in jail, thereby accruing more and more terms. It would make a huge difference if he continues to commit crimes in prison, thereby prolonging his sentence.[5]

Your final objection is based on Jesus' parable of Lazarus and the rich man. Certainly the rich man in Hades exhibits a repentant heart. The problem here, Trey, is that it is a mistake to press parables to extract Christian doctrine. This is a well-known principle of hermeneutics (literary interpretation). The parables are generally meant to illustrate one central point, in this case that if people won't listen to Moses and the prophets neither will they be moved by miraculous signs, and it's bad exegesis to take doctrine from the circumstantial details of parables. The rich man in the parable is almost a cartoon figure, and it would be a serious mistake to use his situation as a basis for a theology of the damned in hell.

---

4. For more on this, see the question above, "Can People in Heaven Sin?" (pages 259–61).

5. As a side note Dr. Craig notes that analogies are a poor form of argumentation because they cannot prove anything; they serve only to illustrate.

Nonetheless, I completely concur with you that we should not think of a person's rejection of Christ as being the sum total of his individual sins. I, too, am uncomfortable with the idea that the damned could escape hell by repenting and serving out their time (that smacks of purgatory). That's why I went on to offer the second, better solution: that the rejection of Christ as Lord and Savior, being a rejection of God Himself, is a sin of infinite gravity and proportion and, therefore, plausibly does merit infinite punishment. So seen, people are sent to hell, not so much for murder and theft and adultery, but for their rejection of God. Moreover, if God has middle knowledge, then we can say that He allows the damned to pass from this earthly life only once He knows that their rejection of Him is irrevocable. The damned are thus responsible for their own fate and cannot impugn God's justice.

Molinism, the Unevangelized, and Cultural Chauvinism

I feel that William Lane Craig's argument that God has arranged for those whom He knows will respond favorably to the gospel to live in parts of the world where they are most likely to be exposed to the gospel smacks of "cultural chauvinism." It means that swathes of humanity are written off, presumably because even if they had heard they would not have believed. I find C. S. Lewis more convincing on that issue; that Christ's blood can save people who may not necessarily know that it is by Christ's blood that they are saved. Could you correct me if I have understood your position incorrectly?

Roger

Dr. Craig's Response

While I think that you may have understood my position more or less correctly, Roger, I don't think that it has the implications you suggest. Before I explain why, let me clarify my proposal.

The basic problem with which I'm wrestling is the fate of the unevangelized, those who never hear the gospel. I suggest that it's possible that God, desiring that all men should be saved and come to a knowledge of the truth (1 Tim. 2:4), has so providentially ordered the world that anyone who would believe in the gospel if he heard it is born at a time and place in history where he does in fact hear it. In that case, no one could stand before God on the Judgment Day and complain that, while he may not have responded to God's general revelation in nature and conscience and so finds himself condemned, he would have responded to the gospel if only he had had the chance.

C. S. Lewis was an inclusivist who apparently thought that the problem of the unevangelized is solved by adopting the view that people can be saved on the basis of Christ's death by an appropriate response to the light that they do have. You say that you find Lewis "more convincing." I think you should have said "more appealing."

Lewis's view, which I once held to, is inadequate for two reasons:

(1) No honest reading of Romans 1 can give grounds for optimism that very many of the unevangelized will be saved by their response to general revelation. Perhaps a few will (and my own view allows for that), but we can't paint a rosy picture of the fate of the unevangelized after reading this passage. Lewis's view is appealing and comforting, no doubt, but difficult to square with biblical teaching.

INSIGHT

Note this particular objection to Lewis' inclusivism (and any that attempt to mimic it). It doesn't deal with the problem of the unevangelized as a counterfactual problem.

(2) Lewis's inclusivism doesn't really solve the problem. The problem with inclusivism is not that it goes too far but, in truth, that it does not go far enough. For it accords salvation only to those who do respond affirmatively to God's general revelation. But it says nothing about those who reject God's general revelation and so are lost, but who *would have responded* to the gospel and been saved if only they had heard it. The problem of the unevangelized is a *counterfactual problem*: what about those who are damned but who would have been saved if only they had been born at a time and place where they heard the gospel? Their damnation seems to be bad luck, the result of historical and geographical accident. Inclusivism like Lewis's doesn't even speak to this counterfactual problem and thus fails as a satisfactory solution to the problem. That's why I had to go beyond it.

I think it's clear that on my view no one is "written off": every human being is given sufficient grace for salvation, even the unevangelized. Salvation is universally accessible.

But God is too good to allow folks to be damned because they happened to be born at the wrong time and place in history. So He places those who would respond to the gospel if they heard it at times and places in history where they do hear it. He does no injustice toward the unevangelized who reject the light of general revelation and are lost because He knows that they wouldn't have responded to the gospel anyway, even if they had heard it.

So is my view culturally chauvinistic? Before I address that question, let me comment on the weight of the objection. The objection challenges neither the possibility of my solution (which is all I need to solve the problem) nor its truth. It just finds my solution to be unpalatable. I'm not sure how serious such an objection is. After all, if we believe that human persons are individuated by their souls, then my soul could have been placed in a different body so that I should have been a person of a different race or ethnicity born at a different time and place in history. On such an understanding of human personhood, bodily characteristics are of much less significance than on a materialistic view. Still, the Bible tells us that in the *eschaton* there will be people from every tribe and tongue and people and nation (Rev. 5:9), so we should ask if my view precludes this.

The answer is: not at all! Anyone who thinks that evangelical Christianity is a white man's religion is just ignorant of the demographic facts of world Christianity. Did you know that today two-thirds of all evangelicals are living in the Third World, as Christian growth rates are exploding in Asia, Africa, and Latin America? Did you know that in 1987, the number of evangelicals in Asia surpassed the number of evangelicals in North America, and in 1991 the number of evangelicals in Asia surpassed the number of evangelicals *in the entire Western world*? If anything, Christianity today is an Asian religion. It may well turn out that Caucasian, European Christianity was merely the means by which God reached the majority of mankind with the gospel. When you think of the whole of human history from beginning to its end, you see that my view is not at all culturally chauvinistic.[6]

---

6. There is a broader discussion to be noted here in Dr. Craig's writings. For more on this very important issue take a look at ReasonableFaith.org, go to articles, and access "Scholarly Articles: Christian Particularism" or "Popular Articles: Christianity and Other Faiths."

2

ON THE PROBLEM OF EVIL

Skeptical Theism and the Problem of Evil

I wonder if we can rely too much on "skeptical theism." To my understanding, it classically endorses these three theses:

ST1: We have no good reason for thinking that the possible goods we know of are representative of the possible goods there are.

ST2: We have no good reason for thinking that the possible evils we know of are representative of the possible evils there are.

ST3: We have no good reason for thinking that the entailment relations we know of between possible goods and the permission of possible evils are representative of the entailment relations there are between possible goods and the permission of possible evils.

But, true or false: Skeptical theism then undermines any of our judgments about how likely it is that any state of affairs obtain, as God could have reasons to bring such a state about or prevent it.

For example, do you think it's unlikely that God would permit/cause a pink lizard to randomly materialize on top of your head tonight and then explode like a firecracker? Why do you think this is unlikely? Consider the butterfly effect and your complete inability to discern how this would change the course of history! So then, given an unmitigated skeptical theism, you should strip off any expectations you'd have about whether God will cause/permit this to happen tonight.

Blake
United States

269

Dr. Craig's Response

Blake, I've never liked the term "skeptical theism" and don't think I've ever used it to characterize my response to the problem of evil (unless, perhaps, in response to someone who used the term). I think it carries the wrong connotations. Typically, these folks have no positive natural theology to serve as a counterweight to the evidence against God posed by apparently gratuitous evil. But my robust natural theology makes my approach the antithesis of skepticism!

With respect to the apparent gratuity of evil in the world, I prefer simply to assert what seems evident on reflection, namely, that given a God endowed with middle knowledge, we're just in no position to assert with any confidence that probably God doesn't have a morally sufficient reason for permitting some incident of suffering which we experience.

So while you're right that so-called skeptical theists often do affirm ST1 and ST2, these have been no part of my response to the problem of evil. In fact, I've *named* the goods that I think could justify God's permission of moral and natural evils in the world. As for ST3, I'm not sure even skeptical theists would affirm what I take this to state; but I have never affirmed any such thing in my response to the problem of evil. I guess that means that I'm not a skeptical theist!

In any case, I don't think your untoward consequences follow from what I've said or even from skeptical theism. For what one is talking about is evil or suffering in the world. The claim is that we have no basis for saying that any evil we experience is not justly permitted by God. That isn't to say that we don't have good *non-moral* grounds for thinking that certain events won't occur. Take your pink lizard example. If someone were to object to this happening on moral grounds, then I'd agree with you. I have no reason to think that God could not be morally justified in allowing such an explosion on my head. Precisely for that reason when someone does suffer a traumatic head injury, say, on the construction site or in war, we're not in a position to say that God lacks a morally sufficient reason for permitting it. But while we can't exclude such a head injury on moral grounds, couldn't we have other grounds for thinking that such an injury is unlikely to take place tonight by the magical appearance of a pink lizard on my head? It seems to me, for example, that I could have good grounds for thinking that God has created a universe that is endowed with natural laws and that miraculous interventions in it on His part are limited in nature and context. So while I wouldn't rule it out that I might suffer from an explosion over my head,

I have good reason to think that it will not be through the random materialization of a pink lizard as I lie in bed tonight.

The Problem of Evil Once More

Hello Dr. Craig,

I'm a former die-hard Christian who has spent countless hours debating agnostics and atheists using many of your arguments, as well as many of my own. Recently, my faith has been strained, to say the least.

But I wanted to follow up on your answer to questions concerning evil and pain and suffering.

First, you often say that there is no good reason to believe that God doesn't have a significant reason for allowing pain and suffering in this world. But the burden of proof is on you to show or give a significant reason why an all loving and all powerful God would allow certain unnecessary pain and suffering? To say God "may" have a significant reason is somewhat of a cop-out, don't you think? For instance if God did have a significant good reason to allow Hitler and his henchmen to build ovens for human disposal, then we should—what?—rejoice that they were built with God's stamp of approval? Why should we view that act as being inhumane or necessarily evil if God had a significant reason to allow it to happen? It seems to me if God had a significant reason to allow it to happen, then we should rejoice that God's will was done.

Another example: my own mother recently passed away after a long bout with dementia, to the point that toward the end her mind could no longer receive signals from her body to tell her that she was starving to death. The doctors all said a feeding tube would only extend her prolonged suffering. As a recent convert to agnosticism, it's hard to find a significant reason why an all powerful, all loving God would allow such an extended, drawn-out death. Please offer a hypothetical significant good reason. After all, the burden of proof is on you to give a good example of a significant good reason why such things would happen if such an all powerful and all loving God does exist. Again we should rejoice that God allows such pain and suffering if, in fact, He has a significantly good reason for its occurrence.

To me, it also makes the whole concept of prayer seem borderline ridiculous; because it's hard to imagine that such an all powerful and all knowing God would look upon such pain and suffering but choose to only intervene if someone prays the right prayer. Can you really imagine that such a God could look down and say: "I see Mary is in a tremendous amount of pain, but I'm not going to intervene unless someone prays, or prays the right prayer"? Even from our perspective the answer has at least a 50 percent chance of being no, and God in His foreknowledge would already have known the answer; so, there would be no possibility of a different outcome of any given event regardless if the entire world prayed in unity. So it seems to me that the whole concept of prayer is a ridiculous concept, seeing that an all powerful or all loving God would have intervened rather than allow such pain and suffering to go on for months unnecessarily. And if there is a significant reason for God to allow such pain and suffering, then rather than feel empathy or be sorrowful, should we rejoice knowing that God allowed her to suffer for so long because He, without a doubt, had a good and significant reason to prolong her suffering?

Sorry, but that just doesn't meld!

That brings me to my last point: Why would a Christian lose their mental faculties only to have them revived in a world hereafter? If our spirit and conscience goes on to this great beyond, certainly it would be the very mind we entertain now, otherwise if there is no conscience memory of this world in the hereafter, then we have no real good reason to look forward to a heavenly bliss any more than an atheistic view of nothingness, at least from our current perspective of reality! Why should I prefer heaven, if the mind I will have then is not the same mind I have in this world? And if that mind can be deluded or damaged beyond rational and conscience thought in this world, what hope is there that there is a rejuvenation that awaits us in the hereafter? I believe the fact that the circuitry of one's brain "conscience" can be scrambled or deluded and damaged beyond repair despite one's faith, or lack thereof, is evidence enough that the mind or conscience is not eternal.

David
United States

Dr. Craig's Response

My condolences, David, on your mother's recent death. My own father similarly passed away after being reduced to a mere shadow of himself by Parkinson's disease, and it was painful for me to watch.

But in my work on the problem of evil, I've found it very helpful to distinguish between what I call the emotional problem of evil and the intellectual problem of evil.[7] I can't help but wonder if you are not struggling with the emotional problem of evil, David, since your objections, considered purely intellectually, are not very substantive but seem to be predicated on some basic misunderstandings.

First, and most fundamentally, you have a misconception of the dialectical role of the problem of evil in the dialogue between theism and atheism and, hence, of the burden of proof. The problem of evil or suffering is an argument on behalf of atheism. It is offered as a defeater of the theistic claim that "God exists." The atheist wants to prove that statement false on the basis of the evil in the world. So it's up to him to present an argument that the evil in the world is in some way incompatible with the truth of "God exists."

Philosophical atheists have understood this and so have traditionally offered arguments to the effect that the evil in the world makes it either logically impossible or improbable that God exists and that, therefore, God does not exist. As the person offering the argument, the atheist is under obligation to support the premises of his argument. He cannot just *assert* them and then demand that the theist refute them, any more than the theist, when he offers arguments for God's existence, can just assert them and demand that the atheist refute them. Now it is the atheist's turn, and so it is he who has to bear the burden of proof. The theist may respond to the

> **INSIGHT**
>
> This is an important observation and insight. So often, among cultural popularizers of the problem of evil, one gets the impression that the burden is on the theist. But is it? This is not to suggest that the theist is absolved of any responsible answer to the problem. But it is important to recognize whose problem is the problem of evil.

---

7. For more on this, see J. P. Moreland and William Lane Craig, *Philosophical Foundations for a Christian Worldview*, chapter 27.

273

atheist's argument either by trying to show that the atheist's premises are false (a rebutting defeater-defeater) or else by trying to show that the atheist's premises have not been shown to be true (an undercutting defeater-defeater). In the latter case, the theist doesn't need to explain why God actually permits evil (why would he know that?); he will simply show that the atheist has not been able to exclude that God does have morally sufficient reasons for permitting evil to occur.

Now, part of my response to the argument from evil, defended in my published work, is that the atheist makes probability judgments that are simply beyond our capacity to make with any sort of confidence. So, for example, if God had prevented Hitler from coming to power, we have no idea how the course of subsequent world history might have run. Perhaps an empowered and emboldened Josef Stalin would have wrought worse atrocities (he starved 11 million Ukrainians to death to finance his Marxist state) and eventually plunged the world into war anyway. Perhaps there would have been a nuclear war by now. Who knows? Similarly, no one is in a position to know how your mother's or my father's agonizing deaths may affect the course of world history. Perhaps God wants man to find cures for the diseases and infirmities that afflict us rather than constantly tinker with the world with miraculous interventions to cure people, just as He wants us to develop plumbers and electricians and computer scientists rather than magically solve our problems by constant miraculous interventions in the world, which would leave us like immature children rather than mature moral agents. More specifically, God could have some providential reason for your mother's slow decline. Perhaps He knew that it would cause you to wrestle with your faith and to emerge from this crucible a strengthened and more mature Christian. You have no idea of what God might accomplish through your mother's death. It would be presumptuous of you to think that it was in vain.

Now, your response to this is not to deny the point—you tacitly admit that God may well have providential reasons for permitting the terrible evils in the world—but your rejoinder, then, is to say that we should rejoice that these things have happened, which in light of your pain over your mother's death seems, of course, absurd. But your conclusion doesn't follow, David. As you know, the Scriptures teach that we are to give thanks *in* all circumstances, but not necessarily *for* all circumstances. In particular, we don't thank God for and rejoice at sin. We're glad that in His providence God can bring some good out of Hitler's sinful acts, but neither we nor God is glad at Hitler's evil. In the case of natural evil, like our parents' diseases, we can be relieved that God can bring some good out of what they suffered, but it doesn't follow that we are glad that they suffered.

David, your view of prayer and providence are naïve and based upon fallacious reasoning. If God has middle knowledge, then His providence over a world already takes into account what prayers would be offered in various circumstances. Your anthropomorphic deity looking down and making last-minute decisions is a caricature. In asserting that *"God in His foreknowledge would already have known the answer; so, there would be no possibility of a different outcome of any given event regardless if the entire world prayed in unity,"* you have fallen into the fallacious reasoning of fatalism! It is logically fallacious to infer that because God foreknows that some event will occur, there is, therefore, no possibility that the event will not occur. All that follows is that the event will occur, not that it must occur, and were it to fail to occur, then God would have foreknown differently.[8] This is one of those cases where one sees the real cash value of philosophy for the Christian life. Because of your philosophical mistakes you are led to inveigh against prayer as "ridiculous," thereby cutting yourself off from the very source of hope and comfort that you so badly need. *Of course* you should feel empathy and sorrow for those who suffer, and what you rejoice in is that this suffering is not the unredeemed product of blind chance but allowed by a loving and provident God who can bring some good out of it.

Your final point, David, strikes me as very confused. Certainly there is personal identity of the person who lives on in the afterlife and the person in this life. But why should their mental condition be the same? The late Nobel Prize–winning neurologist Sir John Eckles once explained the relationship of the mind to the brain like this: *the mind uses the brain as an instrument for thought.* Just as a pianist cannot produce beautiful music if his piano is broken down and out of tune, even though he, himself, has the innate ability to produce such music, so the mind cannot think properly when the brain is impaired through disease or drugs. But in the afterlife, and especially in the resurrection, we are freed from such infirmities. The wonderful hope of eternal life can give us courage to endure the brief suffering of this earthly life. You ask, *"What hope is there that there is a rejuvenation that awaits us in the hereafter?"* Why, the resurrection of Jesus, of course! His resurrection in advance of ours is the basis of our hope for not only our, but also for your mother's and my father's, healing and restoration.

David, reading your letter, I don't get the impression that you are very familiar with either natural theology or the historical evidence for Jesus' resurrection, despite your

---

8. Readers may also be interested in Dr. Craig's *The Only Wise God* (repr., Eugene, Oreg.: Wipf & Stock, 2000) for more on fatalism and foreknowledge.

characterization of yourself as a "former die-hard Christian." For the above defensive move I make against the argument from evil is only the reverse side of the coin of the powerful offensive case for the existence of God and the resurrection of Jesus. Even if we had no response to the atheistic argument from evil, I think that these positive arguments and evidence simply outweigh the argument from evil. Yet you seem to be unaware of the positive case for Christian theism.

So these arguments you give for rejecting faith in God aren't really very good, David. I'd encourage you to work through the pain and in time begin to study more seriously, not only the problem of evil, but also the positive evidence in support of our hope.

Was the Slaughter of the Canaanites an Act of "Divine Genocide"?

In the ReasonableFaith.org forums, there have been some good questions raised on the issue of God commanding the Jews to commit "genocide" on the people in the Promised Land. As you have pointed out in some of your written work, this act does not fit with the Western concept of God being the big sugar daddy in the sky. Now, we can certainly find justification for those people coming under God's judgment because of their sins, idolatry, sacrificing their children, etc. But a harder question is the killing of the children and infants. Children and infants are innocent of the sins that their society has committed. How do we reconcile this command of God to kill the children with the concept of his Holiness?

Also, I have heard you justify Old Testament violence on the basis that God had used the Israelite army to judge the Canaanites, and their elimination by Israelites is morally right as they were obeying God's command (it would be wrong if they did not obey God in eliminating the Canaanites). This resembles a bit on how Muslims define morality and justify the violence of Muhammad and other morally questionable actions (Muslims define morality as doing the will of God). Do you see any difference between your justification of Old Testament violence and Islamic justification of Muhammad and violent verses of the Qur'an? Is the violence and the morally questionable actions and verses of the Qur'an, a good argument while talking to Muslims?

Thank you,
Steven

Dr. Craig's Response

According to the Pentateuch (the first five books of the Old Testament), when God called forth His people out of slavery in Egypt and back to the land of their forefathers, He directed them to kill all the Canaanite clans who were living in the land (Deut. 7:1–2; 20:16–18). The destruction was to be complete: every man, woman, and child was to be killed. The book of Joshua tells the story of Israel's carrying out God's command in city after city throughout Canaan.

These stories offend our moral sensibilities. Ironically, however, our moral sensibilities in the West have been largely, and for many people unconsciously, shaped by our Judeo-Christian heritage, which has taught us the intrinsic value of human beings, the importance of dealing justly rather than capriciously, and the necessity of the punishment's fitting the crime. The Bible itself inculcates the values that these stories seem to violate.

The command to kill all the Canaanite peoples is jarring precisely because it seems so at odds with the portrait of Yahweh, Israel's God, which is painted in the Hebrew Scriptures. Contrary to the vituperative rhetoric of someone like Richard Dawkins, the God of the Hebrew Bible is a God of justice, long-suffering, and compassion.

You can't read the Old Testament prophets without a sense of God's profound care for the poor, the oppressed, the downtrodden, the orphaned, and so on. God demands just laws and just rulers. He literally pleads with people to repent of their unjust ways that He might not judge them. "As I live, says the Lord God, I have no pleasure in the death of the wicked, but that the wicked turn from his way and live" (Ezek. 33:11 RSV).

He sends a prophet even to the pagan city of Nineveh because of His pity for its inhabitants, "who do not know their right hand from their left" (Jonah 4:11 RSV). The Pentateuch itself contains the Ten Commandments, one of the greatest of ancient moral codes, which has shaped Western society. Even the stricture "an eye for an eye and a tooth for a tooth" was not a prescription of vengeance but a check on excessive punishment for any crime, serving to moderate violence.

God's judgment is anything but capricious. When the Lord announces His intention to judge Sodom and Gomorrah for their sins, Abraham boldly asks,

Will you indeed sweep away the righteous with the wicked? Suppose there are fifty righteous within the city. Will you then sweep away the place and not spare it for the fifty righteous who are in it? Far be it from you to do such a thing, to put the righteous to death with the wicked, so that the righteous fare as the wicked! Far be that from you! Shall not the Judge of all the earth do what is just? (Gen. 18:23–25 ESV)

Like a Middle Eastern merchant haggling for a bargain, Abraham continually lowers his price, and each time God meets it without hesitation, assuring Abraham that if there are even ten righteous persons in the city, He will not destroy it for their sake.

So then what is Yahweh doing in commanding Israel's armies to exterminate the Canaanite peoples? It is precisely because we have come to expect Yahweh to act justly and with compassion that we find these stories so difficult to understand. How can He command soldiers to slaughter children?

Now, before attempting to say something by way of answer to this difficult question, we should do well first to pause and ask ourselves what is at stake here. Suppose we agree that if God (who is perfectly good) exists, He could not have issued such a command. What follows? That Jesus didn't rise from the dead? That God does not exist? Hardly! So what is the problem supposed to be?

I've often heard popularizers raise this issue as a refutation of the moral argument for God's existence. But that's plainly incorrect. The claim that God could not have issued such a command doesn't falsify or undercut either of the two premises in the moral argument as I have defended it:

1. If God does not exist, objective moral values do not exist.
2. Objective moral values do exist.
3. Therefore, God exists.

In fact, insofar as the atheist thinks that God did something morally wrong in commanding the extermination of the Canaanites, he affirms premise (2). So what is the problem supposed to be?

The problem, it seems to me, is that if God could not have issued such a command, then the biblical stories must be false. Either the incidents never really happened but are just Israeli folklore; or else, if they did, then Israel, carried away in a fit of nationalistic fervor, thinking that God was on their side, claimed that God had commanded them to commit these atrocities, when in fact He had not. In other words, this problem is really an objection to biblical inerrancy.

In fact, ironically, many Old Testament critics are skeptical that the events of the conquest of Canaan ever occurred. They take these stories to be part of the legends of the founding of Israel, akin to the myths of Romulus and Remus and the founding of Rome. For such critics the problem of God's issuing such a command evaporates.

Now, that puts the issue in quite a different perspective! The question of biblical inerrancy is an important one, but it's not like the existence of God or the deity of Christ! If we Christians can't find a good answer to the question before us and are, moreover, persuaded that such a command is inconsistent with God's nature, then we'll have to give up biblical inerrancy. But we shouldn't let the unbeliever raising this question get away with thinking that it implies more than it does.

I think that a good start at this problem is to enunciate our ethical theory that underlies our moral judgments. According to the version of divine command ethics that I've defended, our moral duties are constituted by the commands of a holy and loving God. Since God doesn't issue commands to Himself, He has no moral duties to fulfill. He is certainly not subject to the same moral obligations and prohibitions that we are. For example, I have no right to take an innocent life. For me to do so would be murder. But God has no such prohibition. He can give and take life as He chooses. We all recognize this when we accuse some authority who presumes to take life as "playing God." Human authorities arrogate to themselves rights that belong only to God. God is under no obligation whatsoever to extend my life for another second. If He wanted to strike me dead right now, that's His prerogative. What that implies is that God has the right to take the lives of the Canaanites when He sees fit. How long they live and when they die is up to Him.

But did God, in fact, command the Israelis to exterminate the Canaanites? Or rather was His command primarily a command to drive them out of the land? What do we know of God's intention here?

EXTERMINATE THE CANAANITES?

Suppose that God did issue a command to exterminate the Canaanites. What is the problem here? The problem, as we have seen, isn't simply that God ended the Canaanites' lives. The problem is that He commanded the Israeli soldiers to end them. Now, isn't that like commanding someone to commit murder? No, it's not. Rather, since our moral duties are determined by God's commands, it is commanding someone to do something which, in the absence of a divine command, *would have been* murder. The act was morally obligatory for the Israeli soldiers in virtue of God's command, even though, had they

279

undertaken it on their own initiative, it would have been wrong.

On divine command theory, then, God has the right to command an act, which, in the absence of a divine command, would have been sin, but which is now morally obligatory in virtue of that command.

All right; but isn't such a command contrary to God's nature? Well, let's look at the case more closely. It is perhaps significant that the story of Yahweh's destruction of Sodom— along with his solemn assurances to Abraham that were there as many as ten righteous persons in Sodom, the city would not have been destroyed—forms part of the background to the conquest of Canaan and Yahweh's command to destroy the cities there. The implication is that the Canaanites are not righteous people but have come under God's judgment.

In fact, prior to Israel's bondage in Egypt, God tells Abraham:

> Know for certain that your offspring will be sojourners in a land that is not theirs and will be servants there, and they will be afflicted for four hundred years. . . . And they shall come back here in the fourth generation, for the iniquity of the Amorites [one of the Canaanite clans] is not yet complete. (Gen. 15:13, 16 ESV)

Think of it! God stays His judgment of the Canaanite clans 400 years because their wickedness had not reached the point of intolerability! This is the long-suffering God we know in the Hebrew Scriptures. He even allows His own chosen people to languish in slavery for four centuries before determining that the Canaanite peoples are ripe for judgment and calling His people forth from Egypt.

By the time of their destruction, Canaanite culture was, in fact, debauched and cruel, embracing such practices as ritual prostitution and even child sacrifice. The Canaanites are to be destroyed "that they may not teach you to do according to all their abominable practices that they have done for their gods, and so you sin against the Lord your God" (Deut. 20:18 ESV). God had morally sufficient reasons for His judgment upon Canaan, and Israel was merely the instrument of His justice, just as centuries later God would use the pagan nations of Assyria and Babylon to judge Israel.

But why take the lives of innocent children? The terrible totality of the destruction was undoubtedly related to the prohibition of assimilation to pagan nations on Israel's part. In commanding complete destruction of the Canaanites, the Lord says, "You shall not intermarry with them, giving your daughters to their sons or taking their daughters for your sons, for they would turn away your sons from following me, to serve other gods"

(Deut. 7:3–4 ESV). This command is part and parcel of the whole fabric of complex Jewish ritual law distinguishing clean and unclean practices. To the contemporary Western mind many of the regulations in Old Testament law seem absolutely bizarre and pointless: not to mix linen with wool, drawing fine lines of distinction between clean and unclean, etc. The overriding thrust of these regulations is to prohibit various kinds of mixing. Clear lines of distinction are being drawn: *this* and *not that*. These serve as daily, tangible reminders that Israel is a special people set apart for God Himself.

I spoke once with an Indian missionary who told me that the Eastern mind has an inveterate tendency toward amalgamation. He said Hindus upon hearing the gospel would smile and say, "*Sub ehki eh, sahib, sub ehki eh!*" ("All is One, sahib, All is One!" [Hindustani speakers, forgive my transliteration!]). It made it almost impossible to reach them because even logical contradictions were subsumed in the whole. He said that he thought the reason God gave Israel so many seemingly arbitrary commands about clean and unclean was to teach them the Law of Contradiction!

By setting such strong, harsh dichotomies God taught Israel that any assimilation to pagan idolatry is intolerable. It was His way of preserving Israel's spiritual health and posterity. God knew that if these Canaanite children were allowed to live, they would spell the undoing of Israel. The killing of the Canaanite children not only served to prevent assimilation to Canaanite identity but also served as a shattering, tangible illustration of Israel's being set exclusively apart for God.

Moreover, if we believe, as I do, that God's grace is extended to those who die in infancy or as small children, the death of these children was actually their salvation. We are so wedded to an earthly, naturalistic perspective that we forget that those who die are happy to quit this earth for heaven's incomparable joy. Therefore, God does these children no wrong in taking their lives.

So who does God wrong in commanding the destruction of the Canaanites? Not the Canaanite adults, for they were corrupt and deserving of judgment. Not the children, for they inherit eternal life. So who is wronged? Ironically, I think the most difficult part of this whole debate is the apparent wrong done to the Israeli soldiers themselves. Can you imagine what it would be like to have to break into some house and kill a terrified woman and her children? The brutalizing effect on these Israeli soldiers is disturbing.

But then, again, we're thinking of this from a Christianized, Western standpoint. For people in the ancient world, life was already brutal. Violence and war were a fact of life for people living in the ancient Near East. Evidence of this fact is that the people who told these stories apparently thought nothing of what the Israeli soldiers were commanded to do (especially if these are founding legends of the nation). No one was wringing his hands over the soldiers' having to kill the Canaanites; those who did so were national heroes.

Moreover, my point above returns. Nothing could so illustrate to the Israelis the seriousness of their calling as a people set apart for God alone. Yahweh is not to be trifled with. He means business, and if Israel apostasizes, the same could happen to her. As C. S. Lewis puts it in Narnia, Aslan is not a tame lion.

DRIVE THE CANAANITES OUT OF THE LAND?

So I think that God had the right to command the Israelis to exterminate the Canaanites. But I have come to appreciate as a result of a closer reading of the biblical text that God's command to Israel was not primarily to exterminate the Canaanites but to drive them out of the land. It was the land that was (and remains today!) paramount in the minds of these ancient Near Eastern peoples. The Canaanite tribal kingdoms that occupied the land were to be destroyed as nation states, not as individuals. The judgment of God upon these tribal groups, which had become so incredibly debauched by that time, is that they were being divested of their land. Canaan was being given over to Israel, whom God had now brought out of Egypt. If the Canaanite tribes, seeing the armies of Israel, had simply chosen to flee, no one would have been killed at all. There was no command to pursue and hunt down the Canaanite peoples.

It is, therefore, completely misleading to characterize God's command to Israel as a command to commit genocide. Rather it was first and foremost a command to drive the tribes out of the land and to occupy it. Only those who remained behind were to be utterly exterminated. There may have been no non-combatants killed at all. That makes sense of why there is no record of the killing of women and children, such as I had vividly imagined. Such scenes may have never taken place, since it was the soldiers who remained to fight. It is also why there were plenty of Canaanite people around after the conquest of the land, as the biblical record attests.

No one had to die in this whole affair. Of course, that fact doesn't affect the moral question concerning the command that God gave, as explained above. But I stand by my claim that God could have commanded the killing of any Canaanites who attempted to remain behind in the land.

ANALOGOUS TO ISLAMIC JIHAD?

Now, how does all this relate to Islamic *jihad*? Islam sees violence as a means of propagating the Muslim faith. Islam divides the world into two camps: the *dar al-Islam* (House of Submission) and the *dar al-harb* (House of War). The former are those lands that have been brought into submission to Islam; the latter are those nations that have not yet been brought into submission. This is how Islam actually views the world!

By contrast, the conquest of Canaan represented God's just judgment upon those peoples. The purpose was not at all to get them to convert to Judaism! War was not being used as an instrument of propagating the Jewish faith. Moreover, the slaughter of the Canaanites represented an unusual historical circumstance, not a regular means of behavior.

The problem with Islam, then, is not that it has got the wrong moral theory; it's that it has got the wrong God. If the Muslim thinks that our moral duties are constituted by God's commands, then I agree with him. But Muslims and Christians differ radically over God's nature. Christians believe that God is all-loving, while Muslims believe that God loves only Muslims. Allah has no love for unbelievers and sinners. Therefore, they can be killed indiscriminately. Moreover, in Islam, God's omnipotence trumps everything, even His own nature. He is, therefore, utterly arbitrary in His dealing with mankind. By contrast, Christians hold that God's holy and loving nature determines what He commands.

The question, then, is not whose moral theory is correct, but which is the true God?

Part 5

QUESTIONS ABOUT JESUS CHRIST AND BEING HIS DISCIPLE

The historical Jesus—His life, ministry, message, miracles, and movement—is, arguably, the most widely addressed idea of human history. One cannot properly address, at least in any spirit of thoroughness, the big questions of life and worldview without encountering Jesus. Of course, He is more than an idea or a theory. For the Christian, He is our very Hero, our Lord, our Savior, our Sage, our Master, Teacher, Prophet, and Risen and Exalted One. But what if all of this is a fabrication, a myth spun by early Christians that plagiarized pagan mythology allusions? What if the historical evidence for Jesus' resurrection is not strong but weak? What if the resurrection accounts in the gospels are a late revision influenced by Pauline theology?

The nine questions of this part explore the above questions and more, confronting them with reason and precision. The topics of the historical Jesus and His bodily resurrection from the dead are not only a central concern for Christianity, but they are also among the more notable topics that Dr. Craig has spent decades researching, studying, and engaging critics at some of the highest levels of scholarship and debate. Moreover, Dr. Craig is one of the few notable Christian scholars who intentionally connects the case for Jesus' resurrection with natural theology arguments for God. Why? Because he is not content to present a mere "generic God." Moreover, if Jesus was actually raised from the dead, that's pretty compelling evidence to think that God must exist, don't you think?

Our view of Jesus is integral to our view of what it means to follow Him in our Father's world. Our view of Him in the world will be reflected in who we are in the world. Jesus did not come to merely inaugurate another religion. He came to bring and announce life-giving life. That life is meant to influence all that we do and say for His name's sake. Even the "ordinary" and "common" are swept up and enlivened as subjects for His purposes. As the nineteenth-century Dutch theologian Abraham Kuyper is famous for declaring, "There is not one square inch of the entire creation about which Jesus Christ does not cry out, 'This is mine! This belongs to me!'" So with that recognition, the totality and all-encompassing scope of Christ's Lordship, questions about marriage, productivity, priorities, and maintaining physical stamina can find their meaningful place. But not just them alone, but also questions about how to deal with spiritual failure, the role of doubt in the life of faith, what even is a reasonable faith, and so much more, gain a context and receive a hearing under the reign of Christ in our hearts.

By interacting with the questions and answers of Part Five, you can benefit in the following ways.

In section 1, you can come to discern
• Why connecting pagan mythology to Jesus is problematic.
• What it means for Jesus to be "the Son of God."
• How the witness of pre-Pauline tradition for the empty tomb is powerful.
• Why the argument for the resurrection of Jesus is not deductive but an inference to the best explanation.

In section 2, you can come to wisely know
• How to deal with doubts and their place in our life and worldview.
• How to protect against spiritual failure.
• How to courageously face ridicule and rejection.

You can discover further background to these issues, grow your understanding, and become even more skillful in your communication of what you learn by interacting with some of these valuable resources:

Dig Deeper into Dr. Craig's Work

BEGINNER

Craig, William Lane. *On Guard: Defending Your Faith with Reason and Precision.* Colorado Springs: David C. Cook Publishers, 2010. Chapters 8–10.

Craig, William Lane. "Evidence for Jesus' Resurrection." Lecture at Southampton Civic Hall, UK., October 24, 2011. http://bit.ly/EvidenceForJesusResurrection.

Craig, William Lane. "Who Does Jesus Think He Was?" National Faculty Leadership Conference, Washington, D.C. (2008). http://bit.ly/WhoJesusWas.

INTERMEDIATE

Craig, William Lane. *Philosophical Foundations for a Christian Worldview*. Downers Grove, Ill.: InterVarsity, 2003. Chapters 29–31.

Craig, William Lane. *Reasonable Faith: Christian Truth and Apologetics*. 3rd ed. Wheaton: Crossway, 2008. Chapters 5–8.

Craig, William Lane. "Craig v. Ehrman: Is There Historical Evidence for Resurrection?" College of the Holy Cross, Worcester, Mass., March 28, 2006. http://bit.ly/CraigEhrman.

Craig, William Lane. "Craig v. Lüdemann: Did Jesus Rise from the Dead," Boston College, Mass. 1997, http://bit.ly/CraigLudemann

ADVANCED

Craig, William Lane. *Assessing the New Testament Evidence for the Historicity of the Resurrection of Jesus*. Lewiston, N.Y.: Edwin Mellen, 2002.

Supplemental Recommended Resources

BEGINNER

Groothuis, Douglas. *On Jesus*. Belmont, Calif.: Wadsworth, 2003.

Koukl, Greg. *Tactics: A Game Plan for Discussing Your Christian Convictions*. Grand Rapids: Zondervan, 2009.

Moreland, J. P. and Klaus Issler. *In Search of a Confident Faith*. Downers Grove, Ill.: InterVarsity, 2008.

Strobel, Lee. *The Case for Christ*. Grand Rapids: Zondervan, 1998.

Willard, Dallas. *Renovation of the Heart*. Colorado Springs: NavPress, 2002.

INTERMEDIATE

Boyd, Gregory. *Cynic, Sage, or Son of God?* Wheaton, Ill.: Victor Books, 1995.

Copan, Paul and William Lane Craig, eds. *Come Let Us Reason: New Essays in Christian Apologetics*. Nashville: B&H Publishers, 2012. Chapters 7–11.

Copan, Paul and William Lane Craig, eds. *Contending with Christianity's Critics*. Nashville: Broadman and Holman, 2009. Chapters 7–12.

Copan, Paul and Ronald Tacelli. *Jesus' Resurrection: Fact or Figment?* Downers Grove, Ill.: InterVarsity, 2000.

Craig, William Lane and Chad Meister, eds. *God Is Great, God Is Good*. Downers Grove, Ill.: InterVarsity, 2009. Chapters 12–13.

Groothuis, Douglas. *Christian Apologetics*. Downers Grove, Ill.: InterVarsity, 2011. Chapters 19–22.

Sweis, Khaldoun A. and Chad V. Meister. *Christian Apologetics: An Anthology of Primary Sources*. Grand Rapids: Zondervan, 2012. Chapters 26–28, 33–39.

ADVANCED

Craig, William Lane and J. P. Moreland, eds. *The Blackwell Companion to Natural Theology*. Malden, Mass.: Wiley-Blackwell Publishing, 2009. Chapters 9, 11.

Eddy, Paul Rhodes and Gregory A. Boyd. *The Jesus Legend: A Case for the Historical Reliability of the Synoptic Jesus Tradition*. Grand Rapids: Baker, 2007.

Evans, Craig. *Fabricating Jesus: How Modern Scholars Distort the Gospels*. Downers Grove, Ill.: InterVarsity, 2006.

Green, Joel B., Scot McKnight, and Howard Marshall, eds. *Dictionary of Jesus and the Gospels*. Downers Grove, Ill.: InterVarsity, 1992.

Keener, Craig S. *Miracles: The Credibility of the New Testament Accounts*. Vols. 1–2. Grand Rapids: Baker, 2011.

Keener, Craig S. *The Historical Jesus of the Gospels*. Grand Rapids: Baker, 2009.

Wright, N. T. *The Resurrection of the Son of God*. Minneapolis: Fortress, 2003.

1

ON JESUS

On Assessing Jesus and Pagan Mythological Allusions

Dr. Craig,

Thank you for your help in all that you do to show the truth that is in Christ. I really only have one question, and, to be honest, it frustrates me to no end. It occurs almost every single time I discuss Christianity with someone.

The question of "Is Jesus a copied myth or real person?" is the source of objection I get most of the time. They put in all of the similarities from Christ to other mythological gods and star constellations and then they say, "See how close they are?"

It seems no matter how I refute a certain similarity between Christ and another mythological belief, they don't take what I say very seriously because they object that I have "Worked way too hard to save my religion."

How sound is their case? Is it even debated at the highest levels of scholarship anymore?

I really would like to hear your insight on this matter because I keep on running into it and I'm frankly tired of trying to refute every single similarity.

Thank you for all that you have done. I was once an atheist, but the argument for objective moral values and duties was the one that led me to Christ.

Kevin

(country not specified)

Dr. Craig's Response

The late Robert Funk, founder of the radical Jesus Seminar, used to complain bitterly of the chasm that exists between high scholarship and popular beliefs about Jesus. Funk was thinking primarily of the insulation of popular piety from historical Jesus scholarship; but nowhere does the chasm yawn wider than between popular impiety and historical Jesus studies.

The Free Thought movement, which fuels the popular objection that Christian beliefs about Jesus are derived from pagan mythology, is stuck in the scholarship of the late nineteenth century. In one sense this is flabbergasting, since there are plenty of contemporary skeptical scholars, like those in the Jesus Seminar, whose work Free Thinkers could avail themselves of in order to justify their skepticism about the traditional understanding of Jesus. But it just goes to show how out of touch with scholarly work on Jesus these popularizers are. They are a hundred years out of date.

Back in the heyday of the so-called History of Religions school, scholars in comparative religion collected parallels to Christian beliefs in other religious movements, and some thought to explain those beliefs (including belief in Jesus' resurrection) as the result of the influence of such myths. Today, however, scarcely any scholar thinks of myth as an important interpretive category for the gospels. Scholars came to realize that pagan mythology is simply the wrong interpretive context for understanding Jesus of Nazareth.

Craig Evans has called this shift the "Eclipse of Mythology" in Life of Jesus research.[1] So James D. G. Dunn begins his article on "Myth" in the *Dictionary of Jesus and the Gospels* with the flat disclaimer, "Myth is a term of at best doubtful relevance to the study of Jesus and the gospels."[2] Sometimes this shift is referred to as "the Jewish reclamation of Jesus." For Jesus and His disciples were first-century Palestinian Jews, and it is against that background that they must be understood. The Jewish reclamation of Jesus has helped to make unjustified any understanding of the gospels' portrait of Jesus as significantly shaped by mythology.

---

1. See Evans' excellent article "Life-of-Jesus Research and the Eclipse of Mythology," *Theological Studies* 54 (1993): 3–36.
2. James D. G. Dunn, "Myth," *Dictionary of Jesus and the Gospels* (Downers Grove, Ill.: InterVarsity, 1993), 566.

This shift is pronounced with respect to the historicity of Jesus' miracles and exorcisms. Contemporary scholars may be no more prepared to believe in the supernatural character of Jesus' miracles and exorcisms than were scholars of previous generations. But they are no longer willing to ascribe such stories to the influence of hellenistic divine man (*theios aner*) myths. Rather Jesus' miracles and exorcisms are to be interpreted in the context of first-century Jewish beliefs and practices. Jewish scholar Geza Vermes, for example, has drawn attention to the ministries of the charismatic miracle workers and/or exorcists Honi the Circle-Drawer (first-century BC) and Hanina ben Dosa (first-century AD), and interprets Jesus of Nazareth as a Jewish *hasid* or holy man. Today the consensus of scholarship holds that miracle-working and exorcisms (bracketing the question of their supernatural character) most assuredly do belong to any historically acceptable reconstruction of Jesus' ministry.

The collapse of the old History of Religions school took place primarily for two reasons. First, scholars came to realize that the alleged parallels are spurious. The ancient world was a virtual cornucopia of myths of gods and heroes. Comparative studies in religion and literature require sensitivity to their similarities and differences, or distortion and confusion inevitably result. Unfortunately, those who adduced parallels to Christian beliefs failed to exercise such sensitivity. Take, for example, the story of the Virgin Birth, or, more accurately, Jesus' virginal conception. The alleged pagan parallels to this story concern tales of gods assuming bodily form and having sexual intercourse with human females to sire divine-human progeny (like Hercules). As such, these stories are exactly the opposite of the gospel story of Mary's conceiving Jesus apart from any sexual relations. The gospel stories of Jesus' virginal conception are, in fact, without parallel in the ancient Near East.

Or consider the gospel event of most interest to me: Jesus' resurrection from the dead. Many of the alleged parallels to this event are actually apotheosis stories, the divinization and assumption of the hero into heaven (Hercules, Romulus). Others are disappearance stories, asserting that the hero has vanished into a higher sphere (Apollonius of Tyana, Empedocles). Still others are seasonal symbols for the crop cycle, as the vegetation dies in the dry season and comes back to life in the rainy season (Tammuz, Osiris, Adonis). Some are political expressions of emperor worship (Julius Caesar, Caesar Augustus). None of these is parallel to the Jewish idea of the resurrection of the dead. David Aune, who is a specialist in comparative ancient Near Eastern literature, concludes, "no parallel to them [resurrection traditions] is found in Graeco-Roman biography."[3]

3. David Aune, "The Genre of the Gospels," in *Gospel Perspectives II*, R. T. France and David Wenham, eds. (Sheffield: JSOT Press, 1981), 48.

In fact, most scholars have come to doubt whether, properly speaking, there really were any myths of dying and rising gods at all! In the Osiris myth, one of the best known symbolic seasonal myths, Osiris does not really come back to life but simply continues to exist in the nether realm of the departed. In a recent review of the evidence, T. N. D. Mettinger reports: "From the 1930s . . . a consensus has developed to the effect that the 'dying and rising gods' died but did not return or rise to live again. . . . Those who still think differently are looked upon as residual members of an almost extinct species."[4] Mettinger himself believes that myths of dying and rising did exist in the cases of Dumuzi, Baal, and Melqart; but he recognizes that such symbols are quite unlike the early Christian belief in Jesus' resurrection:

> The dying and rising gods were closely related to the seasonal cycle. Their death and return were seen as reflected in the changes of plant life. The death and resurrection of Jesus is a one-time event, not repeated, and unrelated to seasonal changes. . . . There is, as far as I am aware, no *prima facie* evidence that the death and resurrection of Jesus is a mythological construct, drawing on the myths and rites of the dying and rising gods of the surrounding world. While studied with profit against the background of Jewish resurrection belief, the faith in the death and resurrection of Jesus retains its unique character in the history of religions. The riddle remains.[5]

Notice Mettinger's insight that the belief in Jesus' resurrection may be profitably studied against the background of *Jewish* resurrection beliefs (not pagan mythology). Here we see that shift in New Testament studies I flagged above as the Jewish reclamation of Jesus. The spuriousness of the alleged parallels is just one indication that pagan mythology is the wrong interpretive framework for understanding the disciples' belief in Jesus' resurrection.

Second, the History of Religions school collapsed as an explanation of the origin of Christian beliefs about Jesus because there was no causal connection between pagan myths and the origin of Christian beliefs about Jesus. Take, for example, the resurrection. Jews were familiar with the seasonal deities mentioned above and found them abhorrent. Therefore, there is no trace of cults of dying and rising gods in first-century

4. Tryggve N. D. Mettinger, *The Riddle of Resurrection: "Dying and Rising Gods" in the Ancient Near East* (Stockholm, Sweden: Almquist & Wiksell International, 2001), 4, 7.
5. Ibid., 221.

Palestine. For Jews, the resurrection to glory and immortality would not take place until the general resurrection of all the dead at the end of the world. It boggles the imagination to think that the original disciples would have suddenly and sincerely come to believe that Jesus of Nazareth was risen from the dead just because they had heard of pagan myths about dying and rising seasonal gods.

But, in a sense, all this is irrelevant to your main question, Kevin. For, as you indicate, the people you're talking to are impervious to scholarship. When you point out to them the spuriousness of the alleged parallels, then you're accused of "working too hard to save your religion." This is a no-win situation for you. So I'm inclined to say that you should not go about "trying to refute every single similarity." Rather I think a more general and dismissive attitude on your part may be more effective.

When they say that Christian beliefs about Jesus are derived from pagan mythology, I think you should laugh. Then look at them wide-eyed and with a big grin, and exclaim, "Do you really believe *that*?" Act as though you've just met a flat earther or Roswell conspirator. You could say something like, "Man, those old theories have been dead for over a hundred years! Where are you getting this stuff?" Tell them this is just sensationalist junk, not serious scholarship. If they persist, then ask them to show you the actual passages narrating the supposed parallel. They're the ones who are swimming against the scholarly consensus, so make them work hard to save their religion. I think you'll find that they've never even read the primary sources.

> **INSIGHT**
> Notice the cleverness and wisdom of this approach. Sometimes this really is the best means of letting the pretentious air out of the room.

If they ever do cite a primary source passage, I think you'd be surprised what you find. For example, in my debate on the resurrection with Robert Price, he claimed that Jesus' healing miracles were derived from mythological healing stories like those concerning Asclepius. I insisted that he read to us a passage from the primary sources showing the purported parallel. When he did so, the tale he produced bore no resemblance whatsoever to the gospel stories of Jesus' healing miracles! It was the best proof that the stories were not genealogically related.

Remember: anyone pressing this objection has a burden of proof to bear. He needs to show that the narratives are parallel and, moreover, that they are causally connected. Insist that they bear that burden if you are to take their objection seriously.

On What It Means for Jesus to Be the Son of God

Hello, Dr. Craig!

First of all, I'd like to introduce myself. I'm from Pakistan, and it's been a spell that I'm listening to you and watching your debates with intellectuals whose beliefs are on the contrary to yours. I am literally thrilled by your standard of epistemology, reasoning, and knowledge. The good news is that I have embraced Christ Jesus and trying my best, day by day, to walk in Him.

I saw your debate with the Muslim scholar, namely Dr. Badawi, and saw him objecting that the central Christian word, i.e., "Trinity" is not recorded in the Bible. But that was an arbitrary argument from Dr. Badawi's side because he knows that the word "Tawheed"—which is the central word for the concept of God in Islam and is one of the five pillars upon which Islam is erected—*does not* exist in the Qur'an! So, does that make that word unacceptable for Muslims? No. Likewise, if a Muslim objects to the concept of the Trinity merely because it's not written by name in the Bible, literally, then that Muslim has to abandon and revoke the concept of Tawheed, since it doesn't exist in the Qur'an.

As usual, you formulated your arguments in a very compelling, coherent, and eloquent manner and Dr. Badawi couldn't address those issues. That was quite evident.

My question to you is: "Jesus is called God's Son in the Bible just like other righteous people. So, what makes Jesus different than others when it comes to the entitlement of sonship of God?"

M.

Dr. Craig's Response

I'm thrilled that you've come to believe in Christ Jesus as your Savior and Lord, M.! (I've abbreviated your name just in case you're still in Pakistan.) You are correct that the validity of a theological concept doesn't in any way depend upon the vocabulary used to express it. The question you raise is an important and interesting one, which I address in the third edition of my *Reasonable Faith*. I'll draw upon that discussion in answering your question here.

As I mentioned in the debate with Dr. Badawi, we have good historical grounds for thinking that Jesus understood Himself to be and claimed to be the Son of God. First, Jesus' parable of the wicked tenants of the vineyard (Mark 12:1–9) tells us that Jesus thought of Himself as God's only son, distinct from all the prophets, God's final messenger, and even the heir of Israel itself. Notice that one cannot delete the figure of the son from the parable as an inauthentic, later addition, for then the parable lacks any climax and point. Moreover, the uniqueness of the son is not only explicitly stated but inherently implied by the tenants' stratagem of murdering the heir in order to claim possession of the vineyard. So this parable discloses to us that the historical Jesus believed and taught that He was the *only* Son of God.

Second, Jesus' self-concept as God's Son comes to explicit expression in Matthew 11:27 (RSV) (cf. Luke 10:22), "All things have been delivered to me by my Father; and no one knows the Son except the Father, and no one knows the Father except the Son and any one to whom the Son chooses to reveal him." Here Jesus claims to be the exclusive Son of God and the only revelation of God the Father to mankind. This saying tells us that Jesus thought of Himself as God's Son in an absolute and unique sense and as having been invested with the exclusive authority to reveal His Father God to men.

Finally, Jesus' saying concerning the date of the consummation: "But of that day or that hour no one knows, not even the angels in heaven, nor the Son, but only the Father" (Mark 13:32 RSV) again speaks of the Son in terms implying uniqueness.

On the basis of these three sayings, we have good evidence that Jesus thought of Himself as the unique Son of God. It's true that Jewish kings were referred to as God's sons (2 Sam. 7:14; 1 Chron. 17:13; 22:10; Psalm 2:6–7; 89:26–27), and in wisdom literature the righteous man could be characterized as God's child, having God as his father (Wisdom 2:13, 16, 18; 5:5; Sirach 4:10; 51:10). Such generic usage is, however, irrelevant to Jesus' claim to divine Sonship, given the uniqueness and exclusivity of His claim. Jesus thought of Himself as God's Son in a singular sense that set Him apart even from the prophets who had gone before.

But what was that sense? We must not conclude too hastily that the title was an implied claim to divinity. It might be that Jesus thought of Himself as God's unique Son in the sense that He was the promised Messiah. The Jewish pseudepigraphal work IV Ezra

7:28–29 speaks of Messiah as God's son but nonetheless as mortal. The Dead Sea scrolls also show that the Messiah was thought to be God's son (4Q174; 4Q246; 1QSa 2:11-12). The uniqueness of Jesus' Sonship could be a function of the uniqueness of the Messiah.

On the other hand, it must be said in all honesty that these Jewish texts do not even approach the sort of absoluteness and exclusivity claimed by Jesus of Nazareth in the sayings mentioned above. There's nothing in Dead Sea texts to suggest that the Messiah would be the unique Son of God. Being the Messiah might set Jesus apart from all the prophets who had come before Him and make Him the heir of Israel, as claimed in the parable of the wicked tenants of the vineyard, but being Messiah would not give Him exclusive knowledge of the Father and absolute revelatory significance, as claimed in Matt. 11:27. Moreover, the saying in Mark 13:32 not only discloses Jesus' sense of unique sonship but also presents us with an ascending scale of status from men to angels to the Son to the Father. Jesus' sense of being God's Son involved a sense of proximity to the Father that transcended that of any mortal man (such as a king or prophet) or any angelic being.

Such an exalted conception of God's Son is not foreign to first-century Judaism. The New Testament itself bears witness to this fact (Col. 1:13–20; Heb. 1:1–12). In IV Ezra 13, Ezra sees a vision of a man arising out of the sea who is identified by God as "my Son" (13:32, 37) and who proceeds to subdue all the nations. Ezra asks,

> O sovereign Lord, explain this to me: Why did I see the man coming up from the heart of the sea?
>
> He said to me, "Just as no one can explore or know what is in the depths of the sea, so no one on earth can see my Son or those who are with him, except in the time of his day." (IV Ezra 13:51–52; cf. 13:26)

That there are other persons presently with the Son prior to His earthly appearance suggests that the Son is a pre-existent, heavenly figure. This becomes quite clear in 14:9 when Ezra is told that his own life is about to end and that he is going to be with God's Son until He is revealed at the end of time: "You shall be taken up from among men, and henceforth you shall live with my Son and those who are like you, until the times are ended." It's intriguing that there is a differentiation made between the pre-existent Son and the righteous, human dead like Ezra who are with him. The Son is clearly set apart as a supernatural figure.

Moreover, as I show in *Reasonable Faith*, the title "Messiah" itself was also a title that could be infused with connotations of divinity. Titles like "the Son of God" and "the Messiah" were multivalent and, therefore, inherently ambiguous without a context. In order to understand the meaning that Jesus invested in such self-descriptions we need to look at the context of His whole life and proclamation, and when we do, it becomes clear that He was claiming superhuman status.

On Assessing Independent Sources for Jesus' Burial and Empty Tomb

Dr. Craig,

I am having a difficult time understanding something that you have said with respect to the historicity of Jesus' resurrection. You say that the four gospels are "independent" attestations of events and, therefore, things like Jesus' burial in a rock-hewn tomb and the discovery of that rock-hewn tomb empty are virtually certain to be historical. But couldn't the gospels all be dependent on common oral traditions or on those gospels written first (i.e., didn't at least Matthew and Luke have Mark available to them?). Basically, my question is: How do you arrive at your conclusion that the four gospels are independent instead of dependent attestations of events?

Dave

Dr. Craig's Response

I'm glad to clarify this issue, Dave, because some people seem to have misunderstood me when I argue that Jesus' burial and empty tomb are independently attested in multiple sources. The claim here is not the naïve assertion that because these events are mentioned in more than one gospel they thereby enjoy multiple, independent attestation.

Rather as I stated in my recent debate with Richard Carrier, the burial account is part of Mark's source material for the story of Jesus' Passion. This is a very early source, which is probably based on eyewitness testimony and dates to within several years of Jesus' crucifixion. Moreover, Paul in his first letter to the church of Corinth also cites an extremely early source for Jesus' burial which most scholars date to within a few years or even months of the crucifixion. Independent testimony to Jesus' burial by Joseph is also found in the special sources used by Matthew and Luke and in the Gospel of John. Historians consider themselves to have hit historical pay dirt when they have *two* independent accounts of the same event. But we have the remarkable number of at least five independent sources for Jesus' burial, some of which are extraordinarily early.

Mark's Passion source didn't end with Jesus' burial, but with the story of the empty tomb, which is tied to the burial account verbally and grammatically. Moreover, Matthew and John rely on independent sources about the empty tomb. Jesus' empty tomb is also mentioned in the early sermons independently preserved in the Acts of the Apostles (2:29–31; 13:36–37), and it's implied by the very old tradition handed on by Paul in his first letter to the Corinthian church (1 Cor. 15:4). Thus, we have multiple, early attestation of the fact of the empty tomb in at least four independent sources.

Notice the focus is on the early, independent *sources* used by the New Testament authors. First and foremost is the Passion source that Mark used in writing his gospel. Whereas most of Mark's gospel consists of short anecdotal stories strung like pearls on a string, when we get to the final week of Jesus' life we encounter a continuous narrative of events from the Jewish plot during the Feast of Unleavened Bread through Jesus' burial and empty tomb. The events of the Last Supper, arrest, execution, burial, and empty tomb were central to the identity of early Christian communities. According to James D. G. Dunn, "The most obvious explanation of this feature is that the framework was early on fixed within the tradition process and remained so throughout the transition to written gospels. This suggests in turn a tradition rooted in the memory of the participants and put into that framework by them."[6] The dominant view among NT scholars is, therefore, that the Passion narratives are early and based on eyewitness testimony.[7] Indeed, according to Richard Bauckham, many scholars date Mark's Passion narrative no later than the 40s (recall that Jesus died in AD 30).[8] So we're dealing here with an extraordinarily early source.

Now, Matthew and Luke probably knew Mark's gospel, as you note, and used it as one of their sources. But the differences between Mark and the other Synoptics point to other independent sources behind Matthew and Luke. These differences are not plausibly explained as

---

6. J. D. G. Dunn, *Jesus Remembered* (Grand Rapids: Eerdmans, 2003), 765–66.

7. Mark Allen Powell, "Book Review of *The Birth of Christianity*," JAAR 68:1 (2000): 171.

8. Richard Bauckham, *Jesus and the Eyewitnesses* (Grand Rapids: Eerdmans, 2006), 243.

due to editorial changes introduced by Matthew and Luke because of (i) their sporadic and uneven nature (*e.g.*, Mark: "tomb which had been hewn out of rock"; Matthew: "tomb which he hewed in the rock"; (ii) the inexplicable omission of events like Pilate's interrogating the centurion; and (iii) Matthew and Luke's agreeing in *their* wording in contrast to Mark (*e.g.*, Matt. 27:58 = Luke 23:52) "This man went in to Pilate and asked for the body of Jesus." Also the phrase translated "wrapped it in linen" is identical in Matthew and Luke. How could Matthew and Luke have *independently* chosen exactly the same wording in contrast to Mark? They both probably had another source. Indeed, as we'll see when we get to the empty tomb account, differences between Matthew and Luke emerge that suggest multiple sources.

Moreover, John is generally believed to be independent of the Synoptic gospels. As Paul Barnett points out, "Careful comparison of the texts of Mark and John indicate that neither of these gospels is dependent on the other. Yet they have a number of incidents in common: For example . . . the burial of Jesus in the tomb of Joseph of Arimathea."[9]

Finally, the old tradition handed on by Paul to the Corinthian church, which is among the earliest traditions identifiable in the NT, refers to Jesus' burial in the second line of the tradition. That this is the same event as the burial described in the gospels becomes evident by comparing Paul's tradition with the Passion narratives on the one hand and the sermons in the Acts of the Apostles on the other. The four-line tradition handed on by Paul is a summary of the central events of Jesus' crucifixion, burial by Joseph of Arimathea, the discovery of His empty tomb, and His appearances to the disciples.

What about the empty tomb account? First, it was also part of the pre-Markan Passion narrative. The empty tomb story is syntactically tied to the burial story; indeed, they are just one story. For example, the antecedent of "him" (Jesus) in Mark 16:1 is in the burial account (15:43); the women's discussion of the stone presupposes the stone's being rolled over the tomb's entrance; their visiting the tomb presupposes their noting its location in 15:47; the words of the angel "see the place where they laid him" refer back to Joseph's laying Jesus' body in the tomb.

As for the other gospels, that Matthew has an independent tradition of the empty tomb is evident not only from the non-Matthean vocabulary (*e.g.*, the words translated "on the next day," "the preparation day," "deceiver," "guard [of soldiers]," "to make secure," "to seal"; the expression "on the third day" is also non-Matthean, for he everywhere else uses "after

9. Paul Barnett, *Jesus and the Logic of History* (Downers Grove, Ill.: InterVarsity, 1997), 104–5.

three days"; the expression "chief priests and Pharisees" never appears in Mark or Luke and is also unusual for Matthew), but also from Matt. 28:15: "this story has been spread among Jews till this day," indicative of a tradition history of disputes with Jewish non-Christians. Luke and John have the non-Markan story of Peter and another disciple inspecting the tomb, which, given John's independence of Luke, indicates a separate tradition behind the story. Moreover, we have already seen that John's independence of Mark shows that he has a separate source for the empty tomb.

The early sermons in Acts are likely not created by Luke out of whole cloth but represent early apostolic preaching. We find the empty tomb implied in the contrast between David's tomb and Jesus': "David died and was buried and his tomb is with us to this day." But "this Jesus God has raised up" (2:29–32; cf. 13:36–37). Finally, the third line of the tradition handed on by Paul summarizes, as I have said, the empty tomb story. The German NT critic Klaus Berger concludes: "Without a doubt the grave of Jesus was found to be empty, and, moreover, the texts about it are not in general dependent upon Mark."[10]

Thus, the burial and empty tomb of Jesus enjoy multiple, early, independent attestation. While some of these traditions could be variations on a common tradition (such as Luke and John's tradition of the disciples' inspection of the empty tomb in response to the women's report), they cannot all be so regarded because they narrate different events. Even in the case of variations on a common tradition, we are pushed back so early, as Dunn emphasizes, that we must now ask what events occurred to leave such an early impression on the tradition, and the obvious explanation is the burial of Jesus in the tomb and the discovery of the empty tomb. While multiple, independent attestation alone would not render the burial and empty tomb "virtually certain," keep in mind that this is but one line of evidence among many, so that the cumulative case for these facts is very powerful, indeed.

10. From *Zeitschrift fur katholische Theologie* (1993), 436.

On the Significance of the Witness of the Pre-Pauline Tradition to the Empty Tomb

Dr. Craig,

I have a few questions regarding some of your arguments in your article, "The Historicity of the Empty Tomb of Jesus."[11] My questions center around your claims that we can establish that Paul believed and knew about the empty tomb.

First off, you discuss the formula that Paul uses in 1 Cor. 15:3–5, and you claim that it is a very old Christian formula that Paul probably received on his visit to Jerusalem following his conversion. Therefore, you say that this formula can probably be dated back to within five years of Christ's death. You base your belief that this formula is an old Christian tradition on its "Semitic and non-Pauline characteristics" and on Paul's claim that this gospel formula is something that he received.

However, in Paul's epistle to the Gal. (3:11–12, 15–18) he says,

But I certify you, brethren, that the gospel which was preached of me is not after man. For I neither received it of man, neither was I taught it, but by the revelation of Jesus Christ . . . But when it pleased God who separated me from my mother's womb, and called me by his grace, to reveal his Son in me that I might preach him among the heathen; immediately I conferred not with flesh and blood; Neither went I up to Jerusalem to them which were apostles before me; but I went into Arabia, and returned again unto Damascus. Then after three years I went up to Jerusalem to see Peter . . .

Paul seems to claim that he didn't receive the gospel which he preached and specifically outlined in 1 Cor. 15:3–5 from man, but from God in some special revelation. Therefore, how do you reconcile your belief that Paul received and consequently preached the old Christian formula of 1 Cor. 15:3–5 with what Paul says in Galatians 3? In

11. This article can be accessed for free at ReasonableFaith.org (http://bit.ly/HistoricityOfEmptyTomb).

addition, what are the Semitic and non-Pauline characteristics that are exhibited in 1 Cor. 15:3–5?

Lastly, you conclude that Paul's claim that Christ rose "on the third day" is indicative of a physical resurrection and, consequently, an empty tomb. You say that colloquial usage of the phrase "on the third day" in the formula and within Christian writings is probably "a time indicator for the events of Easter, including the empty tomb, employing the language of the Old Testament concerning God's acts of deliverance and victory on the third day, perhaps with texts like Jonah 2:11 and Hos. 6:2 especially in mind." However, it seems to me that the dating of the resurrection on the third day could also just as easily have been the result of Christ appearing to the disciples (not even necessarily on the third day) and their remembrance numerous claims that He would rise on the third day (e.g., Matt. 12:39–40; 16:21; 17:22–23; 20:17–19; 27:63, etc.). How do you know that the development of the phrase "on the third day" was not the result of many predictions to His disciples and others that He would rise on the third day? Sorry for the long question. I've just been studying your arguments for the resurrection, and these are some questions that I can't seem to resolve.

Jacob
(country not specified)

Dr. Craig's Response

The evidence that Paul is not writing in his own hand in 1 Cor. 15:3–5 is so powerful that all New Testament scholars recognize that Paul is here passing on a prior tradition. In addition to the fact that Paul explicitly *says* as much, the passage is replete with non-Pauline characteristics, including, in order of appearance: (i) the phrase "for our sins" using the genitive case and plural noun is unusual for Paul; (ii) the phrase "according to the Scriptures" is unparalleled in Paul, who introduces scriptural citations by "as it is written"; (iii) the perfect passive verb "has been raised" appears only in this chapter and in a pre-Pauline confessional formula in 2 Tim. 2:8; (iv) the phrase "on the third day" with its ordinal number following the noun in Greek is non-Pauline; (v) the word "appeared" is found only here and in the confessional formula in 1 Tim. 3:16; and (vi) "the Twelve" is not Paul's nomenclature, for he always speaks of the twelve disciples as "the apostles."

Now, the visit during which Paul may have received this tradition is the visit you mention three years after his conversion on the road to Damascus (Gal. 1:18). This puts the tradition back to within the first five years after Jesus' death in AD 30. So there's not even an apparent inconsistency with Paul's appropriating the language of the formula to encapsulate the gospel he was already preaching during those first three years in Damascus.

The only way there would be even an apparent tension would be if Paul received the tradition while in Damascus at the very beginning. In that case, in light of the evidence, we'd have to say that Paul is putting his own "spin" on things to the Galatians to his own advantage.

But does Paul's statement in Gal. 1:11–12 imply that he received no oral tradition like 1 Cor. 15:3–5 while in Damascus? I think not. "His" gospel, of which Paul was so proud, was the gospel of God's grace freely bestowed on Jew and Gentile alike without discrimination. It was this gospel that he later laid before the Jerusalem apostles to make sure that he was not running in vain (Gal. 2:2). But they were happy for Paul to take the gospel to the Gentiles as they had to Jews. Paul's receiving this insight into the gospel by direct revelation is not at all inconsistent with his learning the basic events of Christ's passion rehearsed in the early formula. Indeed, since he had been a persecutor of the early church, he was probably familiar with the basic events already as a non-Christian.

As for the "third day" motif, it is more probable that this is tied to the empty tomb tradition than to the appearance traditions. The phrase appears in the third line of the formula, which is a summary of the empty tomb narrative.[12] It seems to be a theologically loaded rendering of the phrase "the first day of the week," which is used in the empty tomb narrative. Notice, too, that the third day is always associated with the event of Jesus' rising from the dead, never with the appearances.

The problem with reading the third day motif off Jesus' resurrection predictions alone, rather than as a time indicator of when the tomb was discovered empty, is that the prophecies are not as strongly attested historically as the empty tomb itself. Indeed, they're often regarded as having been written after the fact. So if you accept their authenticity, there's no basis remaining for the even more strongly attested fact of the empty tomb. If the early proclaimers of Jesus' resurrection chose to adopt the language of His prophecies, that was because the tomb had, in fact, been discovered empty on the first day of the week, the third day after Christ's crucifixion.

---

12. See comparative chart in *The Son Rises*, 49–50.

Can One Justifiably Infer Jesus' Resurrection on the Basis of Empirical Evidence?

I've been seeing an argument against Jesus' resurrection making the rounds on the Internet. It says basically:

1. If it cannot be established that Jesus transformed into a supernatural body after He rose from the dead, then the Resurrection cannot be established.
2. It cannot be established that Jesus transformed into a supernatural body after He rose from the dead.
3. Therefore, the Resurrection cannot be established.

It seems to say that even if Jesus somehow survived death, there is no evidence whatever that He rose in an immortal/indestructible body. Therefore, the argument grants a resurrection of sorts, but not the supernatural kind the New Testament describes. Thus, the divine claims of Christ cannot be established by resurrection evidence.

An illustration that often accompanies the argument is that of a man who claims to be impervious to gunfire and can melt objects with lasers from his eyes. Even if he demonstrates this, should one believe his further claim that he could withstand a nuclear-bomb blast? The skeptic says no, because a nuke explosion is so much greater than mere gunfire and lasers.

In the same sense, even if Jesus came back to life, that is infinitely inferior to His more amazing claim to be God! Can you help?

Sincerely,

Don

Dr. Craig's Response

The argument seems to assume that one must establish proof of Jesus' resurrection by proving He had a supernatural body after He was raised. This really isn't an argument *against* Jesus' resurrection, Don. Rather it's an attempt to prove that you can't justifiably infer Jesus' resurrection on the basis of empirical evidence. It's an attempt, not to refute the resurrection of Jesus, but to undercut a historical argument for Jesus' resurrection. As such, it's of interest to Christian apologists but needn't be of concern to most Christians, who don't base their belief in Jesus' resurrection on historical evidence.

> **INSIGHT**
> Notice this important clarification and contextualization of the objection.

This objection to a historical case for Jesus' resurrection owes its origin to Greg Cavin, who published an article about it in the journal *Faith and Philosophy* a number of years back.[13] The nerve of the argument is that even if everything the gospels report concerning Jesus is established to be true, the inference to Jesus' resurrection is unwarranted because "resurrection" in the full Jewish sense of that term meant entry into an immortal, indestructible bodily condition. But how could you prove that the post-Easter Jesus could have survived a nuclear bomb blast? If you can't prove that, then you haven't proved His resurrection in the full, theological sense of that term.

I have to say in all candor that this objection has always struck me as a mere cavil. It could be pressed, perversely, even by one of the very eyewitnesses to Jesus' resurrection, such as doubting Thomas, which surely suggests that something has gone awry here.

In fact, the argument goes awry at a number of levels. First, the Christian apologist doesn't claim to have proof of Jesus' resurrection. In fact, the apologist needn't be understood to be arguing for Jesus' resurrection in the full, theological sense of the word. You'll notice that in my own case, what I identify as *the Resurrection Hypothesis* is the statement "God raised Jesus from the dead." That's all I mean by "resurrection." Such a claim is an assertion of a miracle, an event caused by God, which is naturally impossible. As Cavin himself argued in another context,[14] that all the cells in Jesus' body should naturally come back to life is incomprehensibly improbable, so that even his own outrageously improbable Twin Theory (a.k.a. the "Dave" Theory, after the Kevin Kline movie) is preferable to such a naturalistic hypothesis. So if the Resurrection Hypothesis is, as I claim, the best

13. Robert Greg Cavin, "Is There Sufficient Historical Evidence to Establish the Resurrection of Jesus?" *Faith and Philosophy* 12:3 (July 1995): 361–79.

14. See Robert Greg Cavin, "Miracles, Probability, and the Resurrection of Jesus: A Philosophical, Mathematical, and Historical Study," PhD dissertation (Irvine: University of California, 1993).

explanation of the evidence, then one is justified in inferring a supernatural act of God on behalf of Jesus. Whether this event also involved Jesus' risen body being invested with properties of invulnerability, indestructibility, etc., can be left as open questions for theological reflection.

ARGUING AN INFERENCE TO THE BEST EXPLANATION

Second, the objection seems to misconstrue the case for Jesus' resurrection, even in the full sense of that word, as a deductive argument rather than as an inference to the best explanation. The objector seems to think that the Christian apologist needs to be able to deduce logically from the evidence that, for example, Jesus could have survived cholera or an automobile crash. But that's not the way an inductive argument works. For any data set there will be an infinite number of hypotheses that are consistent with the data. To use a well-known example, think of a set of points plotted relative to two axes. There is an infinite number of lines that could be drawn through those same points, some curving wildly before connecting the dots. But does that mean that a scientist drawing a smooth curve through those points is making an unjustifiable inference about the implications of the data? Of course not! He infers that the relatively straight line correctly interprets the data on the grounds of its comparative simplicity.

Similarly, in inferring that Jesus was risen from the dead in the full, Jewish sense of that term, one is inferring to the best explanation of the data. Here, the religio-historical context of the event is the key to its proper interpretation. Given its Jewish context, if the God of Israel has raised Jesus, thereby vindicating His allegedly blasphemous claims by which He put Himself in God's place, then the most natural inference is that Jesus' resurrection has occurred in advance, ahead of the general resurrection which was the Jewish hope. This conclusion is especially manifest if Jesus predicted His death and resurrection by Israel's God, for He was speaking of resurrection in the full Jewish sense. It would be grossly *ad hoc* and un-Jewish to assert that a better explanation was that Jesus was raised but was still susceptible to, *say*, malaria or being electrocuted. Such a hypothesis is consistent with the data but fails hopelessly as an inference to the best explanation.

THE RESURRECTION DEMONSTRATES GOD'S VALIDATION OF JESUS' CLAIMS

Third, this same point applies with respect to justifying Jesus' claims to divinity. The argument is not that only a divine being can be raised from the dead or that Jesus' divinity can be deduced logically from His resurrection. Rather, the claim is that given the religio-historical context of Jesus' own radical self-understanding and blasphemous personal claims, not to mention His activity as a miracle-worker, exorcist, and herald of the inbreaking of God's kingdom, God's raising Jesus from the dead is most plausibly understood as God's ratification of those claims.

I recall a wonderful illustration of this sort of inference related by the Christian philosopher Tom Morris in his book *Making Sense of It All.* Tom writes:

> For many years I did not myself understand how exactly miracles were supposed to function as marks of divine truth until I met a most extraordinary man. I was living in a vacation house out in the woods on seven acres of land with two other graduate students during my first semester at Yale. A man from the adjoining property introduced himself one day and told me that the night before we had moved in, he had found a motorcycle gang camped in the woods between our houses. It was three a.m., he said, when he appeared among them and persuaded them to leave. He explained that he often roamed the woods at night and hunted when he couldn't sleep because of old war injuries. Unzipping his windbreaker, he showed me the .44 magnum long-barreled handgun in a shoulder holster he always carried with him. "Sometimes makes the folks at the bank a little nervous," he added with a smile and a wink.
>
> Subsequent visits and inquiries on my part led to some war stories that were definitely movie material. He was in a special unit trained in all the relevant martial arts. He could kill at a distance with any projectile—a ballpoint pen, a number two pencil. He and a Shoshone Indian were the only members of his unit to make it back from the Second World War. And that was after he had been shot by a tank. I was invited to feel the hole in this bear-of-a-man's shoulder, while the stories grew in drama. Jumping from planes behind enemy lines, slitting open German attack dogs mid-leap, capturing and eliminating Nazi offers with piano wire. The strategies, the close calls, the exciting escapes. Better than in the movies. One day I saw a medallion on the front bumper of his pickup truck inscribed with the name of a town in Connecticut and "Honorary Police Chief." I asked about this.
>
> 'Oh, it was nothing, Tom. I was just drivin' down the street one day a few years ago and I see out behind a building four guys beatin' up some cop they had on the ground. Well, I couldn't let that happen, so I got outta the truck and stopped it. The mayor thought it was nice of me to help out, so he made me honorary chief of police.'

I asked, 'What happened to the four guys?' He replied, 'Let's just say they had a nice long stay in the hospital.'

The stories got more elaborate, and I began to wonder whether they could possibly all be true. We had gone far beyond any of the war and spy stories I had ever heard or seen on the big screen. At a certain point, anyone would become unsure that all this could possibly be true.

Then, one day, sitting on an outdoor deck playing my guitar, I was stung by the largest, most menacing-looking wasp I had ever seen. The sting was extremely painful and the spot on my left calf immediately began to redden and swell. I became dizzy. Within a minute or two I couldn't walk. The pain was terrible, the swelling was huge, and a housemate had to practically carry me over to the neighbor's for a ride to the hospital. Upon opening his back door, he looked at my face and said, 'My God, Tom what's wrong with you?' We explained quickly as he ushered us into his house.

'Sit down,' he said, motioning to an armchair beside us in the den. I did, with pain. I expected him to get his keys, but instead he looked me in the eyes and said, 'Now, don't worry about a thing. I'm going to have to do something to help you out, but you may not want to watch.' I did want to watch. I'm a philosopher. I'm incurably curious. 'We've got to stretch out your leg,' he said as he pulled it by the foot, lifting it and propping it up on his own knee as he squatted in front of me. He then joined his two burly hands, thumbs sticking up, and with a sudden, violent motion, crammed them into the back of my left knee, hitting it so hard I thought I was going to see my kneecap bounce off the ceiling (and only this year, sixteen years later, have I had a little trouble with the knee). He then raked his thumbs down the length of my calf hard, two or three times. Then he looked up and said, 'Stand up. You should be fine within a couple of minutes.' I stood up, unassisted, with almost no pain. I put weight on the leg, testing it. No pain, I looked down and was shocked to see that the swelling was almost gone, a little bump where a large egg-sized hill had been. 'You OK?' he asked. I was OK, and so were all his stories.

'How did you do that?' I asked. He said, 'Oh, it's just a little trick we needed when guys would get screwed up from the night jumps. We had to be able to fix anything.' From that time on I ceased to doubt any of his stories, however dramatic.

And not too long afterward, I realized that there was a connection between how the events of that afternoon had enhanced the credibility of all his extraordinary stories and how miracles were supposed to do the same for Jesus' teaching and for the extraordinary claims about him made by early Christians. Remarkable actions corroborate remarkable stories. If, in order to explain some astonishing deed, you have to postulate that a person is in touch with some source of knowledge and power far beyond the ordinary, and it is just some such rare status that would be needed to render the claims about that person credible, then witnessing that deed or hearing about it from some very trustworthy source can serve to raise the credibility of the stories, even to the point of banishing all practical doubt. This is what happened with me and my neighbor, and it is just what . . . could happen with our judgment about Jesus.[15]

The miraculous act of God's raising Jesus from the dead is plausibly taken to be God's vindication of Jesus' radical personal claims for which He was crucified as a blasphemer. In light of God's raising Jesus, Jesus' personal claims to divinity take on a new credibility. The resurrection is God's imprimatur on those extraordinary claims.

---

15. Thomas V. Morris, *Making Sense of It All* (Grand Rapids: Eerdmans, 1992), 177–80.

2

ON DISCIPLESHIP TO JESUS

On the Hard Yet Rewarding Work of Dealing with Doubts

Dr. Craig,

I would like to first start out by thanking you for all the work you do. Your articles, books, and talks have been a major benefit to my heart and mind. I'm 21 years old and attending my second and final year at film school in Calgary, Alberta, Canada. Upon entering my first year of film school the doubts I had lingering in my head for the summer prior hit me hard. For the next couple months I went through an intense, mind-numbing search for answers. It was probably the most difficult time of my life. I thought my world was caving in and taking me with it. I scoured the bookstores for anything on the existence of God and the historicity of Christianity. I came across numerous titles by authors such as Norman Geisler, J.P. Moreland, Peter Kreeft and many others. I came across your works by searching the endnotes of the books I bought. I have listened to many of your talks and debates and read many of your articles. I look forward to the release of the latest edition of *Reasonable Faith*. I have since come to take a great interest in Philosophy and Apologetics. I am currently considering studying Philosophy after I finish film school.

The main reason I am writing to you is because I have a question for you, but we'll get to that in a moment. Over this past year of doubt and searching I have had high points and many low points. I can't honestly say I'm feeling the security right now in my beliefs I wish I had. There are points when I just get so frustrated with all this thinking/arguing/debating. Sometimes I'll feel like I'm starting to figure it out when I come across some stupid Internet forum posing some argument against Christianity or the existence of God and I slump back down because I don't have an answer to it. (It's at those points when I really want to listen to your talks). It's become this tiring high/low cycle. A friend of mine has been going through a similar situation as me. We finally found out about each other's struggle after a couple months of going through it. He has since become my close companion on this journey. We talk about our doubts, thoughts, questions, and cynicism together and how we both love listening to your talks. (I introduced him to your works and website about half a year ago and he's told me (in a comedic way) that when he's really feeling weighed down by all the questions he'll listen to your podcasts and talks from your site when he goes to bed and says to himself, "Yes Dr. Craig . . . that does make sense . . . maybe God does exist . . . it all makes sense . . ." as he falls asleep). So both he and I are on similar journeys.

While we were talking the other night, we were both wondering if the doubts and insecurity will ever fade away, or minimize to a bearable amount. My question to you is this, when does the doubt/non-belief go away, if ever? Will there ever be a time where I will actually whole-heartedly believe in God? (I understand you can't actually answer that, but I guess what I'm asking is whether or not there comes a point where it's "BAM! I believe in God!"). Right now it feels like I believe in God on a good day but doubt His existence on another day. But even on those good days it only really feels like I take comfort in the prospect of God's existence and it's not that I actually believe in Him. I want to believe in God more than anything. I understand what happens if God doesn't exist and I can't live with thinking that. But the thing is I can't force myself into belief. There will be days when I have to tell myself there's meaning just so I can take joy in being with my family and friends, that it isn't all pointless. It's as if I'm in a balance of belief and non-belief, tipping back and forth as the days go by. It gets frustrating. I was telling my friend that one of the things that keeps me going through this struggle is looking at where I see myself in the future. In the future, I see myself believing in God and raising my family with that belief and conviction, to guide me so I can guide my family. I see it down the road, but I don't know how long it will take me to get there. I've decided that it's something I won't give up on. I won't settle for non-belief. If it takes me until my deathbed I'll fight the non-belief in hopes of being taken over by belief. But the thing is, I don't want to be "pretending" I believe in God until then.

I don't even know if this is making sense. I'm not expecting you to have an answer to all those questions. I guess maybe all you could really do is maybe relate your own journey from non-belief to belief. Was the transition overnight or did it take time from the moment you said you believed in God for you to actually feel the full conviction? I don't know what I'm expecting or hoping to hear from you. I hope some of this is making sense to you. Thanks for any advice/wisdom/reading recommendations you can provide.

Steven

Dr. Craig's Response

Thanks for your very touching letter, Steven. I admire your courage and your honesty in discussing your struggle with faith and doubt. I suspect that there's no simple, quick recipe that if followed will make your doubts vanish like magic. You'll probably have to work through your doubts in a slow and agonizing process. But be assured that many great men and women of God have traveled that same path before you and have not lost faith.

To speak personally, I myself was not raised in an evangelical home, but I became a Christian my third year of high school, not through any careful consideration of the evidence, but because the Christian students who shared the gospel with me seemed to be living on a different plane of reality than I was. Their faith in Christ imparted meaning to their lives along with a joyous peace, which I craved. Unlike you, I remember looking into the future and saying to my Christian friends, "I just can't see Bill Craig as a Christian!" But after an agonizing six-month search for God, I was marvelously born of the Spirit on September 11, 1965, at around 8:00 in the evening. It set my life on a whole new course.

INSIGHT

In the paragraphs that follow, take stock of how Dr. Craig's biography is shaped, including even by the environment of such institutions as Wheaton in the 1960s, and including his aversion to the theological rationalism of "evidentialism." May I say that in this correspondence you get to experience Dr. Craig in a more pastoral or "soul-care" role than what may have been obvious in other exchanges. His response here is one of my favorite in this collection. Pay close attention to how he gets the job done.

313

THE CONFLICT OF THEOLOGICAL RATIONALISM

As a young believer full of enthusiasm and faith, I went off in 1967 to study at Wheaton College. During the sixties Wheaton had become a seedbed of skepticism and cynicism, and I was dismayed to see some of the students whose intellectual abilities I admired lose their faith and renounce Christianity in the name of reason. The prevailing atmosphere was one of theological rationalism (or, as it's sometimes misleadingly called today, "evidentialism"), the view that faith, in order to be rational, must be based on argument and evidence. In my theology courses I learned that none of the classical arguments for the existence of God is sound, and my Bible professors never discussed evidences for the reliability of the gospels. Among the students, doubt was touted as a virtue of the mature Christian life, and one was supposed to follow unflinchingly the demands of reason wherever it might lead. I remember well one of my theology professors insighting that if he were persuaded that Christianity were unreasonable, then he would renounce Christianity.

Now, that frightened and troubled me. For me, Christ was so real and had invested my life with such significance that I could not make the confession of my professor. If somehow through my studies my reason were to turn against my faith, then so much the worse for my reason! It would only mean that I had made some mistake in my reasoning. Thus, I confided to one of my philosophy teachers, "I guess I'm not a true intellectual. If my reason turned against Christ, I'd still believe. My faith is too real."

So I went through a temporary flirtation with Kierkegaardian fideism—though my mind couldn't rest long in the position that I believe Christianity because it is absurd. As often happens in the lives of earnest students, the reading of certain books proved pivotal in my thinking and directed my life along a different route. The first was E. J. Carnell's *Introduction to Christian Apologetics*, which convinced me that reason might be used to show the systematic consistency of Christian faith without thereby becoming the basis of that faith. The second was Stuart Hackett's *Resurrection of Theism*, which stunned me by its demonstration that there were, after all, persuasive, cogent arguments for God's existence.[16] Hackett's book was part of an incomplete project, however, and left one with a sort of deism rather than Christian theism. But then, third, I became acquainted on a popular level with Christian evidences, particularly for the resurrection of Jesus, compiled, for example, by Josh McDowell

---

16. During the course of writing *A Reasonable Response*, I learned Stu Hackett died. Readers may be interested in Dr. Craig's further reflections on Hackett, which he presented at the website of the Evangelical Philosophical Society: "In Memoriam: Stuart Cornelius Hackett (1925–2012): http://bit.ly/WLCHackett.

in *Evidence that Demands a Verdict*. It became evident to me that it was possible to present a sound, convincing, positive case for the truth of Christian theism.

THE DIFFERENCE BETWEEN KNOWING AND SHOWING CHRISTIANITY TO BE TRUE

Still I couldn't embrace the view that argument and evidence constitute the essential foundation for faith, for the fruits of that viewpoint had become forcefully clear to me at Wheaton. I put the issue on the back burner while I pursued other questions during my seminary and doctoral studies in philosophy, but it came to the fore again in 1977 when I was invited by Campus Crusade for Christ to deliver a series of lectures on apologetics to university students in Munich. My opening lecture was to be on faith and reason, and in meditating on this problem, I hit upon a scheme that has proved to be very helpful to me in illuminating the relationship between faith and reason— namely, the distinction between *knowing* Christianity to be true and *showing* Christianity to be true. It has been gratifying to me that what I grasped in a rough and superficial way has been confirmed by the recent work of religious epistemologists, notably Alvin Plantinga.

> **INSIGHT**
>
> Here is one of Dr. Craig's best articulations of his long-standing distinction between showing and knowing.

I hold that argument and evidence play an essential role in our *showing* Christianity to be true, but a contingent and secondary role in our personally *knowing* Christianity to be true. The proper ground of our *knowing* Christianity to be true is the inner work of the Holy Spirit; and in our *showing* Christianity to be true, it is His role to open the hearts of unbelievers to assent and respond to the reasons we present. If you're interested in seeing how I develop this, take a look at my contribution to Steve Cowan's *Five Views on Apologetics*.[17] Better yet, read Plantinga's inspiring book *Warranted Christian Belief*.[28]

I have found this to be both an intellectually and experientially satisfying account of the matter. As I look back on my Wheaton days, I see now how infected with theological rationalism our community was and how perverse a concept I had of what it meant to be a "true intellectual." It was the testimony of Christ's Spirit within me that gave me the fundamental assurance that my faith was true; and my refusal to give this up in the face of

17. Steve Cowan, ed., *Five Views on Apologetics* (Grand Rapids: Zondervan, 2000).
18. Alvin Plantinga, *Warranted Christian Belief* (Oxford: Oxford University Press, 2003).

potential defeaters was not a *sacrificium intellectus* but was wholly in accord with the deliverances of reason.

If this approach is correct, then it has tremendously important practical implications in the struggle between faith and doubt. One of the most pernicious problems with theological rationalism is that it is deleterious to one's spiritual life. It leads precisely to the sort of agony you describe, where one's faith hangs in the balance with every new issue of *The Philosophical Review* or turn of the archaeologist's spade. God has provided a more secure foundation for our faith than the shifting sands of evidence and argument. He has given us the inner testimony of the Holy Spirit as the proper foundation for our knowledge of the great truths of the gospel.

FAITH AND DOUBT—THE NECESSITY OF GOD AS A LIVING REALITY IN YOUR LIFE

This implies that we have to be very mindful of our own spiritual formation. First and foremost, you need to be sure that you are a regenerate Christian. If you have not been born anew of the Holy Spirit, then you lack His witness within you and so find yourself cast solely upon such arguments and evidence as you in your limited time and knowledge come across. If that's the case, it's no wonder you feel doubt and uncertainty!

A couple of years ago, when I was out at Talbot School of Theology teaching a two-week course, a fellow from the San Francisco Bay Area who was visiting his family in San Diego dropped by to talk with me about doubts that were troubling him. As we chatted, I sensed that he had not yet come to have a personal relationship with the Lord. So I asked him, "Would you say that your faith in God is just an intellectual belief based on your assessment of the evidence or would you say that God is a living reality in your life?" When he said it was just the former, I asked, "Have you ever really committed your life to Christ and invited Him to be your Savior and Lord?" When he replied that he really hadn't, I asked him, "Well, would you like to right now?" He said that he would, and so we bowed our heads together in prayer and he prayed with me to ask Christ into his life. After we had prayed, he was so grateful; it was just the step he had needed to take.

If you've never been born anew, then I'd urge you to go to God in repentance for your sin, tell Him that you believe He sent His Son to die for your sin and to restore the relationship with Him that you were created to have, and invite the Holy Spirit to come and make you spiritually alive.

THE NECESSITY OF CULTIVATING CHRISTIAN VIRTUES

But perhaps you're already a regenerate Christian. Then you need to cultivate the work of the Holy Spirit in your life. You can grieve the Holy Spirit through sin and quench His leading and power by not allowing Him full reign in your life. Confess sin as soon as you're aware of it, and allow the Holy Spirit to empower and direct you. Be sure to maintain a devotional life, with regular times alone of prayer and Bible study. Take your doubts to God and ask Him to give you grace to persevere. Cultivate the Christian virtues in your life, and then you can claim the promise of 2 Peter 1:5–11 (RSV): "if you do this *you will never fall.*"

Make sure you participate in truly meaningful corporate worship in the setting of a local church. Lone Ranger Christians generally don't make it, and even a small group setting is no substitute for the church, which is the body of Christ locally, replete with all His gifts. Be sure you're exercising your own spiritual gift in the context of a local church, so that you are serving others. I assume that you've followed through on your conversion by being baptized and regularly celebrate the Lord's Supper. Be intentional about sharing your faith with unbelievers, despite your doubts (they'll probably respect your transparency and vulnerability!). Nothing will so infuse your spiritual life with excitement as seeing God use you to lead another person to a saving knowledge of Himself.

Be on guard for Satan's deceptions. Never lose sight of the fact that you are involved in a spiritual warfare and that there is an enemy of your soul who hates you intensely, whose goal is your destruction, and who will stop at nothing to destroy you. Which leads me to ask: why are you reading those infidel websites anyway, when you know how destructive they are to your faith? These sites are literally pornographic (evil writing) and so ought, in general, to be shunned. Sure, somebody has to read them and refute them; but why does it have to be you? Let somebody else, who can handle it, do it. Remember: Doubt is not just a matter of academic debate or disinterested intellectual discussion; it involves a battle for your very soul, and if Satan can use doubt to immobilize you or destroy you, then he will.

INSIGHT

Dr. Craig rightly discerns the spiritual formation implications of doubt. This isn't a game. It is not about mere intellectual sport. It is not something that we merely tolerate or prize. Rather, we must come to ruthlessly address our doubts so that they do not remain as obstacles or hindrances to a confident faith in God.

I firmly believe, and I think the bizarro-testimonies of those who have lost their faith and apostatized bear out, that moral and spiritual lapses are the principal cause for failure to persevere, rather than intellectual doubts. But intellectual doubts become a convenient and self-flattering excuse for spiritual failure because we thereby portray ourselves as such intelligent persons rather than as moral and spiritual failures. I think that the key to victorious Christian living is not to have all your questions answered—which is probably impossible in a finite lifetime—but to learn to live successfully with unanswered questions. The key is to prevent unanswered questions from becoming destructive doubts. I believe that can be done by keeping in mind the proper ground of our knowledge of Christianity's truth and by cultivating the ministry of the Holy Spirit in our lives.

DEALING WITH UNANSWERED QUESTIONS

The point is this: the secret to dealing with doubt in the Christian life is not to resolve all of one's doubts. One will always have unanswered questions. Rather, the secret is learning to live victoriously with one's unanswered questions. By understanding the true foundation of our faith and by assigning the proper role to argument and evidence, we can prevent unanswered questions from turning into destructive doubts. In such a case, we shall not have answers to all our questions, but in a deeper sense that won't matter. For we shall know that our faith is true on the basis of the Spirit's witness, and we can live confidently even while having questions we cannot answer. That's why it is so important to keep in mind the proper relationship between faith and reason.

Finally, I'd encourage you to pursue your doubts into the ground. I said that the secret to handling doubt in our lives is to learn to live victoriously with unresolved questions. Any thinking Christian will have a "question bag" filled with unresolved difficulties he must learn to live with. But from time to time, as you have opportunity, it's good to take the bag down from the shelf, select one of the questions, and go to work on answering it. Indeed, I can say that working hard on an unresolved question and pursuing it until you finally find an answer that satisfies you intellectually is one of the most exhilarating experiences of the Christian life. To resolve a doubt that has troubled you for some time brings a wonderful sense of intellectual peace and inspires confidence that there are solutions to the remaining difficulties in your question bag.

When you have a doubt or a question about a particular issue, set aside time to study that specific issue by reading books or articles on the subject. Libraries at Christian colleges and seminaries can be particularly helpful, if those are available where you live. Even public libraries can order what you need through their inter-library loan service. Find out what Christian scholars have written in the area you are exploring and write to them—or, if possible, visit them to discuss your question. Seek out and talk with those members of the body of Christ who have studied the subject. In that way, the members of the body will be helping to build each other up. But don't let your doubts just sit there: pursue them and keep after them until you drive them into the ground.

I don't know the answer to your question of whether your doubts will suddenly come to an end. That's probably very person-relative. But I don't think that's the most important thing. The really important thing is learning to live with unanswered questions without allowing them to become destructive doubts. That, I believe, is, by God's grace, possible.

What Does It Mean to Have a Relationship with God?

Dr. Craig,

I am a philosophy student and an ex-Christian. I lost my faith during my undergraduate education upon realizing that I had accepted my faith without reflection. Like many others my age, I abandoned my worldview and embarked upon a search for answers. The search quickly took on an intellectual character that eventually led me to the joys of philosophy (which, I am happy to say, I have chosen as my career path). And having had a taste of good philosophy and good apologetics, my doubts about Christianity have been intellectually satisfied.

Yet despite my admission that God exists and that Christ was resurrected, I have absolutely no idea what it means to have a relationship with God; the concept is completely mysterious to me. What does it mean to trust God? And for what? Why talk to God? What would one say? What would one hear? What is expected of me and what should I expect of God? Is there a unique experience to such conversations or should one pray despite the feeling that no one is listening?

What's worse, however, is the feeling that I am motivated not by love but by expectation. That is, I grew up in the Church and had it impressed upon me that a

319

relationship just comes with the territory of belief. I now believe, so I am expected to begin a relationship; I don't otherwise feel led to cultivate a relationship to God.

The things the Bible says about the matter seem mysterious or rely too heavily on a human relationship analogy (e.g., surely the Father-son analogy only goes so far given God's hiddenness and permission of suffering). And as for Christ's death, I must admit that I have difficulty feeling grateful for His sacrifice since many parts of the justification story are in tension with my intuitions on justice (e.g., substitutionary atonement).

I understand that these aren't very well formulated questions but that simply indicates my confusion on the matter. Any reply will be greatly appreciated.

Thank you,

Mark

Dr. Craig's Response

INSIGHT

It is important to keep in mind why we seek to help someone deal with their (intellectual) questions, and it is not for the purpose of satisfying their curiosities. We serve in our capacity as question answerers in order to enable people to be free to learn how to enter into a new and living relationship with the one true God.

It was so heartening to receive your letter, Mark, and to learn of your return to belief! I hope you're drinking deeply from the well of Alvin Plantinga, especially *Warranted Christian Belief*, which has a good deal of material which is relevant to your question, particularly his discussion of the religious affections.

As I read your question, I couldn't help but wonder if you might not find yourself in the situation of someone who has returned intellectually to belief in a Christian worldview but who has not yet come into a saving relationship with God. Forgive me if I'm wrong, but since I don't know your story, I can only guess at what seems to be amiss.

One of my concerns about a ministry like mine, which focuses on the truth of the Christian worldview and arguments for it, is that people may not realize that the Christian faith is not just about having a change of mind and coming to accept a new worldview. It's about coming into a new relationship and becoming a new person. That's easy to miss when we're so focused on defending propositional truth.

The Christian faith is about coming into a saving relationship with God. Obviously, we're all related to God in certain ways, such as creature to Creator, but the Christian faith emphasizes that on a personal level we do not naturally find ourselves properly related to God. Instead, we find ourselves spiritually alienated from God due to the sin (moral evil) that pervades our lives. We do not fulfill our moral duties, toward God, toward others, toward ourselves: we have done what we ought not to have done, and we have not done what we ought to have done. As a result we find ourselves morally guilty before a holy God and under His just judgment. Our personal relationship to God has thus been ruptured. Like a Father and a son who are estranged from each other because of the son's rebellion, so we find ourselves estranged from God. God did not create us in order to stand in a relation of condemnation to us, but of welcoming acceptance, nor were we created to stand to God in a relationship of indifference or even hostility, but one of love and adoration. Thus, I think you can see how ruined and twisted our relationship with God is. Instead of friendship, there is alienation and enmity. That's what it means to lack a personal relationship with God.

So God has set about restoring the personal relationship with Him that He created us to have. Since we are, according to the Bible, spiritually dead in our sinful condition, that is, lacking a proper relationship with God and powerless to do anything about it, God must quicken us spiritually in order to restore us to a right relationship with Him. The Bible calls this "regeneration" (in popular piety, it is called being "born again," which is just what "regenerate" means). This takes place by the action of the Holy Spirit in response to a person's placing his faith in Christ for salvation.

Now, "faith," as the Reformer Martin Luther emphasized, is a multivalent word. At the most basic level, faith involves what Luther called *notitia*, which is simply cognizance or understanding of a proposition. Next comes what he called *assensus*, which is assent to the proposition in question. Finally, there is *fiducia*, which is trust in the relevant person or thing. All three are involved in saving faith. First, there is understanding the great truths of the gospel, such as that God exists, that I am morally guilty before God, that God sent His Son Jesus Christ to die on my behalf in order to reconcile me to Himself, that forgiveness and moral cleansing are available through Christ, and so on. Next, I must not merely understand but believe these truths. Finally, I must place my trust in Christ as my personal Savior and Lord in order to be saved from sin and separation from God.

"What does it mean to trust God, and for what?" It means that you place your life, your well-being, wholly in His hands, relying upon Him and Him alone to save you. It is making a wholehearted commitment to follow Christ as His disciple, to allow Him to reshape you to become the kind of person that He wants you to be. It means saying to God, "Not my will, but Thine be done. I am no longer my own man; I am Yours, to be and do what You will."

When you make such a commitment to Christ, the Holy Spirit regenerates you spiritually and restores you to the proper relationship with God that you were meant to have. Not only so, but in some mysterious way you are actually indwelt by God's Spirit, and as we yield daily to Him He transforms our character to make us become more Christ-like and directs our paths according to God's providential plan.

How this new relationship plays itself out experientially varies from person to person and over time. Sometimes one may sense God's presence in a very real way; other times one will hardly be aware of it, but one walks by faith, not by sight. Minimally, you should experience an assurance of salvation, a sense of being rightly related to God as His child, forgiven and restored. As you walk in the power of the Spirit you should experience joy, peace, love, and the other fruit of the Spirit in the life of a regenerate person who is yielded to Christ.

"Why talk to God?" Because you love Him! (This is like asking, why talk to your wife!) Of course, you needn't talk out loud, since He reads your mind. And of course, you don't need to provide Him with any information, since He knows everything. But you should communicate with your heavenly Father. "What would one say?" Tell Him you love Him; tell Him how thankful you are for saving you; offer Him praise for what He has done and is doing in your life; ask Him to guide you, to strengthen you, to help you to resist temptation.

"Should one pray despite the feeling that no one is listening?" You should talk to God, or pray, whether you sense His presence or not. It is part of your life of faith. "What would one hear?" Some people claim to hear from God almost audibly, but most of the time He "speaks" to us through the inspired writings collected into the Bible. When reading the Bible reflectively, you'll sometimes find that a passage will strike you powerfully in a new way, perhaps convicting you, or encouraging you, or inspiring you, or directing you. We should expect God to speak to us in this way, through His Word.

"What is expected of me and what should I expect of God?" The answer to the first part of your question is: Everything! Look at Jesus' parable of the unworthy servants (Luke 17:7–10 RSV). Jesus says, "So you also, when you have done all that is commanded you, say, 'We are unworthy servants; we have only done what was our duty.'" We're to give God His legal right—namely, all that we have and are. We are to be as a matter of course totally dedicated to God and filled with the Holy Spirit.

The answer to the second part of your question is that God bestows upon us, positionally, as we are in Christ, forgiveness of sins, eternal life, adoption as sons, and the availability of unlimited help and power for Christian living. Moreover, He gives to us, experientially, as we are Spirit-filled, the fruit of the Spirit: love, joy, peace, patience, kindness, goodness, faithfulness, gentleness, and self-control. When our relationship with God is healthy, the product in our lives will be righteousness, and the result of righteousness is happiness. Happiness is a by-product of holiness, as God's righteousness is realized in us.

If you don't feel led to cultivate a relationship with God, Mark, it may be because you're not yet a regenerate Christian. You may have come only so far in faith as *assensus* but have not yet reached *fiducia*. You've not yet fallen in love with God, and so your heart is cold toward Him. Jesus said that he who has been forgiven much loves much. I'd encourage you to meditate on your own sinfulness and on how much God has forgiven (or will forgive) you and what it cost Christ to win your salvation—He was willing to die for you! Appreciating this doesn't require that you have some theory of the atonement in mind. Whatever theory of the atonement you accept, the fact remains that Jesus went to the cross for you and your redemption—a sacrifice, even on a purely human level, that is hard to fathom.

If you're not yet a regenerate Christian, then I encourage you to go to God in solitude and offer a prayer of commitment like the following:

God, I really need You. I recognize that I am sinful and wretched and in need of Your forgiveness. I believe that Jesus died on the cross to save me from my sins. And right now, in the best way I know how, I open the door of my life and invite You to come in and be my Savior and Lord. Forgive my sins, take the throne of my life, and make me into the kind of person You want me to be. I give myself to You.

Then, like a spiritual newborn, begin to receive the nourishment that comes through God's Word, meaningful corporate worship, prayer, confession and restitution, sharing your faith with others, and other spiritual disciplines.

It's not enough just to believe the truths of the Christian worldview. Our relationship with God needs to be restored and healed. That will come only through the regenerating work of the Holy Spirit in response to trust and commitment.

On Protecting Against Spiritual Failure

Dear Dr. Craig,

Let me just say I love your work; it has helped numerous times. Anyway, my question is regarding spiritual failure. I have heard your recent Reasonable Faith podcast regarding this topic. You were talking about ex-Christians losing their faith. I will be straightforward: Ever since I started to doubt, it has taken a toll on my spiritual life and I feel that I am heading the same way the ex-Christians went. Ever since I started studying more and more apologetics I have become intellectually proud or vain. Anyway, I would like some advice on how not to fall away from faith.

Sincerely,

Christopher

Dr. Craig's Response

I think the most hopeful aspect of your question, Christopher, is your honesty in recognizing your own intellectual pride and vanity and realizing that it is precisely factors of this nature, rather than purely intellectual issues, that pose the greatest danger to our persevering in the faith. Scripture warns, "God opposes the proud but gives grace to the humble" (James 4:6 NIV). How dreadful it would be to find God actually opposing us because of our pride and ambition!

One of my greatest concerns as a Christian is that I might somehow fall away from the faith and so betray Christ. It would be the height of folly and presumption to think that this could not happen. Think of what happened to Judas. It's amazing that a man who was one of the original twelve disciples, who had been for years in such close proximity to Jesus, should in the end turn against Him. Is it then any wonder that we can similarly fall away and betray Christ? Paul speaks of several whom he knew who had left the faith (1 Tim. 1:20; 2 Tim. 2:17; 4:10). He warns, "Let anyone who thinks that he stands take heed lest he fall" (1 Cor. 10:12 ESV). Paul included himself in that admonition, "lest after preaching to others I myself should be disqualified" (1 Cor. 9:27 ESV). If someone of Paul's spiritual stature and commitment took seriously this danger, how much more should we? Paul urges us, "Examine yourselves, to see whether you are holding to your faith" (2 Cor. 13:5 RSV).

IMPORTANT GUIDELINES FOR STAYING STRONG IN THE FAITH

So how can we avoid falling away? I don't think there is any sort of simple recipe, but 2 Pet. 1:5–11 (RSV) provides some important guidelines:

> For this very reason make every effort to supplement your faith with virtue, and virtue with knowledge, and knowledge with self-control, and self-control with steadfastness, and steadfastness with godliness, and godliness with brotherly affection, and brotherly affection with love. For if these things are yours and abound, they keep you from being ineffective or unfruitful in the knowledge of our Lord Jesus Christ. For whoever lacks these things is blind and shortsighted and has forgotten that he was cleansed from his old sins. Therefore, brethren, be the more zealous to confirm your call and election, for if you do this you will never fall; so there will be richly provided for you an entrance into the eternal kingdom of our Lord and Savior Jesus Christ.

Look at the promise here: "If you do this, *you will never fall.*" What a wonderful promise! This is exactly what we are looking for, and so we need to pay close attention to the text. What is striking about the conditions of this promise is that they are primarily moral and spiritual in nature. We are advised to supplement our faith with seven character qualities:

Faith	virtue
+	knowledge
	self-control
	perseverance
	godliness
	brotherly kindness
	love

Moreover, we are to pursue this character formation with utmost diligence: "make every effort ..." This is intentional; it doesn't just happen.

Now, what are these qualities? I'd encourage you to do a biblical study of them.

- *Virtue* means moral excellence. We're to become good persons, reflecting God's holiness.
- *Knowledge* implies a solid grasp of Christian doctrine. This is part of spiritual maturity, as Paul emphasizes, "that we may no longer be children, tossed to and fro and carried about with every wind of doctrine" (Eph. 4:14 RSV). This is the one intellectual quality in the list.
- *Self-control* means self-mastery, which implies the ability to control one's lusts, temper, tongue, and desires. We all know how easy it is to be just carried along by one's passions rather than having them under one's own control! But just as an athlete in training exercises self-control in all things, so we are to bring our passions under our control (1 Cor. 9:5).
- *Perseverance* connotes endurance, being in it for the long haul, despite the ups and downs of life. We need to be long distance runners, not just sprinters, or we'll burn out.
- *Godliness* implies having a spiritual orientation to one's life rather than having a materialistic, consumer mentality which values and focuses on worldly goods (1 Tim. 6:6–11).
- *Brotherly kindness* involves having a genuine affection and care for fellow Christians (Rom. 12:10; 1 John 3:16–20a). Do we really care about them as persons, or are they just means to our ends?
- *Love* is described in 1 Cor. 13:4–7. We should strive to fit the description that Paul gives there. If we are diligent about inculcating this kind of character into ourselves, we are promised that we shall not be ineffective or unfruitful in the knowledge of Christ.

INSIGHT

Notice these helpful descriptions. It is worthwhile to ponder what these mean and their implications for our lives.

THE FRUIT OF THE SPIRIT AIDS OUR SPIRITUAL DEVELOPMENT

Now, this might seem so daunting a task that it puts us under the pile rather than comforts us! How can we who are so weak and flawed realize these sorts of character qualities in ourselves? It might seem hopeless.

Ah, but here it's very interesting to compare this list of character qualities with the list Paul provides of the fruit of the Holy Spirit in our lives (Gal. 5:22–23)! Paul says the fruit of the Spirit is

- love
- joy
- peace
- patience
- kindness
- goodness
- faithfulness
- gentleness
- self-control.

Here many of the same character traits are said to be the work of the Holy Spirit as we are submitted to Him: love, kindness, goodness, self-control.

Furthermore, notice that faithfulness and patience in combination add up to perseverance. Moreover, since these qualities are the fruit of the Spirit, to have these qualities just is to have a spiritual orientation, or to be godly. So as we are filled with the Holy Spirit, that is, yielded and empowered by Him, He will produce the fruit of these qualities in our lives. We are not just on our own, gutting it out by our own efforts. Rather the key to character formation is being filled with the Holy Spirit.

Interestingly, the one exception seems to be knowledge. That's something that we have to acquire through study of God's truth. But as we seek to gain knowledge, what can we do to combat the sin of intellectual pride?

First, we need to realize the primacy of love over knowledge in God's economy. Socrates said that he was the wisest man in Athens because he knew that he knew nothing! The apostle Paul, when confronted with Greek Gnostics, who touted the importance of knowledge, took a similar line. "Knowledge," he warned, "puffs up, but love builds up. The man who thinks he knows something does not yet know as he ought to know. But the man who loves God is known by God" (1 Cor. 8:1b–3 NIV). According to Paul, if we think we're so smart that we've got it all figured out about God, then in fact we don't know anything. We're just inflated intellectual blowhards. By contrast, the person who loves God is the one who has truly come to know Him. This has shattering implications for our proud intellectual attainments. It means that the simplest child of God who lives in love is wiser in God's sight than the most brilliant Bertrand Russell the world has ever seen.

Second, we need to realize the feebleness and finitude of our human knowledge. I can honestly testify that the more I learn, the more ignorant I feel. Further study only serves to open up to one's consciousness all the endless vistas of knowledge, even in one's own field, about which one knows absolutely nothing. I resonate with a statement Isaac Newton once made, reflecting back on his discoveries laid out in his great treatise on physics, the *Principia Mathematica*. He said that he felt "like a boy playing on the sea-shore, and diverting myself now and then finding a smoother pebble or a prettier shell than ordinary, whilst the great ocean of truth lay all undiscovered before me." How feeble, uncertain, and unstable are our own intellectual attainments!

Finally, third, I want to pass on some advice from Hugh of St. Victor, who wrote in his *Didascalicon* (1125),

Now, the beginning of study is humility. Although the lessons of humility are many, the three which follow are of especial importance for the student: First, that he hold no knowledge and no writing in contempt; second, that he blush to learn from no man; and third, that when he has attained learning himself, he not look down upon everyone else.

On Facing Fear of Ridicule and Rejection

Dear Dr. Craig,

My question is more personal. I hope you can answer it as I think it may be useful to a lot of Christians, particularly in heavily secular/non-Christian environments.

What advice would you give to us who struggle against this fear of attack/persecution/ ridicule/fear of man in the context of evangelism and apologetics, in the light of the good evidence and reasons for our Christian worldview?

Maybe you could share what your mindset is whilst debating, or the way you think about non-Christians when speaking with them. How do you feel/react to attacks? What do you think about them even before they occur?

I'm sure that if many of us were able to conquer this and be bold and clear in our witness and conversations, we'd see a lot of fruit for the gospel in our lives.

Yours faithfully in Christ,

Rohit

United Kingdom

Dr. Craig's Response

Rohit, I remember your name from a few years ago, and it's good to hear from you again. Thanks for your encouraging words! Let me share a few thoughts in response to your question.

Think of what Christ endured for you. Jesus was willing to go through unspeakable torture and what in Jewish thinking was the most humiliating of deaths for us. He hung on the cross naked, in a public display of humiliation and shame, an object of ridicule and derision, for your sake and mine. How could we possibly be embarrassed of Him when He was willing to endure such depths of scorn for us? Recall Jesus' words: "Whoever is ashamed of me and my words, of him will the Son of Man be ashamed when he comes in his glory and in the glory of the Father and of the holy angels" (Luke 9:26). Can you imagine that Christ would be ashamed of you as His disciple? May it never be!

Great blessing is promised those who are abused for Jesus' name. Jesus said, "Blessed are you when people insult you, persecute you, and falsely say all kinds of evil against you because of me. Rejoice and be glad, because great is your reward in heaven, for in the same way they persecuted the prophets who were before you" (Matt. 5:11–12). What a promise! I think of this in debate situations. When people heap insults upon you, be thankful and glad because they are really heaping blessings upon you. Would you forfeit those blessings?

Think of what others have suffered for Christ. When believers in China and various Islamic countries are being imprisoned, tortured, and even killed for their faith in Christ, it is nothing short of scandalous that we in the West should shrink from enduring so much as even verbal abuse or embarrassment for Christ's sake! How could we dare to look our brothers and sisters in the face when our commitment is so paltry, so weak, compared to theirs? We suffer nothing by comparison with what they endure. Reflecting on what they have borne and do bear for Christ's name can give us the resolve to embrace what small amount of suffering we are called upon to shoulder.

Ask God to fill you with love for your adversaries. Jesus said, "Love your enemies and pray for those who persecute you" (Matt. 5:44 NIV). God loves them so much He sent His Son to die for them. They are lost and dying without Christ. When I hear some unbelievers railing against me, I think of the apt aphorism: "I could no more be angry with him than if a blind man had stepped on my foot." Pray that God would remove their spiritual blindness. We are involved in a desperate battle to rescue them from everlasting ruin. Ask God to give you a heart of compassion for the lost so that, like Paul, you feel constrained to speak out (2 Cor. 5:14).

Remember that to respond in kind is counter-productive. Our goal is to win people, not arguments. So even though we may be tempted to respond to sarcasm with sarcasm, that will usually backfire and only push the other person further away. Try to respond graciously and substantively. Now, I do think there is a place for confrontation and termination of an unfruitful conversation, if you sense the other person is insincere and just wants to argue. But it should always be done calmly and in love.

These suggestions will be much easier to carry out if we are ourselves well-equipped to provide positive reasons for why we believe as we do and solid answers to unbelievers' questions and objections. Being so equipped will give us a quiet confidence that will serve us well in dialogue. Since we know the answers, there's just no reason to get all hot and bothered about the unbeliever's attacks. I think that being well-trained plus keeping the above points in mind can embolden our witness for Christ, so that just as He treated the shame of the cross with scorn (Heb. 12:2), so we, too, can treat dismissively the ridicule unbelievers might hurl our way.

INSIGHT

Notice the valuable insights and wisdom in these paragraphs. They are rich with advice for a thick civil discourse and genuine tolerance.

Part 6

QUESTIONS ABOUT
ISSUES OF CHRISTIAN PRACTICE

Some believe that our practices or the "practical" does not merit our thoughtful attention because it consists of intellectually unserious business. But that is a myth. For those of us who operate in academic contexts, one can be tempted to think that the most important intellectual ideas are those that are studied in a classroom, in a publication, or in a research lab alone. But that is often not the case. How we live, including our habits and practices, require as much of a mind to reason as do solving the great questions of the universe. For the Christian, it is scandalous if we fail to drink deeply from the waters—no, ocean!—of Christian wisdom and understanding and not apply such insight to the relevancy of thinking Christianly about the manner in which we live; to fail in this area is, perhaps, to be swayed by the temptation that the "Christian mind" merely equals "thinking as a Christian about academic ideas."

The questions in this part reveal how Dr. Craig seeks to cultivate and apply Christian reflection to issues of practical import. I am especially pleased to present his answers in this part because (1) I think they help to show he has something practical to say that can be beneficial to others and (2) it models how a seasoned intellect of his caliber (for goodness' sake, the guy has two PhDs!) can care and contribute to knowledge and wisdom on matters that affect us all, or at least affect those that we know.

By interacting with the questions and answers of Part Six, you can benefit in the following ways.

In section 1, you can come to discern
- The value and benefits of accurately diagnosing the movements of our society.
- Why we do not really live in a "postmodern society."
- Why it is costly to marry a non-Christian.
- Why self-control and not being defined by the fulfillment of our desires is a calling for both the homosexual Christian and the heterosexual Christian.

In section 2, you can come to experience
- How to maintain physical stamina.
- How to prepare for marriage.

You can discover further background to these issues, grow your understanding, and become even more skillful in your communication of what you learn by interacting with some of these valuable resources:

Dig Deeper into Dr. Craig's Work

BEGINNER

Craig, William Lane. "Vision in Life." Biola University, La Mirada, Calif.: http://bit.ly/VisionInLife.

Craig, William Lane. "On a Healthy Marriage and Grad School." National Faculty Leadership Conference (June 1, 2008). http://bit.ly/HealthyMarriage.

Craig, William Lane. "What Is the Meaning of Failure for a Christian." Johnson Ferry Baptist Church, Marietta, Ga. (2007). http://bit.ly/FailureJFBC.

INTERMEDIATE

Craig, William Lane. "A Christian Perspective on Homosexuality." (http://bit.ly/PerspectiveOnHomosexuality.

Craig, William Lane. "*Creatio ex nihilo*: A Critique of the Mormon Doctrine of Creation." http://bit.ly/MormonCritique.

Craig, William Lane. "Who Is the Real Jesus? The Jesus of the Bible or the Jesus of the Qur'an?" http://bit.ly/JesusQuran.

Supplemental Recommended Resources

BEGINNER

Cabal, Ted, gen. ed. *Apologetics Study Bible*. Nashville: Holman Bible Publishers, 2007.

Moreland, J. P. *Love Your God with All Your Mind*. Rev. ed. Colorado Springs: NavPress, 2012.

INTERMEDIATE

Austin, Michael W. and R. Douglas Geivett, eds. *Being Good: Christian Virtues for Everyday Life.* Grand Rapids: Eerdmans, 2012.

DeYoung, Rebecca Konyndyk. *Glittering Vices: A New Look at the Seven Deadly Sins and Their Remedies.* Grand Rapids: Brazos, 2009.

Groothuis, Douglas. *Christian Apologetics.* Downers Grove, Ill.: InterVarsity, 2011. Chapters 6–7, 23–24, 26.

Rae, Scott B. *Moral Choices: An Introduction to Ethics.* 3rd ed. Grand Rapids: Zondervan, 2009.

Sire, James W. *The Universe Next Door.* 5th ed. Downers Grove, Ill.: InterVarsity, 2009.

Smith, R. Scott. *Truth and a New Kind of Christian.* Wheaton, Ill.: Crossway Books, 2005.

Sweis, Khaldoun A. and Chad V. Meister. *Christian Apologetics.* Grand Rapids: Zondervan, 2012. Chapters 51–54.

ADVANCED

Kelly, Stewart E. *Truth Considered and Applied: Examining Postmodernism, History and Christian Faith.* Nashville: B&H Publishers, 2011.

Penner, Myron B., editor. *Christianity and the Postmodern Turn.* Grand Rapids: Brazos, 2005.

Roberts, Robert C. and W. Jay Wood. *Intellectual Virtues: An Essay in Regulative Epistemology.* Oxford: Clarendon Press; New York: Oxford University Press, 2007.

1

ON SOCIAL-MORAL ISSUES

Do We Live in a Postmodern Society?

In your 2008 *Christianity Today* cover article you said:

However all this may be, some might think that the resurgence of natural theology in our time is merely so much labor lost. For don't we live in a postmodern culture in which appeals to such apologetic arguments are no longer effective? Rational arguments for the truth of theism are no longer supposed to work. Some Christians, therefore, advise that we should simply share our narrative and invite people to participate in it.

This sort of thinking is guilty of a disastrous misdiagnosis of contemporary culture. The idea that we live in a postmodern culture is a myth. In fact, a postmodern culture is an impossibility; it would be utterly unlivable. People are not relativistic when it comes to matters of science, engineering, and technology; rather, they are relativistic and pluralistic in matters of religion and ethics. But, of course, that's not postmodernism; that's modernism! That's just old-line verificationism, which held that anything you can't prove with your five senses is a matter of personal taste. We live in a culture that remains deeply modernist.[1]

I asked a friend to comment and he said:

I think we need to both accept and reject part of Craig's hypothesis here. We certainly live in a culture in which relativism is accepted and absolutes are being seriously

---

1. William Lane Craig, "God Is Not Dead Yet," *Christianity Today*, July 1, 2008, 22–27. This can also be accessed at ChristianityToday.com (http://bit.ly/WLC-CT).

questioned, but just because we are living a more modernist than literally postmodernist culture does not mean the postmodernism is not present in our culture as it is defined today.

What Craig makes clear here is that even though people claim a postmodern mindset, we only operate in that way within certain spheres of our lives. I agree with Craig that while the majority of postmodern influence is on the more relativistic (real or perceived) areas of culture (religion, art, music, ethics, movies, etc.), we do live in a world that is marked by a tendency to see no big story line in history (a meta-narrative) in which there is logical and realistic cohesion from beginning to end. Instead this, too, has been relativised and so many of the rational arguments which are still valid are cast aside because they imply (rightly so) a true meta-narrative which exists for life.

I think he got it right. Do you agree?

John

INSIGHT

Notice the distinction Dr. Craig is drawing between our culture at large (society) and powerful currents in our culture. The distinction is subtle yet meaningful. Perhaps we might say that we live in a late modern society, which is to say that there are real attempts to move beyond the Enlightenment project. If postmodernism is as Dr. Craig has characterized it, then yes, he is right to discern the "unlivability" factor.

Dr. Craig's Response

No, I don't, John. I'm convinced that Western culture, as the stepchild of the Enlightenment, remains at heart deeply modernist and so must be addressed as such. This is not to say, of course, that there aren't powerful currents of postmodernism flowing in our culture. Postmodernism is entrenched in the university subculture in departments of literature, women's studies, and, significantly, religious studies. But with respect to our culture at large these radicals are relatively isolated—indeed, even within the university as a whole they are a minority. I'm proud that my field, philosophy, has stoutly resisted the encroachment of postmodernism.

Most people don't for a minute think that there are no objective standards of truth, rationality, and logic. As I said in the article, a postmodern culture is an impossibility; it would be utterly unlivable. Nobody is a postmodernist when it comes to reading the labels on a medicine bottle versus a box of rat poison. (If you've got a headache, you better believe that texts have objective meaning!) The idea that we live in a postmodern culture is, I fear, a myth perpetuated in our churches by misguided youth ministers.

Your friend seems to think that while people live their lives as modernists in most spheres, still we see the postmodern influence "on the more relativistic (real or perceived) areas of culture (religion, art, music, ethics, movies, etc.)." But what I am contending is that the relativism in those areas of culture is *precisely* an expression of modernism. The first half of the twentieth century was dominated by a philosophy of meaning called *verificationism*. On this view anything that cannot, in principle, be verified through the five senses, that is, through science, is meaningless. Since religious and ethical statements cannot be so verified, it follows that they have no factual content whatsoever. They are merely expressions of personal taste and emotions.

The influential book *Language, Truth, and Logic* by the British philosopher A. J. Ayer served as a sort of manifesto for this movement. Ayer was very explicit about the theological implications of his verificationism. If by the word "God" you mean a transcendent being, says Ayer, then the word "God" is a metaphysical term, and so "it cannot be even probable that a god exists." He explains, "To say that 'God exists' is to make a metaphysical utterance which cannot be either true or false. And by the same criterion, no sentence which purports to describe the nature of a transcendent god can possess any literal significance."

I hope you grasp the significance of this view. On this perspective, statements about God do not even have the dignity of being false. They're just meaningless words or sounds uttered in the air. If you say to someone, "God loves you and has a wonderful plan for your life," you've said nothing more meaningful than if you had proclaimed, "'Twas brillig; and the slithey toves did gyre and gimble in the wabe."

It wasn't just theological statements that Ayer regarded as meaningless. Ethical statements—statements about right and wrong, good and evil—were also declared to be meaningless. Such statements are simply emotional expressions of the user's feelings. Ayer says, "If I say 'Stealing money is wrong,' I produce a statement which has no factual meaning. . . . It is as if I had written, 'Stealing money!!' . . . It is clear that there is nothing said here which can be true or false." So he concludes that value judgments "have no objective validity whatsoever." The same goes for aesthetic statements concerning beauty and ugliness.

According to Ayer, "Such aesthetic words as 'beautiful' and 'hideous' are employed . . . not to make statements of fact, but simply to express certain feelings . . . "

Now, can you appreciate the impact such a philosophy would have upon religion, art, and ethics? It would produce the relativistic and anarchic chaos that besets Western culture today. Crucifixes in urine become objects of art and sexual libertinism is unleashed. Given that religious statements are not statements of fact, it's perfectly appropriate for the unbeliever to respond to the gospel by saying, "That may be true for you, but it's not true for me." Such a response would be crazy with regard to the engineering technology that goes into building a bridge or even a hairdryer, but it makes perfect sense with respect to expressions of personal taste. Christians (or Muslims) who claim that their religious view is the objective truth and that those who disagree with them are wrong will be perceived as closed-minded and dogmatic bigots, on a par with someone who says, "Vanilla tastes better than chocolate, and anyone who thinks otherwise is wrong." As a subjective expression of personal taste, such a judgment has no objective truth, and the person who thinks that it does is misguided.

So my point is that it is precisely modernism that has spawned the relativism and pluralism in those areas of culture mentioned by your friend.

But what about his point that "we do live in a world that is marked by a tendency to see no big story line in history (a meta-narrative) in which there is logical and realistic cohesion from beginning to end"? Is that a product of postmodernism? Not at all. It is again the direct fruit of a modernist perspective that sees man and the universe as the accidental by-products of blind forces of chance and necessity. Look at the poignant words of Bertrand Russell penned in 1903:

> . . . even more purposeless, more void of meaning, is the world which Science presents for our belief. Amid such a world, if anywhere, our ideals henceforward must find a home. That Man is the product of causes which had no prevision of the end they were achieving; that his origin, his growth, his hopes and fears, his loves and his beliefs, are but the outcome of accidental collocations of atoms; that no fire, no heroism, no intensity of thought and feeling, can preserve an individual life beyond the grave; that all the labours of the ages, all the devotion, all the inspiration, all the noonday brightness of human genius, are destined to extinction in the vast death of the solar system, and that the whole temple of Man's achievement must inevitably be buried beneath the debris of a universe in ruins—all these things, if not quite beyond dispute, are yet so nearly

certain, that no philosophy which rejects them can hope to stand. Only within the scaffolding of these truths, only on the firm foundation of unyielding despair, can the soul's habitation henceforth be safely built.[2]

It was scientific naturalism that destroyed modern man's hope of meaning and significance. The despair of Western culture flows out of the scientific naturalism that shapes its view of the way the world really is.

All of this is important because an effective response to our culture requires an accurate diagnosis of that culture. In the minds of some Christians, since we live in a postmodern culture, we should abandon any attempt to commend our faith rationally as the truth about reality. Instead we just share our narrative and invite people to join in it. If I am right, however, this is a suicidal course of action. It will destroy any sense of the church's claim to have the truth about the way the world is—that will be given by scientific naturalism—and Christianity will be seen as mere mythology.

INSIGHT
Notice the important implications of thinking and acting as if the diagnosis is one thing but it turns out to be another; practices often develop based on a mistaken diagnosis.

My colleague J. P. Moreland has warned of the danger that lies before us:

[Such] a church . . . will become . . . impotent to stand against the powerful forces of secularism that threaten to bury Christian ideas under a veneer of soulless pluralism and misguided scientism. In such a context, the church will be tempted to measure her success largely in terms of numbers—numbers achieved by cultural accommodation to empty selves. In this way . . . the church will become her own grave digger; her means of short-term "success" will turn out to be the very thing that marginalizes her in the long run.[3]

"This calls for a mind that has wisdom" (Rev. 17:9).

---

2. Bertrand Russell, "A Free Man's Worship," in *Why I Am Not a Christian* (New York: Simon & Schuster, 1967), 106–7.
3. J. P. Moreland, *Love Your God with All Your Mind: The Role of Reason in the Life of the Soul*, rev. ed. (Colorado Springs: NavPress, 2012), 108.

How Might We Think about a Christian Marrying a Non-Christian?

Dr. Craig,

In your article on failure,[4] which I otherwise find excellent, you state that marrying a non-Christian is a sin:

> By failure in the Christian life, I mean a failure in a believer's relationship and walk with God. For example, a Christian might experience disappointment and failure due to a refusal to heed God's calling, or by succumbing to temptation, or through marrying a non-Christian. Failure of this type is due to sin. It is essentially a spiritual problem, a matter of moral and spiritual failure.

I would like to know how you can be so certain that marriage to non-believers is sinful. Certainly I can think of no instance of Christ saying any such thing. Paul's command to "be not unequally yoked together with unbelievers" obviously refers to "infidels" (idol worshipers, for example) rather than an agnostic struggling for faith.

I personally believe that the telling word here is "unequally"—certainly a Christian should never submit his or her belief to that of the non-believer. And if Paul were speaking strictly of marriage in 2 Corinthians, then he has clearly contradicted the statement in 1 Corinthians:

> But to the rest speak I, not the Lord: If any brother hath a wife that believeth not, and she be pleased to dwell with him, let him not put her away. And the woman which hath an husband that believeth not, and if he be pleased to dwell with her, let her not leave him. For the unbelieving husband is sanctified by the wife, and the unbelieving wife is sanctified by the husband.

Comments?

Judith

---

4. This can be accessed for free at ReasonableFaith.org (http://bit.ly/ChristianFailure).

Dr. Craig's Response

As you rightly surmised, Judith, I'm thinking of Paul's directives in 2 Cor. 6:14ff. I think we'd agree that to consciously do something contrary to a scriptural command is sinful. As James says, "Whoever knows what is right to do and fails to do it, for him it is sin" (James 3:17). So the only question is whether Paul does command Christians not to marry non-believers.

Look, then, at what Paul says: "Do not be mismatched with unbelievers" (v. 14). What could be clearer? The word here for unbeliever is *apistos*, someone who is without faith. To be sure, most unbelievers would at that time also have been involved in the worship of pagan deities (1 Cor. 10:27). But *apistos* doesn't mean "idolater." The word for idolater is *eidololatres* (1 Cor. 6:9). An unbeliever is anyone who lacks saving faith, including but not limited to idol worshipers.

Take a look at how Paul uses the word "unbeliever" elsewhere in his letters. Notice how in 1 Cor. 14:22–25 he uses "unbeliever" as synonymous with "outsider," someone who stands outside the Christian community. In 1 Cor. 6:6, in prohibiting lawsuits between Christians, Paul is scandalized that disputes should be taken before unbelievers rather than before Christian brethren. In 1 Cor. 7:12–13 he addresses the situation of someone who has a spouse who is, as you note, an "unbeliever," that is, who is not saved (v. 16). I think it's evident that an unbeliever is someone who lacks saving faith and so is not part of the body of Christ.

Is there, then, a contradiction with Paul's commands in 1 Cor. 7:12–16? Not at all! Paul is speaking there to couples who were both unbelievers but one of whom has since become a Christian and so finds himself or herself with an unbelieving spouse. That this is the situation is evident in Paul's overriding principle, also applied to slaves and uncircumcised, "Let everyone lead the life which the Lord has assigned to him and in which God has called him" (v. 17). "Everyone should remain in the state in which he was called" (v. 20). So if you were married when you were called, Paul tells you not to leave your non-believing partner. Stay married, just as you were when called to follow Christ, unless the unbelieving partner desires to separate.

But Paul prohibits Christian believers to marry unbelievers. Why? In 1 Cor. 6:15 he says: "Or what has a believer in common with an unbeliever?" One might be tempted to answer Paul's question, "Well, we're both really into sports and the outdoors," or "We both love finance and business." But Paul would have regarded such an answer as betraying an utter lack of understanding of the marriage union. For Paul, common faith in Christ was central to the marriage relationship. Take that away and you've taken the heart out of the marriage. That so few of our marriages between Christians today exhibit the centrality of Christ is shameful testimony to the extent to which we have become assimilated to the world's view of marriage. Is it little wonder, then, that divorce rates among Christian couples is as high as among non-Christians?

It's been my privilege to be married for over thirty years to a woman whose first and foremost love is to know and serve the Lord Jesus Christ. Our common desire to know and serve Him has bound us tightly together. I can't imagine what it would be like to be married to someone who didn't share that common first love. It has seen us through the ups and downs of life.

I don't know your personal situation, Judith, but if you're contemplating marrying a nonbeliever, I'd urge you not to do so, no matter how much you love him. Obey God, give Him time to work in your boyfriend's heart, and in the meantime strive to become the woman that Christ wants you to be, as His character is formed in you.

On the other hand, if you've already married a nonbeliever, then you should confess your sin, claim the Lord's forgiveness, and then obey scriptural commands on how a believing wife married to a non-Christian should deport herself (1 Pet. 3:1–6).

Can Someone Be a "Christian Homosexual"?

In our Young Adult Sunday school class my husband and I have been utilizing your book *Hard Questions, Real Answers* to address many of the difficult issues the church faces today, and in particular, college students begin to struggle with. Our class has had some lively discussions and, ultimately, is beginning the process of reasonably understanding their faith to more accurately and adequately defend the truth in today's unbiblical culture.

We have come across some strong differences of opinion and a great deal of confusion regarding the topic of homosexuality; specifically, the concept that the Bible condemns homosexual acts or behavior, but not having a homosexual orientation (secondary to orientation being a modern concept). The phrase in your book, "It is perfectly possible to be a homosexual, and a spirit-filled Christian" has also caused some confusion, as many believe that God would not "create" a person to be a homosexual.

The main questions that came from this are:

1. Is defining yourself as homosexual in itself sinful? If so, how can the above statement be valid?
2. Does this refer to someone who considers himself or herself homosexual, but does not engage in homosexual acts? If the initial concept is of the acts/behavior being sinful and not the orientation, this could make sense.
3. Is calling someone a homosexual feeding into an unbiblical cultural norm that is permeating society?

There was an example given of a friend of one our Sunday school students who does not consider himself heterosexual, but also says that he is not homosexual. He is from a Christian home, and knows that homosexuality is wrong, but is not attracted to women, and doesn't believe that will change.

The other thought that came up, which relates to the thoughts above, was that it was unbiblical to say that anybody was born as a homosexual, and that we are all created as heterosexuals. This, then, gets into the idea of whether homosexuality is a choice. Now, in your book, you do mention that regardless of genetics or choice, it does not matter; the behavior is a sin. This may be a matter of semantics, however, it is an area that must be addressed.

Additionally, if homosexuality is something that is inherited and not a choice, is it reasonable to say that this was a "choice" made in the garden of Eden? Does it come down to inheriting a sin nature? In Romans 1, it says:

For the wrath of God is revealed from heaven against all ungodliness and unrighteousness of men who suppress the truth in unrighteousness because what is known about God is evident within them; for God made it evident to them ... Therefore God gave them over in the lusts of their hearts ... Therefore God gave them to degrading passions ... And just as they did not see fit to acknowledge God any longer, God gave them over to a depraved mind ...

Therefore, is it a choice only for those who know God and not a choice for those who don't, as their mind is closed to His evidence?

Also, when reaching out to "homosexual Christians" who are attempting to live a pure life and struggle with this sin, how does one lovingly assist them if one believes that by saying they are homosexual that that in itself is a sin? I liken it to the recovering alcoholic who every day sometimes every hour has to pray that the desire to drink be taken from them. This then addresses the issue of unanswered prayers as well. If one believes themselves to be homosexual and prays consistently, fervently, and with the leading of the Holy Spirit that God takes this from them, and He chooses not to make them heterosexual at this time/or ever, how can we address this?

I know this is lengthy. We have taken the matter to our church pastors so that this is a matter that can be addressed with the whole church and not just hidden under the rug. My husband and I very much hope that there will be time to have these questions examined by you and your staff.

Thank you so much. God Bless.
Krista

Dr. Craig's Response

Thank you for taking the time and making the effort to minister to college students! This is a crucial time in their lives, and it sounds as if your students are fortunate to have you and your husband guiding them through tough issues.

Before I address your three questions, let me clarify what I meant in saying, "It is perfectly possible to be a homosexual and a Spirit-filled Christian." I'm taking homosexuality to be an orientation or inclination of one's sexual desires. Someone who is heterosexual is attracted sexually to members of the opposite sex; someone who is homosexual is attracted sexually to members of the same sex. So my sentence meant that it's possible to be sexually attracted to members of one's own sex and yet be a Spirit-filled Christian.

So understood, that fact seems to me rather obvious. Whether the result of nurture or nature, one's sexual inclination is not typically something one chooses but just finds himself with. So one may find himself with such an orientation but in the power of the Holy Spirit refuse to act out on it, knowing that to do so would be sinful. That does not mean staying in the closet. One can be open about one's situation, just as someone struggling with, say, voyeurism might be open about his problem and refuse to act out on the desires he has.

To say this obviously doesn't imply that such persons were "created" by God to have these desires; what I said is consistent with such desires' being the product of one's upbringing. In any case, if homosexuality should prove to have a biological basis, I think it would be naïve to say that God wouldn't "create" someone with such a predisposition. God creates people with genetic defects all the time (I myself have such a genetically based syndrome). This is just a part of the broader question which philosophers call the problem of evil, specifically, natural evil.

So in answer to your questions:

1. *Is defining yourself as homosexual in itself sinful?* No, although I wouldn't use the word "defining." Part of the agenda of proponents of the homosexual lifestyle is to portray sexual orientation as a defining characteristic of who you are, part of your very identity. We shouldn't fall into that trap. Rather, I would speak of "describing" oneself in a certain way. Descriptions can change (for instance, we grow older and fatter) and so need not define who we are.

2. *Does this refer to someone who considers himself homosexual but does not engage in homosexual acts?* Right. I'm talking about someone who is like the person who stands up in an AA meeting and says, "I am an alcoholic, but I've been dry for 15 years, thank God!"

3. *Is calling someone a homosexual feeding into an unbiblical cultural norm that is permeating society?* Maybe so. It might be better not to buy into such labels, since that could encourage the idea that one's homosexual desires are constitutive of one's identity. Maybe it would be better just to say, "I'm struggling with homosexual desires," or "I feel attracted to members of my same sex."

As to your comments, I agree that no one is born as a homosexual, as I defined the term, but by the same token no one is born as a heterosexual either, so defined. Remember, I defined those words in terms of one's sexual attractions. Babies and little children don't feel sexually attracted to other persons. Those desires are awakened later. So be careful not to think of homosexuality and heterosexuality like genders. Most all of us are born with a clearly manifest gender as male or female, but what our sexual preference will be won't manifest itself until much later. That's obviously true even if it has a biological basis. But whether our orientation is the result of biology or upbringing, what we have a choice about is whether we act out on our desires. God commands us to live chastely and to reserve sexual activity for heterosexual marriage. The nature or nurture debate isn't just semantics; it's an interesting scientific question about two very different views. But my point is that our choices about how to live remain the same regardless.

If homosexuality has a biological basis, I don't think we need attribute it to the fall in any direct sense. It would just be like a birth defect or a genetically based disease. It's interesting that in Paul's day most of the people involved in homosexual acts were probably people who were heterosexual in orientation, as such acts were condoned by prominent ancient philosophers. Whether a person knows God or not, sin involves a choice for which that person is responsible.

As to your last question, I don't think it is a sin for Christians who feel attracted to members of the same sex to say that they are homosexuals. But I do take your point that such a label may be unhelpful and may encourage them to think that this disorientation is part of their identity.

As for unanswered prayer, every young, heterosexual, Christian male will tell you that he has prayed again and again that God would help him conquer lust, and those prayers go repeatedly unanswered! Sanctification is not an instantaneous affair. It takes time and discipline, guarding one's eyes and thought life, staying away from certain places, minding even what sort of clothing you wear and music you listen to.

This brings to mind a spiritual discipline almost never talked about today in the church: mortification of the flesh. Paul tells us as Christians to put to death the evil desires in us and not to feed the desires of the flesh (Col. 3:5). This may conjure up images of asceticism and self-flagellation, but that's not the idea. Rather it means that as Christians we should intentionally do things to keep our sexual passions in check, for example, being careful about what movies we see or magazines we read or TV shows we watch, actively taking precautions to prevent us from sinning in this area, such as getting a filter on our Internet access. Over time we can become more holy, and many will testify that with counseling and discipline even one's homosexual orientation can be largely corrected and normal heterosexual relations in marriage enjoyed.

2

ON PRACTICAL ADVICE

On How to Maintain Physical Stamina

Dr. Craig,

From watching you, reading your writings, and even being in some of your classes over the years, I can't help but wonder if there is some advice you could give concerning the physical dimension of nurturing and caring for the mind. In other words, when I compare you to other scholars what I see in you is a calmness of mind, a diligence in maintaining your own physical health, and a sharpness and discipline that I find impossible to imagine in a person who has low physical stamina. You've given some great advice for one who wishes to follow in your footsteps, but as I try to pursue my academic interests with the same rigor, I find I lack the energy to do so. Do you take vitamins daily? Do you run daily? Do you meditate/pray to help calm your mind? Do you eat a well-balanced diet? Or is it all will-power?

God bless,
Peter

Dr. Craig,

I've heard you briefly reference the fact that you have suffered from a neuromuscular illness for some time, which affects your extremities. I've also heard you say that you feel God has used this illness to help you accomplish great things in your life. I was hoping that perhaps you wouldn't mind sharing the name and nature of your illness, as well as how God has used it in your walk with Him.

Thanks, and keep up the good work.

Matt

Dr. Craig's Response

Occasionally I like to take a personal question like these two to share something of my own life's experiences by way of encouragement. In fact, Jan and I are only too happy to give personal advice to anyone who asks!

Paul says, "Bodily exercise profits a little" (1 Tim. 4:8 NKJV). Now, notice that Paul didn't say that bodily exercise is of no value, just that compared to godliness, which holds promise not only for the earthly life but also for the life to come, it is of little value. Moreover, we live in a sedentary society vastly different from the society in which Paul lived and wrote. Much of people's daily lives at that time consisted of what we would call exercise. Just think how Jesus walked all over Palestine! People in that day and age weren't the couch potatoes we tend to be today.

Look around: it's so difficult to stay in shape. I'm told that once you hit 35, you begin to lose a pound of muscle per year and to gain a pound and a half of fat. That sure seems to be true. Moreover, people my age are unbelievably medicated in an effort to solve their physical problems. I'm sure most of these folks would rather not be taking blood thinners, anti-cholesterol medicine, weight loss pills, etc.

In 2003 the *Mayo Clinic Health Letter* carried the following troubling report on "Exercise and Your Health":

> In 1996, more than 60 percent of Americans were getting no regular physical activity, despite years of prodding by government agencies and organizations that had issued statements on disease prevention and the role of exercise. In fact, a quarter of the adult population wasn't active at all. That's the year the U. S. Surgeon General released specific recommendations for physical activity.

The Surgeon General's 1996 report recommended accumulating at least 30 minutes of moderately intense activity on most or all days of the week. During activities of moderate intensity, your breathing should allow you to carry on a conversation, but with some effort. Behind the recommendation was considerable data demonstrating the many benefits of staying physically active. These include helping:

• Reduce the risk of premature death, particularly from cardiovascular disease

- Reduce the risk of developing diabetes and colon cancer
- Reduce the risk of developing high blood pressure or reduce already elevated blood pressure
- Promote psychological well-being and reduce depression and anxiety
- Control weight
- Build and maintain healthy muscles, bones, and joints
- Improve the strength of older adults and their ability to move without falling.

Then came yet another alarm from the Surgeon General in 2001—excess weight and obesity in the United States had reached epidemic proportion. Among adults, 61 percent were overweight or obese.

Then, in late 2002, the National Academy of Sciences released its recommendations. Considering the size of many Americans and their exercise—or lack of exercise—habits, the Academy reported that thirty minutes of moderately intense daily activity generally isn't enough to maintain a healthy weight or prevent weight gain. The Academy, basing its findings on an internal database, recommended upping moderate activity time to an hour a day to help prevent weight gain and enhance health benefits.

Can you imagine? An hour a day!

Now, this is really challenging for those of us who don't have an athletic bone in our bodies. My attitude toward exercise was nicely summed up by the crack: "Whenever I feel like exercising, I just lie down until it goes away!"

But the incentive to exercise was given to me by the neuromuscular disorder mentioned above by Matt. I, like my mom and brother, have Charcot-Marie-Tooth Syndrome, a hereditary disorder that involves the slow disintegration of the myelin sheaths around the nerves in the forearms and legs, resulting in progressive muscular atrophy. Some people afflicted with this condition are terribly disabled, but my case is quite light, affecting mainly my hands and in recent years my calves. It principally means that I can't go bowling or type—big deal, Jan says! But I could see what was coming (though, I must say, my mom is currently eighty-seven years old and still going strong), and this has spurred me to try to stay in shape and tone my muscles to stave off as much as I reasonably can the effects of the inevitable atrophy.

So I've disciplined myself to exercise six days a week. The key to doing this successfully is to realize that you are making a lifestyle choice, not just embarking on a temporary regimen. This is *for life*. You want to make your exercise time habitual so that it just becomes a part of your daily routine and you don't have to psych yourself up to do it each time. So every day except Sunday, after my devotional time of prayer and Bible reading, I exercise for around an hour each morning.

Oddly enough, one of the greatest—perhaps the greatest—benefits of such strenuous exercise is, as the Mayo Clinic letter mentioned, *psychological*. You just feel good in your own skin. It gives you such a sense of confidence and well-being to feel your body toned. It gives you the feeling you're ready to take on the world.

A really great program that I'd recommend is Bill Phillips' *Body for Life*. It combines very sensible weight training with aerobic activities. It's realistically doable, is balanced, can be done at home, and gives real results. (I don't look like one of the "after" photos in his books, but I was really tickled when a recent blogger described my physique as "athletic"! Ha!—me, with CMT Syndrome!) I lift weights three days a week and jog or stair-step three days a week. I'd encourage you to buy a few weights so that you can exercise at home and don't have to get yourself up to go out to a gym.

Now, coupled with regular exercise is a nutritional diet. I have the great fortune of being married to someone who is very interested in healthy cooking. We eat a high protein diet with a lot of seafood. We try to balance carbohydrates with protein in about a 3/4 ratio. You can do this roughly by having about a fistful of food high in carbohydrates with a fistful of protein. We don't eat a lot of sugar, and Jan cooks with natural ingredients (you should try her buckwheat pancakes made from scratch with real maple syrup and strawberries!). We don't take any vitamins, as that's unnecessary if you eat right.

In recent years I've found it useful to take an occasional siesta after lunch. I feel a little embarrassed about doing this, but when we lived in France, we found that a two-hour lunch break was the norm there because folks slept after lunch. It really refreshes you! I follow this pattern especially when I'm traveling and speaking because I need to be really sharp for the evening lecture or debate. At home it's optional, depending on whether I find myself slowly dozing off as I try to read some dry treatise on abstract objects or theories of reference!

Having CMT Syndrome has affected me in ways other than physical. Having this disorder as a child was hard because other kids made fun of me for the way I walked. I was always one of the last few chosen for an athletic team in P.E. class when we'd pair off. (Why teachers subject kids to this humiliating ritual is beyond me!) Because I couldn't succeed in anything physical, I threw myself into intellectual and academic pursuits, where I found I could succeed. Having this disease made me very goal-oriented, determined to show those who had mocked me that I could succeed. Since becoming a Christian, I've come to see that this sort of drivenness is the wrong motivation, but the goal orientation and the desire to succeed remains part of who I am. My CMT is now like an old friend, my "thorn in the flesh," which God has used to shape and prepare me for His service and for which I give Him thanks.

On Preparing for Marriage

Dear Dr. Craig,

Marriage is in the foreseeable future, and I would like to ask you for any advice before it happens. Can we avoid any mistakes? Would it be helpful to meet with a pastor for premarital counseling? Are there any helpful tips you could give from a Christian perspective or from your own experience? Thank you in advance!

Zareen

Dr. Craig's Response

Jan and I just returned from Texas, where I had the privilege of marrying our son John and his fiancée Christine, so your question seems quite apropos at this time! Jan and I are more than happy to give advice when asked, so let me share some thoughts that I hope will be of help to you.

When I got married, I thought that the inevitable adjustments that everyone said to expect were basically trivialities like one person's squeezing the toothpaste tube in the middle and the other person's squeezing it at the end, or one person's being neat and tidy and the other person's leaving dirty clothes lying around, and so on. These sorts of adjustments are the stuff of jokes. I had no idea that the real adjustments in marriage were far more serious and profound.

The real adjustments in marriage stem from the deep brokenness that we all bring into the relationship. Even the most psychologically healthy of us bring into the marriage a residue of experiences since childhood that have left us scarred in different ways and to different degrees: lack of self-esteem, insensitivity, inferiority complex, drivenness, suspiciousness, insecurity, temper, and on and on. With so many people now coming out of broken

351

homes and dysfunctional families, these kinds of problems will be even more manifold among newlyweds today.

I've heard marriage compared to two great rivers, which at some point come together. Where they meet, there will be turbulence and whitewater for some time. But later on downstream the rivers truly become one, and it flows smoothly on its course. This comparison is apt. It may take you five to eight years to work through the adjustment phase before coming to a peaceful, harmonious relationship. I don't mean to discourage you but rather to open your eyes to what's ahead so that when it comes, you won't give up but will say to each other, "We can, with God's help, get through this to find the marriage God wants us to have!" The first few years of marriage, which in the Hollywood portrayal are supposed to be idyllic, are—if you handle them incorrectly—often the worst, and the later years are the best.

So what advice can I give you to help you successfully through that phase to a happy, healthy relationship? Let me mention several points.

First, resolve that there will be no divorce. Remember that according to the Scriptures God hates divorce. It is sin and, therefore, must be avoided at all costs. Therefore, no matter how hard things get, neither of you will bail. You will work it out. You will do whatever it takes to resolve your problems. Individually, you will be the man of God or the woman of God that you have been called to be regardless of what your spouse does. You resolve to seek holiness rather than happiness (though you know that holiness is actually the secret to happiness!) and, therefore, will bear the pain rather than seek the easy way out.

Ironically, by choosing the more difficult path of permanent commitment, you greatly increase the chances of building a happy marriage relationship because you will provide the sort of security for your spouse which allows love to flourish.

Second, delay having children. The first years of marriage are difficult enough on their own without introducing the complication of children. Once children come, your attention is necessarily diverted, and huge stresses come upon you both. Spend the first several years of marriage getting to know each other, working through your issues, having fun together, and enjoying that intimate love relationship between just the two of you. Jan and I waited ten years before having our first child, Charity, which allowed me to finish graduate school, get our feet on the ground financially, establish some roots, and enjoy and build our love relationship until we were really ready to take on the responsibilities of parenthood.

The qualifier here is that if the wife desperately wants children now, then the husband should accede to her wish to become a mother, rather than withhold that from her. Her verdict should be decisive. But if you both can agree to wait, things will probably be much easier.

Third, confront problems honestly. When we meet a young married couple, Jan will sometimes shock them by commenting, "Well, we hope you're fighting a lot!" (They usually are.) Fighting with your spouse is so emotionally wrenching and painful, and yet it is the necessary means by which problems get resolved and you become one. The couple that is in real danger is not the one that is fighting but the one that is not confronting. In order to avoid the pain, it's easier to sweep things under the rug and try to forget about it. But then the problems do not get resolved, and bitterness and resentment can secretly begin to grow until the marriage becomes poisoned. Don't let this happen. Screw up your courage, resolve to bear the hurt, and confront your issues squarely.

Now, please understand that when I talk about "fighting," I'm not talking about physical violence and abuse. I mean arguing. And when you argue, you should exercise self-control so that you fight fairly. Never call your spouse names or say things designed to wound, things that you will later regret. That is inconsistent with love. Rather keep in mind, even in the heat of an argument, that *the purpose of the argument is to resolve the problem*, not to hurt the other person with clever zingers. Always keep asking yourself, "How can we solve this?" rather than how you can win the argument. You win by resolving the problem and coming out of an argument with a partner who loves you and is not emotionally damaged by your hurtful remarks.

Fourth, seek marital counseling. An excellent counselor can see things in you that you are simply blind to and so don't even realize about yourself. It can be quite eye-opening! He or she can help you as a couple to adopt strategies for building your relationship, working through problems, and dealing with your children. Never be ashamed to seek counseling. On the contrary, it tells your spouse how serious you are about building your relationship and how you are ready to humble yourself and change if necessary. Having said that, I caution you against poor counselors. If your counselor isn't revealing penetrating insights into yourself and your spouse and your relationship, if the sessions are just grinding on without profit, get out and find another counselor! Ask around to find out who in your area is really good, and don't waste time and money on a poor counselor.

Fifth, take steps to build intimacy in your relationship. Wives: You need to realize what your husband's number-one need in marriage is, what he wants most from you: sex! Yes, frequent, enthusiastic sex! If you do this, you will have a happy hubby, indeed. Unfortunately, here we confront one of those huge disconnects between men and women (you know, the

Venus and Mars thing). A man achieves intimacy with the woman he loves *through* sexual intercourse; but a woman views intimacy as a *prerequisite* for sexual intercourse. So if you're sensing emotional distance from your spouse, what do you do? You seem to be at an impasse. If you find yourselves in this situation, then my advice is that it is the wife who should yield and be open to her husband's advances. Otherwise what you're doing is using sex as a weapon: saying in effect, "You first meet my emotional needs or I'm going to withhold sex from you." That's manipulative and unloving. Sometime after having sex, you can then raise the issues with him that you feel have created an emotional distance between you and seek to resolve them.

Husbands: For your part, you need to remember what you're asking your wife to do in letting you have sexual intercourse with her: you're asking her to let you literally enter her body. It's hard to imagine an act that displays more vulnerability and surrender than that. Therefore you need to do all you can to build a relationship of intimacy and trust that enables her to yield to you happily. So how do you do that? Romance? Sure; but here we encounter another huge disconnect. When I as a man think of romance, I think of candlelight dinner, soft music, a moonlight walk on the beach. But to my wife those things are just externals. None of those things is to her the heart of romance. For her, the heart of romance is . . . talking to her! Yes, just taking the time to talk with her and so to connect on an emotional level. That means setting aside, say, a half hour a day just to talk with her. The problem is, that can itself also become just one more thing to do, one more external. What's key is that during that time you connect emotionally with each other.

What we've learned is that marriage is really about *being*, not *doing*. You can be doing all the right things prescribed in the marriage handbooks and still not be "being" together. What is "being"? It's lowering one's invisible, defensive walls that we've each built around us to protect us from hurt. It means having permeable boundaries to one's spouse. Less metaphorically, it means *vulnerability* and *transparency* in relating to the other. Relating in this way to your spouse builds an emotional connection which fosters intimacy.

So how can we tell, given our blind spots and proclivity toward self-deception and rationalization, if we're just "doing" rather than "being"? Well, for one thing your spouse can tell you! But a barometer you can use to gauge this yourself is to explore your feelings and see if you feel resentment for all the effort you're putting into your marriage. If you sense feelings of resentment, that's a sure sign you're just doing rather than being.

Both of you: Perhaps the greatest enemy of a successful marriage is "growing separateness." That is to say, eventually you begin to lead two separate lives and so grow further and further apart. This is especially dangerous if the wife has a career independent of her husband. You just begin to live in two different worlds. Although it is politically incorrect, I'd, therefore, encourage your wife not to pursue an independent career but to be a homemaker or to be partnered with you in a common cause. That will give you so much more of your lives to share rather than following independent trajectories.

I hope I haven't laid too much on you, Zareen, but you did ask! I wish you and your wife-to-be a wonderful Christ-centered marriage that will be greatly used by God in the extension of His kingdom!

Conclusion

WHERE DO WE GO FROM HERE?

By Joseph E. Gorra

Perhaps as a result of reading *A Reasonable Response* you are compelled to ask, "How can I personally grow in learning to study the 'big questions' and be prepared to offer compelling answers?" In one sense, it's easy to interpret a question like that as "what degree do I need?" And, maybe for some that is a question to be seriously considered.[1] But the experience of completing a degree will come and go. At best, that may only be "preparation" for some vocation or some role. But what about after the degree; then what? Or, for the rest of us who want to grow but do not want or need to get a degree in order to be educated, how might we proceed? Well, I suppose another recommendation to be made would include reading some great books and obtaining some educational resources on a topic. The introductions at the beginning of the six parts are full of some worthwhile recommendations.

But even here, in-taking knowledge is not enough. To help toward an answer to the above lead question, I commend to you a framework for thinking about these matters, whether pursuing a degree or accomplishing some self-study. I recommend the following:

1. Read and study widely as a *spiritual discipline*, being ordered unto genuine and fruitful love for God and love for neighbor.
2. Converse routinely with different people as a means for exploring how God is at work through His Spirit in your conversations.
3. Learn deeply from the practice and "on the way."

---

1. If you are interested in pursuing a degree in philosophy, Christian apologetics, or theology, you may wish to consider these mainstream evangelical institutions: Biola University (California), Calvin College and Seminary (Michigan), Denver Seminary (Colorado), Gordon-Conwell Theological Seminary (Massachusetts), Houston Baptist University (Texas), Moody Theological Seminary (Chicago and Michigan), Multnomah University and Seminary (Oregon), Talbot School of Theology (California), Trinity Evangelical Seminary (Illinois), Union University (Tennessee), and Wheaton College (Illinois).

A Framework for Growth

For your own personal growth, may I suggest that you take the above three recommendations as consisting of its own unique "curriculum" where you can learn to prosper your understanding. Give it some structure and various means for engagement. We are learners first, then spokespersons. But too many of us just want to be spokespersons. Some are a little too PR-happy. Perhaps we crave people to listen to and follow us and so we become deaf to what we need to hear in order to learn. People who intend to serve long-term in the ministry of answering people's questions must themselves cultivate skill, temperance, patience, and care for the practice of asking and answering questions. We must dedicate ourselves to being lifelong learners as leaders who seek to serve others.

Practically speaking, to practice (1) may look like learning to read well and understand how to engage authorities on a relevant topic, for example. It may also mean growing as a learner who seeks to be dependent on and expectant of the Spirit of God to work through your mind and heart in order to reveal wisdom and discernment as you read and converse with others. For more on this and so much more, I commend to you J. P. Moreland's *Love Your God with All Your Mind*, revised and updated anniversary edition (NavPress, 2012), and James Sire's *Habits of the Mind: Intellectual Life as a Christian Calling* (InterVarsity, 2000). Here's the bottom line: study for the sake of being a valuable resource to those whom you serve.

To practice (2) may mean more than just simply being able to do tit-for-tat kinds of Q&A's with a dialogue partner. It may mean learning to deeply listen to another, including for what is beyond or behind the inquiry itself; that which reveals the abundance of the heart. What do people reveal when they ask their deepest questions? What is their longing like? Learning to listen and discern for that is a great way to grow in this area. I might also add that engaging worldview-oriented fiction or movies, for example, can be helpful for cultivating the imagination, considering such questions like how would I engage a religious pluralist type of character in a story if I were his interlocutor? Here, I commend to you Craig Hazen's apologetics novel, *Five Sacred Crossings* (Contend Publishing Group, 2012).[2]

2. To date, the serious role of the imagination in apologetics is an underdeveloped area. Thankfully, leaders like Holly Ordway at Houston Baptist University are attempting to forge some renewed direction in this area with her emphasis on "literary apologetics." See her interview with Brian Auten (of Apologetics315.com), http://bit.ly/LiteraryApologetics. As conceived by Ordway, "literary apologetics" can be seen as an area of "cultural apologetics" where an important goal is to show via literature "the truth of the Christian faith." This is not a new endeavor per se but an underdeveloped area of contemporary apologetics study and ministry (see also Andrew Davison, ed., *Imaginative Apologetics: Theology, Philosophy, and the Catholic Tradition* (Grand Rapids: Baker, 2012).

I also think that we do well to consider taking a sacramental view of our conversations. For a framework on this, I have in mind the helpful work by Jerry Root and Stan Guthrie in their book *The Sacrament of Evangelism*, where they emphasize "a way of looking at life and the world that is open to God's presence everywhere."[3] Thus, "to discover God's work in the world is to engage in a sacramental activity."[4] In short, it is to discern and to acknowledge how the presence and power of the Spirit of Christ is at work in our midst.

The contexts for our conversations with others may vary with different people. For example, it may be in an online context like on some social media platform. Or, it may be in the context of family or with friends at a coffee shop (for some further tips in these areas, see the appendixes). The point being is that we want to consider how to think about conversations in these different contexts and the opportunities and challenges that they may afford.

To practice (3) may mean that we routinely take stock—study, really, in the spiritual discipline sense—of our endeavors in this area in order to learn how we need to continue to grow; where greater dependence on God is needed; how we need to deal with pride, or ignorance, or a critical spirit, etc. Working this out in the context of small, local Christian fellowship is important for our health and long-term growth.

The Value of Thinking and Living Vocationally

To do this ministry well and to endure in it for a very long time, we need to reckon with the scope of our vocations and be prepared to work within their range in light of what we care about. What does that mean? Well, for one thing, it means acknowledging that you are not Bill Craig, nor are you called to live his life. Bill is just fine living his own life. That's what he is called to do, in the name of Jesus Christ. But now you have your life to live. Your life is not Bill's life. The exact texture, intent, scope, and experience of Bill's vocation is not yours. This does not mean that he is not an exemplar for us. But it does mean that you do not need to be pressured into thinking that you need to size up to Bill's accomplishments and endeavors in order to be fruitful.

What are your vocations? Maybe it is being a parent or a student or a pastor? Maybe your vocations are worked out through your life as a professional? You are likely to swerve

3. Jerry Root and Stan Guthrie, *The Sacrament of Evangelism* (Chicago: Moody, 2011), 15.
4. Ibid., 49.

into some worthwhile feature of a vocation at work in your life by being in touch with answers to these sorts of questions:

What do I care about?
How do I approach intentionally living my life?
How does God accomplish His mission in His world through His people like me?
Through my network of friends and associations, how might God call me to care for them in this season of my life?
What do I have to offer to those whom I love?

I like to think of vocations as consisting of the *scope of our callings* in this life in view of the needs of our neighbors and our care for them. Ultimately, all followers of Jesus are called to be His witnesses in the world. That is what we might identify as our primary calling. So that with Paul, we declare that you are "God's workmanship, created in Christ Jesus to do good works" (Eph. 2:10). And, as Martin Luther has allegedly said, "God does not need your good works. But your neighbor does."

Vocation addresses the meaning of our whole-life for the good of others. There is no sacred vs. secular false dichotomy here, where vocation just refers to supposedly sacred (religious or churchy) activities. Jesus did not call His disciples to dedicate their religious lives. He called them to consider the cost of their whole life. In that regard, blooming in our vocation as a disciple of Jesus is integral to fulfilling the purpose of our life. For vocation is attuned to this beautiful fact: How God is *calling* you to *bless* others with *who you are* and with *the resources you have* for other people's *edification*. Theologian Steven Garber has it right when he observes:

The word vocation is a rich one, having to address the wholeness of life, the range of relationships and responsibilities. Work, yes, but also families, and neighbors, and citizenship, locally and globally—all of this and more is seen as vocation, that to which I am called as a human being, living my life before the face of God. It is never the same word as occupation, just as calling is never the same word as career. Sometimes, by grace, the words and the realities they represent do overlap, even significantly; sometimes, in the incompleteness of life in a fallen world, there is not much overlap at all.[5]

5. Steven Garber, "Vocation Needs No Justification," *Insight Magazine*, September 1, 2010 (http://bit.ly/Garber Vocation).

I emphasize the value of vocation for a variety of reasons. For one thing, it is important to recognize that we are not called to be burdened by wearing other people's callings even if (1) ours overlaps with theirs and (2) we deeply admire the callings of others and aspire to be like them. If anything, we ought to celebrate that we are on the "same team" and that God has called us each to be about our work in whatever capacity that may be. Fruitfulness is not defined by doing what has been fruitful for other people. Fruitfulness is defined by our faithful obedience to what God has called us to fulfill through our lives. That's what good stewardship requires.

Why is any of this important to the ministry of answering people's questions? It is important in order to recognize the unique, wonderful, and intelligently designed place and purpose of this ministry in your life. Take stock of your life.

- Who are you?
- What do you have to give away to others? (e.g., maybe smarts, skills, gifting, relational network, encouragement, hospitality, financial resources, seasoned experience, etc.)
- Consider how to bless those who are in relationship with you, whether they are family members, friends, or acquaintances. What do they need from you? Maybe it is only a listening ear, an attitude that is earnest for their good. Whatever it is, learn to give it away.

It is precisely this context—the occasion to bless others through our vocations—where we locate the ministry of answering people's questions. Otherwise, we risk thinking and living as if this ministry is just some "add-on" to an already busy religious life. What does personal growth look like in this ministry? It involves earnestly integrating this ministry from within our everyday, actual lives. It most likely functions at least at the level of a habit. But even more, it is what ought to characterize the orientation of our way of life before God and others: *open to the call of God and the sincere inquiries of our neighbor, earnestly loving and responsive to both.*

Amen.

Appendix 1: Tips on Using This Book
for Small Group Study

Appendix 2: On Fostering Question-Asking and
Answer-Seeking Environments

Appendix 3: Civility Guidelines for (Online)
"Third Places"

Developed by Joseph E. Gorra
Founder and Director, Veritas Life Center

Veritas Life Center is committed to the promotion of Christianity
as a wisdom and knowledge tradition relevant for life.
www.VeritasLifeCenter.org

Appendix 1

TIPS ON USING THIS BOOK FOR SMALL GROUP STUDY

A Reasonable Response *can be useful toward small group discussion. In this appendix, I suggest some perspective on how such a group might be organized along with five settings where* A Reasonable Response *could be discussed.*

FEATURES OF A SMALL GROUP

Objective: With *A Reasonable Response*, to foster dialogue around relevant questions and answers for the sake of learning and growing.

Size: Three people (ideally), or at most, maybe five people, not including a leader.

Leader: Someone who has familiarity with the overall terrain of theology and apologetics, whether by formal or informal study. It is important that the leader is someone who is competent in these areas but who is also teachable, flexible, and eager to contextualize answers in a discussion of a topic and not just offer automated responses.

Environment: This is a *discussion group*, not a lecture hall. It is meant to be a learning environment for mutual dialogue and not for "grandstanding" by either the leader or a member of the group. Hospitality, trust, and eagerness to encourage should mark the gathering.

Tone: A welcoming, belonging presence aimed at encouraging people to attend to their cares and concerns as expressed in their questions. The tone should be non-contentious and non-alienating even if there are disagreements.

Frequency: Decide on a realistic routine to meet together at a time that is not only convenient for each member but also appropriate for giving people the space to chew and digest on material between the times of meeting. That may mean once a week or once a month, for example.

Outcomes: Try to patiently and faithfully achieve any or all of these depending on the needs of the group:

- Evidence of learning how to deal with questions-as-objections that stand between one's confidence in God.

- Renewed confidence that there are worthwhile answers to questions.

- Strengthened know-how regarding how to skillfully ask and answer questions.

FIVE SMALL GROUP OPTIONS

There are various occasions to discuss *A Reasonable Response* in a small group. I suggest five occasions to consider. With each one, I suggest *a goal* to have with the particular setting. Local group leaders will know better what are the actual needs and relevant goals with members of a group.

1. **Read as part of a theology, philosophy, or apologetics-oriented reading group.**

   Goal: To focus on some top apologetics and theology issues in the book that would be relevant to further study in light of the purpose of the group.

   - Pick your top questions and choose a helpful supplemental text (e.g., *On Guard* or *Reasonable Faith*, depending on the needs of the members of the group) to expound the content in the answers.

   - Discern how Dr. Craig's answer to a question contributes to the relevant literature also on that topic and to the understanding of the group's members.

2. **Read with nonbelievers who are seeking answers to questions similar to those raised in this book.**

   Goal: To focus on questions that closely resonate with any objections to trust in God in order to gain a perspective on how a Christian scholar might respond to such objections.

   - Help nonbelievers work through clarifying and understanding their own questions and objections.

   - Understand any further questions they may have toward Dr. Craig's answers.

- Gently help them become aware of any "reasons of the heart" that might shape their attitude and perspective toward understanding an answer to their objections.

  - If they are willing, consider introducing them to other examples of Christian scholarship where they might have need or interest.

3. Read with pastors and local church small group leaders.

Goal: To focus on questions that closely resonate with common or prominent questions that seem to be before the minds of many members in this season of the life of the group.

- Encourage leaders to attend to the existentially relevant questions of their members and the theological, biblical, and philosophical understanding of their questions.

- Try to discern how the Holy Spirit might be at work in surfacing such questions and direction for how to answer.

- Discover ways in which Dr. Craig's answers in the book might be fruitfully applied and contextualized for the questions that people are in fact surfacing.

- Discern areas of long-term need for understanding.

4. Read with high school and college students and their teachers.

Goal: To focus on questions that are either currently confronting students or likely to confront students as they mature as adults, go to college, etc.

- Help them discover their presuppositions relevant to their main questions.

- Consider with them how character formation and development of specific intellectual virtues might serve them well as they deepen their maturation as an adult.

- Discern with them how the Holy Spirit might be speaking to them through Bill Craig as a model of confident faith.

5. Read with parents of teenagers and of young adults.

Goal: To focus on whole sections of questions which most resonate with fellow parents in light of their own season of parenting the intellectual and spiritual needs of their children.

- Encourage parents to connect with other parents about the kinds of common questions their kids might surface. Maybe this means moms connecting with moms, for example, regarding a specific area of inquiry.

- Discover common or overlapping training needs among parents in the relevant areas of interest.

- Find ways for parents to receive intergenerational support and counsel from seasoned parents.

Appendix 2

ON FOSTERING QUESTION-ASKING
AND ANSWER-SEEKING ENVIRONMENTS

Question-asking and answer-seeking has more to do with a *way of life* than a program, group, role, or title. We work it out by attending to the needs and opportunities through our friendships and acquaintances with others. Our associational life is often varied and rich with possibilities for dialogue with believers and nonbelievers alike. The purpose of this appendix is to help encourage a little further reflection about some of the possibilities and significance of fostering question-answering environments in our family, church, places of work, and "third places."[1]

APOLOGETICS AND THE FAMILY

What might it mean to foster intentional places for asking/answering questions through our family life? How might care and formation through a home shape the environment for studying and doing apologetics? Initially, an answer to this question may involve an issue of time, which often reflects values and priorities, in light of one's season of life and age-specific children needs. How might parents gain a perspective for fostering question-asking and answering possibilities through our family?

1. Recognize the significance of how the family acts as a "forming center."[2]

As parents, you are part of a forming center, especially for your children and their development. All families are broken at some level. The goal is not to raise perfect

---

1. To this list we could add the valuable contribution of Christian education as an integral context and means for fostering a question-answering environment. By Christian education, I have in mind everything from home-schooling, to private grade school, college, and graduate work. It is valuable in this main way: it is a normative historical practice that both *transmits* and *translates* Christian thought and practices as a knowledge and wisdom tradition.

2. For more on this idea, see Marjorie Thompson, *Family: The Forming Center* (Nashville: Upper Room Books, 1996), 22, 41.

children or to parent perfectly. But a goal should be to foster a *climate* of *trust, safe-keeping,* and *belonging* for the sake of intentionally helping children attend to the *process* of their own development and progress in growth. Parents have a unique calling to nurture children in what is good; children need regular "soul nourishers," as Timothy Jones has written, which often come in the form of encouragement, being present, and guiding and teaching their hungry souls to feed on what is life-giving.[3] Family as a forming center is a fertile context for fostering question-seeking and answering practices.

But family life can often be hectic and dictated by the tyranny of the moment and the needs and demands therein. If so, some of the most consequential lead-questions to consider when thinking about family as forming center may involve periodically asking, "How can our family routines be arranged in such a way so as to be more conducive to fostering intentional formation?" Answering that may inevitably involve thinking about how our own busyness or other people's demands on us are prohibitive to family as forming center. Formation requires intentionality about stewardship of time and resources. It also involves communication and care. It does not just happen on its own. Perhaps consider what a typical week looks like, and consider if and how there are occasions in a day to connect and communicate as a whole family, whether to play together, eat together, work together, or simply share some experience of each other's mutual presence in a tangible way.

2. Parent with attentiveness for "teachable moments."

Parents are to look for teachable moments since "all of life packs lessons about the divine," says philosopher James Spiegel in his instructive book *Gum, Geckos, and God.* "Every domain of human experience can serve as the laboratory of faith."[4] If so, there is nothing quite like in-the-moment or on-the-go instruction, and not merely when behavior or beliefs needs to be corrected. Attending to children in their moments of inquisitiveness, yearning for answers and questions, or just simply helping them to identify their various emotional states, are powerful occasions for letting them experience the personal presence of their parent. Some opportunities for teachable moments can include the following:

---

3. See the helpful perspective of Timothy Jones, *Nurturing a Child's Soul* (Nashville: Word, 2000).

4. James S. Spiegel, *Gum, Geckos, and God: A Family's Adventure in Space, Time, and Faith* (Grand Rapids: Zondervan, 2008), 9.

- When a child hears about and tries to process suffering, pain, or evil in our world.
- When a child does not get what he or she wants, it can be an occasion to help a child begin to understand the profound effect of desire on our lives, how it can be life-shaping, and how we can be OK even if we don't always get what we want, etc.
- Experiences at a local church can prompt questions or at least curiosities. Maybe children observe our practices and wonder why we do what we do.
- When kids play together, there is much opportunity to help them appreciate and understand the value of cooperation, friendship, imagination, and a whole range of communication issues. Helping them identify their thoughts and emotions/feelings, for example, about others can be a rewarding opportunity for them to experience some of their own self-knowledge.
- Whenever there are encounters with a story, whether via a book, movie, or game, it is almost always the case that there is something meaningful to talk about regarding character development, decision-making, virtues/vices, cause and effect, etc.

3. Find ways to *reason with* or *alongside* a child.

Sometimes the experience of reasoning in the midst of others can often feel condescending or controlling. But it need not be that way. In age-appropriate ways, you can reason alongside a child so that you can actually enable your son or daughter to feel respected as a contributor to the process of thinking about some issue. There is something dignifying to a child for them to experience an adult reasoning with them. For example, with our five-year-old son and three-year-old daughter, my wife and I will sometimes do the following:

- If they want something nonessential, and especially *demand* something (e.g., to go buy a new toy now!), we will sometimes ask them for their best reasons for wanting it. We don't expect much of an answer to their "because," but we are trying to help them pause, and subject the desire/want to a consideration of why they may want it. In most cases, their reasons are inadequate, which often leads to a discussion about why that is the case.
- My son is at the stage where he loves recalling a story he heard or a movie he watched. By simply asking him basic who, what, where, why, and how questions along the way, we can prod him along to further reflect about something he already

knows or doesn't know or enables him to want to know.

- Learning to "reason alongside" a child earlier in their development can help foster trust, mutuality, openness, and intentional space to be involved in some of the thought processes of their own mind. The benefit to be gained can be reaped in their development.

4. Foster an environment that empowers study in the home.

In one sense, it may be easy to immediately imagine home schooling as the ideal for fostering an environment that empowers the discipline of study at home. But one does not have to be involved in home schooling in order to do this. The goal is to help foster habits within our children that enable them to regularly practice being attentive to how God is at work in their life and in the lives of others—in their knowing, loving, doing, serving, etc. (You may want to review what I say about study in my introduction.) This is not merely a cultivation of religious knowledge per se, but it is at the very least a cultivation of a kind of spiritual and moral knowing, which can permeate other areas of knowledge, including literature, science, psychology, economics, politics, history, etc.

- Reading worthwhile books can be an important way to connect us with the thoughts and experiences of others, whether they are fiction or nonfiction works. But so-called "book learning" is only one among many means for facilitating study.
- Other means for studying include having good conversations with others, self-knowledge through circumspection about one's life, and apprenticing ourselves to trustworthy examples of the kind of person we want to become.
- Teaching our children to pray, to openly, dependently, and responsively learn to attune their heart and mind to our Father through His Son and by the Spirit, can be one of the most consequential ways we can help them study. Even more, we can help them integrate the practice of prayer in both contexts of solitude and silence and in the midst of their work in the world. Study and prayer are integral; our soul is meant to run on prayer, just as our body needs to breathe in and breathe out.

5. Look for ways to include other moral-spiritual exemplars for your children's lives.

Even as early as their middle school years, explore ways for there to be other moral-spiritual exemplars regularly inputting in your children's lives. They can benefit by knowing how life is done by seeing it at work in others beyond what they see from their parents. Maybe for middle school years, it is a trustworthy teenager through your local church who would enjoy hanging out with your kids. For junior high or high school children, maybe a college or graduate student can help bless them. There are real needs and opportunities here for how junior high, high school, and college-aged kids are pastored to serve others younger than them.

6. **Aim to find ways to integrate intellectual formation with character formation.**

J. P. Moreland talks about helping people form an "apologetic character," or we might describe this as a winsome character that is confident and hospitable in sharing understanding about why, how, and what is believed. J. P. says an apologetic character involves "those habits of excellence that constitute what it means for a believer to flourish as a convinced disciple, an attractive, skilled defender of the faith, and a persuasive ambassador for Christ."[5] For example, development in this area would involve helping children notice, identify, and grow in how truth-seeking is related to honesty, how humility is related to open-mindedness and non-defensiveness, and how ardor is associated with vigilance and fortitude. Such training and planning for intellectual and character development requires far more than reading a book, taking a class, or attending a conference. It is a commitment to fostering a way of life that is aimed at becoming a particular kind of person.

7. **Expose older students to solid training about some of life's deepest questions.**

If you have junior high or high school students, consider the following opportunities and material:

- Sean McDowell's *GodQuest* DVD curriculum (www.seanmcdowell.org)
- *Apologetics Study Bible for Students*, edited by Sean McDowell
- Focus on the Family's TrueU Curriculum (www.trueU.org)
- RZIM's Interactive Youth Apologetics (www.rzimask.org)

5. J. P. Moreland, "Developing an Apologetic Character," ACSI *Leadership Academy Report* (2001): http://www.jpmoreland.com/articles/developing-an-apologetics-character.

- *On Guard* DVD Series Companion (www.bit.ly/OnGuardDVD)

- Summit Ministries (www.summit.org)

- Impact 360 (www.impact360.net)

- Stand to Reason's Brett Kunkle (www.str.org)

- Mark Matlock's Wisdom Works Ministries (www.wisdomworks.com)

- Jonathan Morrow's Think Christianly (www.thinkchristianly.org)

- *Salvo* Magazine (www.salvomag.com)

- Ratio Christi (for Christian college apologetics training and networking) (www.ratiochristi.org)

8. Acquaint students with the rich work of Christian scholars and their popularizers.

Introduce your high school students, especially eleventh and twelfth graders, to the varied work of Christian scholars and their "translators" and popularizers who work on behalf of Christian thought and witness in the world. Credible networks of Christian scholars exist in all the main academic disciplines that one would find in a typical college or university setting.[6] One of the most popular content resources to have developed in this area has been "Christian worldview studies." Enjoy the following resources:

- Sean McDowell, *ETHIX: Being Bold in a Whatever World* (2006)

- Jonathan Morrow, *Think Christianly* (2011) and *Welcome to College: A Christ-Follower's Guide for the Journey* (2008)

- David Horner, *Mind Your Faith* (2011)

- James Sire, *The Universe Next Door*, 5th edition (2009)

- Crossway Books' series of short books on "Reclaiming the Christian Intellectual Tradition"

---

6. For a substantial microcosm of such resources, readers might be interested in my Appendix 1 and 2 of "Recommended Resources and Organizations," in J. P. Moreland's *Love Your God with All Your Mind*, revised and updated edition (Colorado Springs, CO: NavPress, 2012).

- The Veritas Forum (www.veritas.org)

- For a survey of other resources, see the list from Brian Auten's Apologetics315. com blog.

APOLOGETICS AND THE CHURCH

What if a local church had the reputation of being *the* go-to place in a local community where it was known to be a confident yet non-defensive context to openly ask the tough-minded big questions about reality and learn how the Christian tradition has thought about both the answers and the very questions themselves? What if local pastors were known in a community for taking seriously the fact that they are in possession of a body of moral and spiritual knowledge that is not only good for the "house of faith" but for all people? Can you imagine?[7]

THE CHURCH'S PRIMARY PURPOSE: PREPARING FOR MINISTRY

Based on passages like Ephesians 4, the primary purpose of local church pastors/teachers is to equip others for service or ministry in Jesus' name through their vocations in the world. A central feature of that equipping is helping to *transmit* and *translate* Christian understanding and wisdom of reality to members in order for them to minister to others and not merely passively support the professional pastor who allegedly does all the real work of ministry. But how can this equipping/training come about? One way to think about that has been to see apologetics as an essential contribution to the task of local church leadership equipping.[8]

"Apologetics in the local church" has continued to receive renewed attention in recent years whether through conferences, online discussions, or the simple yet consequential result of people trying to practice this endeavor and report on their successes and failures.[9]

---

7. You can "imagine" more, and with inspiration and specificity, from Dallas Willard's last chapter in *Knowing Christ Today* titled, "Pastors as Teachers of the Nations" (San Francisco: HarperOne, 2009).

8. For various discussions on this, see J. P. Moreland's chapter 10, "Recapturing the Intellectual Life in the Church," from the 2012 revised and updated *Love Your God with All Your Mind,* and then also the final chapter, "Pastors as Teachers of the Nations," from Dallas Willard's *Knowing Christ Today.*

9. Some interesting and helpful discussion can be accessed through Brian Auten's popular Apologetics315 blog: www.apologetics315.com.

In one sense, a good case could be made that training in apologetics properly belongs to the teaching ministry of the church. But a dominant image usually colors what teaching ministry in a local church looks like; the idea conveyed is usually one of "pulpit ministry" or teaching in some sort of Sunday school class. Of course, these areas of implementation are not bad, but they are only some among many ways to think about apologetics in a local church.

What are we attempting to produce by training people how to think about and engage the "big questions" about reality? Mere intellectual development and accomplishment? Students of contemporary, professional apologists? To me these seem inadequate as outcomes, if not short-lived. I suggest that a significant goal of training people in this area, and in general for works of ministry, is to help them develop into a particular kind of person and leader of others. With respect to the role of apologetics in such training, J. P. Moreland has written about the value of disciples of Jesus developing an "apologetic character":

So understood, an apologetic character is not a set of answers a person memorizes and adds to a life otherwise defined without regard to the apologetic mandate. No, an apologetic character is a way of being present in the world, an approach to life, a part of the very structure of one's embodied soul. Just as there is a difference between someone who can spit out answers from one's home medical book and a skilled physician who sees the world as a doctor, so there is a difference between one who memorizes a set of answers to certain apologetic questions and one who has an apologetic character. An apologetic character is part of the very warp and woof of one's journey, of one's very life as a disciple. So understood, it will increasingly exemplify a set of virtues and exhibit mastery of a range of skills. . . . The development of an apologetic character cannot be reduced to mastery of a set of questions and answers, to a set of skills, or even to a list of virtues. While such a set or list is very helpful for focusing one's training efforts, we must never forget that the whole is greater than the sum of its parts. Training believers to exemplify an apologetic character includes, but goes far beyond, any list of answers, skills, or virtues. It is an entire way of living. Thus, such training will always require role models who are themselves examples of an apologetic character. As a result, it is far more important for a Christian school to help its faculty to grow as apologists than it is to learn skills for teaching "apologetic techniques" to students.[10]

10. Moreland, "Developing an Apologetic Character."

What would it mean to cultivate this character in a congregation, through our families and Christian schools? Surely, it would involve more than just the efforts of self-identified "apologists" alone, right? Pastors are poised to be, and must be, "stakeholders" of this cultivation. In view of J. P.'s concept, apologetics looks weird without pastoral care through the local church, and the local church without apologetics looks defenseless.

But *how* do we *do* apologetics training and work through a local church? That's an important question to be considered for this appendix. A common way to answer that question has been to reply with just *content* suggestions or training resources to be studied in a local church context. The idea seems to be that if we can just convey the right material for the right people and drop that into the right local church context, then the material alone will work its magic. To be sure, utilizing quality content can be helpful, but it can also miss a bigger opportunity of thinking strategically and organizationally/institutionally about the "how" question:

First, while there are some exemplary training and learning resources that address quintessential apologetics issues, they are mostly designed for *conveying information* and are only rarely, if ever, capable of *forming character* in the sense above. Why? Well, it's hard to do that kind of forming via a DVD, book, online course, etc. It takes more than consuming a product, even a good product!

Second, training in apologetics involves far more than mastering a body of knowledge, literature, and conversation. It involves cultivating a way of life and becoming a particular kind of person who is a credible, competent, and character-rich spokesperson for Jesus, attuned to understanding and answering people's relevant and life-shaping questions.

Third, just dropping stellar apologetics-oriented content in the context of a local church is often a failure to think organizationally about how such content can be appropriated through extant and relevant structures, habits, practices, and leadership roles. In that respect, it can be a real failure of imagination.

THREE IMPORTANT DISTINCTIONS

I think there are three important distinctions to keep in mind when thinking about *how* to *do* apologetics in a local church. In some sense, these distinctions act like rudimentary building blocks toward *thinking organizationally* about apologetics in a local church.

First, there is *the difference between a church congregationally "gathered" versus the church "scattered" throughout a neighborhood* with members associated with different communities. I am inclined to emphasize the latter, which includes the former. For the church is more than that which is gathered or congregated, just as pastoring involves more than merely performing church duties at the church. This is not to diminish the significance of what happens when a church is congregated. But how we imagine church surely shapes how we think about what it is like to do something *at, in,* or *through* a local church. The prepositions are theologically potent, whether we acknowledge it or not. Why does that matter? It can shape how we understand apologetics *in* a local church.

Second, there is *the difference between "program" and "environment" for enacting the ministry* of answering people's questions in a local church.

If apologetics work is done *in* a church, it does not follow that it has to be made part of a program or given its own program stature in a congregation in order to be present and accessible to members. There's nothing wrong with being programmatic per se.[11] But sometimes congregants imagine that if something is not arranged programmatically in a church, it must mean that it is unimportant or somehow unreal. To be sure, items which have program status can feel like they are more important than not. But part of this has to do with how a congregation communicates about such things and how *communication operates within a church's overall ecology*. For something can also be important and present in a congregation at the level of ethos or environment yet not part of an official program. For example, is a congregation typified by an ethos of commitment to know what is true and worth believing *and* an openness to genuine inquiry and understanding? That can shape both the *tone* and *texture* of how programs are experienced in a congregation. Perhaps we need some strategic thinking about forming environments conducive to understanding questions and seeking answers through our local churches.

Third, there is *a difference between community and programs*.

Sometimes congregants fail to appreciate how community must be formed often prior to establishing a program. At other times, programs can help give impetus toward forming community. Bottom line: there is a difference between community and a program (including

---

11. In general, we do well to be mindful of how we define "success" or "progress" in view of programs. In the American church context, where there seems to be a greater propensity to be attracted to the allure of pragmatism, it is often the case that success is defined by "demonstrable outcomes"—outcomes that one can measure, if not control. Programs, or programmatic thinking, can be poised to deliver demonstrable outcomes. If people want something done in a church or if they want change to take place, very often they seek to "move" their groups or community by a new program. But the question is, with Eugene Peterson, are programs adequate "Kingdom means" for getting the job done? More often than not, is it the case that we need to decouple "fruitfulness" from "demonstrable outcomes" relative to programs? How we understand these issues will shape how we understand, assess, and decide about apologetics as a program in a local church.

even groups formally associated with a program). I am reminded by an insight that Eugene Peterson has often said by suggesting that community is not made or constructed but it is discovered (this is at least my paraphrase of Peterson). Why? Well, we discover community through working together, cooperating and collaborating, for example. It's more than the sum of our shared interests or having affinity around a common cause. Community is the result of mutual service for or with each other. There may be ways to develop and establish *conditions* that could be *conducive* toward forming community. But community is not directly willed into existence.

In other words, establishing apologetics-oriented programs does not equal a community of apologists per se. Why does that matter? For one thing, it is significant because the work of apologetics can be accomplished in communities through a local church even if such endeavors are not the result of church programs.

Most models that attempt to "get apologetics" in a local church (almost as if it were a conspiracy or a subversive act) operate with a common emphasis on privileging apologetics as a program or product placement through a group(s) in contrast to attempting to form and flourish an environment hospitable to genuine inquiry and openness to understanding.

The pages that follow for this discussion on apologetics in the local church are in some sense the result of (unofficially) observing dozens of churches (various denominations) and interviewing dozens of pastors and church staff, educators, graduate apologetics students, and professionals over the last ten years in such places as Oregon, California, Texas, Georgia, Rhode Island, Maryland, and Wisconsin. I do not claim any unique authority on what I say beyond what I have only been able to hear, see, discuss, and understand with locals. I have tried to seriously reflect on these experiences and then (hopefully) account for some of their features.

NINE MODELS FOR APOLOGETICS AND THE LOCAL CHURCH

How might we consider the work of apologetics in a local church? One way is to consider what different models one can offer in this area. I can identify at least six common organizational models for local church apologetics work, and three other models that are rarely tried. In each of these models, "apologetics work" can refer to a range of possible endeavors, including training/equipping, leadership, resourcing with content (for example), study, outreach, engagement with evangelism, etc.

1. A distinct training program with its own educational priorities and objectives

In some significant way, this model is what tends to commonly come to mind for most enthusiastic apologists who want to see their work occur in a local church. Undergraduate or graduate students in apologetics tend to implement this training as classroom experience in a local church context. The idea might be, why not foster a classroom-like experience, including lectures and readings, for people to attend as a distinct program? That frame of reference is not surprising since that is probably how such students learned apologetics. But the challenge with this model is that it can become (even unintentionally) a niche group of people, perhaps even isolated from other educational and serving endeavors of the church. Moreover, the form may only be accessible to academically inclined learners and limited in its scope and application. It might lend credence to the impression that apologetics really is only for "eggheads" or the "smarties" in a church. With this model, it is often hard to appreciate that education does not have to occur in a classroom or a quasi-classroom in order for it to be educational.

2. An outreach ministry linked to evangelism

Linked to evangelism efforts, this apologetics model is less about something that happens *inside* the church but is more of a veritable practice in the real-world, public marketplace of ideas and interactions. Maybe it is viewed as a means for gathering and inviting people back into the church. Perhaps it is a practical and tangible extension of how a church participates in evangelism. Training in apologetics looks more like learning to have prepared answers in hand or utilization of skills to know how to deflect objections. A challenge for this model is frequent temptation toward reducing apologetics to a mere communication technique. Moreover, apologists can become so outward outcome-based that inner transformation (e.g., character development) can be considered less important to attend to, versus winning souls by winning arguments.

3. A demographic-specific small group ministry

This model is so supportive of the value of apologetics as a program in a local church that it sees demographic-specific training groups as a fundamental way to convey education in this area. So, for example, one might see groups centered around "apologetics for women" or "apologetics for young adults." The benefit of such groups is that they may be more conducive to hearing demographic-specific questions and needs regarding apologetics issues. The challenge, like most anything else that is defined by demography, is that it can become niche, individualistic, and isolated. It can also limit learners from growing in collaboration with learners from a different background.

4. Training via guest speakers or apologetics curriculum

This model recognizes a need for program-oriented apologetics training, but a local church may not have adequate in-house resources and laborers to fulfill the need. Thus, resources are sought outside of a local church context for utilization inside the church. Pastors who see the *need* for apologetics study in their church can often feel overwhelmed with how to fulfill it without having to reinvent the proverbial wheel. Today, more than ever, there are excellent resources to utilize, and by and large, professional apologists have a heart for the church and are eager to come speak to a local congregation.

A challenge, though, is to discern what to do once the conference leaves town, or the professional is no longer in one's midst. How do you learn to attend to the need to form an environment, indeed a culture, of study, of learning, and of growing in ways to help people find answers to their questions? Because the apologetic need is often so great, and due to this model's temporary adequacy, this model often provokes interest and need to implement other models aimed at cultivating a question-answering environment.

5. Ministry associated with members of a church

Such a ministry is not formally dependent on the organizational intention and program of a local church. This model recognizes that apologetics in a local church can operate in a non-program-dependent way. It tends to understand apologetics work with a more community-focused framework by emphasizing the work through members of multiple ecclesial and educational institutions. Workers and leaders in apologetics may all represent and contribute to different churches, but they share in a particular work beyond their affiliations to any particular church or educational outlet. In the context of a local church, with this model, apologists participate in a more on-call kind of way.

In my estimation, of the six main models for apologetics training in the local church, this is the most uncommon one that merits further attention. The challenge, though, is that self-identified apologists can feel isolated and remain unconnected to the serious work of sharing in the responsibilities of the teaching ministry of a local church. Why? Well, perhaps the (mis)perception is that such apologists are off doing their own thing.

6. Apologetics enacted primarily through the pulpit ministry

This model also offers a further alternative to program-oriented apologetics endeavors in a local church. It attempts to integrate the good of apologetics leadership, benefits, and understanding through the megaphone of the weekly teaching ministry of the pulpit. In this context, perhaps a pastor/teacher is engaged in apologetic preaching, where the aim is to perhaps expound on a passage of Scripture or a contemporary topic with the intent of offering a defense of Christian truth claims.

The challenge with this model is to discern whether there is a need long-term for a "formation net." That is, it's one thing for congregants to gain an acquaintance of apologetics via the pulpit, but are there further apologetic needs to address that are beyond the capacity of the pulpit? Moreover, while there can be some growth as the result of great apologetic preaching, that's a different kind of experience compared to being a stakeholder of that same content via discussion and directed practices through a small group, for example. These differences of training and opportunity for growth have to be weighed against their alternatives.

A few other models are worth mentioning, even though (in my opinion) they have yet to be thoroughly tried in a local church context.

7. Through local church staff leaders

This model emphasizes the need for a church to invest in leadership development that is attuned to helping people do apologetics through their various vocations. Thus, it is more leadership-oriented and not merely program-oriented. The model banks on the fact that the church has been given teachers so that people may be formed by a Christian understanding of reality. But instead of creating a separate kind of teacher-leader for apologetics training, this model encourages local church teachers to gain perspective on how apologetics work might look from within already established areas and roles, whether they are adult theological training, children's leaders, young adult pastors, etc. This model emphasizes investing in the theological and worldview development of local leaders.

8. As education in Christian public communication skills, character, and practices

This model is more praxis-oriented, not at the exclusion of cultivating leaders to operate with a Christian understanding of the world, but especially attentive to the manifold "how-to" elements of apologetics as embodied, Christian communication. Whether as a way of shaping mental environments, programs, training through various communities, or a way of investing in leaders, this model is designed to help learners practice what apologetics work can look like in local contexts of interrelationship with others.

9. As a background, educational ministry for the sake of informing and forming others

Enthusiasts of apologetics training in a local church often think it has to be represented in the foreground in order for it to be consequential (e.g., having programs, leaders, or groups with reputation for doing apologetics). This model, though, emphasizes that apologetics training is more effectual if it empowers extant educational/training leaders in a local church to think, apply, and communicate apologetics integratively. For example, through discipleship-training and spiritual formation endeavors, apologetics training would operate from within this area of understanding and not separate from it, according to this model. For ministries to families, youth and college students, and adults, this model would attempt to find ways to integrate apologetics training from within these areas. Moreover, on this model and similar to number 7 above, perhaps the church would be willing to invest time and resources in fostering an educational and research support staff chiefly devoted to empowering other leaders in the church to enable them to equip members. This would be an example of supporting this endeavor in the background for the sake of empowering both the environment and programs in a local church.

Depending on the needs, goals, and willingness of church leadership and structure, there may be good reason to develop "eclectic" models for organizing apologetics training in view of the particular season of a church. For many of these models are conducive toward some kind of fusionist approach and model for training.

FIVE RECOMMENDATIONS FOR GENERAL IMPLEMENTATION

Regardless of the model(s) for "doing apologetics in the local church," at the very least a local church may wish to at least engage in the following routine endeavors:

1. Each month or every two months, devote at least one Sunday morning/evening or midweek church gathering to addressing a major worldview or apologetic question that would seem to be relevant to the spiritual and intellectual needs of a congregation. This would be beneficial for both self-identified Christians and unchurched attendees.

2. On a quarterly basis, devote at least one Sunday morning/evening or midweek church gathering to answering biblical/theological or worldview/apologetics relevant questions from the congregation. Maybe these are answered by both pastor(s) and any theology/apologetics professors that attend a congregation. Bottom line: it is enormously beneficial for a pastor to be attuned and responsive to the ongoing and actual questions from a congregation; it's an effectual way to test an important part of the soul of a congregation.

3. Twice a year, invite a guest speaker(s) to come and address a major apologetics/worldview issue for some sustained training that would be beyond the scope of a regular church gathering in order to equip local church leaders from the immediate area. Maybe this is a Saturday morning seminar for two to three hours that is discussion-oriented.

4. If a local church has a bookstore/library, stock it full with quality resources that are attentive to real and felt intellectual needs in the congregation and regularly promote such resources through as-needed book study groups and discussions, one-paragraph reviews through churchwide communication endeavors, and opportunities to connect current theological training needs with bookstore/library resources for further study.

5. Teach lay leaders how to address relevant worldview/apologetics questions through small group ministries in a local church, including how to integrate such training and character development with discipleship-forming endeavors in a group.

SEVEN QUESTIONS FOR CHURCH LEADERS:
DISCERNING THE VALUE OF THE "APOLOGETICS ENDEAVOR"

Here are seven questions to help you determine if an apologetics program might be effective in your church:

1. How will it enhance the *environment* of a teaching/equipping and preaching ministry of a local church?

2. If it is formally part of the organizational intent of a local church, how can it *integrate* with other teaching/equipping endeavors?

3. How will it complement and empower and not distract or compete with the work of other pastors/leaders through a local church?

4. If it is a group, how can the endeavor be arranged to be more discussion oriented rather than lecture oriented?

5. How will it enhance people's leadership and resourcefulness through their vocations?

6. How will it strengthen people's actual confidence in God and enable them to be effectual in their witness to others?

7. How will it enable people to pick up tools or practices or habits in their everyday life that will enable them to do apologetics?

MISTAKES TO AVOID WHEN ADVOCATING
APOLOGETICS TRAINING IN A LOCAL CHURCH

Well-meaning advocates of apologetics sometimes practice several of these seven mistakes when trying to convince pastors to include apologetics training in a local church:

1. *Demanding that apologetics work has to develop your way in order for it to be effectual in a local church.* Organizationally speaking, there is not one way to do apologetics work in and through the local church. The above models are evidence of that. Therefore, it is unfair and unproductive to demand that it has to look a particular way in order for it to work in a particular context. Thinking creatively, strategically, and collaboratively with other church leaders about models can be a positive way forward.

2. *Shaming pastors for not doing their job if they are hesitant about apologetics or see its value differently than you do.* Such shaming is dumb, ineffectual, and manipulative. Instead of shaming, a better approach would be to help pastors understand the value and benefits of apologetics to the role of a pastor and a congregation. Educating, not judging, is a fruitful way forward. Moreover, teachable parishioners do well to consider how other credible Christian leaders view apologetics, including their criticisms, in order to understand how to better communicate in this area. Shaming is a total conversation-killer.

3. *Overselling the value of apologetics in a local church by insisting that it is the most important endeavor that a church could be involved in.* Apologetics training and ministry was never designed to be the end-all be-all; it is a serving discipline and ministry. It comes alongside other areas of thought and life and empowers them for their own good. Rarely is it the case that pastors are convinced of something as a result of overselling some cause, product, program, personality, etc. It can be effectual to convey a confident and measured view of the good of apologetics in a local church.

4. *Attempting to distract from the normal teaching ministry of a local church by hosting apologetics-oriented events at the same time as what a local church is trying to do.* This is the kind of activity that gives apologists and apologetics in the local church a royal black eye. It is self-centered and immature.

5. *Thinking that apologetics in a local church needs to be an "official" part of the programming of a church in order to be valuable and effectual.* Depending on a pastor's leadership style and perspective, and how a church's structure operates, one may be waiting a long time to be engaged in apologetics in a local church if one is waiting for the green light to make apologetics part of the programming of a local church's training effort, for example. My encouragement is to find ways, which may often have a non-glamorous low profile, to strengthen fellow believers with needs in these areas but keep communication channels open with pastors and see how that develops further.

6. *Insisting that graduate-degreed apologists and philosophers be the only or main teachers in any apologetics training opportunities.* One of the most remarkable achievements in evangelical graduate training of the last twenty years is the opportunity for anyone (pastors and parishioners alike) to get formal training in apologetics. The result has been enthusiastic apologetics students wanting to do something with their education through a local church. But self-identified, professionally trained apologists or

philosophers are *not* the only stakeholders of apologetics training. The same could also be said for theologians; they are not the only stakeholders of theology training through a local church. Emerging leaders in apologetics do well to recognize the multi-faceted role of diverse sources of knowledge and expertise on apologetics and find ways to train as collaborative teams.

7. *Concluding that if a pastor doesn't do apologetics the way you think it should be done he doesn't care seriously for the life of the mind.* This is similar to (2) above, but it also has a different bite and a strange nuance to it. For example, if apologetics is crucial to the health and preservation of the "Christian mind," it might be argued, it should be presented by pastors because pastors have a responsibility to cultivate the mind of their parishioners. Therefore, if pastors do not engage in apologetics in some particular way (training, ministry) through their role as pastors, it is concluded that they must not care for cultivating the life of the mind in their parishioners. But, of course, this is nonsense. Truth be told, more often than not, pastors probably do apologetics in some fashion without even being told they do. For example, whenever they attempt to deal with that which hinders confidence in God, or how God's action in the world is meaningful (e.g., answer to prayer) or when they seek to cultivate the apologetic character of their parishioners (even if they don't call it that), they are likely engaged at some level with work within the scope of doing apologetics.

Here are six assumptions to avoid when bringing apologetics training to the local church:

1. *Training is fundamentally the result of substantive lecturing and "book-learning."* What are the contemporary, dominant ways for conveying apologetics content? In text form (especially as books) and doing events/conferences and lectures? If so, it is not surprising that such dominant communication *means* shape what is understood and expected to be main *models* for training in apologetics. Lectures, books, events, and other *products* to experience are not inherently inadequate means, but they are only one among many means. And if apologetics goes beyond merely conveying information and knowledge (content) to include a particular kind of character development, then it behooves leaders and educators in apologetics to convey a strategic imagination about the relevant means to fulfill real and felt training needs in this area.

2. *Training is really learning how to utilize debate tactics against opponents of Christian truth.* If lecturing is not perceived to be the dominant mode of doing communication in apologetics, debating probably is. When people think of apologetics they often think of how to compete and defend someone in a debate. That tends to be the dominant image that pervades their outlook in this area. Sadly, many people often eliminate themselves from engaging in apologetics because they are not good at arguing or engaging in a debate, and because they think that apologetics is all about communicating in debate form, they conclude that apologetics must not be for them but only for those with such command of skills and technique. One can debate the benefits of what debating actually accomplishes. But there should be a widespread recognition among apologetics enthusiasts in a local church that learning apologetics is not equal to learning debate tactics.

3. *Training is all about memorizing apologetics arguments and talking points, to be repeated as needed.* There is something to be said for taking stock and memorizing basic arguments for some claim relevant to the Christian worldview (e.g., arguments for God's existence). But this alone is inadequate as an intention, means, and approach to learning apologetics. For doing apologetics is also about learning to improvise in conversation, listen astutely, cultivate a character that is winsome and virtuous, non-defensive with one's convictions, and trust and cooperate with the Holy Spirit.

4. *Successful training has occurred when students of apologetics sound like great apologists.* Though this aspiration is often unspoken, many think a ready defender of the faith will sound like Lee Strobel, Hank Hanegraaff, William Lane Craig, Ravi Zacharias, J. P. Moreland, Craig Hazen, Norm Geisler, Paul Copan, or any other favorite apologist. In one sense, this aspiration is understandably commendable. There are now more models than ever to have before one's mind and to consider how these models get the job done in apologetics, philosophy, theology, and evangelism. But the ultimate goal of apologetics training and aspiration should *not* be centered on these personalities as models. We are not called to have their calling. We have our own calling, even if it overlaps or resembles theirs. Not only do these models have their own calling but they have their own voice and platform. It is folly to separate calling from voice and platform. The standard should not be to mimic them in that regard. Rather, our training and ministry in apologetics should seek to be attentive to how these models work but also discern what our unique contributions are in this area and how that can get worked out through our various vocations.

5. *Training is ultimately about stockpiling superior intellectual ammunition against non-Christian thinking.* This attitude is incommodious and full of so much myopic thinking about people and ideas.

6. *Training is for self-identified intellectuals (or for those aspiring to be) who otherwise wouldn't have a "home" in a local church.* Self-identified apologists, and Christian scholars in general, often have an accompanying anxiety about the local church that runs something like this: the local church does not appear to prize the life of the mind given the sort of anti-intellectual, simplistic, and cliché-driven pronouncements that fill this environment, especially teaching contexts like the Sunday pulpit or Sunday school. The solution? Perhaps unintentionally or intentionally, scholars and other academic types congregating among themselves as a sub-community or niche group in a church. In one sense, this outcome as a default posture is understandable, if pastors or a church's ethos fail to help academic types belong. However, there is much to be said for academic types being socialized by a local church's environment, where they can regularly enter into interaction and service with and for non-academic types. The problem is making "training" into an insular, self-contained hangout for academic groupies.

The straightforward and consequential goal of local church apologetics work should be to equip people to be resourceful with answers to tough questions through their vocations in the world. So, we want to aim to equip people from within their everyday life.

APOLOGETICS AND PLACES OF EMPLOYMENT

Apologetics in the workplace may often look more covert than not. After all, the main purpose of going to work, whether as an employer or employee, is probably not necessarily to win hearts and souls for Jesus, unless, of course, that is the organizational mission of a workplace. Naturally, we should arrange our lives to be open to the Spirit's work. For we can still bear witness to Jesus and His kingdom while being "on the job," especially in a pluralistic and non-religious context. But how might our witness look with the aim of serving people with the questions they might have about life and reality? Here are some suggestions:

1. *Be an excellent and trustworthy worker*, as one who in everything is "working unto the Lord." The social capital accrued here can go a long way in establishing a hearing for

your "voice" among fellow employees and your employer. The very witness of your life in this context can strengthen or weaken how colleagues and associates experience the plausibility of your beliefs.

2. *Be an available resource.* Maybe you are the person who is good at recommending resources to interested people. Maybe you can help people gain clarity about their own questions. The winsomeness of being known as an available resource to dialogue about the big questions of life and reality is a major way to serve people in the workplace.

3. *Intentionally encourage fellow Christians in the workplace by helping them become an available resource to others.* As colleagues and fellow brothers and sisters, find ways to encourage each other and promote ways in which the plausibility of Christian witness and the message and mission of Jesus can gain a receptive hearing in your workplace. Practice intentional prayer both for coworkers and for the overall environment.

4. *Study how your workplace, along with your organization's goods and services, might shape how people ask and understand their big questions.* This may or may not be a relevant factor all the time or for all people in all work environments. But it is worth attending to. For example, maybe someone is a factory worker and experiences a boss who is not much more than a taskmaster. How does that shape a worker's experience of God? Or, someone is working in sales, and forms the habit of just feeling like everything in life has to be "sold" in order to be convincing. How does that shape someone's experience of God's communication to them through His Word and other people?

5. *Find intentional ways to relate to non–Christian workers so that in due time you can find ways to be with them beyond your shared workspace and hours.* Invite them to your routine third places and let them reciprocate. Attempt to build associations that move to friendships.

6. *With prudence, avoid "foreign entanglements."* Such entanglements consist of discussions or disputes that will gain Christian witness very little in the likelihood of someone wanting to understand and believe what is true. For example, let's say that you work in a politically left-of-center environment. But you self-identify, politically speaking, as a "Christian conservative." Which is more valuable, short-term and long-term: "correcting" your liberal friends on most everything they say that stands in disagreement with your worldview, or being prudent in what you say and how you

say it in order to still earn the right to be heard and to form a sustainable relationship with someone? This is not at all easy, and can easily feel like giving in. But it need not be.

7. *Keep the health of the environment in mind.* The following questions can be kept before your mind: Do non-Christians in my workplace encounter a living Jesus who is known as the wisest person in the world? How is Christian presence experienced in my workplace? How might the mental environment of my workplace shape people's experience of moral-spiritual knowledge of reality?

Appendix 3

CIVILITY GUIDELINES FOR (ONLINE) "THIRD PLACES"

The qualities and habits of *community* are shaped by the qualities and habits of *communication*, and by the overall *character of communicators*. This is important for understanding the "moral ecology" conditions that create an environment of authentic civility. In other words, to appreciate the nature of civility, one cannot abstract it from factors like the value of community, communication, and character. These are not the only conditions that resource civility. But they are certainly most relevant when seeking to gain a perspective of how civility might work in online discussion contexts. What follows in this appendix is only a sketch; a way of trying to paint with some fairly broad strokes in order to possibly envision further fruitful thought and work in this area. First, let us consider the value of a particular kind of place, and indeed, placement of community that would be a conducive environment for regular, substantive discussion.

"THIRD PLACES" AND COMMUNITY FORMATION

"Third places" refer to those common or routine places for gathering with others that are "between" and can sometimes even mediate socializing between work and home. Perhaps common for members of a local community would be coffee shops, parks, or malls as third places; these are common meeting points for all types of people and not just people with a particular demographic background.

Third places "allow people who live or work in the same neighborhood to get to know one another in a nonthreatening way," writes pastor Eric Jacobsen in his insightful book *The Space Between: A Christian Engagement with the Built Environment*. These kinds of places can both (1) reduce estrangement and (2) encourage the development of old and new relationships. Jacobsen goes on to say, "Third places help create connections among residents in an area, they create places where strangers can feel welcome, and they help to socialize us to the rules of our communities."[1]

How might the value of third places enable contexts conducive for conversation and discovery of community? Here are some considerations in light of Jacobsen's observations:

1. *A third place is a* neutral context. It is not inherently partisan or "directed." That is, one does not have to be a member of x, y, or z in order to inhabit and cultivate relationships in this kind of place. It does not matter who is the host or the guest. On that count, a third place is not home, but can be like a home-away-from-home by virtue of similarly experienced feelings of comfort and support.

2. *A third place acts as a* leveler *of social distinctions.* This is not to deny that such distinctions may have place in the larger society, but for the purpose of experiencing conversation and sharing in the experience of mutuality in the *environment* of a third place, social distinctions are not significant identity-markers.

3. *A third place's distinctive character is in virtue of "the regulars."* This does not mean that only regulars are welcomed. There should exist a significant degree of openness and invitation to belong for any newcomers, especially for any newcomers to become regulars.

4. *A third place exists for a main activity:* ongoing lively conversation. This place is not for entertainment purposes (e.g., compared to a sports stadium), nor is it a selling environment (e.g., compared to a retail store) or even a dominant messaging context (e.g., a lecture hall). It is a place where we can be welcomed to be ourselves in conversation with others who are regulars and newcomers.

---

1. Eric Jacobsen, *The Space Between: A Christian Engagement with the Built Environment* (Grand Rapids: Baker, 2012), 245–46. For a snapshot of some of Jacobsen's main themes, see my interview with him for *Christianity Today's* "City Project": http://bit.ly/CTJacobsen. Moreover, Jacobsen is drawing upon the conceptualization of Ray Oldenburg, *The Great Good Place: Cafes, Coffee Shops, Community Centers, Beauty Parlors, General Stores, Bars, Hangouts, and How They Get You Through the Day,* 2nd ed. (New York: Paragon House, 1997), 20–42. In my estimation, third places can be more fully appreciated by understanding their broader historical and societal antecedents and values, by considering the purpose of free associations, subsidiary relationships, and institutions, and the purpose of fraternal societies. For more on this, see David T. Beito's *From Mutual Aid to the Welfare State: Fraternal Societies and Social Services, 1890-1967* (Chapel Hill: Univ. of North Carolina Press, 2000), chapters 1–2, and then, with delight, Alexis de Tocqueville, *Democracy in America,* historical-critical edition of *De la democratie en Amerique,* Eduardo Nolla, ed., James T. Schleifer, trans., vol. 3 (Indianapolis: Liberty Fund, 2010), chapters 4–5, 7.

5. *A third place offers accessible and accommodating hours of operation and a winsome mood.* The goal is to stay open with relatively long hours for the sake of permitting regulars to join in at any opportune time during their week. A lighthearted mood can be disarming even for seriousness of conversation.

ONLINE DISCUSSION CONTEXTS AS A QUASI "THIRD PLACE"

Consider the words of Sherry Tuckle, psychology professor at Massachusetts Institute of Technology:

> We live in a technological universe in which we are always communicating. And yet we have sacrificed conversation for mere connection. . . .
>
> Human relationships are rich; they're messy and demanding. We have learned the habit of cleaning them up with technology. And the move from conversation to connection is part of this. But it's a process in which we shortchange ourselves. Worse, it seems that over time we stop caring, we forget that there is a difference.
>
> We are tempted to think that our little "sips" of online connection add up to a big gulp of real conversation. But they don't. E-mail, Twitter, Facebook, all of these have their places—in politics, commerce, romance and friendship. But no matter how valuable, they do not substitute for conversation. . . .
>
> FACE-TO-FACE conversation unfolds slowly. It teaches patience. When we communicate on our digital devices, we learn different habits. As we ramp up the volume and velocity of online connections, we start to expect faster answers. To get these, we ask one another simpler questions; we dumb down our communications, even on the most important matters. It is as though we have all put ourselves on cable news. Shakespeare might have said, "We are consum'd with that which we were nourish'd by."
>
> And we use conversation with others to learn to converse with ourselves. So our flight from conversation can mean diminished chances to learn skills of self-reflection. These days, social media continually asks us what's "on our mind," but we have little motivation to say something truly self-reflective. Self-reflection in conversation requires trust. It's hard to do anything with 3,000 Facebook friends except connect. . . .
>
> WE expect more from technology and less from one another and seem increasingly drawn to technologies that provide the illusion of companionship without the

demands of relationship. Always-on/always-on-you devices provide three powerful fantasies: that we will always be heard; that we can put our attention wherever we want it to be; and that we never have to be alone. Indeed our new devices have turned being alone into a problem that can be solved.[2]

Social media platforms are arguably the most popular to date modes of online communication, and increasingly so in an always-on, always-connected, 24/7 mobile-device-mediating world. So, I have that in mind mainly when I talk about online communication.

Increasingly, such platforms (e.g., Facebook, Google+) are acting like third places, or at least contexts for *informal* meet-ups among friends, associates, and colleagues. In this appendix, I try to *sketch* a perspective for fostering a civic-minded question-answering environment in online third-place contexts.

At the time of this writing (autumn 2012), Christians and non-Christians alike in many cases are still attempting to understand how online communication shapes our interaction and free associations and the possibilities of experiencing community together in a digital environment. The challenges and opportunities afforded by communication technology will likely increase in the years to come. It is important to think innovatively, clearly, and soberly about such challenges and opportunities.[3]

More than ever, Christians will benefit from theological and ethical understanding wisely applied to this area. While my goal here is not to articulate an explanation or defense of that understanding, I do want to suggest some guidelines for how we might go about thinking of the opportunities and challenges for answering and discussing people's questions in online environments. In one sense, I am attempting to offer a framework, and in another sense, I am trying to offer some recommended practices. But first, I want to draw attention to a behavioral challenge.

---

2. Sherry Tuckle, "The Flight from Conversation," *New York Times,* April 21, 2012, http://bit.ly/NYTuckle.

3. One of the best books in recent years on this topic is John Dyer's resourceful and accessible *From the Garden to the City: The Redeeming and Corrupting Power of Technology* (Grand Rapids: Kregel Publications, 2011).

THREE BEHAVIORAL PROBLEMS
THAT MAY SHAPE ONLINE DISCUSSIONS

Here are some common negative scenarios (behaviors, in many respects) that commonly shape interaction in online environments. Keep these in mind since they tend to dominate much but certainly not all of what is experienced in online discussion contexts.

A. *The "got you" scenario, resulting in "protesting."* This is where some individual, group, or organization makes it their intent online to air dirty laundry; to expose in order to distract, alienate, or cause pressure to mount against a person, their associations, or their ideas. It has a decisive campaign feel to it, whether rallying the troops in support of, or in opposition to, x, y, or z. What's being exposed may be full-blown sin, or heterodox or heretical ideas, but *how* it is done online, has a particular "got you" texture and tone to it.

B. *The "informationally overwhelming" scenario.* This is where an *approach* to a discussion involves "data dumping" arguments on an individual instead of being measured, interactive, and responsive to an inquirer in light of their actual process of understanding. In many ways, this scenario treats others as mere consumers of information. A main practice in this scenario is to basically blast inquirers with information but with no (or very little) guidance, direction, and context.

C. *The "reductionistic" scenario.* This is where attitudes and practices of naming, framing, and categorizing others and their ideas come into play by the tendency of taking up a reductionistic account of another, especially an opponent with whom there is a disagreement. For example, a constant challenge with hotly debated topics is to view people as, essentially, just the sum of their ideas or beliefs, and that's all they really are, and to then draw identity-boundaries around that kind of characterization of them. So, for example, it's one thing to label someone a Calvinist because (a) they self-identify as such or (b) it is practically useful in order to help draw a distinction between their viewpoint in contrast with non-Calvinist viewpoints. But it takes labeling to another level when such descriptors are meant to pigeonhole or strictly define the scope and nature of one's identity (acting as if they are, as individuals, not any more definable than the sum of their ideas or beliefs).

If civility is to have a chance at becoming even a foothold in online discussions, it seems like one would have to try and maintain a particular vigilance against the above three scenarios. They do not help, but only hinder conditions for civility. How? They fail to treat fellow human beings with respect and dignity.

Moreover, with respect to (A) scenarios, one can bring awareness and understanding of views that are not only disagreeable but are in fact aberrant by not doing so in a "got you" vein. It can be done for whoever is willing, and it can be mostly accomplished effectually through private, behind-the-scenes kinds of conversations with others. Online engagement is an engagement with, and an encounter in, multiple publics. It is made for a kind of spectator viewing and performative participation. We have to decide if what is to be exposed really does merit this medium and its values that shape communication practices, message, behavior, and outcomes.

With respect to (B) scenarios, treating inquirers as if they are mostly or only consumers of information, even with valid and sound information, is not dignifying to an inquirer. For they most likely need more than just information; they need care, guidance, wisdom, and understanding. It's not either/or. Inquirers deserve more than mere data-dumps as solutions to their questions.

Finally, with respect to (C) scenarios, labeling or describing someone that goes beyond mere contrasting to comprehensive identity-defining can be unfruitful and damaging. Prudence, not trigger-happy impulsiveness, should guide our naming/labeling. Even if someone does merit the title "heretic," for example, it does not follow that using it in an online discussion is the best use and place for that descriptor. In other words, there are contexts, subsidiary relationships, that may be more conducive to applying that term with an understanding of the significance of that descriptor's meaning.

TEN FACTORS TOWARD A FRAMEWORK FOR CIVILITY

How might Christians think about civility in the context of real and felt disagreements with fellow Christians and non-Christians? What should go into that thinking about civility? I suggest the following ten considerations. These factors are not intended to be comprehensive but hopefully representative of how one might develop thinking in this area for a particular implementation of a framework in distinct context.

1. *Civility is not about mere niceness of manners alone nor is it a kind of rhetorical decorum to public speech.* Civility is "a republican virtue that is a matter of principle and a habit

of the heart. It is a style of public discourse shaped by respect for the humanity and dignity of individuals, as well as for truth and the common good."[4] Understanding a "common good" can be discoverable through a common vision involving a shared "agreement about the rights, responsibilities, and respect that form the common bonds" within a society.[5] Moral knowledge shapes our understanding of a common vision. Disagreements and differences of worldview and different ways of life are inevitable. The question is, how do we live with these differences? Civility—and its relevant framework—can help toward negotiating our differences and settling peacefully. Civility is as much about our philosophy of society, governance, and laws as it is about the manner in which people deal with their differences in a particular context.

2. *Knowledge of reality does not entail cockiness or dogmatism*. Rather, knowledge involves a *responsibility to share what is known*, lived, and communicated in a non-defensive confidence. Discussions and disagreements as a result of just shared opinions or preferences are more prone toward dissension online. Reducing people's claims to only being "everyone's opinions" does not foster dialogue or understanding of disagreements. The solution to cockiness or dogmatism is not ignorance. Nor is the solution, necessarily, to be less committed to what one knows and believes to be true. The solution is to foster and have understanding in humility; of knowledge in love. An indispensable goal of discussion, and especially discussion involving disagreements, is to come to an understanding of each other's perspective or outlook on the world. And if understanding is our goal, we need not fear what other people contribute to our knowledge of what is real.

Of course, to merely claim knowledge of reality is not adequate. Even reality is testable. We can weigh its evidence or reasons or accuracy of how well it represents reality. It is not the same as having mere beliefs, religious or otherwise, that can readily motivate our actions. For we can live consistently with our beliefs even if they are not true beliefs or regardless if they are rooted in good evidence or method, etc. Beliefs, profession, or one's commitment to some conviction can be helpful for identifying what moves us or how we wish to present ourselves before

---

4. Os Guinness, *The Case for Civility* (San Francisco: HarperOne, 2008), 151.
5. Ibid., 141.

others. But they alone are not an adequate basis for deep discussion, if in fact the goal is to move dialogue toward an understanding of reality.[6]

3. *Truth-seeking and truth-telling are not optional but essential for having a sustainable discussion, especially a discussion involving disagreements.* It is not enough to be committed to seeking truth; we want to be able to seek knowledge of what is true. We want to be able to not only tell the truth, but tell the truth knowingly. This does not mean that only one person or group has a monopoly on knowledge of what is true. Rather, it means that if we know anything about what is true, we have a responsibility to share what we know with others, even if only we "know in part" or know without certainty or even know without full assurance of reasons for how we know and why. Knowledge of the truth is made for sharing.

4. *People being made in the image of God demands mutual respect for each other.* Human dignity is not a social construction; it is not the result of personal preferences or agreement of wills as in the case of contractual arrangements. Dignity is pre-contractual. Moreover, it is essentially not the result of State pronouncement and enforcement. It is a pre-State fact of human existence. It is what I am owed from another human being and it is what I am obligated to give to another. It is inherent to the moral obligation that I have toward another human being by virtue of us simply being made in God's image. Dignity and respect is the proper response due. The image of God puts the humane in human. It speaks to the dignity of human embodiment, of having and experiencing each other's personal presence in the world through our encounter with each other's embodiment.

This is what we encounter when we are in the company of other human beings: we experience their integrated embodiment of body and soul.[7] And, although, human beings are corruptible and finite, and act contrary to the image of God, God's mission is to redeem and restore that which is fallen.

---

6. For more on any of this, please see Dallas Willard, *Knowing Christ Today*, especially chapters 1–2.

7. "This connection of body and person, so taken for granted in our experience, is crucial for our coming to know other persons and respecting their dignity. The body is the place of their personal presence. We know them only there, as they likewise know us only as embodied persons." Gilbert Meilander, *Neither Beast Nor God: The Dignity of the Human Person* (New York: Encounter Books, 2009), 27.

5. *Human finitude and fallenness are sufficient reasons for being* open *to the fact that one could be mistaken and incomplete in their knowledge and beliefs of reality*. Open-mindedness as a virtue is relevant here. But open-mindedness is not the same as being anti-intellectual or unthinking, or wishy-washy, or cowardly in the face of opposition to one's beliefs or knowledge, or unwilling to compromise, morally or spiritually speaking. Open-mindedness involves "an ability and willingness to transcend a certain default cognitive standpoint in order to take up or take seriously a distinct cognitive standpoint."[8] It is at one level a kind of intellectual motivation; a "transcending" for the sake of understanding standpoint that is distinct from my own default standpoint. How might that look? Maybe in mutual dialogue it looks like "holding" my standpoint more like a hypothesis and another standpoint also as a hypothesis to be tested, and not merely tested for the sake of being assessed but to be understood. But if a discussion context is characterized as inherently combative, intellectually speaking, it is difficult if not impossible for mutual open-mindedness to be experienced.

6. *It is beneficial to operate with a thick notion of "free exercise," and not merely some thin concept of tolerating differing viewpoints*. Tolerance has come to mean not much more than a willingness (if that) to put up with someone, if one has to do so. In its extreme, contemporary expression, it is tantamount to anarchy; everyone is permitted to do whatever he or she wants. These thin concepts of tolerance are woefully inadequate to foster a free and just society. They often operate with a thin view of freedom too, where freedom is just the ability to do whatever one wants. Whereas, a thick notion of freedom is that freedom is not itself a virtue but a condition for virtue; it is ordered unto a purpose. A thick view of tolerance is not indifference, "but a generous regard and even provision for those who differ from us on points we deeply care about . . . it is not a lack of something, but the expression of a positive vision of what is good and right, a vision taken to be solidly grounded in knowledge of how things really are."[9] A strong basis for a "civil public square" (in the context of a civil society) is a robust notion of a "free exercise" of conscience and the responsibility to respect that individual exercise. But just because people are free to believe it does not

---

8. For more on this important conceptualization, see Jason Baehr, "Open-Mindedness," in *Being Good: Christian Virtues for Everyday Life* (Grand Rapids: Eerdmans, 2012), 36. Baehr's entire chapter is illuminating and merits serious consideration.

9. Dallas Willard, *Knowing Christ Today*, 29.

follow that what they believe is correct or that one is obligated to accept such beliefs as correct. Moreover, "respect for freedom of conscience" means that one has "a responsibility to be right, but with modesty; for we, too, may be wrong. Arrogance is not the claim to be right, but the refusal to admit even the possibility that we might be wrong."[10] Finally, even with respect for freedom of conscience, sometimes we have a duty to disagree with someone (e.g., their claims or actions are unjust or morally reprehensible). But even here, our responsibility is to disagree with them civilly and persuasively, and not as a result of being vindictive.[11]

7. How *one communicates is as important as* what *one communicates and* why. *Communication, online or offline, is a stewardship with responsibilities.* Having correct beliefs or representing reality correctly is not the only matter worth our attention. We must also attend to how we communicate, including both our speech and action. We must give due attention to how communication forms what we communicate and why. Form can include everything from the texture and tone of our communication to the very medium or modes of communication. Communicating online through some sort of chat environment is different than communicating the same content face-to-face. These different experiences are widely recognized but often do not enter into the intentionality and plan for means of communicating with people. But we must be *thoughtful* about *what* we say, *how* we say it, and *where* we say it.

8. Devotion *and* inquiry *are not mutually exclusive.* It is not an oxymoron to be devoted to deep convictions about how things really are and yet genuinely open to inquiry, criticism, and new or fresh understandings of reality. Another way to say this is that maintaining tradition is not opposed to research and discovery. In fact, inquiring from within the scope of a tradition can be most illuminating. As a Christian, I find the Christian tradition to be positively inspiring, animating, and cause for all sorts of entrepreneurial thinking and inquiring. Being faithfully obedient to Jesus and His mission in this world is not in principle at odds with growing in understanding of reality from non-Christian sources of knowledge. In fact, as historian Mark Noll seems to suggest in his *Jesus Christ and the Life of the Mind*, Jesus stands as both a

---

10. Guinness, *The Case for Civility*, 156.

11. For a model attentive to civility in a pluralistic society, please see the "Williamsburg Charter: A Celebration and Reaffirmation of the First Amendment" (from *The Case for Civility*, 177–98).

motivation and guidance for serious learning; He is the center that permeates all kinds of opportunities to integrate knowledge of reality.[12]

9. *Self-regulation through fostering virtues of humility, courage, patience, and love are empowering for fruitful engagement in meaningful disagreements.* Content managers and creators, especially as Christians, should lead in fostering relevant moral virtues and character development education that is integrated with the experience and practices of being a contributor to an online discussion context. This is, in my estimation, one of the most undeveloped contexts for education in moral formation. But consider how opportune such an education could be: training in the craft of web communication and discussion-fostering that is integrated with character formation and training in virtue as a core competency for communicating well.

10. *The power and presence of the kingdom of God is bigger than our differences and the mission of God is the best context for understanding progress and success in dialogue.* We must learn to be open and willing to give place for God to work by His Spirit to convict, convince, and compel people to be transformed, including us, and not just those with whom we disagree. If the Holy Spirit is the Spirit of truth and wisdom, and all truth is God's truth, this should embolden us to have a significant degree of trust in the Spirit to deliver the goods as He sees fitting. This does not mean that we have no part to play or that we are but mere passive agents in the process. If anything, we are called to be active cooperators with His work.

The above considerations are by no means comprehensive. They are meant to help surface relevant factors for thinking and acting toward a relevant framework for civility. Various communication contexts may wish to emphasize and prioritize these in different ways.

TWENTY GENERAL RECOMMENDATIONS TOWARD A MORE CIVIL ONLINE ENGAGEMENT

In light of the above framework and in view of the three scenarios also mentioned above, I suggest the following general principles to be kept in mind when fostering online contexts

---

12. *Jesus Christ and the Life of the Mind* (Grand Rapids: Eerdmans, 2011).

for dialogue and responding in those environments. I encourage content creators, managers, and commenters to consider these recommendations both as a discipline in self-governance and as a means for fostering positive discussions among disagreeing people online. It is my hope that the points below may be a helpful resource toward a new manifesto of online civility among different groups of people. Specifically, I have in mind Christian content creators, managers, and moderators of blogs, forums, and discussion/sharing-oriented platforms (e.g., Facebook).

On the Medium of Communication

1. *Discern the value-laden features of communication technology platforms and devices and how they shape our ability to reflect, respond, and relate to each other.* One of the most important lead questions to ask *before* communicating something online (e.g., whether as a comment, an article, or the beginnings of a discussions thread) is this: *What are the opportunities and limitations of communicating what I want to say in this context* (e.g., online "group") *with this platform* (e.g., Facebook) *on this device* (e.g., an iPad)? Any of these areas have values associated with them, whether at the level of expectations of use(r), or at the level of how the medium shapes the message to be conveyed, both for the recipient and the author.

2. *Where possible, offer occasion to move a discussion from online to offline contexts* (e.g., a local "third place"), or if not possible, at least from a text-only communication context (e.g., blogging) to audio-video contexts (e.g., a Skype discussion). All mediums of communication are not equal. We often belong to multiple kinds of public, whether on Facebook or at our routine third place like a local coffee shop. They each present opportunities but also challenges and even limitations to achieving a desirable communication experience. If so, then we must be intentional and honest about what we can or cannot meaningfully achieve as a result of online discussion and community-building. We each need to reckon with what are the limitations and opportunities for online discussions with respect to them being *enhancements*, *initiations*, and *shapers* of our conversations, if not *contexts* for working out our disagreements. Frequently, the problem is not a lack of options for moving online conversations to offline environment. Rather, the problem is often no *desire to self-discipline* our desires to *want* the ease of online contexts over and above offline contexts. It might be our default *preference* to want to pontificate behind a screen rather than before the face of another. But

is that preference conducive to the aims and desired outcomes of a conversation? We need to be intentional about reckoning with that question before we get knee-deep (or to change metaphors, "screen co-dependent") in our online engagement. In short, we need to discern the *instrumental value* of online means for communicating, and understand which platforms are more likely to help or weaken interim occasions for communicating between offline and online "meet-ups." If we cannot ever connect with someone face-to-face, or connect them face-to-face with others we trust, then could it be that such a limitation should shape the scope and intensity of what we communicate online, especially if it is a discussion regarding disagreements?

3. *Realize the increasingly slim line between "private" and "public" in an age of social media* and the fact that we are known to belong to multiple publics. It is foolish to think that you can easily shoot your mouth off in one context and *not* be discovered to do so in another context. As much as one may want to compartmentalize their private life from their public, in an always-on and always-connected sort of world this is becoming more and more challenging to accomplish. Our online insighting and behavior catches up with us offline.

On Dealing with Disagreements

4. *Abide by the Golden Rule.* As simple as it is, "do to others what you would want them to do to you" can be a resourceful and memorable way to be mindful of the *humane* in human communication. Stewardship of our online behavior is essential and not optional. At the very least, content creators and managers alike should aspire to this value, both as a practice to encourage and reinforce among online discussion contexts.

5. *Implement a covenant framework as a structure for dealing with disagreements.* It is not enough to cast a substantive vision for civility. We must also try to articulate in specific ways how we might address disagreements. With the anticipation of disagreements and disputes commencing in an online context, content managers would be smart to strategically develop a basic framework for addressing disagreements so that there is meaningful discussion for the sake of understanding. That framework could have a covenant or contract-like stature to it, perhaps with different contributor incentives and disincentives built in.

6. *Recognize that disagreements are inevitable and uniformity of thought is not the ultimate goal in a discussion mode.* "Resolving conflict" in a discussion does not necessarily mean achieving uniformity of thought. Perhaps a way to detect the purpose of conflict resolution here is to discern whether resolution is mainly for the sake of fostering homogenized thought and conformity or is for the purpose of fostering belonging with authentic differentiation of viewpoints.

7. *Avoid entering or stirring up controversies for the sake of entertainment or "newsy" value.* Everyone tends to like (if only secretly) some degree of fireworks when controversy looms over a discussion. The controversy doesn't even have to be of a scandalous sort. The controversy could be personality and cause driven (e.g., "Theologian's book boycotted for heretical views about God"). The goal is not so much to avoid or deny controversial issues. Rather, the point is this: it's one thing to soberly and carefully understand how a view is "heretical" on its own merit. It's another matter to understand and generate news (read: social pressures) about a view because of the "controversial" nature of the view. Moreover, it's one thing to assess the weaknesses of a view on its own merit. It's another matter to assess it in a group mob-like mentality. The "controversial" is often what can energize online discussion of a topic or perspective. People can actually become addicted to the energy of the newsy quality that controversy exudes. It's like being on a drama(tic) high! All that to say, the phenomenology of controversy as experienced in online discussion contexts will shape in a significant way how a controversy is understood, let alone judged. As content creators and managers, we must be mindful of this reality and help others understand its significance.

8. *Be discerning of the difference between these two goals relative to a heated discussion: reconciliation to God versus resolving a conflict.* If we as Christians are only stuck in "discussion mode," to borrow from philosopher Paul Moser, we might be more likely to think that we ultimately bear the burden of "resolving" discussions/conflict, or as a result of our discussion efforts, will make/break whether people come to God. This is not to say that Christian witness and presence are inconsequential. Rather, it is an attempt to understand what might be the ultimate goal when discerning the work of Christians in discussion with non-Christians. It's conceivable, and sometimes it is actually the case, that Christians can become so preoccupied with "having the an-

swers" that we can begin to act as if the eternal destiny, or at least the destiny of one's worldview, is somehow in our *control* to determine by virtue of our ability to answer correctly, comprehensively, certainly, and completely. But is that a worthwhile goal, let alone a realistic goal?

9. *We are first and foremost gospel-shaped people—then we are* x. Disagreements and disputes, whether among Christians themselves or among Christians and non-Christians, can be identity-forming in at least one crucial way: we can tend to label and reduce people to their ideas and associations. For example, let's say that there is a disagreement among two groups of people that could be self-described as theologically "conservative" and "liberal." But let's say that both groups of people are earnest to follow Jesus and desire to do so. If so, shouldn't that shape how one frames and understands contributors of these groups? For example, even if someone self-identifies as a "conservative" it does not follow that all that they believe nicely fits into the category of what might be described as a conservative orientation to x, y, or z. That is, they could be "conservative" on most theological issues, except one or two matters (e.g., they have a stronger affinity to theistic evolution than creationism). Given such complexities, it may or may not be useful to hold them to the label "conservative."

But here's an even more important point to consider: are they seeking to have their life be gospel-shaped? If so, shouldn't that value as a label (insofar as labels can be valuable) take precedence or have some sort of priority in identifying them above and beyond a more tertiary descriptor like "conservative"? Why does any of this matter? Because of how we name things, including why we name what we name, has consequence for shaping how we see ourselves in relationship to others. Moreover, such naming shapes how we envision our service to the "other" in our midst who is also under the care of God. Simply put, it may be prudent to let people in discussion, and especially disagreements in discussion, disclose how they would self-identify themselves and their overall perspective. If so, then maybe a goal in this context is to help them realize where their core identity resides relative to a more tertiary self-identification marker.

On Fruitful Discussion Habits

10. *Foster environments with thick notions of freedom and responsibility.* Generally speaking, free expression of speech can be experienced online in most Western contexts. But expression, if not expression*ism*, can remain uncultivated and undisciplined. "Users" often want to feel like they can freely express themselves, regardless if what is expressed is achieved irresponsibly. This is a persistent challenge for discussion online. But for discussion to be a conduit for understanding, the freedom to do it must be bound by a moral responsibility that does not see a disconnect between speech and virtue.

11. *Recognize that the strength of civility will be in proportion to the richness of our associational life.* A rich associational life is not merely equivalent to being a socialite, a social bug, or a social media maven! It is deeply related to how we are present to our neighbors with skillful and attentive care. Moreover, a rich associational life can include an ability to relate to a variety of people in their circumstances and background that are different than ours or of our family. But this is about more than just being an adept communicator. It is as much about the manner in which we are in the world, communally, as a way of life through relevant, life-affirming mediating institutions (e.g., a church) and the manner in which we gather with others in our third places. I mention all this to make this simple observation: how we respond and react in dialogue or dispute with others is often a microcosm of a broader ecology of associations. A challenge with online communication is the temptation to think that we can virtually abstract our "exchange of information" with others from our habits and qualities of our associational life.

12. *Understand how practicing civility is an exercise in self-discipline and care for another.* Dialogue, even with a civil tone, is as much about practicing the skill of being a good conversationalist as it is learning to practice self-restraint at a variety of levels: curbing our inclination for self-interested question-asking and answering (e.g., somehow making the conversation about ourselves or our own significance); self-controlling the impulsiveness to react to something that you find disagreeable. Civility is about not only freely giving a positive good but refraining from unleashing negativity (e.g., a critical spirit, which is different than exercising moral discernment).

13. *For the sake of mutual understanding, endeavor to clarify and articulate one's presuppositions, their relevancy, and why they are* found to be *compelling or convincing.* Most conversations about questions that matter most, if they are to proceed beyond shallow or surfacy dialogue, need to enter into the context of people's presuppositions; of those areas taken as "first principles," "givens," "starting point," or assumptions taken to be true. These are often what reside *behind* a discussion, especially a discussion related to a dispute. But when presuppositions are not clarified and articulated in this context, there is more likelihood for a discussion to miss the point and for dialogue partners to talk past each other even if they are sincerely intended in their communication. Moreover, it is often the case that the mutual sharing of presuppositions is benefited by contexts where real belonging can be experienced and cultivated. This takes time and patience.

14. *Network with others versus having to be the person who answers all questions.* When contributing answers to an online forum or a small group, it might be easy to take on the reputation of being the go-to person who can answer all the questions. But even if one can answer all of them, is it fruitful to do so? In one sense, it can be helpful to an inquirer to know that someone they know can reliably offer answers on a regular basis, or at least stand as a routine conversation partner. On the other hand, even for contributors who are able to answer all questions, it might also be in the interest of an inquirer to benefit hearing answers to their questions from others even if they have a similar point of view. Contributors can do well to try and connect inquirers to other contributors within a group or community. This approach has the added benefit of enabling the contributor to perhaps have a more realistic view of their work in community with other contributors who can support the learning of inquirers.

15. *Avoid trigger-happy "naming" and "framing."* When controversies and provocations erupt online, it is very challenging to avoid reacting with impulsive naming (e.g., "Liberals are socialist wolves in sheep's clothing") or framing ("Arminianism is a failure because it does not take seriously divine sovereignty in the way that Calvinism does"). Such acts are, at the very least, conversation-inhibitors, if not conversation-stoppers. They are cheap shots that do not enable the spokesperson to gain credibility among objectors. Sometimes it is the case that impulsive naming and framing acts as a particular blind spot of character or of mental outlook. If that is the case, helping someone become aware of this must be done with intentionality, patience, and gentleness.

16. *Have zero tolerance for informal fallacies and jargon.* Is there anything more that really does need to be said? Online contexts for discussion can be poised to *educate* others in this area if content creators and managers were to take seriously their stewardship of content as a public good. Can you imagine how much understanding might be made accessible if our discourse were not cluttered by informal fallacies and jargon?

17. *Offering a perspective, not mere opinion, is more conducive to dialogue.* For the purpose of dialogue, opinions, especially "educated" ones, are more useful than mere guesses or implausible speculations. Nonetheless, opinions, even shared opinions, are not all that worthwhile as a basis for dialogue, especially if a discussion amounts to not much more than a dispute about opinions. One can start off with their opinions, but discussion will not likely be sustained for the sake of growth in understanding if all that contributors articulate are their respective opinions. To elevate the discussion, encouragement should be made for communicating a point of view. That is material from which much work can be accomplished. A point of view, observes essayist Joseph Epstein, "is a reasonably settled sense of what is and isn't significant in life."[13]

18. *Listen first, then foster dialogue by practicing "perspective-taking."* The experience of interacting online is, generally speaking, not all that conducive to forming listening habits. The orientation of "everyone is a first-responder" (which pretty much sums up most of the habits of discussion mode online) whenever something appears to be "breaking" in the news, trending in society, or initiated as a hot button topic, is fuel for all sorts of impulsive thinking and reacting. But how might our discussions be better served by learning to value the practice of perspective-taking? "Central to perspective taking," write communication experts Tim Muehlhoff and Todd Lewis, "is an attempt to distance ourselves from our views long enough to explore and understand the views of another."[14] Can you see how authentic open-mindedness is a virtue, and empowering to perspective-taking?

13. Joseph Epstein, "A Man without Opinions," *The Weekly Standard,* July 14, 2003, 4.

14. Tim Muehlhoff and Todd V. Lewis, *Authentic Communication: Christian Speech Engaging Culture* (Downers Grove, Ill.: InterVarsity, 2010), 59.

19. *The value and significance of prudential judgments in "public."* In heated online discussions and disputes, prudence and a measured tone are often the first casualties. Perhaps what replaces them can include a personalization of claims or objections and brash either/or thinking. But prudence honors realism about the world, accurate perception, and honest representation. Prudence discerns whatever good can be accomplished. Prudential judgments involve a willingness to discern that good, to decide to take right action and implement such decisions effectively.[15] Can you imagine how much more valuable and effectual discussions about disagreements would be if they were salted with prudence? Imprudence is the cause of all sorts of noise in our very tone-deaf world.

20. *Discern the power of peer feedback prior to posting content online.* How might a peer-review process shape the content and tone of discussions of disagreement in an online context? There are various ways that this could be administered. For content managers of a forum or a blog, why not have reviewers available to assess solicited or unsolicited contributions? This is not rocket science, but it is a value that can and needs to be nurtured. If done effectually, some sort of filter like this can go a long ways toward minimizing "group think" and egregious mistakes of content and presentation in an online environment.

GENERAL TIPS FOR FOSTERING
ONLINE "THIRD PLACES" FOR CIVIL DISCUSSION

Depending on our vocation, most of us spend major chunks of our week either at some place of employment or at home or both. But we also meet with others in third places. Sometimes, though, these contexts are an online environment, such as a Facebook group, a group blog, a forum, a chat room, etc. These different contexts have different factors associated with them that may or may not be conducive to what you want to accomplish. Here are some features to foster for an online third place:

1. *It is moderated and monitored.* The goal is not to micromanage discussion or even to direct it in some way as much as to encourage engagement, to act as a referee amidst warring parties where necessary, and to reinforce any framework for civility.

---

15. Clarke D. Forsythe, *Politics for the Greatest Good* (Downers Grove, Ill.: InterVarsity, 2009), chapter 1.

2. *It can be either open or closed in its group membership* but developed with earnest intent to not allow mere "trolls" to enter and disrupt.

3. *It is intent on engaging all who are willing to engage* (the smaller the group, the more likely for this to be feasible), and not content to settle with either having dominant voices alone or dominant onlookers.

4. *It fosters an environment of belonging in mutual trust.*

5. *It encourages transparency of identity.*

   (a) It refuses to see freedom as a virtue, but *a condition for* virtue, indeed, virtuous conversations.

   (b) It is maintained by an effectual insight and posting policy/contract among contributors and readers alike (see below for an example).

There is very little hope for sustainable "civic" discussions in online contexts *if* contributors do not have the *character* to morally discern the opportunities, challenges, and limitations of these contexts and their relevancy for our common public life. The above recommendations and overall framework are an *attempt* to help shape how online environments might become more conducive and effectual for dialogue, inquiry, and discussion of disagreements that would be befitting to human dignity. Our common public life together, whether online or offline, and the manifold instances of dialogue within that shared life, require a particular moral ecology. That is what I have tried to give attention to and hopefully sketch in this appendix.

EXAMPLE OF A COMMENTING POLICY

(with fun, from JPMoreland.com)

We encourage your routine, thoughtful, and constructive comments about all of the content at J. P. Moreland's website.

Posting a comment is not a right but a privilege. If you think it is a right, then you have a sordid view of freedom and entitlement (read relevant parts in *Kingdom Triangle* to understand the distinction between classical and contemporary views of freedom).

J. P. Moreland or Eidos Christian Center are free to reply to comments through whatever communication means they wish and they are free to ignore comments as they see fit.

Posting an insight does not guarantee a response from them. Absence of comments does not mean that they have not read a comment or have not adequately considered its meaning and significance. But due to Dr. Moreland's schedule and family commitments (he has four grandchildren now!), he has adopted a general policy not to comment on things online unless there are significant overriding reasons to do so.

In order to help facilitate civility, the following policy and perspective will be enforced.

1. All comments must be encouraging and for the purpose of edification, even if they are "critical" comments meant to question or challenge what someone thinks or believes (read *The Lost Virtue of Happiness* for the importance of having a healthy background tone to our lives).

2. A comment will not be posted, and either deleted or asked for a revision, if it is

   • Loquacious

   • Off-topic from a post/page's focus.

   • Contains profanity, vulgarity, or harsh or demeaning speech.

   • Attacking someone's character instead of dealing with the merit of a claim.

   • Exercising guilt-by-association reasoning or exhibiting conspiratorial thinking to any degree (brush-up on your reasoning by reading the chapter on Logic in *Philosophical Foundations for a Christian Worldview*).

   • A comment that is better handled by private communication due to the sensitive nature of the topic.

3. Usage policy: By commenting at the website, you are giving J. P. Moreland and the Eidos Christian Center global permission to present, utilize, and duplicate your remarks, however they wish to do so without end (on the basis of an A-theory of time and the endurance of personal identity through time).

SUBJECT INDEX

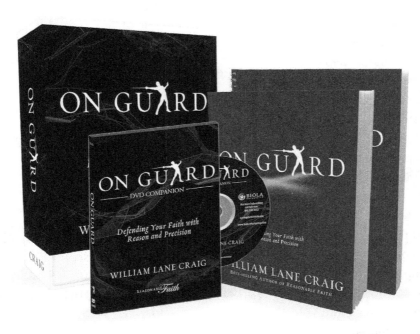

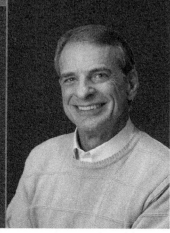